The Irony of Democracy

An Uncommon Introduction
to American Politics

The Irony of Democracy

An Uncommon Introduction to American Politics

Fourth Edition

Thomas R. Dye
Florida State University
L. Harmon Zeigler
University of Oregon

Duxbury Press

North Scituate, Massachusetts

Library of Congress Cataloging in Publication Data

Dye, Thomas R
  The irony of democracy.

  Bibliography: p.
  Includes index.
    1. Elite (Social sciences)—United States.
2. United States—Politics and government.
3. Pluralism (Social sciences)   I. Zeigler, Luther Harmon, 1936-   joint
author.   II. Title.
JK271.D92   1978   301.5'92'0973   77—20154
ISBN 0—87872—148—7

Duxbury Press
A Division of Wadsworth Publishing Company, Inc.

The Irony of Democracy, 4th edition was edited and prepared for composition by Kevin Gleason. Interior design was provided by Richard Spencer and the cover was designed by Joseph Landry.

L.C. Cat. Card No.: 77—20154
ISBN 0—87872—148—7
Printed in the United States of America

 2 3 4 5 6 7 8 9 - 82 81 80 79 78

Contents

To the Student

An instructor who has asked you to read this book wants to do more than teach about "the nuts and bolts" of American government, for this book has a "theme": Only a tiny handful of people make decisions that shape the lives of all of us, and, despite the elaborate rituals of parties, elections, and interest group activity, we have little influence over these people. This theme is widely known as the theory of "elitism." Your instructor may not believe completely in this theory, but may instead believe that power in America is widely shared among many groups of people, that competition is widespread, that there are checks against the abuse of power, and that the individual citizen can personally affect the course of national events by voting, supporting political parties, and joining interest groups. This theory is widely known as "pluralism," and characterizes virtually every American government textbook now in print—except this one. Your instructor, whether personally agreeing with the "elitist" or with the "pluralist" perspective, is challenging you to confront our arguments and to deal directly with some troubling questions about democracy in America.

It is far easier to teach "the nuts and bolts" of American government—the constitutional powers of the president, Congress, and courts; the functions of parties and interest groups; the key cases decided by the Supreme Court, and so on—than to tackle the question: How democratic is American society? It is easier to teach the "facts" of American government than to search for their explanations. While this book does not ignore such facts, its primary purpose is to interpret them—to provide an understanding of *why* American government works *as it does*.

Pluralism portrays the American political process as competition, bargaining, and compromise among a multitude of interest groups vying for the rewards distributed by the political system. Any individual seeking any portion of such rewards can effectively gain them only by joining (or organizing) such a group. Moreover, pluralists argue, most individuals are members of more than one kind of organized group. Thus, the multiplicity of such groups and the overlap of their memberships are believed to be insurance against the eventual emergence of any one group as a dominant elite.

While pluralists highly value individual dignity, they nevertheless accept giant concentrations of power as inevitable in a modern, industrial, urban society. Realizing that the unorganized individual is no match for giant corporate bureaucracy, pluralists hope that "countervailing" centers of power will balance each other and thereby protect the individual from abuse. It is by organized groups and coalition of groups (parties) that individuals gain access to the political system and insure that government is held responsible. The essential value becomes participation in, and competition among, organized groups. Pluralism contends that the American system is open and accessible to the extent that any interest held by a significant portion of the populace can find expression through one or more groups.

Elitist theory, on the other hand, contends that all organizations tend to be governed by a small minority of their membership, and that the backgrounds and values of the leaders across all groups tend to be similar—so similar, in fact, that they constitute an American sociopolitical elite. The members of this elite determine the society's values and control its resources. They are bound as much—if not more—by their elite identities as they are by their specific group attachments. Thus, instead of constituting, as pluralists see them, a balance of power system within American society, organized interest groups are seen by elitists as platforms of power from which the elite effectively governs the nation. These leaders are more accommodating than competitive toward each other. They share a basic consensus about preserving the system essentially as it is, and they are not really held accountable by the members of their groups. Members have little or nothing to say about policy decisions. In fact, leaders influence followers far more than followers influence leaders. Each of these assertions conflicts with pluralist beliefs.

A generation or more of Americans have been educated in the pluralist tradition. We do not claim that they have been educated poorly (if for no other reason than that we are among them); nor do we argue that pluralism is either "wrong" or "dead," for clearly it contains much of value and commands many perceptive adherents. In short, this book was not undertaken to "attack the pluralists." Our primary concern is to make available to students and teachers of political science an introductory analysis of American politics that is not based on pluralist theory.

The *Irony of Democracy* explains American political life by means of an elitist theory of democracy. In organizing historical and social science evidence from the American political system, we have sacrificed some breadth of coverage to present a coherent exposition of the elitist theory. An encyclopedic presentation of the "facts" of American government must be sought elsewhere. Nor do we present a "balanced," or theoretically eclectic, view of American politics. The student can find democratic-pluralist interpretations of American politics everywhere.

The *Irony of Democracy* is not necessarily "anti-establishment." This book challenges the prevailing pluralistic view of democracy in America, but it neither condemns nor endorses American political life. America's governance by a small, homogeneous elite may be interpreted favorably or unfavorably according to one's personal values. Each reader is individually free to decide whether the political system described in these pages ought to be preserved, reformed, or restructured.

The fourth edition covers a number of new topics, and brings some new perspectives to old, important topics. It includes:

An entire new chapter on "The Newsmakers"—the men who control the flow of information to the masses through newspapers and television.

A revised chapter on "protest movements"—examining black politics and the women's movement from an elitist perspective.

An expanded discussion of the role of the voter in shaping public policy—an inquiry into whether parties and elections give the individual a genuine role in deciding the nation's future, or whether they provide only "symbolic reassurance."

A discussion of Jimmy Carter's rapid rise to power—and the reasons why the nation's leadership bypassed established politicians to put "A New Smile on the Face of the Establishment."

A full explanation of the fall of Richard Nixon—the first president to resign from office—which focuses not on the petty burglary of Democratic party's Watergate headquarters, but rather on the whole record of distrust, suspicion, and repression which surrounded the Nixon White House.

ACKNOWLEDGMENTS

We would like to express our sincere thanks to those many instructors who have used the first three editions and have volunteered their reactions and comments and relayed those of their students. We found such comments very helpful and have incorporated many of their suggestions into the fourth edition.

We would like to express our gratitude to the people who reviewed the book in the preparation of the fourth edition: Joel D. Barkan (University of Iowa), Ron Hadian (Santa Monica College), Robert O'Connor (Penn State University), and Marc A. Triebwasser (Saint Lawrence University).

We are especially grateful to Robert Leonard (Georgia State University); Arthur Miller (University of Michigan) for giving us access to a wealth of valuable data about electoral behavior; Warren Miller (University of Michigan) who spent more time than he should have pondering information and clarifying our thinking about elections; James Nathan and James Oliver (University of Delaware) who were unusually generous with their time and shared fully their many insights about Congress; John Pickering (Memphis State University); and Edward G. Weston (University of Florida).

The Irony of Democracy 1

Elites, not masses, govern America. In an industrial, scientific, and nuclear age, life in a democracy, just as in a totalitarian society, is shaped by a handful of men. In spite of differences in their approach to the study of power in America, political scientists and sociologists agree that "the key political, economic, and social decisions are made by 'tiny minorities.'"[1]

An *elite* is the few who have power; the *masses* are the many who do not. Power is deciding who gets what, when, and how; it is participation in the decisions that allocate values for a society. Elites are the few who participate in the decisions that shape our lives; the masses are the many whose lives are shaped by institutions, events, and leaders over which they have little direct control. Harold Lasswell writes, "the division of society into elite and mass is universal," and even in a democracy "a few exercise a relatively great weight of power, and the many exercise comparatively little."[2]

Elites need not be conspiracies to oppress or exploit the masses. On the contrary, elites may be very "public-regarding" and deeply concerned with the welfare of the masses. Membership in an elite may be

1

relatively open to ambitious and talented individuals from the masses, or it may be closed to all except top corporate, financial, military, civic, and government leaders. Elites may be competitive or noncompetitive; they may agree or disagree over the direction of foreign and domestic policy. Elites may form a pyramid, with a top group exercising power in many sectors of the society; or plural elites may divide power, with separate groups making key decisions in different issue areas. Elites may be responsive to the demands of the masses and influenced by the outcome of elections, or they may be unresponsive to mass movements and unaffected by elections. But whether elites are public-minded or self-seeking, open or closed, competitive or consensual, pyramidal or pluralistic, responsive or unresponsive, it is elites and not the masses who govern the modern nation.

Democracy is government "by the people," but the survival of democracy in fact rests on the shoulders of elites. This is the irony of democracy: Elites must govern wisely if government "by the people" is to survive. If the survival of the American system depended on the existence of an active, informed, and enlightened citizenry, then democracy in America would have disappeared long ago; for the masses of America are apathetic and ill-informed about politics and public policy, and they have a surprisingly weak commitment to democratic values— individual dignity, equality of opportunity, the right to dissent, freedom of speech and press, religious toleration, due process of law. But fortunately for these values and for American democracy, the American masses do not lead; they follow. They respond to the attitudes, proposals, and behavior of elites. V. O. Key wrote:

dig up examples

The critical element for the health of the democratic order consists of the beliefs, standards, and competence of those who constitute the influentials, the political activists, in the order. That group, as has been made plain, refuses to define itself with great clarity in the American system; yet analysis after analysis points to its existence. If democracy tends toward indecision, decay, and disaster, the responsibility rests here, not with the mass of people. [3]

Although the symbols of American politics are drawn from democratic political thought, the reality of American politics can often be better understood from the viewpoint of *elite theory*. The questions posed by elite theory are the vital questions of politics: Who governs America? What are the roles of elites and masses in American politics? How do people acquire power? How are economic and political power related? How open and accessible are American elites? How do American elites change over time? How widely is power shared in America?

How much do elites really compete? What is the basis of elite consensus? How do elites and masses differ? How responsive are elites to mass sentiments? How much influence do masses have over policies decided by elites? How do elites accommodate themselves to mass movements?

This book, *The Irony of Democracy*, is an attempt to explain American political life by means of elite theory. It attempts systematically to organize the evidence of American history and contemporary social science to come to grips with the central questions posed by elite theory. But before we turn to this examination of American political life, it is ✳ important that we understand the meaning of *elitism, democracy,* and *pluralism.*

The Meaning of Elitism

The central proposition of elitism is that all societies are divided into two classes—the few who govern and the many who are governed. The Italian political scientist Gaetano Mosca expressed this basic concept as follows:

In all societies—from societies that are very underdeveloped and have largely attained the dawnings of civilization, down to the most advanced and powerful societies—two classes of people appear—a class that rules and a class that is ruled. The first class, always the less numerous, performs all of the political functions, monopolizes power, and enjoys the advantages that power brings, whereas the second, the more numerous class, is directed and controlled by the first, in a manner that is now more or less legal, now more or less arbitrary and violent. [4]

For Mosca it was inevitable that elites and not masses would govern all societies. Elites are not a product of capitalism, or socialism, or industrialization, or technological development. *All* societies—socialist and capitalist, agricultural and industrial, traditional and advanced—are governed by elites. All societies require leaders, and leaders acquire a stake in preserving the organization and their position in it. This motive gives leaders a perspective different from that of the organization's members. An elite, then, is inevitable in any social organization. As the French political scientist Roberto Michels put it: "He who says organization, says oligarchy." [5] The same is true for societies as a whole. According to political scientist Harold Lasswell, "The discovery that in all large-scale societies the decisions at any given time are typically in the hands of a small number of people" confirms a basic fact: "Government is always government by the few, whether in the name of the few, the one, or the many." [6]

Elitism also asserts that the few who govern are not typical of the masses who are governed. Elites control more resources—power, wealth, education, prestige, status, skills of leadership, information, knowledge of political processes, ability to communicate, and organization. And members of the elites in America are drawn disproportionately from among wealthy, educated, prestigiously employed, socially prominent, white, Anglo-Saxon, and Protestant groups in society. In short, elites are drawn from a society's upper classes, from those who own or control a disproportionate share of the societal institutions—industry, commerce, finance, education, the military, communications, civic organizations, and law.

On the other hand, elitism does not necessarily mean that individuals from the lower classes cannot rise to the top: elite theory admits of some social mobility that enables nonelites to become elites. In fact, a certain amount of "circulation of elites" (upward mobility) is essential for the stability of the elite system. Openness in the elite system siphons off potentially revolutionary leadership from the lower classes, and an elite system is strengthened when talented and ambitious individuals from the masses are permitted to enter governing circles. However,

"All right folks, we'll be landing in a few minutes. You first-class passengers gather on my left. You huddled masses and wretched refuse gather on my right."

Drawing by O'Brian; © 1973 The New Yorker Magazine, Inc.

social stability requires that the movement of individuals from nonelite to elite positions be a slow, continuous assimilation rather than a rapid or revolutionary change. Moreover, only those nonelites who have demonstrated their commitment to the elite system itself and to the system's political and economic values can be admitted to the ruling class.

Elites share a *consensus* about the fundamental norms of the social system. They agree on the basic "rules of the game," as well as on the continuation of the social system itself. The stability of the system, and even its survival, depends upon this consensus. According to David Truman, "Being more influential, they (the elites) are privileged; and being privileged, they have, with few exceptions, a special stake in the continuation of the system in which their privileges rest."[7] Elite consensus does not mean that elite members never disagree or never compete with each other for preeminence; it is unlikely that there ever was a society in which there was no competition among elites. But elitism implies that competition takes place within a very narrow range of issues *party differences* and that elites agree on more matters than they disagree on. Disagreement usually occurs over *means* rather than *ends*.

In America, the bases of elite consensus are the sanctity of private property, limited government, and individual liberty. Richard Hofstadter writes about American elite struggles:

The fierceness of political struggles has often been misleading; for the range of vision embodied by the primary contestants in the major parties has always been bounded by the horizons of property and enterprise. However much at odds on specific issues, the major political traditions have shared a belief in the rights of property, the philosophy of economic individualism, the value of competition; they have accepted the economic virtues of capitalist culture as necessary qualities of man.[8]

Elitism implies that public policy does not reflect demands of "the people" so much as it reflects the interests and values of elites. Changes and innovations in public policy come about when elites redefine their own values. However, the general conservatism of elites—that is, their interest in preserving the system—means that changes in public policy will be incremental rather than revolutionary. Public policies are often modified but seldom replaced.

Basic changes in the political system occur when it is threatened by events. Elites, acting on enlightened self-interest, institute reforms to preserve the system and their place in it. Their motives are not necessarily self-serving; the values of elites may be very "public-regarding," and the welfare of the masses may be an important element in elite decision making. Elitism does not mean that public policy will ignore or oppose the welfare of the masses but only that the responsibility for the mass welfare rests upon the shoulders of elites, not upon the masses.

Finally, <u>elitism assumes that the masses are largely passive, apathetic, and ill-informed.</u> <u>Mass sentiments are manipulated by elites more often than elite values</u> are influenced by the sentiments of the masses. For the most part, communication between elites and masses flows downward. Government policies are seldom decided by the masses through elections or by the presentation of policy alternatives by political parties. For the most part, these "democratic" institutions—<u>elections and parties</u>—have only symbolic value: <u>They help tie the masses to the political system by giving them a role to play on election day and a political party with which they can identify.</u> Elitism contends that the masses have at best only an indirect influence over the decision-making behavior of elites.

Mass Media as an example [handwritten margin note]

Naturally, elitism is frequently misunderstood in America, because the prevailing myths and symbols of the American system are drawn from democratic theory rather than elite theory. Therefore, it is as important to emphasize what elitism is *not* as to briefly restate what it *is*.

Elitism does not mean that those who have power are continually locked in conflict with the masses or that powerholders always achieve their goals at the expense of the public interest. Elitism is not a conspiracy to oppress the masses. Elitism does not imply that power is held by a single impenetrable monolithic body, or that powerholders always agree on public issues. Elitism does not pretend that power in society does not shift over time or that new elites cannot emerge to compete with old elites. Elites may be more or less monolithic and cohesive or more or less pluralistic and competitive. Power need not rest exclusively on the control of economic resources but may rest instead on other leadership resources—organization, communication, or information. Elitism does not imply that the masses *never* have any impact on the attitudes of elites but only that elites influence masses more than masses influence elites.

Elite theory can be summarized as follows:

1. Society is divided into the few who have power and the many who do not. Only a small number of persons allocate values for society; the masses do not decide public policy.

2. The few who govern are not typical of the masses who are governed. Elites are drawn disproportionately from the upper socioeconomic strata of society.

3. The movement of nonelites to elite positions must be slow and continuous if stability is to be maintained and revolution avoided. Only nonelites who have accepted the basic elite consensus are admitted to governing circles.

4. Elites share a consensus on the basic values of the social system and the preservation of the system. They disagree only on a narrow range of issues.

5. Public policy does not reflect demands of masses but rather the prevailing values of the elite. Changes in public policy will be incremental rather than revolutionary.

6. Active elites are subject to relatively little direct influence from the apathetic masses. Elites influence masses more than masses influence elites.

The Meaning of Democracy

Ideally, democracy means individual participation in the decisions that affect one's life. John Dewey wrote, "The keynote of democracy as a way of life may be expressed as the necessity for the participation of every mature human being in formation of the values that regulate the living of men together."[9]

In traditional democratic theory, popular participation has been valued as an opportunity for individual self-development: Responsibility for the governing of one's own conduct develops one's character, self-reliance, intelligence, and moral judgment—in short, one's dignity. Even if a benevolent despot could govern in the public interest, he would be rejected by the classic democrat. The English political philosopher J. S. Mill asks, "What sort of human beings can be formed under such a regime? What development can either their thinking or active faculties attain under it?" The argument for citizen participation in public affairs is based not upon the policy outcomes it would produce but on the belief that such involvement is essential to the full development of human capacities. Mill argues that persons can know truth only by discovering it for themselves.[10]

Procedurally, popular participation was to be achieved through majority rule and respect for the rights of minorities. Self-development means self-government, and self-government can be accomplished only by encouraging each individual to contribute to the development of public policy and by resolving conflicts over public policy through majority rule. Minorities who have had the opportunity to influence policy but whose views have not succeeded in winning majority support would accept the decisions of majorities. In return, majorities would permit minorities to openly attempt to win majority support for their views. Freedom of speech and press, freedom to dissent, and freedom to form opposition parties and organizations are essential to insure meaningful individual participation. This freedom of expression is also necessary for ascertaining what the majority views really are.

The underlying value of democracy, then, is individual dignity. Human beings, by virtue of their existence, are entitled to life, liberty, and property. A "natural law," or moral tenet, guarantees to every person both liberty and the right to property; and this natural law is morally superior to man-made law. John Locke, the English political philosopher whose writings most influenced America's founding elites, argues that even in a "state of nature"—that is, a world in which there were no governments—an individual possesses inalienable rights to life, liberty, and property. Locke meant that these rights are independent of government—that these rights are not given to the individual by governments, and that no governments may legitimately take them away.[11]

Locke believed that the very purpose of government was to protect individual liberty. People form a "social contract" with each other in establishing a government to help protect their rights; they tacitly agree to accept government activity in order to better protect life, liberty, and property. Implicit in the social contract and the democratic notion of freedom is the belief that government activity and social control over the individual must be kept to a minimum. This involves removing any external restrictions, controls, and regulations on the individual that do not violate the freedom of other citizens.

Moreover, since government is formed by the consent of the governed to protect individual liberty, it logically follows that government cannot violate the rights it was established to protect. Its authority is limited. Locke's ultimate weapon to protect individual dignity against abuse by government was the right of revolution. According to Locke, whenever governments violate the natural rights of the governed, they forfeit the authority placed in them under the social contract.

Another vital aspect of classic democracy is a belief in the equality of all people. The Declaration of Independence expresses the conviction that "all men are created equal." Even the Founding Fathers believed in equality for all persons *before the law,* notwithstanding the circumstances of the accused. A person was not to be judged by social position, economic class, creed, or race. Many early democrats also believed in *political equality*—equal access of individuals to political influence, that is, equal opportunity to influence public policy. Political equality is expressed in the concept of "one man, one vote."

Over time, the notion of equality has also come to include *equality of opportunity* in all aspects of American life—social, educational, and economic, as well as political. Roland Pennock writes:

The objective of equality is not merely the recognition of a certain dignity of the human being as such, but it is also to provide him with the opportunity—equal to that guaranteed to others—for protecting and advancing his interests and developing his powers and personality.[12]

Thus, the notion of equality of opportunity has been extended beyond political life to include education, employment, housing, recreation, and public accommodations. Each person has an equal opportunity to develop his or her individual capacities to their natural limits.

Remember, however, that the traditional democratic creed has always stressed *equality of opportunity* to education, wealth, and status and not *absolute equality*. Thomas Jefferson recognized a "natural aristoc-racy" of talent, ambition, and industry, and liberal democrats since Jefferson have always accepted inequalities that are a product of individual merit and hard work. Absolute equality, or "leveling," is not a part of liberal democratic theory.

In summary, democratic thinking involves the following ideas:

1. popular participation in the decisions that shape the lives of individuals in a society;
2. government by majority rule, with recognition of the rights of minorities to try to become majorities. These rights include the freedom of speech, press, assembly, and petition and the freedom to dissent, to form opposition parties, and to run for public office;
3. a commitment to individual dignity and the preservation of the liberal values of life, liberty, and property;
4. a commitment to equal opportunity for all individuals to develop their own capacities.

The Meaning of Pluralism

Political rhetoric in America emphasizes citizen participation in decision making, majority rule, our protection of minorities, individual rights, and equality of opportunity. Nevertheless, no scholar or commentator, however optimistic about life in this country, would contend that these conditions have been fully realized in the American political system. No one contends that citizens participate in *all* the decisions which shape their lives, or that majority preferences *always* prevail. Nor do they argue that the rights of minorities are *always* protected, or that the values of life, liberty, and property are *never* sacrificed, or that *every* American has an equal opportunity to influence public policy.

However, modern *pluralism* seeks to reaffirm that American society is democratic by asserting that:

1. Although citizens do not directly participate in decision making, their many leaders do make decisions through a process of bargaining, accommodation, and compromise.
2. There is competition among leadership groups which helps to protect the interests of individuals. Countervailing centers of power—for example, competition among business leaders, labor leaders, and government leaders—can check each other and keep each interest from abusing its power and oppressing the individual.
3. Individuals can influence public policy by choosing among competing elites in elections. Elections and parties allow individuals to hold leaders accountable for their action.
4. While individuals do not participate directly in decision making, they can join organized groups and exert influence by participating in them.
5. Leadership groups are not closed; new groups can be formed and gain access to the political system.

6. Although political influence in society is unequally distributed, <u>power is widely dispersed</u>. Access to decision making is often determined by how much interest people have in a particular decision; and because leadership is fluid and mobile, power depends on one's interest in public affairs, skills in leadership, information about issues, knowledge of democratic processes, and skill in organization and public relations.

7. There are multiple leadership groups within society. Those who exercise power in one kind of decision do not necessarily exercise power in others. <u>No single elite dominates decision making in all issue areas</u>.

8. Public policy is not necessarily majority preference, but it is an equilibrium of interest interaction, that is, competing interest group influences are more or less balanced and the resultant policy is therefore a reasonable approximation of society's preferences.

<u>*Pluralism*, then, is the belief that democratic values can be preserved in a system of multiple, competing elites who determine public policy through a process of bargaining and compromise, in which voters exercise meaningful choices in elections and new elites can gain access to power.</u>

✱How Pluralism Differs from Democracy

<u>But pluralism, even if it accurately describes American society, is *not* the equivalent of classical democracy.</u> Let us explain why. <u>First, the pluralist notion of decision making by elite interaction is not the same as the democratic ideal of direct *individual* participation in decision making.</u> Pluralists recognize that in a complex, urban, industrial society individual participation in decision making is not possible, and has inevitably and necessarily given way to interaction—bargaining, accommodation, and compromise—among leaders of institutions and organizations in society. Individuals are represented in the political system only insofar as they are members of institutions or organizations whose leaders participate in policy making. Government is held responsible not by individual citizens but by leaders of institutions, organized interest groups, and political parties. The principal actors are leaders of corporations and financial institutions, elected and appointed government officials, the top ranks of military and governmental bureaucracies, and leaders of large organizations in labor, agriculture, and the professions.

<u>Yet, decision making by elite interaction, whether it succeeds in protecting the individual or not, fails to contribute to individual growth and development. In this regard, modern pluralism diverges sharply from classic democracy, which emphasizes as a primary value the personal development that would result from active participation in decisions that affect the individual's life.</u>

<u>Pluralism stresses that power is fragmented throughout society and that public opinion and elections influence the behavior of elites. But</u>

this fragmentation of power is not identical with the democratic ideal of political equality. Who rules, in the pluralist view of America? According to political scientist Aaron Wildavsky, "different small groups of interested and active citizens in different issue areas with some overlap, if any, by public officials, and occasional intervention by a larger number of people at the polls."[13] This is not government by the people. While citizen influence can be felt through leaders who anticipate the reaction of citizens, decision making is still in the hands of the leaders—the elites. According to the pluralists, multiple elites decide public policy in America, each in their own area of interest.

Traditional democratic theory envisions public policy as a rational choice of individuals with equal influence, who evaluate their needs and reach a decision with due regard for the rights of others. This traditional theory does not view public policy as a product of elite interaction or interest group pressures. In fact, interest groups and even political parties were viewed by classical democratic theorists as intruders into an individualistic brand of citizenship and politics.

Federalist Papers #51?

There are several other problems in accepting pluralism as the legitimate heir to classical democratic theory. First of all, can pluralism assure that membership in organizations and institutions is really an effective form of individual participation in policy making? Robert Presthus argues that the organizations and institutions on which pluralists rely "become oligarchic and restrictive insofar as they monopolize access to government power and limit individual participation."[14] Henry Kariel writes, "The voluntary organizations or associations which the early theorists of pluralism relied upon to sustain the individual against a unified omnipotent government, have themselves become oligarchically governed hierarchies."[15] Individuals may provide the numerical strength for organizations, but what influence does each have on the leadership? Rarely do corporations, unions, armies, churches, government bureaucracies, or professional associations have any *internal* mechanisms of democracy. They are usually run by a small elite of officers and activists. Leaders of corporations, banks, labor unions, churches, universities, medical associations, and bar associations remain in control year after year. Very few people attend meetings, vote in organizational elections, or make their influence felt within their organization. The pluralists offer no evidence that the giant organizations and institutions in American life really represent the views or interests of their individual members.

Also, can pluralism really assume that the dignity of the individual is being protected by elite competition? Since pluralism contends that different groups of leaders make decisions in *different* issue areas, why should we assume that these leaders compete with each other? It seems more likely that each group of leaders allows other groups of leaders to

govern their own spheres of influence without interference. <u>Accommo-</u>
<u>dation, rather than competition, may be the prevailing style of elite</u>
<u>interaction</u>.

Pluralism answers with the hope that the power of diverse institutions and organizations in society will roughly balance out and that the emergence of power monopoly is unlikely. Pluralism assures us that no interests can ever emerge the complete victor in political competition. Yet inequality of power among institutions and organizations is commonplace. Examples of narrow, organized interests achieving their goals at the expense of the broader, unorganized public are quite common. Furthermore, producer interests, bound together by economic ties, usually dominate less-organized consumer groups and groups based on noneconomic interests. The pluralists offer no evidence that political competition can prevent monopoly or oligopoly in political power.

Finally, pluralism must explain how private, nongovernment elites can be held accountable to the people. Even if *government* elites can be held accountable through elections, how can corporation elites, union leaders, and other kinds of private leadership be held accountable? Pluralism usually dodges this important question by focusing primary attention on *public*, government-elite decision making and largely ignoring *private*, nongovernment-elite decision making. Pluralists focus on rules and orders which are enforced by *governments*, but certainly citizens' lives are vitally affected by decisions made by private institutions and organizations—corporations, banks, universities, medical associations, newspapers, and so on. In an ideal democracy, individuals would participate in *all* decisions which significantly affect their lives; but pluralism largely excludes individuals from participation in many vital decisions by claiming that these decisions are "private" in nature and not subject to public accountability.

In summary, pluralism diverges from classical democratic theory in the following respects:

1. Decisions are made by elite interaction—bargaining, accommodation, compromise—rather than by direct individual participation.
2. Key political actors are leaders of institutions and organizations rather than individual citizens.
3. Power is fragmented, but inequality of political influence among powerholders is common.
4. Power is distributed among government and nongovernment institutions and organizations, but these institutions and organizations are generally governed by oligarchies rather than by their members in democratic fashion.
5. Institutions and organizations divide power and presumably compete among themselves, but there is no certainty that this competition guarantees political equality or protects individual dignity.
6. *Government* elites are presumed to be accountable to the masses through elections, but many important decisions affecting the lives of individuals are made by *private* elites, who are not directly accountable to the masses.

Confusion often arises in distinguishing *pluralism* from *elitism.* Pluralists say that the system they describe is a reaffirmation of democratic theory in a modern, urban, industrial society. They offer pluralism as "a practical solution" to the problem of achieving democratic ideals in a large, complex social system where direct individual participation and decision making is simply not possible. But many critics of pluralism assert that it is a disguised form of elitism—that pluralists are closer to the elitist position than to the democratic tradition they revere. Thus political scientist Peter Bachrach describes pluralism as "democratic elitism":

Until quite recently democratic and elite theories were regarded as distinct and conflicting. While in their pure form they are still regarded as contradictory, there is, I believe, a strong if not dominant trend in contemporary political thought incorporating major elitist principles within democratic theory. As a result there is a new theory which I have called democratic elitism. [16]

Mass Threats to Democracy

Democratic theory assumes that its fundamental values—individual dignity, equality of opportunity, the right of dissent, freedom of speech and press, religious toleration, and due process of law—are best protected by the expansion of mass political participation. Historically, the masses and not elites were considered the guardians of liberty. For example, in the eighteenth and nineteenth centuries, the threat of tyranny arose from corrupt monarchies and decadent churches. But in the twentieth century, it has been the masses who have been most susceptible to the appeals of totalitarianism.

It is the irony of democracy in America that elites, not masses, are most committed to democratic values. Despite a superficial commitment to the symbols of democracy, the American people have a surprisingly weak commitment to individual liberty, toleration of diversity, or freedom of expression for those who would challenge the existing order. Social science research reveals that most persons are not attached to the causes of liberty, fraternity, or equality. On the contrary, support for free speech and press, for freedom of dissent, and for equality of opportunity for all is associated with high educational levels, prestigious occupations, and high social status. Authoritarianism is stronger among the working classes in America than among the middle and upper classes.

Democratic values have survived because elites, not masses, govern. Elites in America—leaders in government, industry, education, and civic affairs; the well-educated, prestigiously employed, and politically active—give greater support to basic democratic values and "rules of the game" than do the masses. And it is because masses in America respond to the ideas and actions of democratically minded elites that liberal values are preserved. Summarizing the social science research on mass behavior in American democracy, Bachrach writes:

A widespread public commitment to the fundamental norms underlying the democratic process was regarded by classical democratic theorists as essential to the survival of democracy . . . today social scientists tend to reject this position. They do so not only because of their limited confidence in the commitment of non-elites to freedom, but also because of the growing awareness that non-elites are, in large part, politically activated by elites. The empirical finding that mass behavior is generally in response to the attitudes, proposals and modes of action of political elites gives added support to the position that responsibility for maintaining "the rules of the game" rests not on the shoulders of the people but on those of the elites. [17]

In short, it is the common person, not the elite, who is most likely to be swayed by antidemocratic ideology; and it is the elite, not the common person, who is the chief guardian of democratic values.

If elites are to fulfill their role as guardians of liberty and property, they must be insulated from the antidemocratic tendencies of the masses. Too much mass influence over elites threatens democratic values. Mass behavior is highly unstable. Usually, established elites can depend on mass apathy; but occasionally the masses become activated, and their activism is extremist, unstable, and unpredictable. Mass activism is usually an expression of resentment against the established order, and it usually occurs in times of crisis, when a counterelite, or demagogue, emerges from the masses to mobilize them against the established elites.

Democracies, in which elites are dangerously accessible to mass influence, can survive only if the masses are absorbed in the problems of everyday life and are involved in groups which distract their attention from mass politics. In other words, the masses are stable when they are absorbed in their work, family, neighborhood, trade union, hobby, church, recreational group, and so on. It is when they become alienated from their home, work, and community—when existing ties to social organizations and institutions become weakened—that mass behavior becomes unstable and dangerous. It is then that the attention and activity of the masses can be captured and directed by the demagogue, or counterelite. The demagogue can easily mobilize for revolution those elements of the masses who have few ties to the existing social and political order.

These ties to the existing order tend to be weakest during crisis periods, when major social changes are taking place. According to social psychologist William Kornhauser:

. . . communism and fascism have gained strength in social systems undergoing sudden and extensive changes in the structure of authority and community. Sharp tears in the social fabric caused by widespread unemployment or by major military defeat are highly favorable to mass politics.[18]

Counterelites are mass-oriented leaders who express hostility toward the established order and appeal to mass sentiments—extremism, intolerance, racial identity, anti-intellectualism, equalitarianism, and violence. Counterelites can easily be distinguished from elites: *Elites,* whether liberal or conservative, support the fundamental values of the system—individual liberty, majority rule, due process of law, limited government, and private property; *counterelites,* whether "left" or "right," are antidemocratic, extremist, impatient with due process, contemptuous of law and authority, and violence-prone. The only significant difference between "left" and "right" counterelites is their attitude toward change: "Right" counterelites express mass reaction against change—political, social, economic, technological—while "left" counterelites demand radical and revolutionary change.

All counterelites claim to speak for "the people," and whether "left" or "right," assert *the supremacy of "the people"* over laws, institutions, procedures, or individual rights. Right-wing counterelites, including fascists, justify their policies as "the will of the people," while left-wing radicals cry "all power to the people" and praise the virtues of "people's democracies."

Extremism is another characteristic of mass politics—the view that compromise and coalition-building are immoral. Indeed "politics" and "politicians" are viewed with hostility, because they imply the possibility of compromising mass demands.[19] Occasionally counterelites will make cynical use of politics, but only as a short-term tactical means to other goals.

Counterelites frequently charge that a deliberate *conspiracy* exists among established elites to perpetuate evil upon the people. The "left" counterelite charges that the established order knowingly exploits and oppresses the people for its own benefit and amusement; the "right" counterelite charges that the established order is falling prey to an international communist conspiracy whose goal is to deprive the people of their liberty and property and to enslave them. Richard Hofstadter refers to this phenomena as "the paranoid style of politics."[20] A related weapon in the arsenal of the counterelite is *scapegoatism*—the designation of particular minority groups in society as responsible for the evils suffered by the people. Throughout American history various scapegoats have been designated —Catholics, immigrants, Jews, blacks, communists, intellectuals, "Wall Street bankers," munitions manufacturers, etc.

The masses define politics in *simplistic* terms. The masses want simple answers to all of society's problems, regardless of how complex these problems may be. Thus, black counterelites charge that "white racism" is responsible for the complex problems of undereducation, poverty, unemployment, crime, delinquency, ill-health, and poor housing of ghetto dwellers. In a similar fashion the white counterelites dismiss ghetto disturbances as a product of "communist agitation." These simplistic answers are designed to relieve both black and white masses of any difficult thinking about social issues and to place their problems in simple, emotion-laden terms. Anti-intellectualism and antirationalism are an important part of mass politics.

Counterelites often reflect mass *propensities toward violence.* Rap Brown inspired black masses in Cambridge, Maryland, in 1967 with:

"Don't be trying to love that honky to death. Shoot him to death. Shoot him to death, brother, 'cause that's what he's out to do to you. Like I said in the beginning, if this town don't come around, this town should be burned down, it should be burned down, brother."[21]

Early in his political career, George C. Wallace's references to violence were only slightly more subtle:

Of course, if I did what I'd like to do I'd pick up something and smash one of these federal judges in the head and then burn the courthouse down. But I'm too genteel. What we need in this country is some Governors that used to work up here at Birmingham in the steel mills with about a tenth-grade education. A Governor like that wouldn't be so genteel. He'd put out his orders and he'd say, "The first man who throws a brick is a dead man. The first man who loots something what doesn't belong to him is a dead man. My orders are to shoot to kill."[22]

The similarity between the appeals of black and white counterelites is obvious.

In summary, elite theory views the critical division in American politics as the division between elites and masses. "Left" and "right" counterelites are similar. Both appeal to mass sentiments; assert the supremacy of "the people" over laws, institutions, and individual rights; reject compromise in favor of extremism; charge that established elites are a conspiracy; designate scapegoat groups; define social problems in simple emotional terms and reject rational thinking; express equalitarian sentiments and hostility toward men who have achieved success within the system; and express approval of mass violence.

While elites are more committed than masses to democratic values, elites themselves frequently abandon these values in crisis periods and become repressive. Antidemocratic mass activism has its counterpart in elite repression. Both endanger democratic values.

Mass activism and elite repression frequently interact to create multiple threats to democracy. Mass activism—riots, demonstrations, extremism, violence—generate fear and insecurity among elites, who respond by curtailing freedom and strengthening "security." Dissent is no longer tolerated, the news media are censored, free speech curtailed, potential counterelites jailed, and police and security forces strengthened—usually in the name of "national security" or "law and order." Elites convince themselves that these steps are necessary to preserve liberal democratic values. The irony is, of course, that in trying to preserve democracy the elites make society less democratic.

In short, neither elites nor masses in America are totally and irrevocably committed to democratic values. Elites are generally more committed to democratic procedures than the masses. This is true for several reasons: First, persons who are successful at the game of democratic politics are more amenable to abiding by the rules of the game than those who are not. Second, many elite members have internalized democratic values learned in childhood. Finally, the achievement of high position may bring a sense of responsibility for, and an awareness of, societal values. However, elites can and do become repressive when they perceive threats to the political system and their position in it.

Repressive behavior is typical of elites who feel threatened in crises, as events in American history show. Some notable examples: (1) the Alien and Sedition Acts (1798) in the administration of John Adams, which closed down Jeffersonian newspapers and jailed their editors; (2) Abraham Lincoln's suspension of due-process rights and imposition of military law in many areas, both North and South, where citizens opposed his efforts to preserve the Union; (3) the "red scare" roundup (1919–1920) of suspected Bolsheviks in the administration of Woodrow Wilson, even after World War I was over; (4) the mass imprisonment of thousands of Japanese-American families in West Coast detention camps by the Roosevelt administration; (5) the persecution of suspected communists and "fellow travelers" during the Truman and Eisenhower administrations—including dismissal from their jobs, blacklisting, and occasionally jailing. Moreover, federal security agencies have long used such practices as wire-tapping, monitoring of mail, use of paid informants, surveillance of suspected subversives, infiltration of radical organizations, and "surreptitious entry" (burglary). Investigations of the domestic "intelligence" activities of the FBI, CIA, National Security Agency, and IRS confirmed that these practices began with the Roosevelt administration and continued through the Truman, Eisenhower, Kennedy, Johnson, and Nixon years.[23] These agencies frequently employed illegal methods in their "surveillance" of antiwar organizations, civil rights advocates, and other individuals and groups who were *not* the objects of criminal investigations. Covert tactics were employed to corrupt and discredit these groups, and derogatory information collected was passed on to other government agencies, the president, and private employers. A special FBI effort was made to expose the personal life of Martin Luther King, Jr., while Robert F. Kennedy was Attorney General.

Watergate: Elite Fears versus Democratic Values

The Watergate affair provides an even more spectacular illustration of elite reaction to mass unrest, and the tendency of elites to resort to repression when threatened. The events of "Watergate" (the break-in at Democratic party headquarters in the Watergate apartments, Washington, D.C., in June 1972, and subsequent White House attempts at a "cover-up" of those involved) grew out of a more general atmosphere of fear and repression that surrounded the White House in the early 1970s. During this period of mass unrest there were disruptive antiwar demonstrations in Washington, D.C. (as in other cities), campus violence, a wave of bombing and arson associated with extreme "Weathermen" radicals, and the theft and leaking to the newspapers of Defense and State Department documents, known as the "Pentagon Papers." This unrest convinced President Nixon and his top aides that special "security" measures should be taken against individuals and groups perceived to be threats to the political system. Thus began a series of what later came to be called White House "horrors."

The Watergate hearings (before the Senate Select Committee on Campaign Practices, chaired by Senator Samuel Ervin, Jr.), together with the Watergate tapes (recordings of presidential conversations in the White House relevant to the Watergate break-in and cover-up), provide significant insight into the origins of government repression. We will neither describe the full history of the Watergate affair nor examine the guilt or innocence of anyone involved. Our interest is the process by which governing elites decide that repressive tactics are necessary and

© Szep, *The Boston Globe*

proper to preserve the political system: We are concerned with the origin of the *policy* of repression—in this case, with the series of repressive tactics (the White House "horrors") that preceded the Watergate break-in.

Let us turn first to the testimony of H. R. "Bob" Haldeman, former White House chief of staff, to understand the origins of Watergate in elite fears about mass disruption:

It has been alleged that there was an atmosphere of fear at the White House regarding security matters. I can state categorically that there was no climate of fear at all. There was, however, a healthy and valid concern for a number of matters in the general area of national security and for a number of other matters in the general area of domestic security. . . .

With regard to leaks of information, especially in the area of national security, it became evident in 1969 that leaks of secret information were taking place that seriously jeopardized a number of highly sensitive foreign policy initiatives. . . . In order to deal with these leaks, a program of wiretaps was instituted in 1969 and continued into early 1971.

In 1970, the domestic security problem reached critical proportions as a wave of bombings and explosions, rioting and violence, demonstrations, arson, gun battles, and other disruptive activities took place across the country—on college campuses primarily, but also in other areas.

In order to deal with this problem, the president set up an interagency committee consisting of the directors of the FBI, the CIA, the Defense Intelligence Agency, and the National Security Agency. This committee was instructed to prepare recommendations for the President . . . for expanded intelligence operations.[24]

This interagency committee submitted a forty-three-page report calling for (1) intensified electronic surveillance of both domestic security threats and foreign diplomats, (2) monitoring of American citizens using international communications facilities, (3) increased legal and illegal opening and reading of mail, (4) more informants on college campuses, (5) the lifting of restrictions on "surreptitious entry" (burglary), and (6) the establishment of an interagency group on domestic intelligence. The president approved the report, but FBI Director J. Edgar Hoover later objected to it—not because he opposed such measures, but because the FBI was not given exclusive control of the program. Hoover's opposition resulted in formal withdrawal of the plan, but the plan itself clearly reflected elite thinking about the appropriate means of dealing with threats to the political system.

The White House continued to believe that the political system was endangered by disruptive and subversive elements, and that "extraordinary" measures were required to protect it. One such measure was the Special Investigation Unit created within the White House and placed under the supervision of John Ehrlichman and his assistant Egil Krough. This "plumber's unit" (so named because it was designed to fix "leaks") soon included former CIA agent and author of spy novels E. Howard Hunt, Jr. and former FBI agent G. Gordon Liddy. The "plumber's unit" worked independently of the FBI and the CIA (although it received occasional assistance from the CIA) and reported directly to John Ehrlichman. It undertook a variety of repressive activities, including: the investigation of Daniel Ellsberg and the burglary of his psychiatrist's office to learn more about his motives in the theft of the Pentagon Papers; investigation of (and later the forgery of) the record of the events surrounding the assassination of South Vietnam's President Diem during the administration of John F. Kennedy; investigation of national security leaks which affected the U.S. negotiating position in the SALT talks; and other undisclosed domestic and foreign intelligence activities.

There is additional evidence that the "plumber's unit" also undertook investigations of other White House domestic "enemies," including antiwar protesters; critical reporters and television commentators; assorted liberals and radicals; and even an investigation of the Chappaquiddick scandal and Senator Edward M. Kennedy.

The Watergate break-in itself—the burglarizing and wiretapping of the Democratic National Headquarters in the Watergate apartment building in Washington, D.C.—was an outgrowth of earlier elite fears and repressive measures. The work of the "plumber's unit" tapered off at the end of 1971, and Hunt and Liddy found new jobs with the president's reelection campaign organization, the Committee to Re-elect the President (CRP), headed by former Attorney General John M. Mitchell. The security coordinator for CRP was James W. McCord, Jr., who had served seven years as an FBI agent and nineteen years as a CIA agent. It was easy for Hunt, Liddy, and McCord to confuse threats to national security with threats to the reelection of the incumbent president, and to employ well-known "national security" tactics, including bugging and burglary, against the president's opponents. Hence, on the night of June 17, 1972, five men, including McCord and Bernard L. Barker, were discovered in the offices of the Democratic National Committee, in the Watergate, with burglary and wire-tapping tools, and were arrested. Later a grand jury charged these five men, together with Hunt and Liddy, with burglary and wire-tapping; at a trial in January 1973, all seven were convicted.

The Watergate "cover-up" was designed not only to protect White House aides and John Mitchell from implication in the burglary, but also to prevent exposure of these "national security" activities. (See "Watergate and the Resignation of Richard Nixon," in Chapter 10.) There is no evidence that the White House "horrors" were undertaken for the personal financial gain of any of the major figures. Rather, they were undertaken out of a genuine belief that the political system was threatened and that extraordinary measures were required to preserve it. The mass media, the Democratic opposition, and the academic community may contend that the Nixon administration was especially blameworthy; we do not dispute this contention. But assertions that Watergate is unique or unprecedented are either partisan or naive. Elite repression is a continuing threat to democratic values. And this threat will always be greater in periods of mass unrest, when elites convince themselves that their repressive acts are necessary to preserve the political system.

[1]Robert A. Dahl, "Power, Pluralism, and Democracy: A Modest Proposal," paper delivered at 1964 annual meeting of the American Political Science Association, p. 3. See also Peter Bachrach, *The Theory of Democratic Elitism* (Boston: Little, Brown and Co., 1967).

References

[2]Harold Lasswell and Abraham Kaplan, *Power and Society* (New Haven, Conn.: Yale University Press, 1950), p. 219.

[3]V. O. Key, Jr., *Public Opinion and American Democracy* (New York: Alfred A. Knopf, 1961), p. 558.

[4]Gaetano Mosca, *The Ruling Class* (New York: McGraw-Hill Book Co., 1939), p. 50.

[5]Roberto Michels, *Political Parties: A Sociological Study of the Oligarchical Tendencies of Modern Democracies* (New York: The Free Press, 1962), p. 70. (First published 1915.)

[6]Harold Lasswell and Daniel Lerner, *The Comparative Study of Elites* (Stanford, Calif.: Stanford University Press, 1952, p. 7.

[7]David Truman, "The American System in Crisis," *Political Science Quarterly* (December 1959), 489.

[8]Richard Hofstadter, *The American Political Tradition* (New York: Alfred A. Knopf, 1948), p. viii.

[9]John Dewey, "Democracy and Educational Administration," *School and Society* (April 3, 1937).

[10]John Stuart Mill, *Representative Government* (New York: E. P. Dutton, Everyman's Library), p. 203.

[11]For a discussion of John Locke and the political philosophy underlying democracy, see George Sabine, *A History of Political Theory* (New York: Holt, Rinehart and Winston, 1950), pp. 517–541.

[12]Roland Pennock, "Democracy and Leadership," in William Chambers and Robert Salisbury (eds.), *Democracy Today* (New York: Dodd, Mead & Co., 1962), pp. 126–127.

[13]Aaron Wildavsky, *Leadership in a Small Town* (Totawa, N.J.: Bedminster Press, 1964), p. 20.

[14]Robert Presthus, *Men at the Top* (New York: Oxford University Press, 1964), p. 20.

[15]Henry Kariel, *The Decline of American Pluralism* (Stanford, Calif.: Stanford University Press, 1961), p. 74.

[16]Peter Bachrach. *The Theory of Democratic Elitism* (Boston: Little, Brown and Co., 1967), p. xi.

[17]*Ibid.*, pp. 47–48.

[18]William Kornhauser, *The Politics of Mass Society* (New York: Free Press, 1959), p. 99.

[19]See John H. Bunzel, *Anti-Politics in America* (New York: Knopf, 1967).

[20]Richard Hofstadter, *The Paranoid Style of American Politics* (New York: Knopf, 1965).

[21]U.S. Congress, Senate, Committee on the Judiciary, Hearings on H.R. 421, "Anti-riot Bill," 90th Congress, 1st Session, 2 August 1967, p. 32.

[22]Quoted in Seymour Martin Lipset and Earl Raab, *The Politics of Unreason* (New York: Harper and Row, 1970), p. 356.

[23]See *Report of the Senate Select Committee on Intelligence*, April 28, 1976 (Washington, D.C.: Government Printing Office, 1976).

[24]Testimony of H. R. Haldeman, former White House Chief of Staff, before the U.S. Senate Select Committee on Campaign Practices, July 30, 1973, reprinted in *Congressional Quarterly Weekly Report* August 4, 1973, pp. 2125–2134.

The Founding Fathers: The Nation's First Elite 2

The Founding Fathers—those fifty-five men who wrote the Constitution of the United States and founded a new nation—were a truly exceptional elite, not only "rich and wellborn" but also educated, talented, and resourceful. When Thomas Jefferson, then the nation's minister in Paris, first saw the list of delegates to the Constitutional Convention of 1787, he wrote to John Adams, the minister to London: "It is really an assembly of demigods."[1] The men at the Convention were drawn from the nation's intellectual and economic elites—possessors of landed estates, large merchants and importers, financiers and moneylenders, real estate and land speculators, and owners of public bonds and securities. Jefferson and Adams were among the very few of the nation's "notables" who were *not* at the Convention.

Needless to say, the Founding Fathers were not representative of the four million Americans in the new nation, most of whom were small farmers, debtors, trades people, frontier dwellers, servants, or slaves. However, to say that these men were not representative of the American people, or that the Constitution was not a very democratic document, does not discredit the Constitution or the Founding Fathers. To the aristocratic society of eighteenth-century Europe, the Founding Fathers were dangerous revolutionaries, who were establishing a government in which men with the talent of acquiring property could rise to political power even though not born into the nobility. And the Constitution has survived the test of time, providing the basic framework for an ever-changing society.

Elites and Masses in the New American Nation

Many visitors from the old aristocratic countries of Europe remarked about the absence of a nobility in America, and about the spirit of equality that prevailed. Certainly farmers or frontier dwellers in America gave much less open deference to their "betters" than did the peasants of Europe. Yet there were class lines in America; at the top of the social structure was a tiny elite, composed mostly of the wellborn, although some were self-made. This elite group dominated the social, cultural, economic, and political life of the new nation. The French chargé d'affaires reported in 1787 that although there were "no nobles" in America, there were "gentlemen" who enjoyed a kind of "preeminence" because of "their wealth, their talents, their education, their families, or the offices they hold."[2] Some of these prominent "gentlemen" were Tories and had been forced to flee America after the Revolution; but there were still the Pinckneys and Rutledges in Charleston; the Adamses, Lowells, and Gerrys in Boston; the Schuylers, Clintons, and Jays of New York; the Morrises, Mifflins, and Ingersolls of Philadelphia; the Jenifers and Carrolls of Maryland; and the Blairs and Randolphs of Virginia.

Below this thin layer of educated and talented merchants, planters, lawyers, and bankers was a substantial body of successful farmers, shop keepers, and independent artisans—of the "middling" sort, as they were known in Revolutionary America. This early middle class was by no means a majority in the new nation; it stood considerably above the masses of debt-ridden farmers and frontier dwellers who made up most of the population. This small middle class had some political power, even at the time of the Constitutional Convention; it was entitled to vote, and its views were represented in governing circles, even if they did not prevail at the Convention. The middle class was especially well represented in state legislatures and was championed by several men of prominence in the Revolutionary period—Patrick Henry, Luther Martin, and Thomas Jefferson.

The great mass of white Americans in the Revolutionary period were "freeholders," small farmers who worked their own land, scratching out a bare existence for themselves and their families. They had little interest in, or knowledge about, public affairs. Usually, the small farmers who were not barred from voting by property-owning or tax-paying qualifications were too preoccupied with debt and subsistence, or too isolated in the wilderness, to vote anyhow. Nearly eight out of ten Americans made a marginal living in the dirt; one in ten worked in fishing or lumbering; one in ten was engaged in commerce in some way, from the dockhand and sailor to the lawyer and merchant.

At the bottom of the white social structure in the new republic were the indentured servants and tenant farmers; this class comprised perhaps 20 percent of the population at this time. There is no evidence that this group exercised any political power at all. Finally, still further below were the Negro slaves. While they also comprised almost 20 percent of the population and were an important component of the American economy, they were considered property, even in a country that proclaimed the natural rights and equality of "all men."

Elite Dissatisfaction with the Confederation: The Stimulus to Reform

In July 1775, Benjamin Franklin had proposed to the Continental Congress a plan for a "perpetual union"; and, following the Declaration of Independence in 1776, the Congress appointed a committee to consider the Franklin proposals. The committee, headed by John Dickinson, made its report in the form of Articles of Confederation, which were debated for more than a year before finally being adopted by the Congress on November 15, 1777. It was stipulated that the Articles of Confederation would not go into effect until every state had approved; Delaware withheld its consent until 1779, Maryland until 1781.

The Articles of Confederation, effective from 1781 to 1789, established a "firm league of friendship" among the states "for their common defense, the security of their liberties, and their mutual and general welfare." Each state was reassured of "its sovereignty, freedom, and independence, and every power, jurisdiction, and right, which is not by this confederation expressly delegated to the United States, in Congress assembled." The powers expressly delegated to the Confederation included power to declare war, to send and receive ambassadors, to make treaties, to fix standards of weights and measures, to regulate the value of coins, to manage Indian affairs, to establish post offices, to borrow money, to build and equip an army and navy, and to make requisitions (requests) upon the several states for money and manpower. The powers not delegated to Congress remained with the states, and these included two of the most important powers of government—the power to regulate commerce and the power to levy taxes. And Congress had no authority to compel the states to honor its requisitions for revenues. Moreover, since Congress could not regulate commerce, the states were free to protect local trade and commerce even at the expense of destroying the emerging national economy.

Thus, the United States under the Articles of Confederation was comparable to an international organization of thirteen separate and independent governments. The national government was thought of as an alliance of separate *states*, not a government "of the people"; and the powers of the national government were dependent upon state governments.

The Founding Fathers were very critical of the first government of the United States under the Articles of Confederation, but the government was not a failure. In the years between 1774 and 1789, the American Confederation declared its independence from the world's most powerful colonial nation, fought a successful war, established a viable peace, won powerful allies in the international community, created a successful army and navy, established a postal system, created a national bureaucracy, and laid the foundations for national unity.

But despite the successes of the Confederation in war and diplomatic relations, the political arrangements under the Articles were found unsatisfactory, even threatening, by the American elites. Generally, the "weaknesses" of the Articles most lamented by the Founding Fathers were the political arrangements that threatened the interests of merchants, investors, planters, real estate developers, and owners of public bonds and securities. Some of these "weaknesses," and the way they threatened America's elite, are described below.

The inability of Congress to levy taxes under the Articles of Confederation was a serious threat to those patriots who had given financial backing to the new nation during the Revolutionary War. The war had been financed with money borrowed by the Continental Congress and the states through the issuance of bonds and securities. The United States government owed about $10 million to foreign investors and over $40 million to American investors; in addition, individual states owed over $20 million as a result of their efforts in support of the war.*

Congress was unable to tax the people for funds with which to pay off these debts; and the states became less and less inclined, as time passed, to meet their obligations to the central government. Only one-tenth of the sums continually requisitioned by Congress under the Articles was ever paid by the states; and during the last years of the Articles, the United States was unable even to pay interest on its foreign and domestic debt. The result was that the bonds and notes of the United States government lost most of their value, sometimes selling on the open market for only one-tenth of their original value. Investors who had backed the American war effort were left holding the bag.

Without the power to tax, and with the credit of the United States ruined, the prospects of the central government for future financial

---

*A debt of $70 million is very small by today's standards, but the total taxable land value in all of the thirteen states in 1787 was only about $400 million. Thus, the public debt was about 20 percent of the total value of all of the lands in the thirteen states.

support—and for survival—looked dim. Naturally, the rich planters, merchants, and investors who held public securities had a direct financial interest in helping the central government acquire the power to tax and to pay off its debts.

The inability of Congress under the Articles to regulate commerce among the states and with foreign nations, and the practice of the states of laying tariffs on the goods of other states as well as on those of foreign nations, were creating havoc among commercial and shipping interests. "In every point of view," Madison wrote in 1785, "the trade of this country is in a deplorable condition."[3] The American Revolution had been fought, in part, to defend American commercial and business interests from oppressive regulations by the British government. Now the states themselves were interfering with the development of a national economy. Merchants and shippers with a view toward a national market and a high level of commerce were vitally concerned that the central government acquire the power to regulate interstate commerce and that the states be prevented from imposing crippling tariffs and restrictions on interstate trade.

State governments under the Articles posed a serious threat to investors and creditors through the issuance of cheap paper money and the passage of laws impairing the obligations of contract. Paper money issued by the states permitted debtors to pay off their creditors with money worth less than the money originally loaned. Even the most successful farmers were usually heavily in debt, and many of these farmers were gaining strength in state legislatures. They threatened to pass laws delaying the collection of debts and even abolishing the prevailing practice of imprisonment for unpaid debts. Obviously, creditors had a direct financial interest in the establishment of a strong central government that could prevent the states from issuing public paper or otherwise interfering with debt collection.

The political success of debtors in Rhode Island particularly alerted property holders to the need for action that would offset the potential power of the agrarian classes. In Rhode Island, the paper-money faction secured a majority in the legislature and issued so much state currency that Rhode Island money was almost valueless. When merchants and creditors refused to accept Rhode Island paper money as "legal tender," the Rhode Island legislature passed a law making such refusal a punishable offense. In one of the first exercises of judicial review in history, the Rhode Island Supreme Court, still safe in the hands of propertied men, declared the law in violation of the Rhode Island Constitution. But the lesson to America's elite was clear: Too much democracy could threaten the rights of property, and only a strong central government with limited popular participation could safeguard property from the attacks of the masses.

A strong central government would help to protect creditors against social upheavals by the large debtor class in America. In several states, debtors had already engaged in open rebellion against tax collectors and sheriffs attempting to repossess farms on behalf of creditors. The most serious rebellion broke out in the summer of 1786 in Massachusetts, when bands of insurgents—composed of farmers, artisans, and laborers—captured the courthouses in several western districts and momentarily held the city of Springfield. Led by Daniel Shays, a veteran of Bunker Hill, the insurgent army posed a direct military threat to the governing elite of Massachusetts. Shays' Rebellion, as it was called, was put down by a small mercenary army, paid for by well-to-do citizens who feared that a wholesale attack on property rights was imminent.

The growing radicalism in the states was intimidating the propertied classes, who began to suggest that a strong central government was needed to "insure domestic tranquility," guarantee "a republican form of government," and protect property "against domestic violence." The American Revolution had disturbed the tradition among the masses of deferring to those in authority. Extremists, like Thomas Paine, who had reasoned that it was right and proper to revolt against England because of political tyranny, might also call for revolt against creditors because of economic tyranny. If debts owed to British merchants could be legislated out of existence, why not also the debts owed to American merchants? Acts of violence, boycotts, tea parties, and attacks on tax collectors frightened all propertied men in America.

A strong central government with enough military power to oust the British from the Northwest and to protect western settlers against Indian attacks could open the way for the development of the American West. In addition, the protection and settlement of Western land would skyrocket land values and make rich men of land speculators.

Men of property in early America very actively speculated in western land. George Washington, Benjamin Franklin, Robert Morris, and even the popular hero Patrick Henry were involved in land speculation. During the Revolutionary War, the Congress had often paid the Continental soldiers with land certificates. After the war, most of the ex-soldiers sold these certificates to land speculators at very low prices. The Confederation's military weakness along its frontiers had kept the value of western lands low, for ravaging Indians discouraged immigration to the lands west of the Alleghenies, and the British threatened to cut off westward expansion by continuing to occupy (in defiance of the peace treaty) seven important fur-trading forts in the Northwest. The British forts were also becoming centers of anti-American influence among the Indians.

The development of a strong American navy was also important to American commercial interests; for the states seem to have been ineffective in preventing smuggling, and piracy was a very real danger at the time and a vital concern of American shippers.

Manufacturing was still in its infant stages during the Revolutionary era in America, but farsighted investors were anxious to provide protection for infant American industries against the importation of British goods. While it is true that all thirteen states erected tariff barriers against foreign goods, state tariffs were unlikely to provide the same degree of protection for industry as a strong central government with a uniform tariff policy, because foreign goods could be brought into low-tariff states and then circulated throughout the country.

Finally, a strong sense of nationalism appeared to motivate America's elites. While the masses directed their attention to local affairs, the educated and cosmopolitan-minded leaders in America were concerned with the weakness of America in the international community of nations. Thirteen separate states failed to manifest a sense of national purpose and identity. The United States were held in contempt not only by Britain, as evidenced by the violations of the Treaty of Paris, but even by the lowly Barbary states. Hamilton expressed the indignation of America's leadership over its inability to swing weight in the world community:

There is something . . . diminutive and contemptible in the prospect of a number of petty states, with the appearance only of union, jarring, jealous, and perverse, without any determined direction, fluctuating and unhappy at home, weak and insignificant by their dissentions in the eyes of other nations.[4]

In short, America's elite wanted to assume a respectable role in the international community and exercise power in world affairs.

The Formation of a National Elite

In the spring of 1785, delegates from Virginia and Maryland met at Alexandria, Virginia, to resolve certain difficulties that had arisen between the two states over the regulation of commerce and navigation on the Potomac River and Chesapeake Bay. It was fortunate, indeed, for the new nation that the most prominent man in America, George Washington, took a personal interest in this meeting. As a rich planter and land speculator who owned over 30,000 acres of western lands upstream on the Potomac, Washington was keenly aware of commercial problems under the Articles. He lent great prestige to the Alexandria meeting by inviting participants to his home at Mount Vernon. Out of this conference came the idea for a general economic conference for all of the states. The Virginia legislature issued a call for such a convention to meet at Annapolis in September 1786.

Judged by its publicly announced purpose—securing interstate agreement on matters of commerce and navigation—the Annapolis

Convention was a failure; only twelve delegates appeared, representing five commercial states: New York, New Jersey, Pennsylvania, Delaware, and Virginia. But these twelve men saw the opportunity to use the Annapolis meeting to achieve greater political successes. Alexander Hamilton, with masterful political foresight, persuaded Egbert Benson, John Dickinson, George Reed, Edmund Randolph, James Madison, and others in attendance to strike out for a full constitutional solution to all of the ills of America. The Annapolis Convention adopted a report, written by Hamilton, which outlined the defects in the Articles of Confederation and called upon the states to send delegates to a new convention to suggest remedies for these defects. The new convention was to meet in May 1787 in Philadelphia. It was rumored at the time that Hamilton, with the behind-the-scenes support of James Madison in the Virginia legislature, intended that the Annapolis Convention should fail in its stated purposes, and had planned all along to make Annapolis a stepping stone to larger political objectives.

Shays' Rebellion could not have been better timed for men like Hamilton and Madison, who sought to galvanize America's elite into action. Occurring in the fall of 1786, after the Annapolis call for a new convention, the rebellion convinced men of property in Congress and state legislatures that there was cause for alarm. Even George Washington, who did not frighten easily, expressed his concern: "I feel... infinitely more than I can express... for the disorders which have arisen. . . . Good God! Who besides a Tory could have foreseen, or a Briton have predicted them!"

On February 21, 1787, Congress confirmed the call for a convention to meet in Philadelphia

for the sole and express purpose of revising the Articles of Confederation and reporting to Congress and the several legislatures such alterations and provisions therein as shall, when agreed to in Congress and confirmed by the states, render the federal Constitution adequate to the exigencies of government and the preservation of the union.

Delegates to the Convention were appointed by the legislatures of every state except Rhode Island, the only state in which the debtor classes had won political control.

The fifty-five men who met in the summer of 1787 to establish a new national government quickly chose George Washington, their most prestigious member—indeed, the most prestigious man on the continent—to preside over the assembly. Just as quickly, the Convention decided that its sessions would be held behind closed doors and that all proceedings would be a carefully guarded secret. This decision was closely adhered to, and neither close friends nor relatives were informed of the nature of the discussions underway. Apparently the Founding Fathers were aware that elites are most effective in negotiation, compromise, and decision making when operating in secrecy.

The Convention was also quick to discard its congressional mandate to "revise the Articles of Confederation"; and without much hesitation, it proceeded to write an entirely new constitution. Only men self-confident of their own powers and abilities, men of principle and property, would be capable of proceeding in this bold fashion. Let us examine the characteristics of the nation's first elite more closely.

The Founding Fathers were, first of all, men of prestige and reputation. Washington and Franklin were men of world fame; and Johnson, Livingston, Robert Morris, Dickinson, and Rutledge were also well known in Europe. Gorham, Gerry, Sherman, Ellsworth, Hamilton, Mifflin, Wilson, Madison, Wythe, Williamson, Whitney, and Mason were men of continental reputations; and the others were major figures in their respective states.

It is hardly possible to overestimate the prestige of George Washington at this time in his life. As the commander-in-chief of the successful Revolutionary army and founder of the new nation, he had overwhelming charismatic appeal among both elites and masses. Not only preeminent as soldier, statesman, and founder of the nation, he was also one of the richest men in the United States at this time. Despite all the years that he had spent in the Revolutionary cause, he had refused any payment for his services. He often paid his soldiers from his own fortune. In addition to his large estate on the Potomac, he possessed many thousands of acres of undeveloped land in western Virginia, Maryland, Pennsylvania, Kentucky, and the Northwest Territory. He owned major shares in the Potomac Company, the James River Company, the Bank of Columbia, and the Bank of Alexandria. Finally, he held large amounts in United States bonds and securities. In short, Washington stood at the apex of America's elite structure.

The Founding Fathers had extensive experience in governing. These same men had made all the key decisions in American history from the Stamp Act Congress to the Declaration of Independence to the Articles of Confederation. They controlled the Congress of the United States and had conducted the Revolutionary War. Dickinson, Rutledge, and Johnson had been instrumental in the Stamp Act Congress at the very beginning of Revolutionary activity. Eight delegates—Sherman, Robert Morris, Franklin, Clymer, Wilson, Gerry, Reed, and Wythe— had signed the Declaration of Independence. Langdon, Livingston, Mifflin, Rutledge, Hamilton, Dayton, McHenry, Mercer, A. Martin, Davie, and Pierce had all served as officers in Washington's army. Forty-two of the fifty-five Founding Fathers had already served in the Congress of the United States, and Gorham and Mifflin had served as president of the Congress. Even at the moment of the Convention, more than forty delegates held high offices in state governments; Franklin, Livingston, and Randolph were governors. The Founding Fathers were unexcelled in political skill and experience.

In an age when no more than a handful of men on the North American continent had ever gone to college, the Founding Fathers were conspicuous for their educational attainment. Over half the delegates had been educated at Princeton, Yale, Harvard, Columbia, Pennsylvania, William and Mary, or in England. The tradition of legal training for political decision makers, which has continued in America to the present day, was already evident in Philadelphia. About a dozen delegates were still active members of the bar in 1787, and about three dozen had been trained in law. Aristotle, Plutarch, Cicero, Locke, and Montesquieu were familiar names in debate. The Founding Fathers continually made historical and comparative references to Athenian democracy, the Roman republic, the Belgian and Dutch confederacies, the German empire, the English constitution, and even the Swiss cantons. The Convention was as rich in learning as it was in property and experience.

The fifty-five men at Philadelphia formed a major part of the nation's economic elite. The personal wealth represented at the meeting was enormous. Even Luther Martin, more sympathetic to the debtors of the nation than anyone else in attendance, was a Princeton graduate, successful attorney, planter, slaveowner, and bondholder, although his fortune was modest compared to those of his fellow delegates. It is difficult to determine accurately who were the richest men in America at this time, because the finances of the period were chaotic and because wealth assumed a variety of forms—land, ships, credit, slaves, business inventories, bonds, and paper money of uncertain worth (even George Washington had difficulty at times in converting his wealth in land into hard cash). But at least forty of the fifty-five delegates were known to be holders of public securities; fourteen were land speculators; twenty-four were moneylenders and investors; eleven were engaged in commerce or manufacturing; and fifteen owned large plantations.[5] (See Table 2–1.)

Robert Morris was perhaps the foremost business and financial leader in the nation in 1787. This Philadelphia merchant owned scores of ships that traded throughout the world; he engaged in iron manufacturing, speculated in land in all parts of the country, and controlled the Bank of North America, in Philadelphia, probably the nation's largest financial institution at the time. In business and financial dealings, he associated with many other eminent leaders, including Hamilton, Fitzsimons, G. Morris, Langdon, Clymer, and John Marshall. He earned his title "the patriot financier" by underwriting a large share of the debts of the United States during and after the Revolutionary War. George

Washington was later to ask Morris, described as Washington's most intimate friend and closest companion, to become his first Secretary of the Treasury, but Morris declined in order to pursue his personal business interests. Later in his life, his financial empire collapsed, probably because of overspeculation, and he died in debt. But at the time of the Convention, he stood at the apex of the financial structure of America.

Perhaps what most distinguished the men at Philadelphia from the masses was their cosmopolitanism. They approached political, economic, and military issues from a "continental" point of view. Unlike the masses, members of the elite extended their loyalties beyond their states; they experienced the sentiment of nationalism half a century before it would begin to seep down to the masses. Professor John P. Roche summarizes the characteristics and strengths of this national elite:

A small group of political leaders with the continental vision and essentially a consciousness of the United States' international impotence, provided the matrix of the movement. To their standard other leaders rallied with their own parallel ambitions. Their great assets were (1) the presence in their caucus of one authentic "father figure," George Washington, whose prestige was enormous; (2) the energy and talent of

Public Security Interests		Real Estate and Land Speculation	Lending and Investments	Mercantile, Manufacturing, and Shipping	Planters and Slaveholders
Major	Minor				
Baldwin	Bassett	Blount	Bassett	Broom	Butler
Blair	Blount	Dayton	Broom	Clymer	Davie
Clymer	Brearley	Few	Butler	Ellsworth	Jenifer
Dayton	Broom	Fitzsimons	Carroll	Fitzsimons	A. Martin
Ellsworth	Butler	Franklin	Clymer	Gerry	L. Martin
Fitzsimons	Carroll	Gerry	Davie	King	Mason
Gerry	Few	Gilman	Dickinson	Langdon	Mercer
Gilman	Hamilton	Gorham	Ellsworth	McHenry	C. C. Pinckney
Gorham	L. Martin	Hamilton	Few	Mifflin	C. Pinckney
Jenifer	Mason	Mason	Fitzsimons	G. Morris	Randolph
Johnson	Mercer	R. Morris	Franklin	R. Morris	Read
King	Mifflin	Washington	Gilman		Rutledge
Langdon	Read	Williamson	Ingersoll		Spaight
Lansing	Spaight	Wilson	Johnson		Washington
Livingston	Wilson		King		Wythe
McClurg	Wythe		Langdon		
R. Morris			Mason		
C. C. Pinckney			McHenry		
C. Pinckney			C. C. Pinckney		
Randolph			C. Pinckney		
Sherman			Randolph		
Strong			Read		
Washington			Washington		
Williamson			Williamson		

Table 2–1
Founding Fathers Classified by Known Membership in Elite Groups

their leadership (in which one must include the towering intellectuals of the time, John Adams and Thomas Jefferson, despite their absence abroad) and their communications "network," which was far superior to anything on the opposition side; (3) the preemptive skill which made "Their Issue" "The Issue" and kept the locally oriented opposition permanently on the defensive; (4) the subjective consideration that these men were spokesmen of a new and compelling credo: American nationalism, that illdefined but none the less potent sense of collective purpose that emerged from the American Revolution.[6]

Elite Consensus in 1787

By focusing on the debates within the Convention, many historical scholars tend to overemphasize the differences of opinion among the Founding Fathers. True, many conflicting views had to be reconciled in Philadelphia and innumerable compromises had to be made; yet the more striking fact is that the delegates were in almost complete accord on the essential questions of politics.

1. *Protecting liberty and property* They agreed that the fundamental end of government was the protection of liberty and property. They accepted without debate many of the precedents set by the English constitution and by the constitutions of the new states. Reflecting what were the advanced ideas of their times, the Founding Fathers were

"We hold these truths to be self serving . . . no, make that self evident. . . ."

Aaron Bacall

much less devoutly religious than most Americans today. Yet they believed in a law of nature with rules of abstract justice to which human laws should conform. They believed that this law of nature endowed each person with certain inalienable rights that were essential to a meaningful existence: the right to life, liberty, and property; and these rights should be recognized and protected by law. They believed that all people were equal, in that they were entitled to have their natural rights respected regardless of their station in life. Most of the Founding Fathers were even aware that this belief ran contrary to the practice of slavery and were embarrassed by this inconsistency in American life.

But "equality" did *not* mean to the Founding Fathers that people were equal in birth, wealth, intelligence, talent, or virtue. Inequalities in wealth and property were accepted as a natural product of human diversity. It was definitely not the function of government to reduce these inequalities; in fact, "dangerous leveling" was a serious violation of the right to property, the right to use and dispose of the fruits of one's own industry. On the contrary, it was the very function of government to protect property and to prevent "leveling" influences from reducing the natural inequalities of wealth and power.

2. *Government as contract*   The Founding Fathers agreed that the origin of government is an implied contract among men. They believed that people pledged allegiance and obedience to government in return for protection of their natural rights, the maintenance of peace, and protection from foreign invasion. The ultimate legitimacy of government—that is, sovereignty—rested with the people themselves, and not with gods or kings; and the basis of government was the consent of the governed.

3. *Republicanism*   The Founding Fathers believed in republican government. They were opposed to hereditary monarchies, the prevailing form of government in the world at the time. While they believed that persons of principle and property should govern, they were opposed to an aristocracy or a governing nobility. By "republican government" they meant a representative, responsible, and nonhereditary government. But they certainly did *not* mean mass democracy, with direct participation by the people in decision making. They expected the masses to consent to government by men of principle and property out of recognition for their abilities, talents, education, and stake in the preservation of liberty and order. The Founding Fathers believed that the masses should have only a limited part in the selection of government leaders. There was some bickering over how much direct participation should take place in the selection of decision makers, and some bickering over the qualifications of public office. But there was general agreement that the masses should have only a limited, indirect role in selecting decision

makers, and that decision makers themselves should be men of wealth, education, and proven leadership ability.

4. *Limited government*   The Founding Fathers believed in limited government. Government should be designed so that it would not become a threat to liberty or property. Since the Founding Fathers believed that power was a corrupting influence and that the concentration of power was dangerous, they believed in dividing government power into separate bodies capable of checking, or thwarting, each other should any one branch pose a threat to liberty or property. Differences of opinion among honest men, particularly differences among elites located in separate states, could best be resolved by balancing representation of these several elites in the national government and by a system of decentralization that permitted local elites to govern their states as they saw fit, with limited interference from the national government.

It should be noted that the laissez-faire principles of Adam Smith were *not* a part of elite consensus in 1787. Quite the contrary, the men who wrote the Constitution believed that government had the obligation not only to protect private property but also to nourish it. They expected government to foster trade and commerce, protect manufacturing, assist in land development, and provide other positive economic assistance. And, to protect the rights of property, they expected government to enforce contracts, maintain a stable money supply, punish thievery, assist in the collection of debts, record the ownership of property in the form of deeds, punish counterfeiting and piracy, protect copyrights and patents, regulate the value of money, establish courts, and regulate banking and commerce.

5. *Nationalism*   Finally, and perhaps most importantly, the Founding Fathers believed that only a strong national government, with power to exercise its will directly on the people, would be able to "establish justice, insure domestic tranquility, provide for the common defense, promote the general welfare, and secure the blessings of liberty."

The differences requiring compromise in the Convention were dwarfed by this consensus on fundamentals. It was the existence of a national elite and its agreement on the fundamentals of politics that enabled the American government to be founded. If there had been any substantial cleavage among elites in 1787, any substantial competition or conflict, or any divergent centers of influence, a new government would never have emerged from the Philadelphia convention. Elite consensus in 1787 was profoundly conservative, in that it wished to preserve the status quo in the distribution of power and property in America. Yet, at the same time, this elite consensus was radical in comparison with the beliefs of other elites in the world at this time. Nearly every other government of the time adhered to the principle of hereditary monarchy and privileged nobility, while American elites were committed to republicanism. Other elites asserted the divine right of kings, while American elites talked about government by the consent of the governed. While the elites in Europe rationalized and defended a rigid caste system, American elites believed in equality with respect to inalienable human rights.

On May 25, 1787, sessions of the Constitutional Convention opened in Independence Hall, Philadelphia. After the selection of Washington as president of the Convention and the decision that the proceedings of the Convention should be kept secret, Governor Edmund Randolph, speaking for the Virginia delegation, presented a draft of a new constitution.

An Elite in Operation— Conciliation and Compromise

The Representation Compromise

Under the Virginia Plan, little recognition was given to the states in the composition of the national government. The plan proposed a two-house legislature, the lower house to be chosen by the people of the several states with representation according to population. The upper house was to be chosen by the first house. This Congress would be empowered to "legislate in all cases in which the separate states are incompetent, or in which the harmony of the United States may be interrupted by the exercise of individual legislation." Moreover, Congress would have the authority to nullify state laws that it felt violated the Constitution, thus insuring national supremacy. The Virginia Plan also proposed a parliamentary form of government, with members of the executive and judiciary branches chosen by the Congress.

It is interesting that the most important line of cleavage at the Convention was between elites of large states and elites of small states over the representation scheme in the Virginia Plan. This was not a great question of economic interest or ideology, since delegates from large and small states did not divide along economic or ideological lines. But the Virginia Plan did not provide certainty that elites from small states would secure membership in the upper house of the legislature.

After several weeks of debate over the Virginia Plan, delegates from the small states presented a counterproposal, in a report by William Patterson of New Jersey. The New Jersey Plan may have been merely a tactic by the small state elites to force the Convention to compromise on representation, for it was debated only a week before it was set aside, and despite this defeat the small state delegates did not leave the Convention nor did they seem particularly upset with their defeat. The New

Jersey Plan proposed to retain the representation scheme in Congress under the Articles, where each state was accorded a single vote. But separate executive and judiciary branches were to be established, and the powers of Congress were to be greatly expanded to include the right to levy taxes and regulate commerce.

The New Jersey Plan was *not* an attempt to retain the Confederation. Indeed, the plan included words that were later to appear in the Constitution itself as the famous "national supremacy clause":

This constitution, and the laws of the United States which shall be made in pursuance thereof, and all treaties made, or which shall be made, under the authority of the United States shall be the Supreme Law of the Land; the judges in every state shall be bound thereby, anything in the Constitution or laws of any state to the contrary notwithstanding.

Thus, even the small states did not envision a confederation. Both the Virginia and New Jersey plans were designed to strengthen the national government; they differed only on how much it would be strengthened and on its system of representation.

On June 29, William Samuel Johnson of Connecticut proposed the obvious compromise; namely, *that representation in the lower house of Congress be based upon population whereas representation in the upper house would be equal*—two senators from each state. The Connecticut Compromise also provided that equal representation of states in the Senate could not be abridged, even by constitutional amendment.

The Slavery Compromises

The next question to be compromised, that of slavery and the role of slaves in the system of representation, was more closely related to economic differences among America's elite. It was essentially the same question that 75 years later was to divide that elite and provoke the nation's bloodiest war. Planters and slaveholders generally believed that wealth, particularly wealth in slaves, should be counted in apportioning representation. Nonslaveholders felt that "the people" should only include free inhabitants. The decision to apportion direct taxes among the states in proportion to population opened the way to compromise, since the attitude of slaveholders and nonslaveholders was just the reverse as to which person should be counted for the purposes of apportioning taxes. The result was the famous Three-Fifths Compromise, in which *three-fifths of the slaves of each state would be counted for the purposes both of representation and apportioning direct taxes.*

Finally, a compromise had to be reached on the question of trading in slaves. On this issue, the men of Maryland and Virginia, states that were already well supplied with slaves, were able to indulge in the luxury of conscience and support proposals for banning the further importation of slaves. But the less-developed Southern states, particularly South Carolina and Georgia, could not afford to be so moral, since they still wanted additional slave labor. Inasmuch as the Southern planters were themselves divided, the ultimate compromise permitted Congress to prohibit *the slave trade—but not before the year 1808*. This twenty-year delay would allow the undeveloped Southern states to acquire all the slaves they needed before the slave trade was cut off.

The Export Tax Compromise

Agreement between Southern planters and Northern merchants was still relatively easy to achieve at this early date in American history. But latent conflict could be observed on issues other than slavery. While all the elite groups agreed that the national government should regulate interstate and foreign commerce, Southern planters had some fear that the unrestricted power of Congress over commerce might lead to the imposition of export taxes. Export taxes would bear most heavily on the Southern states, which were dependent upon foreign markets for the sale of indigo, rice, tobacco, and cotton. However, planters and merchants were able to reach another compromise in resolving this issue: *no tax or duty should be levied on articles exported from any state.*

The Voter Qualification Compromise

Another important compromise, one which occupied much of the time of the Convention although it has received little recognition by later writers, concerned qualifications for voting and holding office in the new government. While no property qualifications for voters or officeholders appear in the text of the Constitution, the debates revealed that members of the Convention generally favored property qualifications for voting and almost unanimously favored property qualifications for officeholding. The delegates showed little enthusiasm for mass participation in democracy. Elbridge Gerry of Massachusetts declared that "the evils we experience flow from the excess of democracy." Roger Sherman protested that "the people immediately should have as little to do as may be about the government." Edmund Randolph continually deplored the turbulence and follies of democracy, and George Clymer's notion of republican government was that "a representative of the people is appointed to think for and not with his constituents." John Dickinson considered property qualifications a "necessary defense against the dangerous influence of those multitudes without property and without principle, with which our country like all others, will in time abound." Gouverneur Morris also insisted upon property qualifications: "Give the votes to the people who have no property and they will sell them to the rich who will be able to buy them." Charles Pinckney later wrote to Madison, "are you not . . . abundantly depressed at the theoretical nonsense of an election of Congress by the people; in the first instance, it's clearly and practically wrong, and it will in the end be the means of bringing our councils into contempt." Many more such statements could be cited from the records of the Convention.[7]

There was even stronger agreement that property qualifications should be imposed for senators and for the president. The Senate, according to C. C. Pinckney, "was meant to represent the wealth of the country. It ought to be composed of persons of wealth." He also proposed that no pay be given presidents or senators, because "if no allowance was made, the wealthy alone would undertake the service."

In the light of these views, how then do we explain the absence of property qualifications in the Constitution? Actually, a motion was carried in the Convention instructing a committee to fix property qualifications for officeholding, but the committee could not agree upon the nature of the qualifications to be imposed. Various propositions to establish property qualifications were defeated on the floor, not because they were believed to be inherently wrong but, interestingly enough, because of differences in the *kind* of property represented by elites at the Convention. Madison pointed this out in the debate in July, when he noted that a requirement of land ownership would exclude from Congress the mercantile and manufacturing classes, who would hardly be willing to turn their money into large quantities of landed property just to make them eligible for a seat in Congress. Madison rightly observed that "landed possessions were no certain evidence of real wealth. Many enjoyed them to a great extent who were more in debt than they were worth." The objections by merchants and investors led to a defeat of the "landed" qualification for congressmen. Also, a motion to disqualify persons from public office who had "unsettled accounts" with the United States (an early-day version of conflict-of-interests law) was also struck down by an overwhelming vote of the delegates.

Thus, the Constitution was approved *without any property qualifications on voters, except those which the states themselves might see fit to impose.* Failing to come to a decision on this issue of suffrage, the delegates merely returned the question to state legislatures by providing that "the electors in each state should have the qualifications requisite for electors of the most numerous branch of the state legislatures." At the time, it did not seem that this expedient course of action would result in mass democracy. Only one branch of the new government, the House of

Representatives, was to be elected by popular vote anyhow. The other three controlling bodies—the President, the Senate, and the Supreme Court—were removed from direct voter participations. Finally, the delegates were reassured by the fact that nearly all of the state constitutions then in force included property qualifications for voters.*

The text of the Constitution, together with interpretive materials in *The Federalist* papers written by Hamilton, Madison, and Jay, provides ample evidence that elites in America benefited both politically and economically from the adoption of the Constitution. While both elites and nonelites—indeed, all Americans—may have benefited by the adoption of the Constitution, elites benefited more directly and immediately than nonelites. And it is reasonable to infer that the advantages contained in the document for America's elite provided the direct, impelling motive for their activities on behalf of the new Constitution. Indeed, if elites had not stood to gain substantially from the Constitution, it is doubtful that this document would have been written or that the new government would have been established. We can discover the elitist consensus by examining the underlying philosophy of government contained in the Constitution.

According to Madison in *The Federalist*, "the principal task of modern legislation" was to *control factions*.[8] A "faction" is a number of citizens united by a common interest that is adverse to the interest of other citizens or of the community as a whole. The causes of factions are found in human diversity:

A zeal for different opinions concerning religion, concerning government, and many other points, as well of speculation as of practice; an attachment to different leaders ambitiously contending for preeminence and power; or to persons of other descriptions whose fortunes have been interesting to human passions.

The Constitution as an Elitist Document

*Historians disagree about the number of people who were disenfranchised by property qualifications in 1787. All states had property-owning or tax-paying qualifications for voting and even higher qualifications for officeholding. But we do not really know how many people met these qualifications. For example, Massachusetts conferred the suffrage on all males owning an estate with an annual income of three pounds or a total value of sixty pounds. And a Massachusetts senator was required to be "seized in his own right of a freehold within this Commonwealth of the value of 300 pounds at least, or possessed of a personal estate of the value of 600 pounds at least, or both to the amount of the same sum." It is difficult to estimate what percentage of Massachusetts males owned an estate with an annual income of three pounds. But whether or not many citizens were *legally* disenfranchised, very few voted.

At the heart of the problem of faction, however, is inequality in the control of economic resources:

But the most common and durable source of factions has been the various and unequal distribution of property. Those who hold and those who are without property have ever formed distinct interests in society. Those who are creditors and those who are debtors fall under like discrimination. A landed interest, a manufacturing interest, a mercantile interest, a monied interest, with many lesser interests, grow up of necessity in civilized nations, and divide them into different classes, actuated by different sentiments and views. [Federalist No. 10]

In Madison's view, the most important protection against mass movements that might threaten property would be a national government. By creating such a government, encompassing a large number of citizens and a great expanse of territory,

you take in a greater variety of parties and interests; you make it less probable that a majority of the whole will have a common motive to invade the rights of other citizens; or if such a common motive exists it will be more difficult for all who feel it to discover their own strength, and to act in unison with each other.

The structure of the new national government was supposed to insure that "factious" issues (those that would generate factions) would be suppressed. And Madison does not hedge on naming the factious issues that must be avoided: "A rage for paper money, for an abolition of debts, for an equal division of property, or any other improper or wicked project . . . ." Note that all of Madison's factious issues are challenges to the dominant economic elites. Madison's defense of the new Constitution was that its republican and federal features would help to keep certain threats to property from ever becoming public issues. In short, the new American government was deliberately designed by the Founding Fathers to make it difficult for any mass political movement to challenge property rights.

Impact of the Constitution on Elites

Now let us examine the text of the Constitution itself and its impact on American elites. There are seventeen specific grants of power to Congress in Article I, Section 8, followed by a general grant of power to make "all laws which shall be necessary and proper for carrying into execution the foregoing powers." The first and perhaps the most important is the "power to lay and collect taxes, duties, imposts, and excises." The *taxing power* is, of course, the basis of all other powers, and it enabled the national government to end its dependence upon states. The taxing power was essential to the holders of public securities, particularly when it was combined with the provision in Article VI that "All the debts contracted and engagements entered into before the adoption of this Constitution shall be valid against the United States under this Constitution as under the Confederation." This meant that the national government would be obliged to pay off all those investors who held bonds of the United States, and the taxing power would enable the national government to do this on its own.

The text of the Constitution suggests that the Founding Fathers intended Congress to place most of the tax burden on consumers in the form of custom duties and excise taxes, rather than direct taxes on individual income or property. Article I, Section 2, required that direct taxes could be levied only on the basis of population; it follows that such taxes could not be levied in proportion to wealth. This provision prevented the national government from levying progressive income taxes, and it was not until the Sixteenth Amendment was passed in 1913 that this protection for wealth was removed from the Constitution.

Southern planters, whose livelihoods depended on the export of indigo, rice, tobacco, and cotton, strenuously opposed giving the national government the power to tax exports. Protection for their interests was provided in Article I, Section 9: "no tax or duty shall be laid on goods exported from any state." However, Congress was given the power to tax imports so Northern manufacturers could erect a tariff wall to protect American industries against foreign goods.

Congress was also given the power to "regulate commerce with foreign nations and among the several states." The interstate commerce clause, together with the provision in Article I, Section 9, prohibiting the states from taxing either imports or exports, created a free trade area over the thirteen states. In *The Federalist* No. 11, Hamilton describes the advantages of this arrangement for American merchants:

The speculative trader will at once perceive the force of these observations and will acknowledge that the aggregate balance of the commerce of the United States would bid fair to be much more favorable than that of the thirteen states without union or with partial unions.

Following the power to tax and spend, to borrow money, and to regulate commerce in Article I, there is a series of specific powers designed to enable Congress to protect money and property. Congress is given the power to make bankruptcy laws, to coin money and regulate its value, to fix standards of weights and measures, to punish counterfeiting, to establish post offices and post roads, to pass copyright and patent laws to protect authors and inventors, and to punish piracies and felonies committed on the high seas. Each of these powers is a specific asset to bankers, investors, and shippers, respectively. Obviously, the Founding Fathers felt that giving Congress control over currency and credit in America would result in better protection for financial interests than would leaving this essential responsibility to the states. Likewise, control over communication and transportation ("post offices and post roads") was believed to be too essential to trade and commerce to be left to the states.

The remaining powers in Article I deal with military affairs—raising and supporting armies, organizing, training, and calling up the state militia, declaring war, suppressing insurrections, and repelling invasions. These powers in Article I—together with the provisions in Article II making the president the commander-in-chief of the army and navy and of the state militia when called into the federal service; and the power of the president to make treaties with the advice and consent of the Senate, and to send and receive ambassadors—all combined to centralize diplomatic and military affairs at the national level. This centralization of diplomatic-military power is confirmed in Article I, Section 10, where the states are specifically prohibited from entering into treaties with foreign nations, maintaining ships of war, or engaging in war unless actually invaded.

It is clear that the Founding Fathers had little confidence in the state militia, particularly when it was under state control; General Washington's painful experiences with state militia during the Revolutionary War were still fresh in his memory. The militia had proven adequate when defending their own states against invasion; but when employed outside their own states, they were often a disaster. Moreover, if western settlers were to be protected from the Indians, and if the British were to be persuaded to give up their forts in Ohio and open the way to American expansion westward, the national government could not rely upon state militia but must instead have an army of its own. Similarly, a strong navy was essential to the protection of American commerce on the seas (the first significant naval action under the new government was against the piracy of the Barbary states). Thus, a national army and navy were not so much protection against invasion (for many years the national government would continue to rely primarily upon state militia for this purpose), but rather for the protection and promotion of its commercial and territorial ambitions.

A national army and navy, as well as an organized and trained militia that could be called into national service, also provided *protection against class wars* and rebellion by debtors. In an obvious reference to Shays' Rebellion, Hamilton warns in *The Federalist* No. 21:

The tempestuous situation from which Massachusetts has scarcely emerged evinces that dangers of this kind are not merely speculative. Who could determine what might have been the issue of her late convulsions if the malcontents had been headed by a Caesar or a Cromwell? A strong military force in the hands of the national government is a protection against revolutionary action.

Further evidence of the Founding Fathers' intention to protect the governing classes from revolution is found in Article IV, Section 4, where the national government guarantees to every state "a republican form of government" as well as protection against "domestic violence." Thus, in addition to protecting western land and commerce on the seas, a strong army and navy would enable the national government to back up its pledge to protect governing elites in the states from violence and revolution.

Protection against domestic insurrection also appealed to the Southern slaveholders' deep-seated fear of a slave revolt. Madison drives this point home in *The Federalist* No. 23:

I take no little notice of an unhappy species of population abounding in some of the states who, during the calm of regular government were sunk below the level of men; but who, in the tempestuous seeds of civil violence, may emerge into human character and give a superiority of strength to any party with which they may associate themselves.

As we have already noted, the Constitution permitted Congress to outlaw the importation of slaves after the year 1808. But most of the Southern planters were more interested in protecting their existing property and slaves than they were in extending the slave trade, and the Constitution provided an explicit advantage of slaveholders in Article IV, Section 2:

No person held to service or labor in one state, under the laws thereof, escaping into another, shall, in consequence of any law or regulation thereof, be discharged from such service or labor, but shall be delivered upon claim of the party to whom such service or labor may be due.

This was an extremely valuable protection for one of the most important forms of property in America at the time. Although the slave trade lapsed in America after twenty years, slavery itself, as a domestic institution, was better safeguarded under the new Constitution than under the Articles.

The restrictions placed upon state legislatures by the Constitution also provided protection to economic elites in the new nation. States were prevented from coining money, issuing paper money, or passing legal tender laws that would make any money other than gold or silver coin tender in the payment of debts. This restriction would prevent the states from issuing cheap paper money, which could be used by debtors to pay off creditors with less valuable currency. The authors of *The Federalist* pointed to this prohibition on paper money in their appeal to economic elites to support ratification of the Constitution:

The loss which America has sustained since the peace from the pestilential effects of paper money on the necessary confidence between man and man, on the necessary confidence in the public councils, on the industry and the morals of the people, and on the character of republican government constitutes an enormous debt against the states chargeable to this unadvised measure, which must long remain unsatisfied, or rather an accumulation of guilt, which can be expiated no otherwise than by a voluntary sacrifice on the altar of justice which has been the instrument of it. [Federalist *No. 44*]

In other words, the states had frequently issued paper money to relieve debtors; they were now to be punished for their "unadvised" behavior by removing their power to issue money. Moreover, the states were prohibited from passing legal-tender laws obliging creditors to accept paper money in payment of debts.

The Constitution also prevents states from passing any law "impairing the obligation of contracts." The structure of business relations in a free-enterprise economy depends upon government enforcement of private contracts, and it is essential to economic elites that the government be prevented from relieving persons from their obligations to contract. If state legislatures could relieve debtors of their contractual obligations, or relieve indentured servants from their obligations to their masters, or prevent creditors from foreclosing on mortgages, or declare moratoriums on debt, or otherwise interfere with business obligations, the interests of investors, merchants, and creditors would be seriously damaged.

Elitism and the Structure of the National Government

The heart of the Constitution is the supremacy clause of Article VI:

This Constitution, and the laws of the United States which shall be made in pursuance thereof, and all treaties made, or which shall be made under the authority of the United States, shall be the Supreme Law of the Land and the judges in every state shall be bound thereby, anything in the Constitution or laws of any state to the contrary notwithstanding.

This sentence made it abundantly clear that laws of Congress would supersede laws of the states, and it made certain that Congress would control interstate commerce, bankruptcy, monetary affairs, weights and measures, currency and credit, communication, and transportation, as well as foreign and military affairs. Thus, the supremacy clause insures that the decisions of the national elite will prevail over those of the local elites in all vital areas allocated to the national government.

The structure of the national government—its republicanism and its system of separated powers and checks and balances—was also designed to protect liberty and property. To the Founding Fathers, a *republican government* meant the delegation of powers by the people to a small number of citizens "whose wisdom may best discern the true interest of their country, and whose patriotism and love of justice will be least likely to sacrifice it to temporary or partial considerations."[11] Madison explains, in classic elite fashion, "that the public voice, pronounced by representatives of the people, will be more consonant to the public good than if pronounced by the people themselves." The Founding Fathers clearly believed that representatives of the people were more likely to be enlightened persons of principle and property than the voters who chose them, and thus more trustworthy and dependable.

Moreover, voters had a very limited voice in the selection of decision makers. Of the four major decision-making bodies established in the Constitution—the House of Representatives, the Senate, the Presidency, and the Supreme Court—only *one* was to be elected by the people themselves. The other bodies were to be at least twice removed from popular control. In the Constitution of 1787, only United States representatives were directly elected by the people, and they were elected for short terms of two years. In contrast, United States senators were to be elected by state legislatures, not by the people, for six-year terms. The president was not elected by the people, but by "electors," who themselves were to be selected as state legislatures saw fit. The states could hold elections for presidential "electors," or the state legislatures could appoint them. The Founding Fathers hoped that presidential "electors" would be prominent men of wealth and reputation in their respective states. Finally, federal judges were to be appointed by the president for life, thus removing these decision makers as far from popular control as possible. Of course, it would be unfair to brand the Founding Fathers as "conservative" because of these republican arrangements. In 1787, the idea of republicanism itself was radical, since few governments provided for *any* popular participation in government, even a limited role in the selection of representatives. While the Founding Fathers believed that government ultimately rested upon the will of the people, they hoped that republicanism could reduce the influence of the masses and help insure government by elites.

The system of separated powers in the national government—separate legislative, executive, and judicial branches—was also intended by the Founding Fathers as a bulwark against majoritarianism (government by popular majorities) and an additional safeguard for elite liberty and property. The doctrine derives from the French writer, Montesquieu, whose *Spirit of Laws* was a political textbook for these eighteenth-century statesmen. *The Federalist* No. 51 expresses the logic of the checks and balances system:

Ambition must be made to counteract ambition. . . . It may be a reflection on human nature, that such devices should be necessary to control the abuses of government. But what is government itself, but the greatest of all reflections on human nature? If men were angels, no government would be necessary. If angels were to govern men, neither external nor internal controls on government would be necessary. In framing a government which is to be administered by men over men, the great difficulty lies in this: you must first enable the government to control the governed; and in the next place oblige it to control itself.

The separation-of-powers concept is expressed in the opening sentences of the first three articles of the Constitution:

All legislative powers herein granted shall be invested in the Congress of the United States. . . . The Executive power shall be vested in a President of the United States. . . . The Judicial power shall be vested in one Supreme Court and such inferior courts as Congress may from time to time ordain and establish.

Insofar as this system divides responsibility and makes it difficult for the masses to hold government accountable for public policy, it achieves one of the purposes intended by the Founding Fathers. Each of the four major decision-making bodies of the national government is chosen by different constituencies—the House by the voters in the several states, the Senate by the state legislatures, the president by electors chosen by the states, and the judiciary by the president and the Senate. Because the terms of these decision-making bodies differ so markedly in length, a complete renewal of government at one stroke is impossible. The House is chosen for two years; the Senate is chosen for six (but not in one election, for one-third go out every two years); the president is chosen every four years; but judges of the Supreme Court hold office for life. Thus the people are restrained from working immediate havoc through direct elections. To make their will felt in all the decision-making bodies of the national government, they must wait years.

Moreover, each of these decision-making bodies has an important check on the decisions of the others. No bill can become law without the approval of both the House and the Senate. The president shares in the legislative power through the veto and the responsibility to "give to the Congress information of the state of the union, and recommend to their consideration such measures as he shall judge necessary and expedient." The president can also convene sessions of Congress. But the appointing power of the president is shared by the Senate; so is the power to make treaties. Also, Congress can override executive vetoes. The president must execute the laws, but cannot do so without relying on executive departments, which must be created by Congress. Moreover, the executive branch cannot spend money that has not been appropriated by Congress. Thus, the concept of "separation of powers" is really misnamed, for what we are really talking about is a sharing, not a separating, of power; each branch participates in the activities of every other branch.

Even the Supreme Court, which was created by the Constitution, must be appointed by the president with the consent of the Senate, and Congress may prescribe the number of judges. More importantly, Congress must create lower and intermediate courts, establish the number of judges, fix the jurisdiction of lower federal courts, and make "exceptions" to the jurisdiction of the Supreme Court over appeals.

All of these checks and counterchecks were defended in *The Federalist* as a means of restraining popular majorities, particularly those which might arise in the House of Representatives. Perhaps the keystone of the system of checks and balances is the idea of *judicial review,* an original contribution by the Founding Fathers to the science of government. In the case of *Marbury* v. *Madison* in 1803, Chief Justice John Marshall argued convincingly that the Founding Fathers intended the Supreme Court to have the power of invalidating not only state laws and constitutions but also any laws of Congress that came in conflict with the Constitution of the United States. Marshall reasoned (1) that the "judicial power" was given to the Supreme Court, (2) that historically the judicial power included the power to interpret the meaning of the law, (3) that the Supremacy Clause made the Constitution the "Supreme Law of the Land," (4) that laws of the United States should be made "in pursuance thereof," (5) that judges are sworn to uphold the Constitution, and (6) that judges must therefore declare void any legislative act that they feel conflicts with the Constitution.

The text of the Constitution nowhere specifically authorizes federal judges to invalidate acts of Congress; at most, the Constitution implies this power. But Hamilton apparently thought that the Constitution contained this power, since he was careful to explain it in *The Federalist* No. 78 prior to the ratification of the Constitution:

The complete independence of the courts of justice is peculiarly essential in a limited constitution. By a limited constitution, I understand one which contains certain specified exceptions to the legislative authority; such, for instance, as that it shall pass no bills of attainder, no ex post facto laws, and the like. Limitations of this kind can be preserved in practice no other way than through the medium of courts of justice, whose duty it must be to declare all acts contrary to the manifest tenor of the constitution void. Without this, all the reservations of particular rights or privileges would amount to nothing. . . . The interpretation of the laws is the proper and peculiar province of the courts. A constitution is, in fact, and must be regarded by the judges as a fundamental law. It therefore belongs to them to ascertain its meaning, as well as the meaning of any particular act proceeding from the legislative body. If there should happen to be an irreconcilable variance between the two, that which has the superior obligation and validity ought, of course, to be preferred; or, in other words, the constitution ought to be preferred to the statute, the intention of the people to the intention of their agents.

Thus, the Supreme Court stands as the final defender of the fundamental principles agreed upon by the Founding Fathers against the encroachments of popularly elected legislatures.

Ratification—An Exercise in Elite Political Skills

When the work of the Constitutional Convention ended on September 17, 1787, the document was sent to New York City, where Congress was then in session. The Convention suggested that the Constitution "should afterwards be submitted to a convention of delegates chose in each state by the people thereof, under the recommendation of its legislature for their assent and ratification." The Philadelphia Convention further proposed that when *nine* states had ratified the new constitution, it should go into effect. On September 28, Congress sent the Constitution to the states without making any recommendations of its own.

The ratification procedure suggested by the Founding Fathers was a skillful political maneuver. The Convention itself had been held in secret, so there was little advance word that the delegates had not merely amended the Articles of Confederation, as they had been instructed, but instead had created a whole new scheme of government. Their ratification procedure was a complete departure from what was then the law of the land, the Articles of Confederation. The Articles provided that all amendments should be made by Congress only with the approval of *all* of the states. But since Rhode Island was firmly in the hands of small farmers, the unanimity required by the Articles was obviously out of the question; and the Founding Fathers felt obliged to act outside of the existing law. Hence the proclamation that only nine states need ratify the new Constitution.

It is important to note that the Founding Fathers also called for special ratifying conventions in the states, rather than risk submitting the Constitution to the state legislatures. This extraordinary procedure gave clear advantage to supporters of the Constitution. Nathaniel Gorham argued effectively at Philadelphia that submitting the plan to the state legislatures would weaken its chances for success:

Men chosen by the people for the particular purpose will discuss the subject more candidly than the members of the legislature who are about to lose the power which is to be given up to the general movement. Some of the legislatures are composed of several branches. It will consequently be more difficult in these cases to get the plan through the legislatures than through a convention. In the states, many of the ablest men are excluded from the legislatures but may be elected to a convention . . . the legislatures will be interrupted by a variety of little business . . . if the last Article of Confederation is to be pursued the unanimous concurrence of the states will be necessary. [9]

In other words, it was politically expedient to by-pass the state legislatures and to ignore the requirement of the Articles for unanimity among the states. Thus, the struggle for ratification began under ground rules designed by the national elite to give them the advantage over any potential opponents.

In the most important and controversial study of the Constitution to date, Charles A. Beard compiled a great deal of evidence in support of the hypothesis "that substantially all of the merchants, money lenders, security holders, manufacturers, shippers, capitalists and financiers, and their professional associates are to be found on one side in support of the Constitution, and that substantially all of the major portion of the opposition came from the non-slaveholding farmers and debtors."[10] While historians disagree over the solidarity of class divisions in the struggle for ratification, most concede that only about 160,000 persons voted in elections for delegates to state ratifying conventions and that not more than 100,000 of these voters favored the adoption of the Constitution. This figure represents about one in six of the adult males in the country, and no more than 5 percent of the population in general. Thus, whether or not Beard is correct about class divisions in the struggle for ratification, one thing is clear: The total number of persons who participated in any fashion in the ratification of the Constitution was an extremely small minority of the population.

Some men of property and education did champion the views of the common people. Men like Patrick Henry and Richard Henry Lee of Virginia vigorously attacked the Constitution as a "counterrevolutionary" document that could undo much of the progress made since 1776 toward freedom, liberty, and equality. According to the opponents of the Constitution, the new government would be "aristocratic," all-powerful, and a threat to the "spirit of republicanism" and the "genius of democracy." They charged that the new Constitution created an aristocratic upper house and an almost monarchical presidency. The powers of the national government could trample the states and deny the people of the states the opportunity to handle their own political and economic affairs. The Antifederalists repeatedly asserted that the Constitution removed powers from the people and concentrated them in the hands of a few national officials who were largely immune from popular control; moreover, they attacked the undemocratic features of the Constitution and argued that state governments were much more representative of the people. Also under attack were the secrecy of the Philadelphia Convention and the actions of the Founding Fathers, both contrary to the law and the spirit of the Articles of Confederation.

While the Antifederalists deplored the undemocratic features of the new Constitution, their most effective criticism centered on the absence of any Bill of Rights. The omission of a Bill of Rights is particularly glaring, since the idea of a Bill of Rights was very popular at the time and most of the new state constitutions contained them. It is an interesting comment on the psychology of the Founding Fathers that the idea of a Bill of Rights was never even mentioned in the Philadelphia Convention until the final week of deliberations; even then it was given little consideration. The Founding Fathers certainly believed in the idea of limited government. A few liberties were written into the body of the Constitution: protection against bills of attainder and *ex post facto* laws; a guarantee of the writ of *habeas corpus*; a limited definition of treason; a guarantee of jury trial—but there was no Bill of Rights labeled as such.

When criticism about the absence of a Bill of Rights began to mount in the states, supporters of the Constitution presented an interesting argument to explain this deficiency: (1) the national government was one of enumerated powers and could not exercise any powers not expressly delegated to it in the Constitution; (2) the power to interfere with free speech or press or otherwise to restrain liberty was not among the enumerated powers in the Constitution; (3) it was therefore unnecessary to specifically deny the new government this power. But this logic was unconvincing; the absence of a Bill of Rights seemed to confirm the suspicion that the Founding Fathers were more concerned with protecting property than with protecting the personal liberties of the people. Many members of elites and nonelites alike were uncomfortable with the thought that personal liberty depended on a thin thread of inference from enumerated powers. Supporters of the Constitution were forced to retreat from their demand for unconditional ratification; the New York, Massachusetts, and Virginia conventions agreed to the new Constitution only after receiving the solemn promise of the Federalists that a Bill of Rights would be added as amendments. Thus the fundamental guarantees of liberty in the Bill of Rights were political concessions by the nation's elite. While the Founding Fathers deserved great credit for the document that they produced at Philadelphia, nonetheless, the first Congress to meet under that Constitution was obliged to submit twelve amendments to the states, ten of which were ratified by 1791.

Historians disagree as to whether class lines were as clearly drawn in the struggle for ratification as Beard contends. But Beard's summary of the strengths and weaknesses of the Federalist and Antifederalist in the struggle over ratification is a classic statement of the political advantages of an elite over a numerically superior mass:

At all events, the disenfranchisement of the masses through property qualifications and ignorance and apathy contributed largely to the facility with which the . . . [Federalists] carried the day. The latter were alert everywhere, for they knew, not as a matter of theory, but as a practical matter of dollars and cents, the value of the new Constitution. They were well informed. They were conscious of the identity of their interests. They were well organized. They knew for weeks in advance, even before the Constitution was sent to the states for ratification, what the real nature of the contest was. They resided for the most part in the towns or in the more thickly populated areas and they could marshal their forces quickly and effectively. . . . Talent, wealth, and professional abilities were, generally speaking, on the side of the Constitutionalists. The money to be spent in the campaign of education was on their side also; and it was spent in considerable sums for pamphleteering, organizing parades and demonstrations, and engaging the interests of the press. A small percentage of the enormous gain to come through the appreciation of securities alone would have financed no mean campaign for those days. [11]

In contrast, Beard describes the plight of the Antifederalists in this struggle:

The opposition, on the other hand, suffered from the difficulties connected with getting a backwoods vote out to the town and country elections. This involved sometimes long journeys and bad weather, for it will be remembered that elections were held in late fall and winter. There were no such immediate personal gains to be made through the defeat of the Constitution, as were to be made by the security holders on the other side. It was true that the debtors knew that they would probably have to settle their accounts in full, and the small farmers were aware that taxes would have to be paid to discharge the national debt if the Constitution was adopted; and the debtors everywhere waged war against the Constitution—of this there is plenty of evidence. But they had no money to carry on their campaign; they were poor and uninfluential—the strongest battalions were not on their side. The wonder is that they came so near defeating the Constitution at the polls. [12]

Summary

Elite theory provides us with an interpretation of the Constitution of the United States and the basic structure of American government. The following propositions can be derived from our analysis of Constitutional politics:

1. The Constitution of the United States was not "ordained and established" by "the people." Instead, it was written by a small, educated, talented, wealthy elite in America, representative of powerful economic interests—bondholders, investors, merchants, real estate owners, and planters.

2. The Constitution and the national government that it established had its origins in elite dissatisfaction with the inability of the central government to pay off its bondholders, the interference of state governments with the development of a national economy, the threat to investors and creditors with state issuance of cheap paper money and laws relieving debtors of contractual obligations, the threat to propertied classes arising from post-Revolutionary War radicalism, the inability of the central government to provide an army capable of protecting western development or a navy capable of protecting American commercial interests on the high seas, and the inability of America's elite to exercise power in world affairs.

3. Ratification of the Constitution was achieved through the political skills of the elite. The masses of people in America did not participate in the writing of the Constitution nor in its adoption by the states, and they probably would have opposed the Constitution had they the information and resources to do so.

4. Founding Fathers shared a consensus that the fundamental role of government was the protection of liberty and property. They believed in a republican form of government by men of principle and property. They opposed an aristocracy or a governing nobility, but they also opposed mass democracy with direct participation by the people in decision making. They were fearful of mass movements that would seek to reduce inequalities of wealth, intelligence, talent, or virtue. "Dangerous leveling" was a serious violation of men's rights to property.

5. The structure of American government was designed to suppress "factious" issues, that is, threats to dominant economic elites. Republicanism, the division of power between state and national governments, and the complex system of checks and balances and divided power were all designed as protections against mass movements threatening liberty and property.

6. The text of the Constitution itself contains many direct and immediate benefits to America's governing elite. Although all Americans, both elite and mass, may have benefited by the adoption of the Constitution, the advantages and benefits in that document for America's elite provided the impelling motive for their activities on behalf of the new Constitution.

References

[1] Lester Cappon (ed.), *The Adams-Jefferson Letters*, Vol. I (Chapel Hill: University of North Carolina Press, 1959), p. 196.

[2] Max Farrand (ed.), *The Records of the Federal Convention of 1787*, Vol. 3 (New Haven, Conn.: Yale University Press, 1937), p. 15.

[3] *Ibid.*, p. 32.

[4] See Clinton Rossiter, *1787, The Grand Convention* (New York: Macmillan Co., 1966), p. 45.

[5] Charles Beard, *An Economic Interpretation of the Constitution of the United States* (New York: Macmillan Co., 1913), pp. 73–151.

[6] John P. Roche, "The Founding Fathers: A Reform Caucus in Action," *American Political Science Review*, 55 (December 1961), 799.

[7] See especially Beard, *Economic Interpretation of the Constitution.*

[8] James Madison, Alexander Hamilton, John Jay, *The Federalist* No. 10 (New York: The Modern Library, 1937).

[9] Beard, *Economic Interpretation of the Constitution*, pp. 217–238.

[10] *Ibid.*, pp. 16–7. Beard's "economic" interpretation differs from an elitist interpretation in that Beard believed the economic elites supported the Constitution and the masses opposed it. Our elitist interpretation asserts only that the masses did not participate in the writing or adoption of the Constitution, and that elites benefited directly from its provisions. Our interpretation does not depend upon showing that the masses opposed the Constitution, but merely upon showing that they did not participate in its establishment. Beard's thesis about class conflict over adoption is a controversial one among historians. Attacks on Beard are found in Forrest McDonald, *We the People: The Economic Origins of the Constitution* (Chicago: University of Chicago, 1963); and Robert E. Brown, *Charles Beard and the Constitution* (Princeton, N.J.: Princeton University Press, 1956). A balanced view is presented in Lee Benson, *Turner and Beard: American Historical Writing Reconsidered* (New York: Free Press, 1960).

[11] *Ibid.*, pp. 251–252.

[12] *Ibid.*, p. 252.

The Evolution of American Elites 3

A stable elite system depends on the movement of talented and ambitious individuals from the lower strata into the elite. An open elite system providing for "a slow and continuous modification of the ruling classes" is essential for continuing the system and avoiding revolution. Of course, only those nonelites who accept the basic consensus of the system can be admitted into the ruling class. Although popular elections, party competition, and other democratic institutions in America have not enabled the masses to govern, these institutions have helped keep the elite system an open one. They have assisted in the circulation of elites, even if they have never been a means of challenging the dominant elite consensus.

In this chapter, an historical analysis of the evolution of American elites, we shall show that American elite membership has evolved slowly, without any serious break in the ideas or values underlying the American political and economic system. America has never experienced a true revolution, in which governing elites were forcefully replaced with nonelites. Instead, American elite membership has been open to those individuals who have acquired wealth and property and who have accepted the national consensus about private enterprise, limited government, and individualism. Thus, industrialization, technological change, and new sources of wealth in the expanding economy have produced new elite members, and America's elite system has permitted the absorption of the new elites without upsetting the system itself.

America's political leadership over the years has been essentially conservative, in that it has accepted the basic consensus underlying the American political and economic system. Whatever the popular political label has been—"Federalist," "Democrat," "Whig," "Republican," "Progressive," "Conservative," or "Liberal"—American leadership has remained committed to the same values and ideas that motivated the Founding Fathers. No drastic revisions of the American system have ever been contemplated by the American elites.

"Religious freedom is my immediate goal, but my long-range plan is to go into real estate."

Drawing by Donald Reilly; © 1974 The New Yorker Magazine, Inc.

While it is true that there have been basic changes in public policy and major innovations in the structure of American government over the decades, we shall argue in this chapter that these changes and innovations have been *incremental* (step-by-step) rather than revolutionary. Public policies have been frequently modified but seldom replaced. Structural adaptations have been made in the constitutional system designed by the Founding Fathers, but the original framework of American constitutionalism remains substantially intact.

Finally, we shall contend that policy changes in America have not come about through demands by "the people." Instead, changes and innovations in public policy have occurred when events have threatened the system and when elites, acting to preserve the system and their place in it, have instituted reforms. Reforms have been designed to strengthen the existing social and economic fabric of society with a minimum of dislocation for governing elites. Political conflict in America has continually centered on a very narrow range of issues; only once, in the Civil War, have American elites been deeply divided over the nature of American society. The Civil War reflected a deep cleavage between Southern elites—dependent upon a plantation economy, slave labor, and free trade—and Northern industrial and commercial elites, who prospered under free labor and protective tariffs.

Hamilton and the Nation's First Public Policies

The most influential figure in George Washington's administration was Alexander Hamilton, Secretary of the Treasury. More than anyone else, Hamilton was aware that the new nation, to survive and prosper, must win the lasting confidence of business and financial elites. Only if the United States were established on a sound financial basis would it be able to attract investors both at home and abroad and to expand its industry and commerce. Great Britain remained the largest source of investment capital for the new nation, and Hamilton was decidedly pro-British. Also, he favored a strong central government as a means of protecting property and stimulating the growth of commerce and industry.

Hamilton's first move was to refund the national debt at face value. Most of the original bonds were no longer in the hands of the original owners but had fallen to speculators who had purchased them for only a fraction of their face value. Since these securities were worth only about 25 cents on the dollar, the Hamilton program for refunding the national debt meant a 300 percent profit for the speculators. But Hamilton's program did not end with refunding the debts owed by the United States; he also undertook to pay the debts incurred by the states themselves during the Revolutionary War. His object was to place the creditor class under a deep obligation to the central government.

Hamilton also acted to establish a Bank of the United States, which would receive government funds, issue a national currency, facilitate the sale of national bonds, and tie the national government even more closely to the banking community. The Constitution did not specifically grant Congress the power to create a national bank, but Hamilton was willing to interpret the "necessary and proper" clause broadly enough to include the creation of a bank to help carry out the taxing, borrowing, and currency powers enumerated in the Constitution. Obviously, Hamilton's broad construction of the "necessary and proper" clause looked in the direction of a powerful central government that would exercise powers not specifically enumerated in the Constitution. Thomas Jefferson, who was Secretary of State in the same Cabinet with Hamilton, expressed growing concern over Hamilton's tendency toward national centralization. Jefferson argued that Congress could not establish the bank because the bank was not, strictly speaking, "necessary" to carry out delegated functions. But Hamilton won out, with the support of President Washington; and in 1791 Congress voted to charter a Bank of the United States. For twenty years the bank was very successful, especially in stabilizing the currency of the new nation.

Not until 1819 was the constitutionality of the Bank of the United States decided by the Supreme Court. In the famous case of *McCulloch* v. *Maryland*, the Supreme Court upheld the broad definition of national power suggested by Hamilton under the "necessary and proper" clause. At the same time, the Court established the principle that when a state law interferes with a national activity the state law will be declared unconstitutional.[1] "Let the end be legitimate," Chief Justice John Marshall wrote, "let it be within the scope of the Constitution, and all means which are appropriate, which are plainly adopted to that end, which are not prohibited, but consistent with the letter and spirit of the Constitution, are constitutional." The McCulloch case firmly established the principle that Congress has the right to choose any appropriate means for carrying out the delegated powers of the national government. The "necessary and proper" clause is now sometimes called the "implied powers" clause or the "elastic" clause, because it gives to Congress many powers that are not explicitly given in the Constitution. Of course, Congress must still trace all of its activities to some formal grant of power, but this is usually not a difficult task.

The Rise of the Jeffersonians

The centralizing effect of Hamilton's programs and their favoring of merchants, manufacturers, and ship builders aroused serious opposition in elite circles. Southern planters and large landowners benefited very little from Hamilton's policies, and they were joined in their opposition by local and state elites who feared that a strong central government threatened their own powers. These agrarian groups were first called "Antifederalists," and later "Republicans" and "Democratic Republicans" when these terms became popular after the French Revolution. When Thomas Jefferson resigned from Washington's Cabinet in protest of Hamilton's program, opposition to the Federalists began to gather around Jefferson.

Jefferson is portrayed in history as a great democrat and champion of the "common man." And it is true that in writing the Declaration of Independence, the Virginia Statute for Religious Freedom, and the famous *Notes on Virginia*, Jefferson expressed concern for the rights of all "the people" and a willingness to trust in their wisdom. But when Jefferson spoke warmly of the merits of "the people," he meant those who owned and managed their own farms and estates. He firmly believed that only those who owned their own land could make good citizens. Jefferson disliked aristocracy, but he also held urban masses in contempt. He wanted to see the United States become a nation of free, educated, landowning farmers. Democracy, he believed, could only be founded on a propertied class in a propertied nation.

Jefferson's political views differed very little from those of the Founding Fathers. In 1788 he wrote to James Madison praising *The Federalist* as "the best commentary on the principles of government which was ever written." He shared the concern of the Founding Fathers about unrestrained rule by the masses. While Jefferson expressed more confidence in the judgment of small landowning farmers than most of his contemporaries, he also believed in republican government with its checks and balances and safeguards against popular majorities. Jefferson was willing to base republican government on large and small landowners, but he distrusted merchants, manufacturers, laborers, and urban dwellers. In 1787 he wrote:

I think our governments will remain virtuous for many centuries; as long as they remain chiefly agricultural; and this will be as long as there shall be vacant lands in any part of America. When they get piled upon one another in large cities, as in Europe, they will become corrupt as in Europe.

Later on he exclaimed: "Those who labor in the earth are the chosen people of God, if ever he had a chosen people." His belief that land ownership was essential to virtuous government explains in part his Louisiana Purchase, which he hoped would provide the American people with land "to the hundredth and thousandth generation."[2]

The dispute between Federalists and Antifederalists in early America was not a dispute between elites and masses. Instead, it was a dispute within elite circles between two kinds of property—merchants and bankers on one side, and plantation owners and slaveholders on the other. As Richard Hofstadter explains:

. . . although democratically minded Americans did stand with Jefferson, the line of division was essentially between two kinds of property, not two kinds of philosophy. The Federalists during Hamilton's service as Secretary of the Treasury had given the government a foundation of unashamed devotion to the mercantile and investing classes . . . the landed interests, however, were in a majority, and it was only a matter of time before they could marshal themselves in a strong party of their own. Jefferson's party was formed to defend specific property interests rather than the abstract premises of democracy, and its policies were conceived and executed in the sober, moderate spirit that Jefferson's generation expected of propertied citizens when they entered the political arena. [3]

The Antifederalists, or "Republicans," did not elect their first president, Thomas Jefferson, until 1800. John Adams, a Federalist, was chosen to succeed Washington in the election of 1796. Yet the election of 1796 was an important milestone in the development of the American political system. For the first time, two candidates, Adams and Jefferson, campaigned not as individuals but as members of political parties. For the first time, the candidates for the electoral college announced themselves before the election as either "Adams's men" or "Jefferson's men." More importantly, for the first time, the American political leaders saw the importance of molding mass opinion in organizing the masses for political action. It was the Republican party that first saw the importance of working among the masses to rally popular support. The Federalist leaders made the mistake of assuming that they could maintain the unquestioning support of the less-educated and less-wealthy without bothering to mold their opinions.

Rather than try, like the Republicans, to manipulate public opinion, the Federalists tried to outlaw public criticism of government officials by means of the Alien and Sedition Acts of 1798. Among other things, these acts made it a crime to conspire to oppose the legal measures of the government or to interfere with their execution, or to publish any false or malicious writing directed against the president or Congress, or to "stir up hatred" against them. These acts directly challenged the newly adopted First Amendment guarantee of freedom of speech and press. But the Supreme Court had not yet asserted itself in declaring laws of Congress unconstitutional, as it would in *Marbury* v. *Madison*[4] a few years later.

In response to the Alien and Sedition Acts, Jefferson and Madison put forward their famous Kentucky and Virginia Resolutions. These measures proposed that the states should assume the right to decide whether Congress has acted unconstitutionally and, furthermore, that the states might properly "interpose" their authority against "palpable and alarming infractions of the Constitution." The Virginia and Kentucky legislatures passed these resolutions and declared the Alien and Sedition Acts were "void and of no force" in these states.

Republicans in Power—The Stability of Public Policy

In the election of 1800, the Federalists finally went down to defeat; Thomas Jefferson and Aaron Burr were elected over John Adams and C. C. Pinckney. Only New England, New Jersey, and Delaware, where commercial and manufacturing interests were strongest, voted Federalist. The vast majority of American people won their living from the soil, and landed elites were able to mobilize these masses behind their bid for control of the government. The Federalists had failed to recognize the importance of agrarianism in the nation's economic and political life. Another half century would pass and America's industrial revolution would be in full swing before manufacturing and commercial elites would reestablish their dominance.

But the real importance of the election of 1800 is *not* that landed interests gained power in relation to commercial and industrial interests. The importance of 1800 is that for the first time in America's history control of the government passed peacefully from the hands of one faction to an opposition faction. This may seem commonplace, but there are few nations in the world today where government office changes hands in orderly or peaceful fashion. The fact that an "out" party peacefully replaced an "in" party is further testimony to the strength of the consensus among the elite of the new nation. Despite bitter campaign rhetoric, Federalists and Republicans agreed to abide by the basic "rules of the game," to view an opposition faction as legitimate, and to accept the outcome of an election. The Federalists relinquished control of the government without fear that the fundamental values of the American society would be destroyed by a new governing faction. There was clearly more agreement among American leaders than there was disagreement.*

*The original text of the Constitution did not envision an opposition faction. Presidential electors were permitted to cast two votes for president, with the understanding that the candidate with the second highest vote total would be vice-president. A total of 73 Republican electors pledged to Jefferson were sent to the electoral college, and 65 Federalists pledged to Adams. Somewhat thoughtlessly, all of the Republicans cast one vote for Jefferson and one vote for

The "Virginia Dynasty"—Thomas Jefferson, James Madison, and finally James Monroe—was to govern the country for a total of six presidential terms, nearly a quarter of a century. Interestingly, once in office, the Republicans made few changes in Federalist and Hamiltonian policy.* No attack was made on commercial or industrial enterprise; in fact, commerce and industry prospered under Republican rule as never before. No attempt was made to recover money paid out by Hamilton in the refunding of national or state debts. Speculations in public lands continued. Instead of crushing the banks, Republicans were soon supporting the financial interests they were sworn to oppose.

When the Bank of the United States expired in 1811, problems of cheap currency and unreliable state banks began to plague Republican men of property; and by 1816, the Republicans themselves chartered a Second Bank of the United States. Soon Republican newspapers were reprinting Alexander Hamilton's arguments in favor of the constitutionality of the First Bank of the United States! Jefferson was an ardent expansionist; to add to America's wealth in land, he purchased the vast Louisiana Territory. Later a stronger army and a system of internal roads were required to assist the development of western land. Jefferson's successor, James Madison, built a strong navy and engaged in another war with England, the War of 1812, to protect American commerce on the high seas. The Napoleonic Wars and the War of 1812, by depressing trade with Britain, stimulated American manufacturing. In 1816 Republicans passed a high tariff in order to protect domestic industry and manufacturing from foreign goods. As for Republican tax policies, Jefferson wrote in 1816:

Aaron Burr, his running mate, with the result that, when the votes were tallied, each man was equally eligible for the presidency. Because of the tie vote, the decision went to the Federalist-controlled House of Representatives, where a movement was begun to elect Burr, rather than Jefferson, in order to embarrass the Republicans. But Alexander Hamilton used his influence in Congress to swing the election to his old political foe Jefferson, suggesting again that their differences were not so deep that either would deliberately undermine the presidency to strike at the other. Once in power, the Republicans passed the Twelfth Amendment to the Constitution, providing that each presidential elector should thereafter vote separately for president and vice-president. This reform was promptly agreed to by both Federalists and Republicans in the states and was ratified in time for the election of 1804.

*The only major pieces of legislation to be repealed by the Republicans were the Alien and Sedition Acts. And it seems clear that in these acts the Federalists had violated elite consensus. Even John Marshall, who was elected as a Federalist congressman in 1798, pledged to support repeal of these acts.

To take from one, because it is thought his own industry and that of his fathers has acquired too much, in order to spare to others, who, or whose fathers have not, exercised equal industry and skill, is to violate arbitrarily the first principle of association, 'the guarantee to everyone of free exercise of his industry and the fruits acquired by it.'[5]

In short, the Republicans had no intention of redistributing wealth in America. Indeed, before the end of Madison's second term, the Republicans had taken over the whole complex of Hamiltonian policies—a national bank, high tariffs, protection for manufacturers, internal improvements, western land development, a strong army and navy, and a broad interpretation of national power. So complete was the elite consensus that by 1820 the Republicans had completely driven the Federalist party out of existence, largely by taking over their programs.

The Rise of the Western Elites

According to Frederick Jackson Turner, "The rise of the New West was the most significant fact in American history."[6] Certainly the American West had a profound impact on the political system of the new nation. People went West because of the vast wealth of fertile lands that awaited them there; nowhere in the world could one acquire wealth so quickly as in the new American West. Because aristocratic families of the eastern seaboard seldom had reason to migrate westward, the western settlers were mainly middle- or lower-class immigrants. With hard work and good fortune, a penniless migrant could become a wealthy plantation owner or cattle rancher in a single generation. Thus, the West meant rapid upward social mobility.

New elites arose in the West and had to be assimilated into America's governing circles. This assimilation had a profound effect on the character of America's elites. No one exemplifies the new entrants into America's elite better than Andrew Jackson. Jackson's victory in the presidential election of 1828 was not a victory of the common man against the propertied classes but rather a victory of the new western elites against established Republican leadership in the East. Jackson's victory forced America's established elites to recognize the growing importance of the West and to open their ranks to the new rich who were settled west of the Alleghenies.

Since Jackson was a favorite of the people, it was easy for him to believe in the wisdom of the common man. But "Jacksonian Democracy" was by no means a philosophy of leveling equalitarianism. The ideal of the frontier society was the self-made man, and wealth and power won by competitive skill was very much admired. It was only wealth and power obtained through special privilege that offended the frontiersmen. They believed in a *natural aristocracy,* rather than an aristocracy by birth, education, or special privilege. Jackson himself best expressed this philosophy in his famous message vetoing the bill to recharter the national bank:

Distinctions in society will always exist under every just government. Equality of talents, of education, or wealth cannot be produced by human institutions. In the full enjoyment of the gifts of heaven and the fruits of superior industry, economy, and virtue, every man is equally entitled to protection by law; but when the laws undertake to add to these natural and just advantages artificial distinctions, to grant titles, gratuities, and exclusive privileges, to make the rich richer and the potent more powerful, the humble members of society—the farmers, mechanics, and laborers,—who have neither the time nor the means for securing like favors to themselves, have a right to complain of the injustice of their government. [7]

Thus it was not absolute equality that Jacksonians demanded but rather a more open elite system—a greater opportunity for the rising middle class to acquire wealth and influence through competition.

Hoping to win a place for themselves in America's governing circles, the new western leaders tried to convince the public that politics and administration should be taken from the hands of social elites and opened to men like themselves, who could boast of natural ability and talent. Jackson himself expressed this philosophy in his first annual message to Congress in December 1829:

The duties of all public offices are, or at least admit of being made, so plain and simple that men of intelligence may readily qualify themselves for their performance, and I cannot but believe that more is lost by the long continuance of men in office than is generally to be gained by experience.

Rotation in office became a leading principle of Jacksonian Democracy.

In their struggle to open America's elite system, the Jacksonians appealed to mass sentiment. Jackson's humble beginnings, his image as a self-made man, his military adventures, his frontier experience, and his rough, brawling style served to endear him to the masses. As beneficiaries of popular support, the new elites of the West developed a strong faith in the wisdom and justice of popular decisions. All of the new western states that entered the Union granted universal white male suffrage, and gradually the older states fell into step. Rising elites, themselves often less than a generation away from the masses, saw in a widened electorate a chance for personal advancement that they could never have achieved under the old regime. Therefore, the Jacksonians became noisy and effective advocates of the principle that all men should have the right to vote and that no restrictions should be placed on officeholding. They also launched a successful attack upon the congressional caucus system of nominating presidential candidates. Having been defeated in Congress in 1824, Jackson wished to sever Congress from the nominating process. In 1832, when the Democrats held their first national convention, Andrew Jackson was renominated by acclamation.

Jacksonian Democracy also brought changes in the method of selecting presidential electors. The Constitution left to the various state legislatures the right to decide how presidential electors should be chosen, and in most cases the legislatures themselves chose the electors. But after 1832 all states selected their presidential electors by popular vote. In most of these states the people voted for electors who were listed under the name of their party and their candidate.

The Jacksonian drive to open America's elite system did not stop with electoral reforms. The western elites also tried to curtail the privileges of the established eastern elites. As a westerner, Jackson despised the Bank of the United States, which was controlled by conservative eastern bankers, and supported the free lending policies of the state banks. State bank men were prominent in Jackson's first administration; Roger Taney, for instance, was a lawyer for and stockholder of the Union Bank of Maryland before Jackson appointed him Chief Justice of the U.S. Supreme Court. Thus when, prior to the election of 1832, easterners Daniel Webster and Nicholas Biddle pushed through Congress a new charter for the Bank of the United States to replace the charter that was to expire in 1836, Jackson vetoed the new charter with a ringing message that cemented his popularity with the masses. He denounced the banks as a "granted monopoly and exclusive privilege." Again, Jackson emerged as the apparent champion of the common man.

Following his reelection in 1832, Jackson decided to make war upon the Bank and its president, Nicholas Biddle. Jackson withdrew all deposits of the United States government from the bank and placed them in selected state banks—"pet banks," as they were called—which were prepared to extend credit to the new empire builders and land speculators of the western states. The result was that money began to move from east to west in America and the way was paved for the rise of new western capitalism. Jacksonian Democracy broke the exclusive monopoly of the eastern elites over money and political power in America.

Yet the evidence is clear that the changes in the character of elites, from the administration of John Adams through Thomas Jefferson to Andrew Jackson, were very minor. Sociologist Sidney H. Aronson's historical research reveals that, contrary to the general assumption,

Jackson's administration was clearly upper class in origin, college educated, prestigiously employed, professionally trained, and probably wealthy. (See Table 3–1). In fact, Jackson's administration is not much different in class character from that of Thomas Jefferson or even that of the Federalist John Adams! Over half of Jackson's top appointees were born into America's distinguished upper-class families, and three-quarters enjoyed high class standing, prior to their appointment, either through birth or achievement.

Elite Cleavage—The Civil War

During its first sixty years America's elites were in substantial agreement about the character and direction of the new nation. Conflicts over the Bank, the tariff, internal improvements (roads, harbors, etc.), and even the controversial war with Mexico in 1846 did not threaten the basic underlying consensus in support of the American political system. In the 1850s, however, the role of the Negro in American society—the most divisive issue in the history of American politics—drove a wedge among America's elites and ultimately led to the nation's bloodiest war. The American political system was unequal to the task of negotiating a peaceful settlement to the problem of slavery because America's elites were themselves deeply divided over the question.

In 1787, the Southern elites—cotton planters, land owners, exporters, and slave traders—had foreseen an end to slavery; but after 1820,

Table 3–1
Social Class Characteristics of Presidential Appointments of Adams, Jefferson, and Jackson

Characteristics	Adams (N = 96)	Jefferson (N = 100)	Jackson (N = 127)
Father held political office	52%	43%	44%
Father attended college	17	13	12
Class I¹ family social position	62	58	51
High-ranking occupation	92	93	90
Political office prior to appointment	91	83	88
Class I¹ social position	86	74	74
Family in America in seventeenth century	55	48	48
Attended college	63	52	52
Professional training	69	74	81
Relative an appointive elite	40	34	34

¹"Class I" is the highest of four classes described as follows:
  Class I: "national and international aristocracy";
  Class II: "prosperous and respectable";
  Class III: "respectable";
  Class IV: "subsistence or impoverished."
Breakdowns by each class are as follows:
  Adams: I: 62%, II: 19%, III: 5%, IV: 1%, unknown: 13%.
  Jefferson: I: 58%, II: 15%, III: 6%, IV: 1%, unknown: 20%.
  Jackson: I: 51%, II: 25%, III: 11%, IV: 2%, unknown: 11%.
Source: Sidney H. Aronson, *Status and Kinship in the Higher Civil Service* (Cambridge: Harvard University Press, 1964), p. 195.

the demand for cotton became insatiable, and cotton could not be profitably produced without slave labor. Over half the value of all American goods shipped abroad before the Civil War was in cotton; and a broad belt of Southern land, ranging in width from about 500 miles in the Carolinas and Georgia to 600 or 700 miles in the Mississippi Valley, was devoted primarily to cotton culture. While Virginia did not depend upon cotton, it sold great numbers of slaves to the cotton states, and "slave raising" itself became immensely profitable. The price of a good slave for the fields increased from $300 in 1820 to over $1,000 in 1860, even though the slave population grew from about a million and a half to nearly four million during this period.

It was the white *elites* and not the white *masses* of the South who had an interest in the slave and cotton culture. On the eve of the Civil War, probably no more than 400,000 Southern families—approximately one in four—held slaves. And many of these families held only one or two slaves each. The number of great planters—men who owned fifty or more slaves and large holdings of land—was probably not more than 7,000. Yet the views of these men dominated Southern politics.

The Northern elites were merchants and manufacturers who depended upon free labor. However, Northern elites had no direct interest in the abolition of slavery in the South. Some Northern manufacturers were making good profits from Southern trade; and with higher tariffs, they stood a chance to make even better profits. Abolitionist activities imperiled trade relations between North and South and were often looked upon with irritation even in Northern social circles. But both Northern and Southern elites realized that control of the West was the key to future dominance of the nation. Northern elites wanted a West composed of small farmers who produced food and raw materials for the industrial and commercial East and provided a market for eastern goods. Southern planters feared the voting power of a West composed of small farmers and wanted western lands for the expansion of the cotton and slave culture. Cotton ate up the land and, because it required continuous cultivation and monotonous rounds of simple tasks, was suited to slave labor. Thus, to protect the cotton economy, it was essential to protect slavery in western lands. This conflict over western land eventually precipitated the Civil War.

Yet despite these differences, the underlying consensus of American elites was so great that compromise after compromise was devised to maintain unity. In the Missouri Compromise of 1820, the land in the Louisiana Purchase exclusive of Missouri was divided between free territory and slave territory at 36° 30'; and Maine and Missouri were admitted as free and slave states, respectively. After the war with Mexico, the elaborate Compromise of 1850 caused one of the greatest debates in American legislative history, with Senators Henry Clay, Daniel Webster,

John C. Calhoun, Salmon P. Chase, Stephen A. Douglas, Jefferson Davis, Alexander H. Stevens, Robert Tombs, William H. Seward, and Thaddeus Stevens all participating. Elite cleavage was apparent, but it was not yet so divisive as to split the nation. A compromise was achieved, providing for the admission of California as a free state; for the creation of two new territories, New Mexico and Utah, out of the Mexican cession; for a drastic fugitive slave law to satisfy Southern planters; and for the prohibition of slave trade in the District of Columbia. Even the Kansas-Nebraska Act of 1854 was intended to be a compromise; each new territory was supposed to decide for itself whether it should be slave or free, with the expectation that Nebraska would vote free and Kansas slave. But gradually the spirit of compromise gave way to cleavage and conflict.

Beginning in 1856, proslavery and antislavery forces fought it out in "bleeding Kansas." Senator Charles Sumner of Massachusetts delivered a condemnation of slavery in the Senate and was beaten almost to death on the Senate floor by Preston Brooks, a relative of Senator Andrew P. Butler of South Carolina. Intemperate language in the Senate became commonplace, with frequent threats of secession, violence, and civil war.

In 1857, the Supreme Court decided, in *Dred Scot* v. *Sanford*,[8] that the Missouri Compromise was unconstitutional because Congress had no authority to forbid slavery in any territory. Slave property, said Chief Justice Roger B. Taney, was as much protected by the Constitution as was any other kind of property.

In 1859, John Brown and his followers raided the United States arsenal at Harpers Ferry, as a first step to freeing the slaves of Virginia by force. Brown was captured by Virginia militia under the command of Colonel Robert E. Lee, tried for treason, found guilty, and executed. Southerners believed that Northerners had tried to incite the horror of slave insurrection, while Northerners believed that Brown had died a martyr.

The conflict between North and South led to the complete collapse of the Whig party and the emergence of a new Republican party composed exclusively of Northerners and westerners. For the first time in the history of American parties, one of the two major parties did not spread across both sides of the Mason-Dixon line. 1860 was the only year in American history that four, rather than two, major parties sought the presidency. The nation was so divided that no party came close to winning the majority of popular votes. Lincoln, the Republican candidate, and Douglas, the Democratic candidate, won most of their votes from the North and West, while Breckenridge, the Southern Democratic candidate, and Bell, the Constitutional Union candidate, received most of their votes from the South. (See Table 3–2.)

More important, the cleavage had become so deep that many prominent Southern leaders announced that they would not accept the outcome of the presidential election if Lincoln won. Threats of secession were not new, but this time it was no bluff. For the first and only time in American history, prominent elite members were prepared to destroy the American political system rather than compromise their interests and principles. Shortly after the election, on December 20, 1860, the state of South Carolina seceded from the Union. Within six months, ten other Southern states had followed.

Yet even in the midst of this disastrous conflict, continued devotion to the principles of constitutional government and private property are evident among both Northern and Southern elites. There were many genuine efforts at compromise and conciliation. Abraham Lincoln never attacked slavery in the South; his exclusive concern was to halt the spread of slavery in the western territories. He wrote in 1845: "I hold it a paramount duty of us in the free states, due to the union of the states, and perhaps to liberty itself (paradox though it may seem), to let the slavery of the other states alone."[9] Throughout his political career he consistently held this position. On the other hand, with regard to the western territories he said: "The whole nation is interested that the best use shall be made of these territories. We want them for homes and free white people. This they cannot be, to any considerable extent, if slavery shall be planted within them."[10] In short, Lincoln wanted the western territories to be tied economically and culturally to the Northern system. As for Lincoln's racial views, as late as 1858 he said:

I will say, then, that I am not, nor ever have been, in favor of bringing about in any way the social and political equality of the white and black races; that I am not, nor ever have been, in favor of making voters or jurors of Negroes, nor qualifying them to hold office, nor to intermarry with white people . . . and in as much as they cannot so live while they do remain together, there must be a position of superior and inferior; and I as

	Percent of Total Vote	Percent of Vote from North and West	Percent of Vote from South
Republicans: Lincoln	40	98.6	1.4
Democrats: Douglas	30	88.0	12.0
Southern Democrats: Breckenridge	18	33.0	67.0
Constitutional Union: Bell	12	13.0	87.0

Table 3–2
The Election of 1860

Source: Robert A. Dahl, *Pluralist Democracy in the United States* (Chicago: Rand McNally, 1966, pp. 312–313; data from W. Dean Burnham, *Presidential Ballots, 1836–1892* (Baltimore: Johns Hopkins Press, 1955).

much as any other man am in favor of having the superior position assigned to the white race. [11]

Lincoln's political posture was essentially conservative: He wished to preserve the long-established order and consensus that had protected American principles and property rights so successfully in the past. He was not an abolitionist, and it was not his goal to destroy the Southern elites or to alter the Southern social fabric. His goal was to bring the South back into the Union, to restore orderly government, and to establish the principle that the states cannot resist national authority with force. At the beginning of the war, Lincoln knew that a great part of conservative Northern opinion supported a fight for the Union but might oppose a war to free Negroes. Lincoln's great political skill was his ability to submerge all the issues of the Civil War into one single overriding theme—the preservation of the Union. On the other hand, he was bitterly attacked throughout the war by radical Republicans who thought that he had "no anti-slavery instincts."

As the war continued and casualties mounted, opinion in the North became increasingly bitter toward Southern slaveowners. Many Republicans joined the abolitionists in calling for emancipation of the slaves simply to punish the "rebels." They knew that the power of the South was based on the labor of slaves. Lincoln also knew that if he proclaimed to the world that the war was being fought to free the slaves, there would be less danger of foreign intervention. Yet even in late summer of 1862, Lincoln wrote:

My paramount object in this struggle is to save the Union. If I could save the Union without freeing any slaves, I would do it; if I could save it by freeing some and leaving others alone, I would also do that. I shall do less whenever I shall believe what I am doing hurts the cause, and I shall do more whenever I believe doing more will help the cause. I shall adopt new views as fast as they shall appear to be true views. [12]

Finally, on September 22, 1862, Lincoln issued his preliminary Emancipation Proclamation. Claiming his right as commander-in-chief of the army and navy, he promised that "on the first day of January 1863, all persons held as slaves within any state or designated part of a state, the people whereof shall then be in rebellion against the United States shall be then, thence forward, and forever free." Thus one of the great steps toward freedom in this nation, the Emancipation Proclamation, did not come about as a result of demands by the people, and certainly not as a result of demands by the slaves themselves. It was a political and military action by the president intended to help preserve the Union. It was not a revolutionary action but a conservative one.

The importance of the Civil War for America's elite structure was the commanding position that the new industrial capitalists won during the course of the struggle. Even before 1860, Northern industry had been altering the course of American life; the economic transformation of the United States from an agricultural to an industrial nation reached the crescendo of a revolution in the second half of the nineteenth century. Canals and steam railroads had been opening new markets for the growing industrial cities of the East. The rise of corporations and of stock markets for the accumulation of capital upset old-fashioned ideas of property. The introduction of machinery in factories revolutionized the conditions of American labor and made the masses dependent upon industrial capitalists for their livelihood. Civil War profits compounded the capital of the industrialists and placed them in a position to dominate the economic life of the nation. Moreover, when the Southern planters were removed from the national scene, the government in Washington became the exclusive domain of the new industrial leaders.

The protective tariff, long opposed by the Southern planters, became the cornerstone of the new business structure of America. The industrial capitalists realized that the Northwest Territory was the natural market for their manufactured goods, and the protective tariff restricted the vast and growing American market to American industry alone. When the passage of the Homestead Act (1862) threw the national domain wide open to settlers, eastern capital hastened to build a system of transcontinental railroads to link expanding western markets to eastern industry. The Northeast was rich in the natural resources of coal, iron, and water power; and the large immigrant population streaming in from Europe furnished a dependable source of cheap labor. The Northeast also had superior means of transportation—both water and rail—to facilitate the assembling of raw materials and the marketing of finished products. With the rise of the new industrial capitalism, power in the United States flowed from the South and West to the Northeast and Jefferson's dream of a nation of free farmers faded.

The new industrial elite found a new philosophy to justify its political and economic dominance. Drawing an analogy from the new Darwinian biology, Herbert Spencer undertook to demonstrate that just as an elite was selected in nature through evolution, so also society would near perfection as it allowed natural social elites to be selected by free competition. In defense of the new capitalists, Herbert Spencer argued: "There cannot be more good done than that of letting social progress go on unhindered; an immensity of mischief may be done in . . . the artificial preservation of those least able to care for themselves."[13] Spencer hailed the accumulation of new industrial wealth as a sign of "the survival of the fittest." The "social Darwinists" found in the law of survival of the fittest an admirable defense for the emergence of a ruthless ruling

The Rise of the New Industrial Elite

elite, an elite which defined its own self-interest more narrowly, perhaps, than any other in American history. It was a philosophy that permitted the conditions of the masses to decline to the lowest depths in American history.

Spencer's social Darwinism forbade restrictive "meddling" legislation. If trusts and monopolies proved to be the natural results of competition, worshippers of competition could not logically prohibit them. Yet, ironically, the industrial elites saw no objection to legislation if it furthered their success in business. Unrestricted competition might prove who was the "fittest"; but as an added precaution to insure that industrial capitalists themselves emerged as the "fittest," these new elites also insisted upon government subsidies, patents, tariffs, loans, and massive giveaways of land and other natural resources.

After the Civil War, businessmen became more numerous in Congress than at any other time in American history. They had little trouble voting high tariffs and hard money (made of or backed by gold), both of which heightened profits. Very little effective regulatory legislation was permitted to reach the floor of Congress. After 1881 the Senate came under the spell of Nelson Aldrich, son-in-law of John D. Rockefeller, who controlled Standard Oil. Aldrich served 30 years in the Senate. He believed that geographical representation in the Senate was old-fashioned and openly advocated a Senate manned officially by representatives from the great business "constituencies"—steel, coal, copper, railroads, banks, textiles, and so on.

As business became increasingly national in scope, only the strongest or most unscrupulous of the competitors survived. Great producers tended to become the cheapest producers, and little companies tended to disappear. Industrial production rose rapidly, while the number of industrial concerns steadily diminished. Total capital investment and total output of industry vastly increased, while ownership became concentrated. One result was the emergence of monopolies and near monopolies in each of the major industries of America. Another result was the accumulation of great family fortunes.[14] (See Table 3–3, which was compiled from 1924 tax returns. Admittedly it fails to record other great personal fortunes, such as Armour and Swift in meat packing, Candler in Coca-Cola, Cannon in textiles, Fleischman in yeast, Pulitzer in publishing, Golet in real estate, Harriman in railroads, Heinz in foods, Manville in asbestos, Cudahy in meat packing, Dorrance in Campbell's Soup, Hartford in A & P, Eastman in film, Firestone in rubber, Sinclair in oil, Chrysler in automobiles, Pabst in beer, and others.)

Typical of the great entrepreneurs of industrial capitalism was John D. Rockefeller. By the end of the Civil War, Rockefeller had accumulated a modest fortune of $50,000 in wholesale grain and meat. In 1865, with extraordinary good judgment, he invested his money in the wholly new petroleum business. He backed one of the first oil refineries in the nation and continually reinvested his profits into his business. In 1867, backed by two new partners—H. M. Flagler and F. W. Harkness—Rockefeller founded the Standard Oil Company of Ohio, which in that year refined 4 percent of the nation's output. By 1872, with monopoly as his goal, he had acquired 20 of the 25 refineries in Cleveland and was laying plans that within a decade would bring him into control of over 90 percent of the oil refineries of the country. Rockefeller bought up pipelines, warehouses, and factories and was able to force railroads to grant him rebates. In 1882, he formed a giant trust, the Standard Oil Company, with a multitude of affiliates. Thereafter, the Standard Oil Company became a prototype of American monopolies. As Rockefeller himself put it: "The day of combination is here to stay. Individualism has gone, never to return."

Perhaps the greatest American success story is that of Andrew Carnegie, a Scottish immigrant boy who came penniless to America. He worked first as a bobbin boy for $1.25 a week in a western Pennsylvania cotton factory, then as a messenger at $2.50 a week in a Pittsburgh telegraph office. Quite soon, he became the private secretary of Thomas A. Scott of the Pennsylvania Railroad and began to amass railway and oil stocks. Then, on a trip to England, he saw steel being made by the new Bessemer process, and he returned to the United States determined to manufacture steel. In Pittsburgh, in 1873, he opened the J. Edgar Thompson Steel Mill (carefully named after the president of the Pennsylvania Railroad). Carnegie soon monopolized the steel industry in Pittsburgh and much of the nation, and steel replaced railroads as the backbone of the new industrialism. Unlike his fellow capitalists Carnegie believed that "The amassing of wealth is one of the worst species of idolatry" and he gave away over $350,000,000. Most of his philanthropy went to public libraries in cities throughout the nation.

At the apex of America's new corporate and industrial elite stood J. Pierpont Morgan, master of industrial finance. In 1901, Morgan knit together the U.S. Steel Corporation, America's first billion dollar corporation, by merging Carnegie Steel and three other steel giants—the Tennessee Coal and Iron Company, the Illinois Steel Company, and Colorado Fuel and Iron. He later established International Harvester Corporation. During World War I, J. P. Morgan and Company was the purchasing agent in America for the Allies at a commission of 1 percent. J. P. Morgan himself was not the wealthiest of America's wealthy men, but the Morgan firm derived its unprecedented power from the combined resources of many families and corporations in which it had an interest. The extent of Morgan power in American industry and finance defies statistical measurement. Direct Morgan *control* of banking and nonbanking corporations often shades into Morgan *dominance,* and Morgan dominance often shades into Morgan *influence.* Morgan partners

Table 3–3
The Industrial Fortunes,
1924

Family and Number of Tax Returns	Primary Source of Wealth	Aggregate 1924 Tax	Approximate Net Aggregate Income Taxed	Net Aggregate Fortune Taxed	Gross Adjusted Fortune after Multiplying by 3	Maximum Estimated Fortune
1. 21 Rockefellers	Standard Oil	$7,309,989	$17,955,000	$359,100,000	$1,077,300,000	$2,500,000,000
2. 34 Morgan Inner Group	J. P. Morgan & Co.	4,796,263	12,620,000	276,000,000‡	728,000,000‡	......
(Including Morgan partners and families and eight leading Morgan corporation executives)						
3. 2 Fords	Ford Motor Co.	4,766,863	11,000,000	220,000,000	660,000,000	1,000,000,000
4. 5 Harknesses	Standard Oil	2,776,735	7,550,000	150,200,000	450,600,000	800,000,000
5. 3 Mellons	Aluminum Company	3,237,876	7,550,000	150,000,000	450,000,000	1,000,000,000
6. 22 Vanderbilts	N.Y. Central R.R.	2,148,892	6,005,000	120,100,000	360,300,000	800,000,000
7. 4 Whitneys	Standard Oil	2,143,992	5,375,000	107,500,000	322,000,000	750,000,000
8. 28 Standard Oil Group	Standard Oil	1,737,857	5,435,000	118,700,000	356,000,000	......
(Including Archbolds, Rogerses, Bedfords, Cutlers, Flaglers, Pratts, and Benjamins, but excepting others)						
9. 20 Du Ponts	E. I. du Pont de Nemours	1,294,651	3,925,000	79,500,000	238,500,000	1,000,000,000
10. 8 McCormicks	Int. Harvester and Chi. Tribune	1,332,517	3,520,000	70,400,000	211,200,000	......
11. 2 Bakers	1st National Bank	1,575,482	3,500,000	70,000,000	210,000,000	500,000,000
12. 5 Fishers	General Motors	1,424,583	3,225,000	64,500,000	193,500,000	500,000,000
13. 6 Guggenheims	Amer. Smelting & Rfg. Co.	817,836	2,185,000	63,700,000	190,100,000	......
14. 6 Fields	Marshall Field & Co.	1,197,605	3,000,000	60,000,000	180,000,000	......
15. 5 Curtis-Boks	Curtis Pub. Co.	1,303,228	2,900,000	58,000,000	174,000,000	......
16. 3 Dukes	Am. Tobacco Co.	1,045,544	2,600,000	52,000,000	156,000,000	......
17. 3 Berwinds	Berwind-White Coal Co.	906,495	2,500,000	50,000,000	150,000,000	......
18. 17 Lehmans	Lehman Brothers	672,897	2,150,000	43,000,000	129,000,000‡	......
19. 3 Wideners	Am. Tob. & Pub. Utilities	772,720	1,975,000	39,500,000	118,500,000	......
20. 7 Reynolds	R. J. Reynolds Tobacco Co.	652,824	1,950,000	39,000,000	117,000,000	......
21. 3 Astors	Real Estate	783,002	1,900,000	38,000,000	114,000,000	300,000,000
22. 6 Winthrops	Miscellaneous	651,188	1,735,000	34,700,000	104,100,000	......
23. 3 Stillmans	National City Bank	623,614	1,700,000	34,000,000	102,000,000	500,000,000
24. 3 Timkens	Timken Roller Bearing Co.	781,435	1,850,000	37,000,000	111,000,000	......
25. 4 Pitcairns	Pittsburgh Plate Glass Co.	752,545	1,660,000	33,200,000	99,600,000	......
26. 8 Warburgs	Kuhn, Loeb & Co.	598,246	1,620,000	32,400,000	97,200,000‡	......
27. 4 Metcalfs	Rhode Island textile mills	623,817	1,510,000	30,200,000	90,600,000	......
28. 3 Clarks	Singer Sewing Mach. Co.	583,087	1,475,000	30,000,000	90,000,000	......
29. 16 Phipps	Carnegie Steel Co.	431,969	1,485,000	29,700,000	89,100,000	600,000,000
30. 4 Kahns	Kuhn, Loeb & Co.	565,608	1,440,000	28,800,000	86,400,000‡	......

#							
31.	2 Greens	Stocks and real estate	443,021	1,200,000	24,000,000	72,000,000	
32.	2 Pattersons	Chicago Tribune, Inc.	365,211	1,015,000	20,300,000	60,900,000	
33.	3 Tafts	Real Estate	329,689	900,000	18,000,000	54,000,000	
34.	3 Deerings	International Harvester	315,701	825,000	16,500,000	49,500,000	
35.	6 De Forests	Corp. law practice	202,013	685,000	13,700,000	41,100,000‡	
36.	5 Goulds	Railroads	154,563	565,000	11,300,000	33,900,000	400,000,000
37.	3 Hills	Railroads	226,827	360,000	7,200,000	21,600,000	150,000,000
38.	2 Drexels	J. P. Morgan & Co.	131,616	350,000	7,000,000	21,000,000	100,000,000
39.	Thomas Fortune Ryan*†	Stock market	791,851	1,800,000	36,000,000	108,000,000	
40.	H. Foster (Cleveland)	Auto parts	569,894	1,700,000	34,000,000	106,000,000	
41.	Eldridge Johnson	Victor Phonograph	542,627	1,250,000	25,000,000	75,000,000	
42.	Arthur Curtiss James	Copper and railroads	521,388	1,200,000	24,000,000	72,000,000	
43.	C. W. Nash	Automobiles	459,776	1,100,000	22,000,000	66,000,000	
44.	Mortimer Schiff	Kuhn, Loeb & Co.	459,410	1,100,000	22,000,000	66,000,000	
45.	James A. Patten	Wheat market	425,348	1,000,000	20,000,000	60,000,000‡	
46.	Charles Hayden*	Stock market	427,979	1,000,000	20,000,000	60,000,000	
47.	Orlando F. Weber	Allied Chemical & Dye Corp.	406,582	900,000	18,000,000	54,000,000	
48.	George Blumenthal	Lazard Frères	415,621	900,000	18,000,000	54,000,000‡	
49.	Ogden L. Mills	Mining	372,827	800,000	16,000,000	48,000,000	
50.	Michael Friedsam*†	Merchandising	292,396	700,000	14,000,000	42,000,000	
51.	Edward B. McLean	Mining	281,125	700,000	14,000,000	42,000,000	
52.	Eugene Higgins	New York real estate	279,265	700,000	14,000,000	42,000,000	
53.	Alexander S. Cochran*†	Textiles	271,542	700,000	14,000,000	42,000,000	
54.	Mrs. L. N. Kirkwood		268,556	625,000	12,500,000	37,500,000	
55.	Helen Tyson		258,086	600,000	12,000,000	36,000,000	
56.	Archer D. Huntington*†	Railroads	226,353	575,000	11,500,000	34,500,000	
57.	James J. Storrow*†	Lee Higginson & Co.	222,571	575,000	11,500,000	34,500,000‡	
58.	Julius Rosenwald†	Sears, Roebuck & Co.	208,812	500,000	10,000,000	30,000,000	
59.	Bernard M. Baruch	Stock market	268,142	625,000	12,500,000	37,500,000	
60.	S. S. Kresge	Merchandising	188,608	500,000	10,000,000	30,000,000	

*Deceased.
†Fortune left to family.
‡Partly theoretical as income consisted in varying measure of fees.
Source: Ferdinand Lundberg, *America's Sixty Families* (New York: Citadel Press, 1937).

or executives were found in dominant positions on the boards of American Telephone and Telegraph Company, U.S. Steel Corporation, General Electric Company, Consolidated Edison Company, United Gas Improvement Company, American & Foreign Power Company, Electric Bond and Share Company, Niagara Hudson Power Corporation, Montgomery Ward and Company, International Telephone and Telegraph Corporation, American Can Company, Kennecott Copper Corporation, Chesapeake and Ohio Railroad, New York Central Railroad, General Motors Corporation, E. I. du Pont de Nemours and Company, and many others. The Morgan firm exercised dominance over the Guarantee Trust Company of New York, the Banker's Trust Company, the First National Bank of New York, and the New York Trust Company. The combined Morgan commercial banks outweighed all other banking interests in total assets, deposits, and resources. As late as 1932, it was estimated that the Morgan interests, with their varying degrees of control, dominance, and influence, totaled more than one quarter of all American corporate wealth. The boards of directors of most of these banks and corporations reveal the same names again and again and point up the close interlocking community of interest among America's industrial elite.

The Political Dominance of the Industrial Elite

The condition of the masses during the age of great industrial expansion was perhaps the lowest in American history. At the turn of the century, American workers earned, on the average, between $400 and $500 a year (or only $1,500 a year by today's standards). Unemployment was frequent and there were no unemployment benefits. A working day of ten hours, six days a week, was taken for granted. Accidents among industrial employees were numerous and lightly regarded by employers. Employment of women and children in industry tended to hold down wages but was an absolute necessity for many families. Child labor was ruthlessly exploited in the cotton mills of the South, in the sweat shops of the East, and in the packing plants of the West.

By 1900, almost 40 percent of the population lived in urban areas in which the living conditions for the masses varied from bad to unspeakable. Very few owned their own homes; from 80 percent to 90 percent rented their dwellings.

Both the Republican and Democratic parties reflected the dominance of the industrial elites. Richard Hofstadter comments on the influence that the industrial capitalists exercised over the party system in America:

The Republicans were distinguished from the Democrats chiefly by being successful. From the war and Reconstruction onwards, when it sought actively to strengthen its social base by espousing policies of American industrialists, the Republican party existed in an unholy and often mutually hostile conjunction with the capitalistic interests. Capitalists, seeking land grants, tariffs, bounties, favorable currency policies, freedom from regulatory legislation, and economic reform, supplied campaign funds, fees, and bribes, and plied politicians with investment opportunities. Seward had said that "a party is in one sense a joint stock company in which those who contribute the most direct the action and management of the concern." [15]

V. O. Key also describes the Republican party machine of the 1870s and 1880s:

The inner strength of Republicanism did not rest on sentiment alone. Sentiment clothed the bonds of substance. To the old soldiers—old Union soldiers—went pensions. To manufacturers of the Northeast went tariffs. To the farmers of the Northwest went free land under the Homestead Act. To railroad promoters went land grants for the construction of railroads that tied together the West and the North—and assured that the flow of commerce would bypass the South. The synthesis of self-interest and glory formed a cohesive combination. The G. O. P. represented a wonderfully effective contrivance, not only for preserving the Union but for holding together East and West, for the magnate and factory worker, homesteader and banker, and the great enterprise of continental unification, development, and exploitation. [16]

The Democratic party under Grover Cleveland was little different from the Republican—with perhaps the one exception that Cleveland called upon businessmen to improve their morals and become trustees of the public interest. Nevertheless, Cleveland used federal troops to break the Pullman strike in 1894 and to help keep down the urban working class. He supported the gold standard and alienated the debt-ridden farmers of the West. He hedged on the tariff question, refusing to adopt the traditional position of landed interests on behalf of low tariffs. He even negotiated a much-publicized gold purchase loan from J. P. Morgan. Hofstadter remarks: "Out of heartfelt conviction he gave to the interests what many a lesser politician might have sold them for a price." [17]

The only serious challenge to the political dominance of eastern capital came over the issue of "free silver." Leadership of the "free silver" movement came from mine owners in the silver states of the Far West. Their campaigns convinced thousands of western farmers that free silver was the answer to their economic distress. The western mine owners did not care about the welfare of small farmers, but the prospect of inflation, debt relief, and expansion of the supply of money and purchasing power won increasing support among the masses in the West and South.

When William Jennings Bryan delivered his famous "Cross of Gold" speech at the Democratic Convention in 1896, he swept the Cleveland "Gold Democrats" out of control of the Democratic party. Bryan was a westerner, a talented orator, an anti-intellectual, and a deeply religious man; he was antagonistic to the eastern industrial interests and totally committed to the cause of free silver. Bryan tried to rally the nation's have-nots to his banner; he tried to convince them they were being exploited by Wall Street finance. Yet it is important to note that he did not severely criticize the capitalist system, nor did he call for increases in the regulatory powers of the federal government. In his acceptance speech he declared, "our campaign has not for its object the reconstruction of society. . . . Property is and will remain the stimulus to endeavor and the compensation for toil."[18] He was uninterested in labor legislation; his only issue was free silver.

The Republican campaign, directed by Marcus Alonzo Hanna of Standard Oil, was aimed at persuading the voters that what was good for business was good for the country. Hanna raised an unprecedented $16,000,000 campaign fund from his wealthy fellow industrialists (an amount that would not be matched in presidential campaigns until the 1960s) and advertised his candidate, William McKinley, as the man who would bring a "full dinner pail" to all. The heavy expenditures of the Republicans suggest that Bryan was considered capable of rallying the masses. Republican machines were mobilized across the nation. As the end of the campaign drew near, threats were cast about freely. Working men were told that the election of McKinley would mean high wages and prosperity, whereas the election of Bryan would bring the loss of their jobs. Some employers bluntly told their employees that if Bryan were elected they could not come back to work. Farmers were told that a Democratic victory might mean their mortgages would not be renewed.

Bryan's attempt to rally the masses was a dismal failure; McKinley won by a landslide. Bryan would run twice again under the Democratic banner, in 1900 and 1908, but he would lose by even greater margins. Although Bryan carried the South and some western states, he failed to rally the masses of the populous eastern states or the people of America's growing cities. Republicans carried working-class, middle-class, and upper-class neighborhoods in the urban industrial states. As V. O. Key explains:

While the election of 1896 is often pictured as a lasting fight between the haves and have-nots, that understanding of the contest was evidently restricted to the plains of leadership and oratory. It did not extend to the voting actions of the electorate. . . . In 1896 the industrial cities, in their aggregate vote at least, moved toward the Republicans in about the same degree as did the rural farming communities . . . the Republicans gained in the working class wards, just as they did in the silk stocking wards, over their 1892 vote. . . . Instead of a sharpening of class cleavages within New England, the voting apparently reflected a more sectional antagonism and anxiety, shared by all classes, expressed in opposition to the dangers supposed to be threatening the West. [19]

In 1882, William H. Vanderbilt of the New York Central Railroad expressed the ethos of the industrial elite in his famous declaration, "The public be damned." There was little sense of public responsibility among America's first generation of great capitalists. They had built their empires in the competitive pursuit of profit. They believed that their success could be attributed to the immutable laws of natural selection, the survival of the fittest; and they believed that society was best served by allowing these laws to operate freely. In 1910, Woodrow Wilson, forerunner of a new elite ethos, criticized America's elite for its lack of public responsibility. At a widely publicized lecture to a meeting of bankers, with J. P. Morgan sitting at his side, Wilson declared:

The trouble today is that you bankers are too narrow-minded. You don't know the country or what is going on in it and the country doesn't trust you. . . . You take no interest in the small borrower and the small enterprise which affect the future of the country, but you give every attention to the big borrower and the rich enterprise which has already arrived. . . . You bankers see nothing beyond your own interests. . . . You should be broader-minded and see what is best for the country in the long run. [20]

Wilson urged America's elite to reject a narrowly self-interested view of things and to take the welfare of others, especially that of "the community," into account as an aspect of its own long-run welfare. Wilson did not wish to upset the established order; he merely wished to develop a sense of public responsibility within the establishment. He believed that the national government should see that industrial elites operated in the public interest, and his New Freedom program reflected these high-minded aspirations. In the Federal Reserve Act, the nation's banking and credit system was placed under public control. The Clayton Antitrust Act attempted to define specific business abuses, such as

The Liberal Establishment: Reform as Elite Self-interest

charging different prices to different buyers, granting rebates, or making false statements about competitors in order to take business away from them. A Federal Trade Commission was established and authorized to function in the "public interest" to prevent "unfair methods of competition and unfair and deceptive acts in commerce." An eight-hour day was established for railroad workers in interstate commerce; and the Child Labor Act attempted to eliminate the worst abuses of children in industry (this act was declared unconstitutional, however, by a much less public-regarding Supreme Court). Wilson's program aimed to preserve competition, individualism, enterprise, opportunity—all things that were considered vital in the American heritage. But he also believed fervently that elites must function in the public interest and that some government regulation might be required to see that they do so.

Wilson's New Freedom was forgotten during America's participation in World War I, and its gains were largely wiped out by the postwar reaction to reform. During the 1920s, America's elite rejected Wilsonian idealism. The established order clung to the philosophy of rugged individualism and rejected Wilson's appeal to a higher public interest.

Herbert Hoover was the last great advocate of the rugged individualism of the old order. The economic collapse of the Great Depression undermined the faith of both elites and nonelites in the ideals of the old order. Following the stock market crash of October 1929, and in spite of elite assurances that prosperity lay "just around the corner," the American economy virtually stopped. Prices dropped sharply, factories closed, real estate values declined, new construction practically ceased, banks went under, wages were cut drastically, and unemployment figures mounted. By 1932, one out of every four persons was unemployed, and one out of every five persons was on a welfare role. Persons who had never known unemployment before lost their jobs, used up their savings or lost them when banks folded, cashed in their life insurance, gave up their homes and farms because they could not continue the mortgage payments. Economic catastrophe struck far up into the ranks of the middle classes. Once a man lost a job, he could not find another. Tramps abounded, panhandlers plied the streets, transients slept on the steps of public buildings, on park benches, on lawns, or on highways. Mines were no longer worked; steel mills, iron foundries, and every variety of industrial plant put out only a fraction of the goods that they could produce; trains ran with only a handful of passengers; stores lacked customers, and many closed their doors; ships stayed in port; hospitals were empty, not because they were unneeded but because people could not afford them.

The election of Franklin Delano Roosevelt to the presidency in 1932 ushered in a new era in American elite philosophy. The Great Depression did not bring about a revolution or the emergence of new elites; but it did have important impact on the thinking of America's governing elites. The economic disaster that had befallen the nation caused American elites to consider the need for economic reform. The Great Depression also gave force to Wilson's advice that elites acquire a greater public responsibility. The victories of fascism in Germany and communism in the Soviet Union and the growing restlessness of the masses in America combined to convince America's elite that reform and regard for the public welfare were essential to the continued maintenance of the American political system and their dominant place in it. In December 1933, John Maynard Keynes wrote an open letter to Roosevelt, emphasizing the importance of saving the capitalist system:

You have made yourself the trustee for those in every country who seek to mend the evils of our conditions by reasoned experiment within the framework of the existing social system. If you fail, rational change will be gravely prejudiced throughout the world, leaving orthodoxy and revolution to fight it out. [21]

And Roosevelt himself was aware of the necessity of saving capitalism from itself:

As I see it, the task of government in its relation to business is to assist the development of an economic declaration of rights, an economic constitutional order . . . . Happily, the times indicate that to create such an order not only is the proper policy of government, but it is the only line of safety for our economic structures as well. [22]

Roosevelt sought to elaborate a New Deal philosophy that would permit government to devote much more attention to the public welfare than did the philosophy of Hoover's somewhat discredited "rugged individualism." The New Deal was not a new or revolutionary system but rather a necessary reform of the existing capitalist system. There was no consistent unifying plan to the New Deal; it was a series of improvisations, many of them adopted very suddenly and some of them even contradictory. Roosevelt believed that more careful economic planning by government was required in order to adapt "existing economic organizations to the service of the people." And he believed that the government must act humanely and compassionately toward those who were suffering hardship. Relief, recovery, and reform, not revolution, were the objectives of the New Deal. Roosevelt called for "full, persistent experimentation. If it fails, admit it frankly and try something else.

But above all try something. The millions who are in want will not stand by silently forever while the things to satisfy their needs are within easy reach."[23]

For anyone of Roosevelt's background, it would have been surprising indeed if he had tried to do other than preserve the existing social and economic order. Roosevelt was a descendant of two of America's oldest elite families, the Roosevelts and the Delanos, patrician families whose wealth predated the Civil War and the industrial revolution. The Roosevelts were not schooled in social Darwinism or the survival of the fittest or the scrambling competition of the new industrialists. From the beginning Roosevelt expressed a public-regarding philosophy. In Hofstadter's words:

At the beginning of his career he took to the patrician reform thought of the progressive era and accepted a social outlook that can best be summed up in the phrase "noblesse oblige." He had a penchant for public service, personal philanthropy, and harmless manifestos against dishonesty in government; he displayed a broad easy-going tolerance, a genuine liking for all sorts of people; he loved to exercise his charm in political and social situations. [24]

Roosevelt's personal philosophy was soon to become the prevailing ethos of the new liberal establishment.

In his first administration, Roosevelt concentrated on relief (a Federal Emergency Relief program, a Public Works Administration program, and a Works Project Administration) and on national economic planning through the National Recovery Administration (NRA). The NRA sought unsuccessfully to organize businessmen for the purposes of self-regulation in the public interest. The NRA failed, as did the Agricultural Adjustment Administration, which had tried to compensate farmers in various ways for reducing output. The National Labor Relations Act of 1935 was not a product of demands by the workers for government protection but rather a scheme for alleviating the depression by protecting unions, in the hope that unions could raise wage rates and hence income levels in the nation. Established leaders of the American Federation of Labor actually opposed the measure at its time of passage, firmly believing that government should be kept out of labor relations. The Social Security Act of 1935 was designed to reduce the burdens of government welfare programs by compelling people to purchase insurance against the possibility of their own poverty. Later, the Housing Act of 1937 and the Fair Labor Standards Act continued the president's efforts to restore the health of capitalism.

In the New Deal, American elites accepted the principle that the entire community, through the agency of the national government, had a responsibility for mass welfare. In Roosevelt's second inaugural address he called attention to "one third of a nation, ill housed, ill clad, ill nourished." Roosevelt succeeded in saving the existing system of private capitalism and avoiding the threats to the established order of fascism, socialism, communism, and other radical movements.

Of course, some capitalists were unwilling to be "saved" by the New Deal. Roosevelt was genuinely hurt by criticisms from American industrialists, whom he felt he had protected with his reforms; he cried out in anger against the "economic royalists" who challenged his policies. He believed that the economic machinery of the nation had broken down and that the political fabric of America was beginning to unravel. He believed he had stabilized the economy and returned politics safely to its normal democratic course. While he had engaged in some novel experiments (including the dangerous concept of public ownership, in TVA), he believed that for the most part he had avoided disturbing vital property interests. He rejected cries to nationalize America's banks during the bank crisis of 1933 and instead merely urged the American people to have greater confidence in their bankers. His basic policies in industry and agriculture had been designed by the large industrial and agricultural interests themselves. He believed that his relief and reform measures were mainly of the kind that any wise and humane conservative would admit to be necessary. He believed he had headed off the demagogues—Huey Long, Father Coughlin, and others—who had attempted to stir up the masses.

Eventually, Roosevelt's philosophy of noblesse oblige—elite responsibility for the welfare of the masses—won widespread acceptance within America's established leadership. The success of Roosevelt's liberal philosophy was in part a product of the economic disaster of the Great Depression and in part a tribute to the effectiveness of Roosevelt himself as a mobilizer of opinion among both elites and masses. But the acceptance of liberal establishment ideas may also be attributed in part to the changes that were occurring in the economic system.

One of these was a decline in the rate of new elite formation. Most of America's great entrepreneurial families had built their empires before World War I. The first-generation industrialists and entrepreneurs were unfriendly toward philosophies of public responsibility and appeals to "the public interest." But among the children and grandchildren of the great empire builders these ideals won increasing acceptance. Those who are born to wealth seem to accept the idea of noblesse oblige more than those who had to acquire wealth for themselves, and available evidence indicates that there were more self-made men in 1900 than in 1950. Table 3–4 shows that only 39 percent of America's richest men in 1900 came from the upper classes, while 68 percent of the nation's richest men in 1950 were born to wealth. Moreover, 39 percent of the

Table 3–4
Social Origins of America's Richest Men, 1900–1950

Social Origin	1900	1925	1950
Upper class	39%	56%	68%
Middle class	20	30	20
Lower class	39	12	9
Not classified	2	2	3

Source: Adapted from C. Wright Wills, The Power Elite (New York: Oxford University Press, 1956), pp. 104–105. The percentages are derived from biographies of the 275 people who were and are known to historians, biographers, and journalists as the richest people living in the United States—the 90 richest of 1900, the 95 of 1925, and the 90 of 1950. At the top of the 1900 group is John D. Rockefeller; at the top in 1925 is Henry Ford I; at the top in 1950 is H. L. Hunt.

richest men in 1900 had struggled up from the bottom, whereas only 9 percent of the richest men of 1950 had done so. This suggests that America's elite in the mid-twentieth century was more receptive to the ideas of responsibility for the common good and concern for the welfare of the masses. In other words, while Wilson's appeals for elite responsibility fell on the deaf ears of John D. Rockefeller in 1910, a sense of public responsibility would motivate the careers of his grandsons—Nelson Rockefeller, former governor of New York and vice president of the United States (appointed); Winthrop Rockefeller, governor of Arkansas; David Rockefeller, president of Chase Manhattan Bank of New York; and John D. Rockefeller III, chairman of the board of the Lincoln Center for Performing Arts in New York City.

Summary

According to elite theory, the movement of nonelites into elite positions must be slow and continuous to maintain stability and avoid revolution. Furthermore, potential elite members must demonstrate their commitment to the basic elite consensus before being admitted to elite positions. Elite theory recognizes competition among elites, but contends that elites share a broad consensus about preserving the system essentially as it is. It views public-policy changes as a response to elite redefinition of its own self-interest, rather than as a product of direct mass influence. Finally, elite theory views changes in public policy as incremental rather than revolutionary. All of these propositions can be supported by America's political history:

1. America's elite membership evolved slowly with no serious break in the ideas or values of the American political and economic system. When the leadership of Hamilton and Adams—Federalists—was replaced by that of Jefferson, Monroe, and Madison—Republicans—the policies of American government changed very little, owing to the fundamental consensus among elite members.

2. As new sources of wealth were opened in an expanding economy, America's elite membership was opened to new groups and individuals who acquired wealth and property and who accepted the national consensus about private enterprise, limited government, and individualism. The West produced new elites, which were assimilated into America's governing circle. Public policies were modified but not replaced. The Jacksonians wanted a more open elite system where the newly wealthy could acquire influence, but they were no more in favor of "dangerous leveling" than the Founding Fathers.

3. The Civil War reduced the influence of the Southern planters in America's elite structure and paved the way for the rise of the new industrial capitalists. The industrial revolution produced a narrowly self-interested elite of industrial capitalists. Mass movements resulted—chiefly free silver—but they met with failure.

4. America's elites have been deeply divided on the nature of American society only once. This elite cleavage produced the Civil War—the nation's bloodiest

conflict. The Civil War was a conflict between Southern elites—dependent on a plantation economy, slave labor, and free trade—and Northern industrial commercial elites—who prospered under free labor and protective tariffs. But before, during, and after the Civil War, Northern and Southern elites continued to strive for compromise in recognition of shared consensus on behalf of liberty and property.

5. Although industrial elites were never ousted from power, they were prevailed upon to assume a more public-regarding attitude toward the welfare of the masses. Economic collapse undermined the faith of elites and nonelites in the rugged individualism of the nineteenth-century industrial elite. But even economic collapse brought neither revolution nor the emergence of new elites. Instead, the Great Depression, the victories of fascism in Germany and communism in the Soviet Union, and growing restlessness of the American masses combined to convince America's elites that a more public-regarding philosophy was essential to the maintenance of the American political system and their prominent place in it.

6. The new liberal establishment sought to preserve the existing social and economic order, not to overthrow it. Eventually, Franklin D. Roosevelt's philosophy of noblesse oblige—elite responsibility for the welfare of the masses—won widespread acceptance within America's established leadership.

7. Political conflict in America has centered on a narrow range of issues. Consensus rather than conflict has characterized America's elite history. Political rhetoric and campaign slogans should not obscure the fundamental consensus of America's elites. Whatever the popular political label has been—"Federalist," "Democratic," "Whig," "Republican," "Progressive," "Conservative," or "Liberal"—America's leadership has been essentially conservative.

8. Policy changes, even those seemingly as revolutionary as the New Deal, did not cause any serious break in the ideals and values of the American system. Nor did they result from demands by "the people." Instead, policy changes, including the New Deal, occurred when events threatened the system; governing elites—acting on the basis of enlightened self-interest—instituted reforms to preserve the system. Even the reforms and welfare policies of the New Deal were designed to strengthen the existing social and economic fabric of society while minimally dislocating elites.

References

[1]*McCulloch* v. *Maryland*, 4 Wheaton 316 (1819).

[2]See Richard Hofstadter, *The American Political Tradition* (New York: Alfred A. Knopf, 1948), pp. 18–44.

[3]*Ibid.*, pp. 32–33.

[4]*Marbury* v. *Madison*, 1 Cranch 137 (1803).

[5]Hofstadter, *American Political Tradition*, p. 38.

[6]Frederick Jackson Turner, "The West and American Ideals," in *The Frontier in American History* (New York: Holt, 1921).

[7]See Hofstadter, *American Political Tradition*, pp. 45–67.

[8]*Dred Scott* v. *Sanford*, 19 Howard 393 (1857).

[9]Hofstadter, *American Political Tradition*, p. 109.

[10]*Ibid.*, p. 113.

[11]*Ibid.*, p. 116.

[12]*Ibid.*, pp. 132–133.

[13]Herbert Spencer, *Social Statics* (1851).

[14]See Gustavus Myers, *A History of the Great American Fortunes*, 3 vols. (Chicago: 1910).

[15]Hofstadter, *American Political Tradition*, p. 170.

[16]V. O. Key, Jr., *Politics, Parties, and Pressure Groups* (New York: Thomas Y. Crowell Co., 1942), pp. 185–186.

[17]Hofstadter, *American Political Tradition*, p. 185.

[18]*Ibid.*, p. 190.

[19]Key, *Politics, Parties, and Pressure Groups*, pp. 189–191.

[20]Hofstadter, *American Political Tradition*, p. 251.

[21]*Ibid.*, p. 332 (emphasis added).

[22]*Ibid.*, p. 330.

[23]*Ibid.*, p. 316.

[24]*Ibid.*, pp. 323–324.

Men at the Top: Positions of Power in America 4

Power in America is organized into large institutions—corporate, government, educational, military, religious, professional, occupational. Positions at the top of the major institutions in American society are sources of great power. True, not all power is anchored in and exercised through institutions; and the potential power of giant institutions is not always exercised by the leadership. But institutional positions provide a continuous and important base of power. Sociologist C. Wright Mills describes the relationship between institutional authority and power as follows:

If we took the one hundred most powerful men in America, the one hundred wealthiest, and the one hundred most celebrated away from the institutional positions they now occupy, away from their resources of men and women and money, away from the media of mass communication that are now focused upon them—then they would be powerless and poor and uncelebrated. For power is not of a man. Wealth does not center in the person of the wealthy. Celebrity is not inherent in any personality.

To be celebrated, to be wealthy, to have power, requires access to major institutions, for the institutional positions men occupy determine in large part their chances to have and to hold these valued experiences. [1]

In this chapter we shall describe the persons who occupy high positions in the major private and government institutions of American society. We include the major *private* institutions—in industry, finance, law, and other "nongovernment institutions"—because we believe that they allocate values for our society and shape the lives of all Americans. Remember, we defined an <u>elite member as anyone who participates in decisions that allocate values for society</u>, not just those who participate in decision making as part of the government. The decisions of steel companies to raise prices, of defense industries to develop new weapons, of banks to raise or lower interest rates, of electrical companies to market new products, of the mass media to determine what is "news," and of schools and colleges to decide what shall be taught—all affect the lives of Americans as much as do government decisions. Moreover, these private institutions have the power and resources to enforce their decisions.

Those at the top of institutional structures need not overtly exercise their power; their values may be reflected even if they do not directly participate in the decisions, because the subordinates who carry on the day-to-day business of industry, finance, government, and so on, know the values of the top elite and understand the great potential for power that the top elite possesses. These subordinates were selected for their jobs in part because they reflected dominant values in their thinking and actions. Whether consciously or unconsciously, their decisions reflect the values of the men at the top.

The institutional structure of society also exercises power when it limits the scope of public decision making to issues that are relatively harmless to the elite. Institutions facilitate the achievement of some values while they obstruct the achievement of other values. For example, we already know that the American government system was deliberately constructed to suppress certain values and issues. James Madison, in *The Federalist* No. 10, defended the structure of the new American government, particularly its republican and federal features, on the grounds that it would suppress "factious issues." And Madison named outright the factious issues which must be avoided: "a rage for paper money, for an abolition of debts, for an equal division of property, or any other improper or wicked project. . . ."[2] It is interesting that all of the issues that Madison wished to avoid involved challenges to the dominant economic interests. To select a nongovernment example: By placing owners of large blocks of company stock on governing boards of directors, and by increasingly allocating large blocks of stock to top management personnel, the American business corporation tends to encourage the values of profit and investment security in corporate decision making. The structure of the American corporation deters it from pursuing a policy of public welfare at the expense of profit.

The fact that institutional structures maximize certain values (private enterprise, limited government, the profit system) while obstructing other values (absolute equality or "leveling," government ownership of industry) is an important aspect of American politics, one which was recognized even by our Founding Fathers. It is another reason for examining the major institutions of society and the men who occupy high positions in them.

The Governing Elites

Politicians specialize in office-seeking. The politician knows how to run for office, but may not know how to run the government. After victory at the polls, the wise politician turns to experienced executive elites to run the government. Both Democratic and Republican presidents turn to essentially the same type of executive elite to staff the key positions in their administrations. These top government executives—Cabinet members, presidential advisors, department officers, special ambassadors—are frequently persons who have occupied key posts in private industry, finance, or law, or who have sat in influential positions in education, in the arts and sciences, or in social, civic, and charitable

Feiffer

Men at the Top: Positions of Power in America   91

associations. They move easily in and out of government posts from their positions in the corporate, financial, legal, and educational world. They often assume government jobs at a financial sacrifice, and many do so out of a sense of public service.

Obviously, there is some overlapping of top leadership in America, but it is difficult to measure precisely *how much*. The plural-elite model of power (described in Chapter 1) suggests that there is very little overlap, that *different* groups of individuals exercise power in different sectors of American life. In contrast, the single-elite model of power envisions extensive overlap, with a single group of men exercising power in many different sectors of American life. To understand position overlap among American elites, let us examine the career backgrounds of several key government executives in recent Democratic and Republican presidential administrations.[3]

Secretaries of State

John Foster Dulles: Secretary of State, 1953–1960; partner of Sullivan and Cromwell (one of twenty largest law firms on Wall Street); member of the board of directors of the Bank of New York, of the Fifth Avenue Bank, of the American Bank Note Company, of the International Nickel Company of Canada, of Babcock and Wilson Corporation, of Gold Dust Corporation, of the Overseas Security Corporation, of Shenandoah Corporation, of United Cigar Stores, of American Cotton Oil Company, of United Railroad of St. Louis, and of European Textile Corporation. He was a trustee of the New York Public Library, of the Union Theological Seminary, of the Rockefeller Foundation, and of the Carnegie Endowment for International Peace; a delegate to the World Council of Churches.

Dean Rusk: Secretary of State, 1961–1968; former president of Rockefeller Foundation.

William P. Rogers: Secretary of State, 1969–1973; U.S. Attorney General during Eisenhower administration; senior partner in Royall, Koegal, Rogers, and Wells (one of the twenty largest Wall Street law firms).

Henry Kissinger: Secretary of State, 1973–1977; former Special Assistant to the President for National Security Affairs; former Harvard Professor of International Affairs, and project director for Rockefeller Brothers Fund and for the Council on Foreign Relations.

Cyrus Vance: Secretary of State, 1977 to date; senior partner in New York law firm of Simpson, Thacher, and Bartlett; a director of IBM and Pan American World Airways; a trustee of Yale University and Chairman of the Board of Trustees of the Rockefeller Foundation, and a member of the Council on Foreign Relations; former Secretary of the Army and Undersecretary of Defense; U.S. negotiator in the Paris Peace Conference on Vietnam.

Secretaries of Defense

Charles E. Wilson: Secretary of Defense, 1953–1957; president and member of the board of directors of General Motors Corporation.

Neil H. McElroy: Secretary of Defense, 1957–1959; former president and member of the board of directors of Procter and Gamble Co.; member of the board of directors of General Electric Company, of Chrysler Corporation, and of Equitable Life Insurance Company; member of the board of trustees of Harvard University, of the National Safety Council, and of the National Industrial Conference.

Thomas S. Gates: Secretary of Defense, 1959–1960, and Secretary of the Navy, 1957–1959; chairman of the board and chief executive officer, Morgan Guaranty Trust Co. (J. P. Morgan, New York); member of the board of directors of General Electric Corp., Bethlehem Steel Corp., Scott Paper Co., Campbell Soup Co., Insurance Co. of North America, Cities Service Co., Smith, Kline and French (pharmaceuticals), and the University of Pennsylvania.

Robert S. McNamara: Secretary of Defense, 1961–1967; president and member of the board of directors of the Ford Motor Company; member of the board of directors of Scott Paper Company; president of the World Bank, 1967 to date.

Clark Clifford: Secretary of Defense, 1967–1969; senior partner of Clifford and Miller (Washington law firm); member of the board of directors of the National Bank of Washington, and of the Sheridan Hotel Corporation; Special Counsel to the President, 1949–1950; member of the board of trustees of Washington University in St. Louis.

Melvin Laird: Secretary of Defense, 1969–1973; former Republican congressman from Wisconsin.

James R. Schlesinger: Secretary of Defense, 1973–1977; former director, Central Intelligence Agency; former chairman, Atomic Energy Commission; former economics professor and research associate, Rand Corporation.

Harold Brown: Secretary of Defense, 1977 to date; former president, California Institute of Technology; member of the board of directors of IBM and the Times-Mirror Corporation; former Secretary of the Air Force under President Lyndon Johnson; and U.S. representative to the SALT talks under President Richard Nixon.

Secretaries of the Treasury

George M. Humphrey: Secretary of the Treasury, 1953–1957; former chairman of the board of directors of the M. A. Hanna Company; member of the board of directors of the National Steel Corporation, of Consolidated Coal Company, of Canada and Dominion Sugar Company; a trustee of the Massachusetts Institute of Technology.

Robert B. Anderson: Secretary of the Treasury, 1957–1961; Secretary of the Navy, 1953–1954; Deputy Secretary of Defense, 1954–1955; member of the board of directors of the Goodyear Tire and Rubber Company; member of the executive board of the Boy Scouts of America.

Douglas Dillon: Secretary of the Treasury, 1960–1965; chairman of the board of Dillon, Reed, and Company, Inc. (Wall Street investment firm); member of the New York Stock Exchange; director of U.S. and Foreign Securities Corporation and of U.S. International Securities Corporation; member of the board of governors of the New York Hospital and of the Metropolitan Museum.

David Kennedy: Secretary of the Treasury, 1969–1971; president and chairman of the board of Continental Illinois Bank and Trust Company; a director of International Harvester Company, of Commonwealth Edison, of Pullman Company, of Abbott Laboratories, of Swift and Company, of U.S. Gypsum, and of Communications Satellite Corporation; and a trustee of the University of Chicago, of the Brookings Institution, of the Committee for Economic Development, and of George Washington University.

John B. Connally: Secretary of the Treasury, 1971–1972; former Secretary of the Navy, governor of Texas, administrative assistant to Lyndon B. Johnson; attorney for Murcheson Brothers Investment (Dallas); former director of New York Central Railroad.

George P. Schultz: Secretary of the Treasury, 1972–1974; former Secretary of Labor and Director of the Office of Management and Budget; former dean of the University of Chicago Graduate School of Business; former senior partner of Salmon Brothers (one of Wall Street's largest portation Company, and Stein, Roe and Farnham (investments).

William E. Simon: Secretary of the Treasury, 1974–1977; former director, Federal Energy Office, and former Deputy Secretary of the Treasury; formerly a senior partner of Salmon Brothers (one of Wall Street's largest investment firms, specializing in municipal bond trading).

Werner Michael Blumenthal: Secretary of the Treasury, 1977 to date; former president of the Bendix Corporation. A trustee of Princeton University and member of the Council on Foreign Relations.

The administrations of Kennedy, Johnson, Nixon, Ford, and Carter all included top business leaders, experienced corporate lawyers, and intellectuals from prestigious universities. There is only slight variation in the mixture of career backgrounds represented in each of these administrations. Kennedy's Secretary of Defense was Robert McNamara, president of *Ford Motors*; while Eisenhower's Secretary of Defense was Charles E. Wilson, president of *General Motors*.

Kennedy brought into government as Special Assistant to the President for National Security, McGeorge Bundy, who was formerly Dean of Arts and Sciences at Harvard University. The Nixon administration replaced Harvard dean McGeorge Bundy with Harvard professor Henry Kissinger. The Carter administration replaced Harvard professor Henry Kissinger with Columbia professor Zbigniew Brzezinski. The Rockefeller Foundation supported the intellectual careers of both Kissinger and Brzezinski, suggesting that little, if any, difference can be expected in national security policy between the Nixon and Carter administrations.

Despite campaign hoopla describing Carter as an "outsider" who would replace traditional establishment figures with many new faces, just the opposite occurred. Cyrus Vance, Wall Street lawyer and chairman of the board of the Rockefeller Foundation, became Secretary of State, bringing with him his experience as President Johnson's Secretary of the Army. Harold Brown, Cal Tech president, became Secretary of Defense, bringing with him his experience as President Johnson's Secretary of the Air Force. Werner Michael Blumenthal, president of Bendix Corporation, became Secretary of the Treasury, and Charles L. Schultze, Director of the Office of Management and Budget under President Johnson, became Chairman of the Council of Economic Advisors (after eight years of grooming for the job at the Brookings Institution). Joseph Califano, Chief Domestic Advisor under President Johnson and author of many of the "Great Society" programs of the 1960s, became Secretary of Health, Education, and Welfare. Indeed, Carter even turned to Nixon's Secretary of Defense James A. Schlesinger, to head up a new Cabinet-level energy administration. In short, the Carter administration is very much in the "establishment" mold. (See Chapter 10 for a detailed examination of Carter's ascent to the presidency.)

The Corporate Elites

Formal control of the nation's economic life is concentrated in the hands of very few: the presidents, vice-presidents, and boards of directors of the nation's corporate institutions. This concentration has occurred chiefly because the economic enterprise is increasingly consolidated into a small number of giant corporations. The following statistics can only suggest the scale and concentration of modern corporate enterprise in America.

There are more than 200,000 industrial corporations in the United States; but the 100 corporations listed below control 52 percent of all industrial assets in the nation. The five largest industrial corporations (Exxon, General Motors, Texaco, IBM, and Mobil Oil) control 10 percent of the nation's industrial assets themselves. (See Table 4–1.) Concentra-

Table 4–1
Top Industrial
Corporations, 1975
(Ranked by Assets)

Rank	Company	Rank	Company
1	Exxon	51	Sperry Rand
2	General Motors	52	W. R. Grace
3	Texaco	53	AMAX
4	IBM	54	Deere
5	Mobil Oil	55	Burroughs
6	Ford Motor	56	National Steel
7	Standard Oil (Calif.)	57	American Brands
8	Gulf Oil	58	Georgia-Pacific
9	ITT	59	Amerada Hess
10	Standard Oil (Chicago)	60	Illinois Central Industries
11	General Electric	61	Allied Chemical
12	U.S. Steel	62	Kennecott Copper
13	Atlantic Richfield	63	McDonnell Douglas
14	Shell Oil	64	Reynolds Metals
15	Tenneco	65	National Cash Register
16	E. I. du Pont de Nemours	66	Litton Industries
17	Chrysler	67	Kaiser Aluminum and Chemical
18	Dow Chemical	68	Republic Steel
19	Union Carbide	69	Penzoil
20	Continental	70	Pfizer
21	Eastman Kodak	71	Anaconda
22	Western Electric	72	Marathon Oil
23	Westinghouse Electric	73	Ashland Oil
24	Bethlehem Steel	74	Champion International
25	Phillips Petroleum	75	Continental Can
26	Xerox	76	LTV
27	Sun Oil	77	Owens-Illinois
28	Standard Oil (Ohio)	78	Celanese
29	Goodyear Tire & Rubber	79	General Foods
30	Union Oil of California	80	PPG Industries
31	RCA	81	Signal Companies
32	Procter and Gamble	82	Inland Steel
33	International Harvester	83	American Can
34	Occidental Petroleum	84	FMC
35	Monsanto	85	Control Data
36	Aluminum Co. of America	86	Warner-Lambert
37	Caterpillar Tractor	87	Singer
38	International Paper	88	Boeing
39	Gulf and Western Industries	89	American Cyanamid
40	R. J. Reynolds Industries	90	Coca-Cola
41	Weyerhaeuser	91	TRW
42	Getty Oil	92	Ingersoll-Rand
43	Cities Service	93	Kraftco
44	Firestone Tire & Rubber	94	Beatrice Foods
45	Phillip Morris	95	Borden
46	Minnesota Mining & Manufacturing	96	Phelps Dodge
47	Rockwell International	97	Lykes-Youngstown
48	United Technologies	98	Uniroyal
49	Armco Steel	99	B F Goodrich
50	Honeywell	100	Merck

Source: Compiled from data obtained from *Fortune* Magazine (May 1976).

tion in utilities, transportation, and communications is even greater! Thirty-three corporations, out of 67,000 in these fields, control 50 percent of the nation's assets in transportation, communication, electricity, and gas. This sector of the nation is dominated by the American Telephone and Telegraph Company (AT&T)—the nation's single largest corporation by total assets. (See Table 4–2.)

The financial world is equally concentrated. Out of 13,500 banks serving the nation, the fifty largest banks control 48 percent of all banking assets; three banks (Bank of America, Citicorp, and Chase Manhattan) control 14 percent of all banking assets. (See Table 4–3.) Out of 1,790 insurance companies, eighteen control two-thirds of all insurance assets. Two companies (Prudential and Metropolitan) control over one-quarter of all insurance assets. (See Table 4–4.)

Control of these corporate resources is officially entrusted to the presidents and directors of these corporations. In 1970 a total of 3,572 persons were listed as presidents or directors of these top corporations. Collectively, these people controlled half the nation's industrial assets, half of all assets in communications, transportation, and utilities, nearly half of all banking assets, and two-thirds of all insurance assets.

A. A. Berle, Jr., a corporation lawyer and corporate director who has written extensively on the modern corporation, explains that corpo-

Table 4–2
The Fifty Largest Utilities (1975)

Rank/Company	Rank/Company
1 American Telephone & Telegraph (New York)	26 Carolina Power & Light (Raleigh)
2 General Telephone & Electronics (Stamford, Conn.)	27 Pennsylvania Power & Light (Allentown)
3 Southern Company (Atlanta)	28 Northern States Power (Minneapolis)
4 Pacific Gas & Electric (San Francisco)	29 Peoples Gas (Chicago)
5 American Electric Power (New York)	30 Baltimore Gas & Electric
6 Consolidated Edison (New York)	31 Union Electric (St. Louis)
7 Commonwealth Edison (Chicago)	32 Ohio Edison (Akron)
8 Southern California Edison (Rosemead)	33 Continental Telephone (Chantilly, Va.)
9 Public Service Electric & Gas (Newark)	34 Houston Lighting & Power
10 Philadelphia Electric	35 Central & South West (Wilmington)
11 Virginia Electric & Power (Richmond)	36 Northern Natural Gas (Omaha)
12 Duke Power (Charlotte)	37 Allegheny Power System (New York)
13 Detroit Edison	38 Long Island Lighting (Mineola, N.Y.)
14 Middle South Utilities (New Orleans)	39 Pacific Power & Light (Portland)
15 General Public Utilities (New York)	40 Consolidated Natural Gas (Pittsburgh)
16 Florida Power & Light (Miami)	41 Potomac Electric Power (Washington, D.C.)
17 Consumers Power (Jackson, Mich.)	42 Transco Companies (Houston)
18 Texas Utilities (Dallas)	43 Coastal States Gas (Houston)
19 Columbia Gas System (Wilmington)	44 Panhandle Eastern Pipe Line (Houston)
20 Northeast Utilities (Berlin, Conn.)	45 Pacific Lighting (Los Angeles)
21 Texas Eastern Transmission (Houston)	46 New England Electric System (Westborough, Mass.)
22 Niagara Mohawk Power (Syracuse, N.Y.)	47 Duquesne Light (Pittsburgh)
23 United Telecommunications (Westwood, Kans.)	48 Florida Power (St. Petersburg)
24 American Natural Resources (New York)	49 Cleveland Electric Illuminating
25 El Paso (Houston)	50 Western Union (Upper Saddle River, N.J.)

Source: Compiled from data obtained from *Fortune* Magazine (July 1976).

rate power is lodged with these corporations' directors and with the holders of large "control blocks" of corporate stock:

The control system in today's corporations, when it does not lie solely in the directors as in the American Telephone and Telegraph Company, lies in a combination of the directors of a so-called control block (of stock) plus the directors themselves. For practical purposes, therefore, the control or power element in most large corporations rests in its group of directors, and it is autonomous—or autonomous if taken together with a control block. . . .This is a self-perpetuating oligarchy. [4]

Table 4–3
Top Commercial Banks (1975)

Rank	Company	Rank	Company
1	BankAmerica Corp. (San Francisco)	26	Texas Commerce Bancshares, Inc. (Houston)
2	Citicorp (New York)	27	Bank of New York Co.
3	Chase Manhattan Corp. (New York)	28	Harris Bankcorp (Chicago)
4	Manufacturers Hanover Corp. (New York)	29	Philadelphia National Corp.
5	J. P. Morgan & Co. (New York)	30	NCNB Corp. (Charlotte, N.C.)
6	Chemical New York Corp.	31	CleveTrust Corp. (Cleveland)
7	Bankers Trust New York Corp.	32	Union Bancorp (Los Angeles)
8	Continental Illinois Corp. (Chicago)	33	Girard Co. (Philadelphia)
9	First Chicago Corp.	34	First Wisconsin Corp. (Milwaukee)
10	Western Bancorp. (Los Angeles)	35	Nortrust Corp. (Chicago)
11	Security Pacific Corp. (Los Angeles)	36	Wachovia Corp. (Winston-Salem)
12	Wells Fargo & Co. (San Francisco)	37	Michigan National Corp. (Bloomfield Hills)
13	Charter New York Corp.	38	Valley National Bank of Arizona (Phoenix)
14	Marine Midland Banks, Inc. (Buffalo)	39	Southeast Banking Corp. (Miami)
15	Crocker National Corp. (San Francisco)	40	Pittsburgh National Corp.
16	Mellon National Corp. (Pittsburgh)	41	BancOhio Corp. (Columbus)
17	First National Boston Corp.	42	DETROITBANK Corp.
18	Northwest Bancorp. (Minneapolis)	43	U.S. Bancorp (Portland, Ore.)
19	National Detroit Corp.	44	BanCal Tri-State Corp. (San Francisco)
20	First Bank System, Inc. (Minneapolis)	45	Citizens & Southern National Bank (Atlanta)
21	First Pennsylvania Corp. (Philadelphia)	46	Fidelcor (Philadelphia)
22	First International Bancshares, Inc. (Dallas)	47	National Bank of North America (New York)
23	Republic of Texas Corp. (Dallas)	48	Manufacturers National Corp. (Detroit)
24	First City Bancorp. of Texas (Houston)	49	National City Corp. (Cleveland)
25	Seafirst Corp. (Seattle)	50	Mercantile Bancorp. (St. Louis)

Source: Compiled from data obtained from *Fortune* Magazine (July 1976).

Table 4–4
Top Insurance Companies (1975)

Rank	Company	Rank	Company
1	Prudential	10	Massachusetts Mutual
2	Metropolitan	11	Mutual of New York
3	Equitable Life Assurance	12	New England Mutual
4	New York Life	13	Teachers Insurance & Annuity
5	John Hancock Mutual	14	Connecticut Mutual
6	Aetna Life	15	Bankers Life
7	Northwestern Mutual	16	Mutual Benefit
8	Connecticut General Life (Bloomfield)	17	Lincoln National Life
9	Travelers	18	Penn Mutual

Source: Compiled from data obtained from *Fortune* Magazine (July 1976).

Corporate power does not rest in the hands of the masses of corporate employees or even in the hands of the millions of middle- and upper-middle-class Americans who own corporate stock.

Corporate power is further concentrated by a system of interlocking directorates and by a corporate ownership system in which control blocks of stock are owned by financial institutions rather than by private individuals. Interlocking directorates, in which a director of one corporation also sits on the board of other corporations, enable key corporate elites to wield influence over a large number of corporations. It is not uncommon for top members of an elite to hold six, eight, or ten directorships.

Concentration of power among corporate elites occurs not only through interlocking directorates but also through the system of ownership in which one corporation or financial institution owns controlling blocks of the common stock of other corporations or financial institutions. It is very difficult to trace the ownership of a corporation. For example, because the Federal Power Commission requires that the ten largest stockholders of electric utilities companies be reported, one might assume that it would be easy to identify the owners of these companies. However, this is not the case, because these utilities are owned by other corporations rather than by individuals. The list of the ten top stockholders of Pacific Gas and Electric, the fourth largest utility in the country, was reported as follows:[5]

1. Merrill Lynch
2. Equitable Life
3. New York Life
4. Savings Fund and Plan
5. Prudential Life
6. King and Company
7. Raymond and Company
8. Sigler and Company
9. Mack and Company
10. Cudd and Company

Some of these companies are identifiable; but others are "street names," or aliases, of leading banks and investment firms, which hold the stock in trust for unnamed individuals. Mack and Company, for example, translates into Mellon National Bank, which represents the interest of the Mellon family, headed by Richard King Mellon.

Economist Gabriel Kolko summarizes what we know about corporate power in America:

The concentration of economic power in a very small elite is an indisputable fact. . . . A social theory assuming a democratized economic system—or even a trend in this direction—is quite obviously not in accord with social reality. Whether the men who control industry are socially responsive or trustees of the social welfare is quite another matter: it is one thing to speculate about their motivations, another to generalize about economic facts. And even if we assume that these men act benevo-

lently toward their workers and the larger community, their actions still would not be the result of social control through a formal democratic structure and group participation, which are the essentials for democracy; they would be an arbitrary noblesse oblige by the economic elite. When discussing the existing corporate system, it would be more realistic to drop all references to democracy. [6]

Drawing by Stan Hunt; © 1975 The New Yorker Magazine, Inc.

Wealth in America

Income inequality is and has always been a significant component of American social structure.[7] The top fifth (20 percent) of income recipients in America receives over 40 percent of all income in the nation, while the bottom fifth receives only about 5 percent. (See Table 4–5.) However, the income share of the top fifth has declined since the pre-World War II years. And the income share of the top 5 percent of families has declined dramatically from 30.0 to 14.4 percent. But the bottom fifth of the population still receives a very small share of the national income. The only significant rise in income distributions has occurred among the middle classes, in the second, third, and fourth income fifths. It is widely believed that the progressive income tax substantially levels incomes, but this is not really so. The best available evidence suggests that taxation has not altered the unequal distribution of income.

Millionaires in America are no longer considered among the really rich of the nation. *Fortune* magazine estimated in 1968 that there were at least 153 Americans who are "centi-millionaires"—worth more than $100,000,000 each—and the numbers of these great fortunes are growing. The editors of *Fortune* reported that in 1957, 45 persons in the United States were centi-millionaires; in the following ten years, the "centi-millionaire" population tripled. *Fortune* also stated that half of the people with $150,000,000 or more inherited most of it and that the Du Ponts, the Fords, the Mellons, and the Rockefellers are among America's wealthiest citizens.

However, despite the scores of "centi-millionaires" in America, *personal* wealth is insignificant in comparison to *institutional* wealth. Individuals may control millions, but institutions control billions. A president of a major corporation may receive an annual salary of $300,000 or $400,000 and possess a net worth of $1 or $2 million; but these amounts are insignificant when compared to the monies that the president may control—say annual revenues of $2 billion and assets worth $10 or $20 billion. The contrast between individual wealth and institutional wealth is even greater when we consider that a bureaucrat in the federal government may make only $50,000 but control an annual budget of $50 billion!

Thus, by far the greatest inequalities are between institutional wealth and personal wealth. Even if the entire personal wealth of every one of America's centi-millionaires were confiscated by the government, the resulting revenue (about $3 billion) would amount to less than 1 percent of the federal budget for a single year! Thus, the greatest disparities in America are not between the rich and poor, but between individuals and institutions. Wealth and power are concentrated in large

Table 4–5
The Distribution of Family Income in America

Quintiles	By Quintiles and Top 5 Percent							
	1929	1936	1944	1950	1956	1962	1972	1975
Lowest	3.5	4.1	4.9	4.8	4.8	4.6	5.5	5.4
Second	9.0	9.2	10.9	10.9	11.3	10.9	12.0	12.0
Third	13.8	14.1	16.2	16.1	16.3	16.3	17.4	17.6
Fourth	19.3	20.9	22.2	22.1	22.3	22.7	23.5	24.1
Highest	54.4	51.7	45.8	46.1	45.3	45.5	41.6	41.0
Total	100.0	100.0	100.0	100.0	100.0	100.0	100.0	100.0
Top 5 Percent	30.0	24.0	20.7	21.4	20.2	19.6	14.4	15.3

Source: U.S. Bureau of the Census, Current Population Reports Series P-60 No. 80; Data for early years from Edward C. Budd, *Inequality and Poverty* (New York: W. W. Norton and Co., 1967).

corporate and government institutions. The people who control power and wealth in this nation do so by virtue of their high positions in these institutions, not because of their personal wealth or income.

The Managerial Elites

Today the requirements of technology and planning have greatly increased industry's need for specialized talent and skill in organization. Capital is something that a corporation can now supply to itself. Approximately three-fifths of industrial capital now comes from retained earnings of corporations; another one-fifth is borrowed, chiefly from banks. Even though the remaining one-fifth of industrial capital comes from "outside" investments, the bulk of these are from large insurance companies, mutual funds, and pension trusts, rather than from individual investors. Thus, the individual capitalist investor is no longer essential to capital accumulation, and therefore no longer in a position of dominance.

American capital is primarily administered and expended by managers of large corporations and financial institutions. Thus there is a shift in power in the American economy from capital to organized intelligence, and we can reasonably expect that this shift will be reflected in the deployment of power in society at large.

Stockholders are supposed to have ultimate power over management, but individual stockholders seldom have any control over the activities of the corporations they own. Usually "management slates" for the board of directors are selected by management and automatically approved by stockholders. Occasionally banks and financial institutions and pension trust or mutual fund managers will get together to replace a management-selected board of directors. But more often than not, banks and trust funds will sell their stock in corporations whose management they distrust, rather than use the voting power of their stock to replace management. Generally, banks and trust funds vote their stock for the management slate. The policy of inaction by institutional investors means that the directors and managements of corporations whose stock they hold become increasingly self-appointed and unchallengeable; and this policy freezes absolute power in the corporate managements.

Most of the capital in America is owned not by individuals but by corporations, banks, insurance companies, mutual funds, investment companies, and pension trusts. A. A. Berle writes:

Of the capital flowing into non-agricultural industry, 60 percent is internally generated through profits and depreciation funds (within corporations). Another 10 or 15 percent is handled through the investment staffs of insurance companies and pension trusts. Another 20 percent is borrowed from banks. Perhaps 5 percent represents individuals who have saved and chosen the application of their savings. This is the system. . . . The capital system is not in many aspects an open market system. It is an administered system. [8]

Of course, the profit motive is still important to corporate managers, since profits are the basis of capital formation within the corporation. Increased capital at the disposal of corporate managers increases their power; losses decrease the capital available to the managers and decrease their power (and perhaps spell eventual extinction for the organization).

There is some evidence that management today is more public-regarding than the capitalist entrepreneurs of a few decades ago were. The management class is more sympathetic to the philosophy of the liberal establishment, to which they belong; they are concerned with the public interest and express a devotion to the "corporate conscience." As Berle explains:

This is the existence of a set of ideas, widely held by the community and often by the organization itself and the men who direct it, that certain uses of power are "wrong," that is, contrary to the established interest and value system of the community. Indulgence of these ideas as a limitation on economic power, and regard for them by the managers of great corporations, is sometimes called—and ridiculed as—the "corporate conscience." The ridicule is pragmatically unjustified. The first sanction enforcing limitations imposed by the public consensus is a lively appreciation of that consensus by corporate managements. This is the reality of the "corporate conscience." [9]

Management fears loss of prestige and popular esteem. While the public has no direct economic control over management, and government control is more symbolic than real, the deprivation of prestige is one of the oldest methods by which any society enforces its values upon individuals and groups. Moreover, most of the values of the prevailing liberal consensus have been internalized by corporate managers themselves; that is, they have come to believe in a public-regarding philosophy.

Economist John Kenneth Galbraith summarizes the changes in America's economic elite:

Seventy years ago the corporation was the instrument of its owners and a projection of their personalities. The names of these principals— Carnegie, Rockefeller, Harriman, Mellon, Guggenheim, Ford—were well known across the land. They are still known, but for the art galleries and philanthropic foundations they established and their descendents who are in politics. The men who now head the great corporations are unknown. Not for a generation did people outside Detroit in the automobile industry know the name of the currect head of General Motors. In the manner of all men, he must produce identification when paying by check. So with Ford, Standard Oil, and General Dynamics. The men who now run the large corporations own no appreciable share of the enterprise. They are selected not by the stockholders but, in the common case, by a board of directors which narcissistically they selected themselves.[10]

Corporate and financial elites have access to government officials which ordinary citizens could never hope to acquire. Several years ago Herbert P. Patterson, president of Chase Manhattan Bank, bemoaned his heavy schedule in Washington and listed a single day's appointments on Capitol Hill:

8:30 A.M.	Arrive National Airport
9:15 A.M.	Sen. Ernest Hollings of South Carolina
9:45 A.M.	Rep. William Widnall of New Jersey
10:30 A.M.	Sen. Warren Magnuson of Washington
11:00 A.M.	Sen. Alan Cranston of California
11:45 A.M.	Rep. Gerald Ford of Michigan, House Minority Leader. (I'm asked to note that if he's delayed at a White House conference the appointment will be rescheduled for 3:45 P.M.)
Noon	Luncheon in House dining room with Rep. Leslie Arends of Illinois, the House Minority Whip, and Rep. Harold Collier of Illinois
1:30 P.M.	Sen. Henry Jackson of Washington
2:00 P.M.	Sen. Wallace Bennett of Utah
2:30 P.M.	Sen. Robert Packwood of Oregon
3:15 P.M.	Rep. Hale Boggs of Louisiana, the House Majority Leader
3:45 P.M.	Rep. Gerald Ford (who *was* delayed at the White House)

Also on the schedule, if time permitted and they could break free, were Rep. Benjamin Blackburn of Georgia and Sen. William Brock of Tennessee.[11]

Needless to say, it is unlikely that very many Americans would ever be able to schedule meetings with so many congressmen in a lifetime, let alone in a single day. Mr. Patterson goes on to note with approval that:

My banking colleague, A. W. Clausen of the Bank of America, is no stranger to Capitol Hill. Men like Edward Cole of General Motors, John Connor of Allied Chemical and Charles Myers of Burlington Industries, among others, have made a real effort to provide legislators with information, to discuss with them problems of mutual interest, and to give them their best judgment as to how particular issues can be handled in the national interest. [12]

In his farewell address to the nation in 1961, President Dwight D. Eisenhower warned of "an immense military establishment and a large arms industry." He observed:

The Military-Industrial Complex

In the councils of government, we must guard against the acquisition of unwarranted influence, whether sought or unsought, by the military industrial complex. The potential for the disastrous rise of misplaced power exists and will persist. We must never let the weight of this combination endanger our liberties or democratic processes. We should take nothing for granted. Only an alert and knowledgeable citizenry can compel the proper meshings of the huge industrial and military machinery of defense with our peaceful methods and goals, so that security and liberty may prosper together. [13]

These words were prepared by political scientist Malcolm Moos, an Eisenhower advisor who was later to become president of the University of Minnesota. But they accurately reflect Eisenhower's personal feelings about the pressures which had been mounting during his administration from the military and from private defense contractors for increased military spending. The "military-industrial complex" refers to the armed forces, the Defense Department, military contractors, and congressmen who represent defense-oriented constituencies.

While some radicals view the military-industrial complex as a conspiracy to promote war and imperialism, it is not really anything like that. Galbraith, a liberal, portrays the military-industrial complex as a far more subtle interplay of forces in American society:

It is an organization or a complex of organizations and not a conspiracy. . . . In the conspiratorial view, the military power is a collation of generals and conniving industrialists. The goal is mutual enrichment; they arrange elaborately to feather each other's nests. The industrialists are the deus ex machina; *their agents make their way around Washington arranging the payoff. . . .* [14]

What indeed are the facts about the military-industrial complex? Military spending runs about $100 billion per year—only one-fourth of the federal budget and about 6 percent of the gross national product. The one hundred largest industrial corporations in the United States depend on military contracts for less than 10 percent of their sales. In other words, American industry does *not* depend upon war or the threat of war for any significant proportion of its income or sales.

Nonetheless, a few companies do depend heavily on defense contracts—Lockheed Aircraft, General Dynamics, McDonald Douglass, Boeing Co., Martin-Marietta Co., Grumman Aircraft, and Newport News Shipbuilding. But in the world of corporate giants, these firms are only medium-sized. None appears in the list of the top 100 corporations in America. While General Electric and American Telephone and Telegraph, among the real corporate giants, appear near the top of defense contracts, their military sales are only a small proportion of total sales. Yet there is enough military business to make it a real concern of certain companies, the people who work for them, the communities in which they are located, and the legislators and other public officials who represent these communities.

A frequent criticism of the military-industrial complex is that defense-oriented industries have become dependent on military hardware orders. Any reduction in military spending would be a severe economic setback for these industries, so they apply great pressure to keep defense spending high. This is particularly true of the industries that are almost totally dependent upon defense contracts. The military, always pleased to receive new weapons, joins with defense industries in recommending to the government that they purchase new weapons. The military identifies and publicizes "gaps" in U.S. weapon strength relative to that of the Soviet Union—the missile gap, the bomber gap, the atomic submarine gap, the surface ship gap—frequently overestimating Soviet military capabilities to obtain new weapons. Finally, legislators from constituencies with large defense industries and giant military bases can usually be counted on to join with the armed forces and defense industries in support of increased defense spending for new weapons. Of course, heavy military spending by the United States prompts the Soviet Union to try to keep pace, thus accelerating the arms race.

But American business is not interested in promoting war or international instability. The defense industry is considered an unstable enterprise—a feast-or-famine business for industrial companies. The price-earnings ratios for military-oriented companies are substantially lower than for civilian-oriented companies. More importantly, corporate America seeks planned, stable growth; secure investments; and guaranteed returns. These conditions are disrupted by war. The stock market, reflecting the aspirations of businessmen, goes *up* when peace is announced, not *down*.

A more rational critique of the relationship between government and business centers on the gradual blurring of the distinction between private and public activity in the economy. In *The New Industrial State,* Galbraith argues effectively that the military-industrial complex is part of a general merger of corporate and government enterprise into a giant "technostructure." Corporate planning and government planning are replacing market competition in America. Corporations avoid vigorous price competition, and the government also endeavors to fix overall prices. Both corporations and governments seek stable relations with large labor unions. Solid prosperous growth is the keynote of the planned economy, without undue, disruptive, old-style competition. Wars, depressions, or overheated inflations are to be avoided in the interest of stable growth. Big government, big industry, and big labor organizations share in this consensus. Within this consensus, the big quietly grow bigger and more powerful. Government protects this secure, stable world of corporate giants, unless they abuse the accepted standards of behavior or openly try to aggrandize their positions.

According to Galbraith:

The industrial system, in fact, is inextricably associated with the state. In notable respects the mature corporation is an arm of the state. And the state, in important matters, is an instrument of the industrial system. This runs strongly counter to the accepted doctrine that assumes and affirms a clear line between government and private business enterprise. . . . In fact, the line between public and private authority in the industrial system is indistinct and in large measure imaginary, and the abhorrent association of public and private organizations is normal. When this is perceived, the central trends in American economic and political life become clear. [15]

Galbraith is concerned with the dangers in this merger of governmental and corporate power. He believes the industrial system has proven its ability to serve our material desires, but that it threatens our industrial liberty. He expresses his fear of this "new industrial state" in his concluding section:

Our wants will be managed in accordance with the needs of the industrial system; the policies of the state will be subject to similar influence; education will be adapted to industrial need; the disciplines required by the industrial system will be the conventional morality of the community. All other goals will be made to seem precious, unimportant or antisocial. We will be bound to the ends of the industrial system. The state will add its moral, and perhaps some of its legal, power to their enforcement. What

*will eventuate, on the whole, will be the benign servitude of the house-
hold retainer who is taught to love her mistress and see her interests as
her own, and not the compelled servitude of the field hand. But it will not
be freedom.* [16]

Elite Recruitment: Getting to the Top

How do people at the top get there? Certainly we cannot provide a
complete picture of the recruitment process in all sectors of society. But
we can learn whether the top leadership in government is recruited from
the corporate world, or whether there are separate and distinct channels
of recruitment.

Biographical information on individuals occupying positions of authority in top institutions in each sector of society reveals that there are
separate paths to authority. Table 4–6 shows the principal lifetime occupational activity of individuals at the top of each sector of society. (This
categorization depended largely on their own designation of principal
occupation in *Who's Who.*)

It turns out that the corporate sector supplies a majority of the
occupants of top positions in only the corporate sector (89.1 percent).
The corporate sector supplied only 37 percent of the top elites in the
public interest sector, and only 16.6 percent of government elites. Top
leaders in government are recruited primarily from the legal profession
(56.1 percent); some have based their careers in government itself (16.7
percent) and education (10.6 percent). This finding is important. Gov-

Table 4–6
Recruitment to Top
Institutional Positions

	Elites		
	Corporate[a]	Public Interest[b]	Governmental[c]
Primary Sector from Which Top Elites Were Recruited:			
Corporate	89.1	37.2	16.6
Public Interest	8.8	50.8	62.1
Governmental	1.7	7.0	16.7
Other (Labor, Press, Religion, etc.)	0.4	5.0	4.6

[a]Presidents and directors of largest corporations in industry, communication, transportation, utilities, banking, and insurance. (See listings in previous tables.)
N = 3,572.
[b]Trustees of prestigious private colleges and universities (see note for Table 4-7);
directors of twelve largest private foundations; senior partners of top law firms,
directors of trustees of twelve prestigious civic and cultural organizations.
N = 1,345.
[c]President and vice president; secretaries and undersecretaries and assistant secretaries of all executive departments; White House presidential advisors; congressional leaders, committee chairmen, and ranking minority members; Supreme Court
justices; Federal Reserve Board; Council of Economic Advisors; all four-star generals
and admirals. N = 286.

ernment and law apparently provide independent channels of recruitment of high public office. <u>High position in the corporate world is *not* a prerequisite to high public office</u>.

What do we know about those who occupy authoritative positions in American society? There are a number of excellent social-background studies of political decision makers,[17] federal government executives,[18] military officers,[19] and corporate executives.[20] These studies consistently show that top business executives and political decision makers are *atypical* of the American public. <u>They are recruited from the well-educated, prestigiously employed, older, affluent, urban, white, Anglo-Saxon, upper and upper-middle class, male population.</u> (See Table 4–7.)

Age

The average age of all of the corporate leaders identified in our study is <u>61. Leaders in foundations, law, education, and civic and cultural organizations are slightly older—average age 64. Top positions in government are filled by slightly younger men.</u>

Sex

The female half of the population is seriously underrepresented at the top of America's institutional structure. Male dominance in top positions

*Table 4–7
Social Characteristics of
Corporate, Government
and Public Interest Elites*

	Corporate	Public Interest	Government
Average Age	61.0	64.0	58.0
Female Percentage	0.3	7.2	1.4
Schools			
Public	81.8	73.2	90.9
Private	7.0	8.8	3.0
Prestigious[a]	11.2	18.0	6.1
Colleges			
Public	31.8	12.8	43.9
Private	13.3	8.4	12.1
Prestigious[b]	55.0	78.8	43.9
Education			
College Educated	90.1	95.7	100.0
Advanced Degree	49.2	75.7	77.4
Urban Percent	89.0	84.9	69.7

[a]Andover, Buckley, Cate, Catlin, Choate, Cranbrook, Country Day, Deerfield, Exeter, Episcopal, Gilman, Groton, Hill, Hotchkiss, Kingswood, Kent, Lakeside, Lawrenceville, Lincoln, Loomis, Middlesex, Milton, St. Andrew's, St. Christopher's, St. George's, St. Mark's, St. Paul's, Shatluck, Taft, Thatcher, Webb, Westminister, Woodbary Forest.
[b]Harvard, Yale, Chicago, Stanford, Columbia, M.I.T., Cornell, Northwestern, Princeton, Johns Hopkins, Pennsylvania, and Dartmouth.

is nearly complete in the corporate world.* The same is true in government: only one woman served in the Cabinet under President Gerald Ford and two in the Cabinet under President Jimmy Carter; one has served as chairperson of a standing committee of either the House or Senate; none has served as a member of the Supreme Court, the Council of Economic Advisors, or Federal Reserve Board. Only in civic and cultural affairs, education, and foundations are women found among the top position-holders.

Race

In 1970, of the five thousand positions of authority surveyed in top-ranked institutions, only two were occupied by blacks; both were in government. One was Thurgood Marshall, associate justice of the Supreme Court, former Solicitor General of the United States, and former director of the Legal Defense and Educational Fund of the NAACP. Only one black served in the Cabinet under President Gerald Ford, and one black, Patricia Roberts Harris, serves in the Carter Cabinet. Andrew Young, former congressman from Atlanta and an early associate of Martin Luther King, Jr., serves as U.S. Ambassador to the United Nations. Young was jailed with King in Birmingham, Alabama, in 1963, and was an early member of the Southern Christian Leadership Conference. Ambassador to the UN is not officially a Cabinet position and is largely a ceremonial role. We were unable to identify any blacks in top institutional positions in industry, banking, communications and utilities, insurance, law, etc., although it is possible that some may have escaped identification in our biographical search. Certainly it is justifiable to conclude that very few blacks are in any positions of authority in America.

Education

Nearly all our top leaders are college educated, and more than half hold advanced degrees. Some 25.8 percent hold law degrees, and 23.8 percent advanced academic or professional degrees. (These are earned de-

---

*Data for this study is from 1970. Recent attention to women's roles in society may result in greater female representation on top corporate boards. In 1972 General Motors Corporation appointed its first woman director, *Ms. Catherine B. Cleary,* president of First Wisconsin Trust, and now a director of AT&T, Kraftco, and Northwestern Mutual Life. *Patricia Roberts Harris,* Washington attorney and former Ambassador to Luxembourg, has been named a director of IBM, Chase Manhattan, and Scott Paper. Barnard College President *Martha E. Peterson* has been named to the board of Metropolitan Life, and Chicago attorney *Jewel Stradford Lafontant* to the board of TWA. *Time,* October 16, 1972.

grees only; the host of honorary degrees were not counted.) Government leaders are somewhat more likely to hold advanced degrees than corporate leaders.

A glance at the precollegiate education of our top elites reveals that about 18 percent of the corporate leaders and 10 percent of the government leaders attended private school. Perhaps the more surprising fact is that 11 percent of corporate leaders and 6 percent of the government leaders attended one of the thirty prestigious prep schools in America. When these men were attending school, only 6 or 7 percent of the U.S. school population attended private school. Needless to say, only an infinitesimal proportion of the population had the benefit of education at a "name" prep school. Even more impressive is that 55 percent of the corporate leaders and 44 percent of the governmental leaders are alumni of twelve prestigious, heavily endowed private universities—Harvard, Yale, Chicago, Stanford, Columbia, M.I.T., Cornell, Northwestern, Princeton, Johns Hopkins, Pennsylvania, and Dartmouth. Elites in America are notably Ivy League (Table 4–7).

Urban Origin

Most of our top leaders were urban dwellers. Government leaders are somewhat more likely to be drawn from rural areas than leaders in business, finance, and law, but, still, less than one-third of key government posts are filled by individuals from rural areas.

These social-background characteristics suggest a slight tendency for corporate elites to be more upper class than government elites. There are somewhat lower proportions of prestigious prep school types and Ivy Leaguers among governmental leaders than among corporate or public interest sector leaders. There is a slight tendency for government leaders to have more advanced professional education.

Elites in America share a consensus about the fundamental values of private property, limited government, individual liberty, and due process of law. Moreover, since the Roosevelt era, American elites have generally supported liberal, public-regarding, social welfare programs, including social security, fair labor standards, unemployment compensation, a graduated income tax, a federally aided welfare system, government regulation of public utilities, and countercyclical fiscal and monetary policies. Today, elite consensus also includes a commitment to equality of opportunity for black Americans and a desire to end direct, lawful discrimination. Finally, elite consensus includes a desire to exercise influence in world affairs, to oppose the spread of communism, to maintain a strong national defense, and to protect pro-Western governments from internal subversion and external aggression.

Elite Consensus: The Liberal Establishment

The prevailing philosophy of America's elite is liberal and public-regarding; that is, it is willing to take the welfare of others into account as an aspect of one's own sense of well-being, and willing to use government power to correct perceived wrongs done to others. It is a philosophy of noblesse oblige—elite responsibility for the welfare of the poor and downtrodden, particularly blacks. Today's liberal elite believes that it can change citizens' lives through the exercise of government power: end discrimination, abolish poverty, eliminate slums, insure employment, uplift the poor, eliminate sickness, educate the masses, and install dominant culture values in everyone. This philosophy is *not* widely shared among America's masses.

Leadership for liberal reform has always come from America's upper social classes—usually from established "old family" segments of the elite, rather than the "new rich," self-made segments. Before the Civil War, abolitionist leaders were "descended from old and socially dominant Northeastern families"[21] and were clearly distinguished from the new industrial leaders of that era. Later, when the children and grandchildren of the rugged individualists of the industrial revolution inherited positions of power, they turned away from the Darwinist philosophy of their parents and moved toward the more public-regarding ideas of the New Deal. Liberalism was championed not by the working class but by men like Franklin D. Roosevelt (Groton and Harvard), Adlai Stevenson (Choate School and Princeton), Averell Harriman (Groton and Yale), and John F. Kennedy (Choate School and Harvard).

The liberal, public-regarding character of America's elite defies simplistic Marxian interpretations of American politics; wealth, education, sophistication, and upper-class cultural values do not foster attitudes of exploitation, but rather of public service and do-goodism. Liberal elites are frequently paternalistic toward segments of the masses they define as "underprivileged," "culturally deprived," "disadvantaged," etc., but they are seldom hostile toward them. Indeed, hostility toward blacks is more characteristic of white masses than of white elites. Political divisions in America do not take the form of upper classes versus lower classes, but rather upper class, allied with certain minority segments of the lower classes, notably blacks, in opposition to the white middle-class and working-class masses.

The liberal philosophy of noblesse oblige—elite responsibility for the welfare of the masses—leads inevitably to a sense of national responsibility for the welfare of the world, which in turn involves the United States in war. The missionary spirit of liberalism strives to bring freedom—self-determination, civil liberty, limited government, and private enterprise—to all the peoples of the world. America's major wars of the twentieth century occurred during the administrations of liberal Democratic presidents—Wilson (World War I), Roosevelt (World

War II), Truman (Korea), and Johnson (Vietnam). Is it accidental that wars occurred during these administrations? Or is it this element of the liberal philosophy which propels the nation toward international involvement and war?

Both World Wars were fought to "make the world safe for democracy." Following World War II, the United States embarked upon a policy of worldwide involvement in the internal and external affairs of nations in an effort to halt the expansion of communism. The "containment policy," as it came to be known, was a commitment by America's liberal elite to halt revolutionary communist movements and to support noncommunist governments attempting to resist revolutionary influences either within or outside their borders.

As a result of this containment policy, the United States acquired a staggering number of international obligations. In addition to numerous specific treaty commitments, the containment policy committed the United States to resist the expansion of communism in every noncommunist nation in the world. We were committed to resist not only overt military aggression, but also internal takeovers, economic penetration, and even successful campaigning in free elections. But many peoples of the world did not wish to accept American social, political, and economic ideals. The "good" that the liberals sought to do throughout the world was neither appreciated nor understood by the elites and masses of many nations. The result was a great deal of bloodshed and violence committed by well-meaning liberal administrations for the finest of motives. An American field commander in Vietnam summed up the liberal dilemma: "It was necessary to destroy the village in order to save it."[22]

The failure of America's political and military leadership to achieve victory in Vietnam seriously undermined the legitimacy of the established elite. The original decision to commit American troops to a land war in Vietnam is widely viewed as a serious mistake—militarily and politically—by both elites and masses. The obvious errors in political and military judgment, the heavy loss of life over a prolonged period, the humiliation of the military establishment in a war with a third-rate power, the revelations of incompetency and brutality, and the moral and philosophical questions posed by American involvement in a distant war, all combined to spawn a rash of criticism of the established leadership.

The Limits of Consensus Among Elites

Elite theory does *not* contend that disagreement never occurs among elites. On the contrary, the multiple bases of power in American society—industry, finance, law, government, mass media, etc.—insure that different segments of America's elite will view public issues from slightly different vantage points. However, <u>elite theory does assert that</u>

disagreement occurs *within* a framework of consensus on fundamental values, that the range of disagreement among elites is relatively narrow, and that disagreement is generally confined to means rather than ends.

We have already suggested the broad outlines of elite consensus on behalf of private enterprise, due process of law, liberal and public-regarding social welfare programs, equality of opportunity, and a strong national defense posture. But let us examine more closely the nature and extent of elite disagreement.

Columbia University's Bureau of Applied Social Research conducted a comprehensive survey of over five hundred top members of elites in business, labor, government, the Democratic and Republican parties, and the news media to identify the boundaries of disagreement among elites. The study first identified a "liberal consensus" on which *all* leadership groups agreed, for example:

More should be done for the poor.
Government spending should increase in a recession.
Federal government should strive for full employment.
Wage-price controls should be imposed when needed.

The study also identified a broad "conservative consensus" on which *all* leadership groups agreed, for example:

There should be no top limit on personal incomes.
Large corporations should remain in private ownership.
There are many opportunities for workers' sons to achieve success.

Disagreement occurred only within the boundaries of these two areas of consensus.

On some questions elites actually divided along the lines suggested by pluralist political theory: Republican politicians and business leaders aligned against Democratic politicians, union leaders, and news media elites. But such questions addressed a relatively narrow range of issues:

Whether to retain the oil depletion allowance.
Federal versus state control of social programs.
Whether income differences should be reduced.

Professor Alan Barton, director of the study, summarized his findings in part as follows:

While there were sharp divisions on some economic policies, there were certain general actions favored by a majority of every one of the groups studied. These include some kind of action to help the poor, deficit spending in times of recession, wage-price controls against inflation, and federal job creation in the public sector for the unemployed. "Keynesian economics" and the welfare state in some form are now orthodoxy among American leaders; so also—since the Republican administration adopted them shortly after our interviewing began—are direct controls on wages and prices in periods of inflation. . . .

Some issues sharply divided the businessmen from the labor and liberal interest-group leaders, with differences of over 50 percentage points on most: the Republicans come close to the business position on all of these issues, while Democrats tend toward the labor position. . . .

Just as there are some things which "everyone" now favors, like Keynesian economics, controls, and the welfare state, there are some things which "everyone" opposes. Three such items rejected by large majorities in every group are: a top limit on incomes, taking big corporations out of private hands, and the belief that a worker's son doesn't have much chance to get ahead in our society. There are very few socialists among American leaders—only one out of every six labor leaders give even qualified support to socializing large corporations, and 90 percent of them subscribe to the Horatio Alger theory.[23]

There are multiple structures of power in American society—industry, utilities, finance, law, government, education, the news media, etc.— and some competition among these separate power centers is inevitable. Moreover, in any society, various leaders will compete with each other for power and preeminence. Finally, the circulation of elites insures that new members are continually admitted to elite circles and these new elites bring slightly different interests and experiences to their roles than older established elites. Elite theory does *not* contend that conflict, competition, and factionalism never occur among elites.

A major source of factionalism among America's elite today is the division between the new-rich, southern and western *Cowboys* and the established, eastern, liberal *Yankees*. This factional split transcends partisan squabbling among Democrats and Republicans. or traditional rifts between Congress and the president, or petty strife among organized interest groups. The conflict between Cowboys and Yankees derives from differences in their sources of wealth and the newness of the elite status of the Cowboys.

The Cowboys are new-money people who acquired their wealth in the post-World War II era of erratic growth and expansion. Their wealth and power were generated in (1) independent oil and natural gas exploration and development; (2) real estate operations in the population-boom areas running from Southern California and Arizona through Texas, and from the "New South" to Florida; (3) aerospace and defense contracting and allied businesses, and in some cases new commercial

Elite Competition: Sunbelt "Cowboys" and Established "Yankees"

Men at the Top: Positions of Power in America 115

inventions. In contrast, the <u>Yankees are men whose fortunes are linked</u> <u>to the great corporate and financial institutions established in the</u> <u>nineteenth century.</u> Many of the Yankees are themselves second-generation descendants of the great entrepreneurial families of the industrial revolution (the Rockefellers, Fords, Mellons, Du Ponts, Kennedys, Harrimans, etc.).Other Yankees have been recruited through established corporate institutions, Wall Street and Washington law firms, eastern banking and investment firms, prestigious foundations, and Ivy League universities.

The Cowboys do not fully share in the liberal, public-regarding values of the dominant eastern establishment. Nor, however, do they exercise power in any way proportional to the overwhelming hegemony of the established Yankees. The Cowboys may have gained influence in recent years—and much of the petty political fighting reported in today's press has its roots in Cowboy-Yankee factionalism—but the liberal establishment remains dominant. And Cowboys and Yankees agree on the overriding importance of preserving political stability and a healthy free-enterprise economy.

The Cowboys are self-made persons who acquired wealth and power in an intense competitive struggle that continues to shape their outlook on life. Their upward mobility, their individualism, and their competitive spirit influence their view of society and the way they perceive their new elite responsibilities. In contrast, Yankees either inherit great wealth or attach themselves to established institutions of great wealth, power, and prestige. The Yankees are socialized, sometimes from earliest childhood, into the responsibilities of wealth and power. They are secure in their upper-class membership, highly principled in their relationships with others, and public-regarding of their exercise in elite responsibilities.

The Cowboys are new to their position; they lack old school ties, and they are not particularly concerned with the niceties of ethical conduct. The Yankees frequently regard the Cowboys with disdain—as uncouth and opportunistic gamblers and speculators, shady wheeler-dealers and influence-peddlers, and uncultured and selfish boors.

The Cowboys are newly risen from the masses—many had very humble beginnings. But it is their experience in *rising* from the masses that shapes their philosophy, rather than their mass origins. The Cowboys, being less public-regarding and social-welfare oriented than the Yankees, tend toward individualistic solutions to social problems—they place primary responsibility for solving life's problems on the individual. Cowboys believe that they made it themselves through initiative and hard work, and they believe that anyone who wants more out of life can get it the same way they did. The Cowboys do not feel guilty about poverty or discrimination—neither they nor their ancestors had any responsibility for these conditions. Their wealth and position were not given to them—they earned it themselves and they have no apologies for what they have accomplished in life. They are supportive of the political and economic system that helped them rise to the top; they are very patriotic, sometimes vocally anticommunist, and moderate to conservative on most national policy issues.

Basically Republicans

An examination of the backgrounds of some of the new-rich sunbelt Cowboys reveals their connections with the oil, defense, and real estate industries.

Clint Murcheson. Murcheson Brothers Investments, Dallas, Texas. A director of the First National Bank of Dallas, Delhi-Australian Petroleum Co., and the Dallas Cowboys professional football team. He owns substantial interest in Atlantic Life Insurance, Transcontinental Bus, Southeastern Michigan Gas, and Holt, Rinehart, and Winston, publishers. He is a former director of the New York Central Railroad, which he purchased with partner Sid W. Richardson. (Trinity College, Texas.)

John B. Connally. Special advisor to President Richard Nixon. Former Secretary of the Treasury, Secretary of the Navy, Governor of Texas, and administrative assistant to Lyndon B. Johnson. Wounded in the assassination fire that killed President John F. Kennedy. Attorney for oilman Sid W. Richardson and formerly a director of New York Central Railroad. (University of Texas.)

Roy Ash. Director, Office of Management and Budget, under President Richard Nixon. Former president and director of Litton Industries. Director of Bank of America, Global Marine Inc., Pacific Mutual Life Insurance; a trustee of California Institute of Technology, Marymount College, Loyola University. Formerly chief financial officer of Hughes Aircraft. (No college.)

Cowboys rose to the top echelons of government in both the Democratic administration of President Lyndon B. Johnson and the Republican administration of Richard M. Nixon. Johnson and Nixon themselves were self-made men, from the South and West respectively. Both devoted many years of their lives to the task of convincing established eastern elites of their trustworthiness—Johnson in the U.S. Senate as a leader in civil rights and poverty legislation, and Nixon as vice-president and Wall Street corporation lawyer. Yet many of the attacks on these two presidents arose from their closeness to the new-wealth components of America's elite, and the resulting distrust of them by influential segments of the eastern liberal establishment.*

*Yankee distrust of Cowboys may have begun with the assassination of President John F. Kennedy in Dallas, Texas, and the rash of conspiracy theories

The Watergate affair and the subsequent movement to impeach President Nixon also involved Cowboy-Yankee conflict. Early in the affair, the eastern liberals were content merely to chastise the President; there was little open talk of impeachment. The President appointed a Yankee, Elliot Richardson (Harvard Law, clerkship under Supreme Court Justice Felix Frankfurter, prestigious Boston law firm, prior government service as Secretary of HEW and Secretary of Defense), as Attorney General to replace Richard Kleindienst (Arizona attorney and former assistant to Senator Barry Goldwater). Richardson appointed, as Special Prosecutor, Yankee Archibald Cox (Harvard Law professor, U.S. Solicitor General under Kennedy and Johnson) to conduct the Watergate investigation. When President Nixon fired Cox over the use of taped presidential conversations, Richardson resigned and the eastern establishment turned against the President.

Eastern liberals in both parties charged that President Nixon had surrounded himself with southern and western sunbelt "wheeler-dealers" whose opportunism and lack of ethics created the milieu for Watergate. Easterners decried the unwholesome influence of many White House staffers whose careers were tied to southern and western interests: H. R. (Bob) Haldeman (California public relations), John Ehrlichman (Seattle lawyer), Ronald Ziegler (California public relations), Herbert Klein (California press executive), Frederick Dent (South Carolina textile millionaire).

The prestigious *New York Times,* voice of the eastern establishment, published an article blaming Watergate on the Cowboys:

The Nixonian bedfellows, the people whose creed the President expresses and whose interests he guards, are, to generalize, the economic sovereigns of America's Southern rim, the "sun-belt," that runs from Southern California, through Arizona and Texas down to the Florida Keys. . . . They are "self-made" men and women in the sense that they did not generally inherit great riches . . . whether because of the newness of their position, their frontier heritage, or their lack of old school ties, they tend to be without particular concerns about the niceties of business ethics and morals, and therefore to be connected more than earlier money would have thought wise, with shady speculations, political influence-peddling, corrupt unions, and even organized crime. . . .

---

linking the assassination to reactionary Texas oil interests. President Johnson acted decisively to discredit these rumors with the appointment of the prestigious Warren Commission, composed mainly of eastern liberals, which assured the liberal establishment and the entire nation that Kennedy's death was the act of a lone gunman.

Other scandals are sure to follow, for it seems obvious that the kind of milieu in which the President has chosen to immerse himself will continue to produce policies self serving at best, shady at average, and downright illegal at worst . . . the new-money wheeler-dealers seem to regard influence-peddling and back scratching as the true stuff of the American dream.[24]*

However, sunbelt power was divided and weakened by Jimmy Carter, who split the South from the West in the 1976 presidential election. Carter's contacts with the established Yankees are extensive. (See Chapter 10 on Carter's establishment ties.) Yet he was able to carry the southeastern states (except Virginia) as a native son. The West voted heavily for Ford; Texas was almost evenly divided but won by Carter. Thus, sunbelt power, which appeared to be growing in unity and influence under Johnson, Nixon, and Ford, was divided by Carter. While Carter's southern origins have frequently worried established Yankees, he has apparently brought the South back into the Democratic coalition and set back Republican hopes of creating a "new majority" based on western and southern unity. In short, Carter has obscured the division between established Yankees and sunbelt Cowboys for the present. But the fundamental division remains in the sources and locations of the wealth of each of these factions. Factional strife between Yankees and Cowboys may break out into the open again.

Summary

Elite theory does not limit its definition of elites to those who participate in *government* decision making. On the contrary, an elite member is anyone who participates in decisions that allocate values for society. Power in America is organized into large institutions, private as well as public—corporations, banks and financial institutions, universities, law firms, churches, professional associations, and military and government bureaucracies. Several propositions were developed in our analysis of power and the institutional structure of America:

1. Great potential for power is lodged in the giant institutions and bureaucracies of American society.

*Of course, this charge overlooks former Attorney General John Mitchell, who as chairman of the Committee to Re-Elect the President was directly responsible for campaign tactics, and who possesses impeccable eastern establishment credentials: senior partner, top Wall Street law firm of Mudge, Rose, Guthrie, Alexander, and Mitchell; specialist in tax-free municipal bond investing (a favorite tax shelter for establishment fortunes).

2. The institutional structure of American society concentrates great authority in a relatively small number of positions. About 3,500 presidents and directors of the nation's largest corporations possess formal authority over half of the nation's industrial assets, half of all assets in communications, transportation, and utilities, nearly half of all banking assets, and two-thirds of all insurance assets.

3. Wealth in America is unequally distributed. The top fifth of income recipients receive over 40 percent of all income in the nation, while the bottom fifth receives about 5 percent. Inequality is lessening very slowly over time.

4. Managerial elites are replacing owners and stockholders as the dominant influence in American corporations. Most capital investment comes from the retained earnings of corporations and bank loans, rather than from individual investors.

5. Despite concentration of institutional power, there is clear evidence of specialization among different elites. Less than 20 percent of top government officeholders are recruited from the corporate world. Most are recruited from the legal profession; some have based their career in government itself and in education. Thus, there are separate channels of recruitment to top elite positions.

6. American elites are recruited disproportionally from the well-educated, prestigiously employed, older, affluent, urban, white, Anglo-Saxon, upper- and upper-middle-class male population.

7. Elites in America share a consensus about the fundamental values of private enterprise, due process of law, liberal and public-regarding social welfare programs, equality of opportunity, and opposition to the spread of communism. The prevailing impulse of the "liberal establishment" is to do good, to perform public services, and to use government power to change lives. In world affairs, this missionary spirit has involved the United States in a great deal of bloodshed and violence, presumably in pursuit of high motives: the self-determination of free peoples resisting aggression and suppression.

8. Disagreement among elites occurs within a framework of consensus on fundamental values. The range of disagreement among elites is relatively narrow, and generally confined to means rather than ends.

9. A major source of factionalism among America's elite today is the division between the new-rich, southern and western sunbelt "Cowboys," and the established, eastern, liberal "Yankees." Their differences in style derive from differences in sources of wealth and the newness of the elite status of the Cowboys. The establishment Yankees remain overwhelmingly dominant in national affairs, but new southern and western elites have gained influence in recent years.

References

[1]Wright Mills, *The Power Elite* (New York: Oxford University Press, 1956), pp. 10–11.

[2]James Madison, Alexander Hamilton, and John Jay, *The Federalist* No. 10 (New York: Modern Library, 1937).

[3]Biographical data in this chapter compiled from various volumes of *Who's Who in America* (Chicago: Marquis Who's Who).

[4]A. A. Berle, Jr., *Economic Power and the Free Society* (New York: Fund for the Republic, 1958), p. 10.

[5]See William Domhoff, *Who Rules America?* (Englewood Cliffs, N.J.: Prentice-Hall, 1967), p. 55.

[6]Gabriel Kolko, *Wealth and Power in America* (New York: Praeger, 1962), pp. 68–69.

[7]See *ibid*, see also Clair Wilcox, *Toward Social Welfare* (Homewood, Ill.: Richard D. Irwin, 1969), pp. 7–24.

[8]A. A. Berle, Jr., *Power Without Property* (New York: Harcourt Brace Jovanovich, 1959), p. 45.

[9]*Ibid.*, pp. 90–91.

[10]John K. Galbraith, *The New Industrial State* (Boston: Houghton Mifflin, 1967), p. 14.

[11]Herbert P. Patterson in *Nation's Business*, February 1971, p. 61.

[12]*Ibid.*

[13]Excerpt from "Farewell to the Nation" speech by President Dwight D. Eisenhower, delivered over radio and television, January 17, 1961.

[14]John Kenneth Galbraith, *How to Control the Military* (New York: Signet Books, 1969), pp. 23–31.

[15]John Kenneth Galbraith, *The New Industrial State* (New York: Signet Books, 1967), pp. 304–305.

[16]*Ibid.*, p. 405.

[17]Donald R Mathews, *The Social Background of Political Decision-Makers* (New York: Doubleday, 1954).

[18]David T. Stanley, Dean E. Mann, and Jameson W. Doig, *Men Who Govern* (Washington, D.C., The Brookings Institution, 1967).

[19]Morris Janowitz, *The Professional Soldier: A Social and Political Portrait* (New York: The Free Press, 1960).

[20]Lloyd Warner and James C. Abegglen, *Big Business Leaders in America* (New York: Harper, 1955).

[21]David Donald, *Lincoln Reconsidered* (New York: Knopf, 1956), p. 33

[22]See David Halberstam, *The Best and the Brightest* (New York: Random House, 1973), for a full account of how U.S. involvement in Vietnam grew out of the "good" motives of "good" men.

[23]Allen H. Barton, "The Limits of Consensus Among American Leaders," Bureau of Applied Social Research, Columbia University, 1972, pp. 8–9.

[24]Kirkpatrick Sale, "The World Behind Watergate," *New York Times Review of Books*, 20, May 3, 1973.

Elites and Masses: The Shaky Foundations of Democracy

5

Many people believe that the survival of democracy depends upon widespread agreement among the American people on the principles of democratic government. However, only a small portion of the people is committed to those principles—freedom of speech and press, tolerance of diversity, due process of law, and guarantees of individual liberty and dignity. While most people voice superficial agreement with abstract statements of democratic values, they do not translate them into actual patterns of behavior. The question is not whether most Americans are in accord with the principles of democracy. The question is how democracy and individual freedom can survive in a country where most people do not support these principles in practice.

It has long been known that the American public is generally willing to restrict the civil rights of deviant groups. As early as 1937 the majority of voters were found to be in favor of banning communist literature and denying communists the right to hold public office, or even to hold public meetings.[1] During World War II, when the United States and the

Antidemocratic Attitudes among Masses

Soviet Union were allies, tolerance of the rights of communists rose somewhat; nevertheless, two out of five Americans would have prohibited any Communist party member from speaking on the radio. This proportion rose during the Cold War years; it was 77 percent by 1952 and 81 percent by 1954.[2] Willingness and, occasionally, eagerness to abridge the civil liberties of groups other than communists is also very much in evidence.

The first systematic examination of the intolerant frame of mind was made by sociologist Samuel Stouffer in 1954.[3] Stouffer realized that he was conducting his surveys of attitudes toward communism and other minority ideologies during one of the characteristic periodic U.S. reactions to communism. He argued, however, that he was concerned not with transient opinions but with deeper attitudes. For example, he measured popular support for freedom of speech, a fundamental democratic value. Stouffer asked a national sample of Americans whether various minorities should be allowed to "speak in your community." The re-

"What it boils down to, Sire, is that they seek a life style more similar to your own."

Drawing by CEM; © 1976 The New Yorker Magazine, Inc.

spondents were not asked to approve sabotage or other conspiratorial behavior; they were asked only whether these minorities should be given the right to speak. Twenty-one percent would not permit a man to speak if his loyalty had been *questioned* before a congressional committee, even if *he swore he was not a communist.* Nearly a third of Stouffer's sample would not permit a socialist to speak; 60 percent would not permit an atheist to speak; and fully two-thirds would not permit a communist to speak. This important study indicates that the American masses are not willing to extend democratic rights to unpopular minorities even for legitimate activities.

Mass support for the liberties of despised minorities is no greater today than during the Cold War. What has changed is simply who the minority groups are. For example, a recent replication of the Stouffer study found substantial increases in the willingness of the masses to tolerate nonconformists as defined by the original study.[4] Thus the threat of communists and "fellow travelers" has subsided, but the masses continue to oppose lawful activities of "extremists"—including demonstrators and protestors of all kinds. Communists have been replaced by protesting blacks and student radicals as "the enemy"; "law and order" is the phrase that now mobilizes mass support for repression. There is a strong mass revulsion against street demonstrations, even among those who have sympathy with the stated goals of the protestors. A substantial majority disapproves of civil disobedience and lawful protest. "Before 1950 a maximum of 49 percent would have allowed an extremist to speak freely. During the 1950s permissiveness towards radicals never climbed above 29 percent. Since 1960 only two in ten would approve free expression to an extreme view."[5]

But what are the attitudes of members of elites? Stouffer's study found community leaders (mayors, school board presidents, political party leaders, etc.) more willing than the general public to tolerate nonconformists. A 1973 replication of the study found virtually identical results. While only half of the general public were classified as "tolerant," 82 percent of the community leaders were so classified.[6] Whatever the focus of hostility, then, there is one consistent pattern: elites exhibit a greater support for tolerance than do masses.

The studies cited above suggest the correctness of former Senator William Fulbright's comment that Americans believe in the right of freedom of speech until someone tries to exercise it.[7] The evidence seems quite clear that "a large proportion of the electorate has failed to grasp certain of the underlying ideas and principles on which the American political system rests."[8] We are left with the question, why does the system survive?

Social Class and Democratic Attitudes

*One possible answer is the distribution of antidemocratic attitudes among various social classes. Upper social classes (from which new members of elites are largely recruited) give greater, more consistent support to democratic values than do lower social classes. Political sociologist Martin Seymour Lipset has observed that "extremist and intolerant movements in modern society are more likely to be based on the lower classes than on the middle and upper classes."[9] Analyzing the ideologies of the lower classes, Lipset notes:

The poorer strata everywhere are more liberal or leftist on economic issues; they favor more welfare state measures, higher wages, graduated income taxes, support of trade unions, and so forth. But when liberalism is defined in noneconomic terms—as support of civil liberties, internationalism, and so forth—the correlation is reversed. The more well-to-do are more liberal; the poorer are more intolerant.[10]

Working Class Authoritarianism

Many surveys show that intolerance is disproportionately concentrated in the lower classes. One study tested for a "cultural intolerance factor": a measure of intolerance of values and beliefs differing from one's own. (See Table 5–1). Cultural intolerance is most heavily concentrated among the poorly educated and economically impoverished, and among those who define their own social-class standing (under "Subjective Class" in the table) as low.

From such findings Lipset formulated the concept of "working class authoritarianism." (Authoritarianism is belief in the need for a strong central authority that compels submission.) Lipset observed that only 30 percent of the manual workers in Stouffer's study were "tolerant," whereas 66 percent of the professionals were. But what aspects of lower-class life make an authoritarian or antidemocratic personality? Lipset argued that a number of elements contribute, such as low education, low participation in political organizations, little reading, economic insecurity, and rigid family patterns.

Many features of the working- and lower-class subculture support the idea of a class-linked, antidemocratic pattern. For example, the lower-class childrearing patterns are substantially more authoritarian than those of the middle and upper classes. Also, the work life of the lower classes is depressing; unskilled workers are far less satisfied than skilled workers with their jobs, and, as a partial result, have a more fatalistic attitude toward life; workers who feel little control over their own lives tend to view the social and political worlds as unchangeable. Unskilled workers are also more likely to view both big business and big government as cynically manipulative. Most important, the skill level in

Table 5–1
Correlates of the Cultural Intolerance Factor (Percentage High)

	Percent
Education	
8th Grade	52%
High School	39
Some College	28
College Graduate	12
Income	
Under $5,000	47%
$5,000 to $9,999	35
$10,000 to $14,999	29
$15,000 and over	27
Subjective Class	
Lower	43%
Middle	37
Upper	27

Source: Seymour Martin Lipset and Earl Raab, *The Politics of Unreason* (New York: Harper and Row, 1971), p. 447.

manual jobs is clearly related to mental health. Anxiety, hostility, negative self-feelings, and social alienation are consistently associated with unskilled labor; and people in skilled occupations have higher mental health scores than those whose jobs require a repetitive unskilled operation.[11] Lipset provides the following depressing summary of the lower-class individual:

He is likely to have been exposed to punishment, lack of love, and a general atmosphere of tension and aggression since early childhood—all experiences which tend to produce deep-rooted hostilities expressed by ethnic prejudices, political authoritarianism, and chiliastic transvaluational religion. His educational attainment is less than that of men with higher socioeconomic status, and his association as a child with others of similar background not only fails to stimulate his own intellectual interests but also creates an atmosphere which prevents his educational experience from increasing his general social sophistication and his understanding of different groups and ideas. Leaving school rather early, he is surrounded on the job by others with a similarly restricted cultural, educational, and family background.[12]

belief in the coming of the millennium (a thou.)

Social Class, Education, and Commitment to Democracy

The circumstances of lower-class life, then, make commitment to democratic ideas very difficult. But how much each of these circumstances—family life, work, or education—contributes to the making of the antidemocratic personality is not clear.

Lipset suggested that lack of education might be more important than any of the other characteristics of lower-class life. By examining the tolerance responses of people of various educational and occupational strata, he found that within each occupational level, higher educational status makes for greater tolerance. He also found that increases in tolerance associated with educational level are greater than those related to occupation. And no matter what the occupation, tolerance and education were strongly related.

Numerous studies also closely relate commitment to free speech with educational levels; college graduates were far more tolerant of the speech of unpopular minorities than were persons with only a grade school or high school education. Kornhauser found that within a given occupation (auto workers), the better the education the less authoritarian the person was.[13]

Examining many surveys of the 1950s, Lewis Lipsitz finds that the upper and middle classes are less authoritarian primarily because of their greater frequency of post-high school education. When education is held constant, very few of the relationships between class and authoritarianism remain strong. Thus, the greater authoritarianism of the working classes is largely a product of low levels of education.[14]

The problem of isolating the effects of education is best illustrated by *simultaneously* examining education and income—that is, by looking at variation in attitude according to education *within* selected income categories. With regard to one indicator of tolerance—willingness to accept the legitimacy of lawful protest—the results suggest an *independent*, strong effect of education (Table 5–2). Within each income group, tolerance increases significantly with education. It is also true, however, that within each education group, tolerance increases with income, but the increases are far less dramatic.

Education affects tolerance by influencing the individual's ability to apply an abstract principle to a concrete situation. It is one thing to agree that peaceful demonstrations are legitimate; it is quite another to allow an unpopular demonstration. For instance, about 66 percent of those with a college education agree that "people should be allowed to hold a protest demonstration to ask the government to act on some issue," while 37 percent of those with grade school education agree. Of that 37 percent, however, 94 percent would allow an antipollution demonstration by a group of neighbors, but two-thirds would *prohibit* a demonstration in favor of legalizing marijuana. Thus, among the few of the poorly educated who are tolerant, most are "deflected" from tolerance by the specific nature of the demonstration. For the highly educated, the deflection is less severe; of the two-thirds who agree with the abstract principle of demonstration, 97 percent would allow a neighborhood antipollution demonstration and 81 percent would allow a promarijuana demonstration:

consistency in applying a general norm does increase with education. . . . college educated respondents rarely abandon their tolerant gen-

Table 5–2
Joint Effects of Income and Education on Support for Lawful Protest

Percent Liberal (of Opinion Holders) on Lawful Protest					
	Education				
Family Income	Non-High School Graduate		High School Graduate		Some College
Under $6,000	27%	(214)	33%	(76)	55%	(61)
$6,000–$9,999	29	(113)	41	(143)	48	(103)
$10,000 and over	39	(57)	44	(140)	71	(181)

Source: Robert S. Erikson and Norman R. Luttbeg, *American Public Opinion: Its Origins, Content, and Import* (1973), p. 176. Used with permission of John Wiley & Sons, Inc.

eral norm. . . . among the less educated, however, inconsistency is far more common. . . . the less educated are . . . considerably more likely than others to abandon a tolerant general norm. [15]

The key, then, to variations in tolerance is education—indeed, more so now than in the 1950s, when the Stouffer study was made. In that study, the correlation between education and tolerance was .44; in the 1973 replication it increased to .55, suggesting considerably more tolerant attitudes among the highly educated. Lest we be overly optimistic, however, note, in Table 5–2, that only among the wealthy, college-educated population is tolerance not very low.

Social Class and the Antidemocratic Personality

The research of Herbert McClosky provides the most thorough inventory available of the psychological underpinnings of a democratic society. [16] McClosky administered a variety of attitude and personality scales to a national cross-section of 1,484 respondents. Most of the scales were also administered by a mail survey to 3,000 Democratic and Republican leaders, ranging from federal officials to local officials and precinct workers.* By dividing the national sample into educational categories, we can compare the responses of both well-educated and poorly educated people with the responses of the sample of national leaders.

McClosky examines both personality and attitude. (See Table 5–3.) A good indicator of elites and mass characteristics is the proportion of each of the three groups that scores high on the rigidity scale. A high scorer on this scale is likely to view the world in black-and-white terms (that is, dichotomously), and is especially given to stereotypes and over-generalizations. The world consists of "them" and "us." "They" are unquestionably bad, while "we" are unquestionably good. A division of the world into two opposing camps simplifies problems that would otherwise require thought and makes the world manageable. Notice that rigidity is higher among low-education groups than among either the leaders or the high-education group.

A clearer measure of dichotomous thinking can be observed in the we-they, chauvinism, ethnocentrism, anti-Semitism, and segregation-integration scales. On all of these scales, elites are distinguished from masses by their rejection of dichotomous thinking. Such simplistic views of the world are compatible with those who have a feeling of mar-

division into 2 parts

---

*One might quarrel with McClosky's definition of leaders; certainly it is not intended to be inclusive. However, political party leaders are at least a part of the elite as well as we have defined it.

ginality, or virtually no power or importance. The alienation scale (which measures feelings of personal isolation), the anomie scale (which measures the degree to which individuals feel society is lacking in direction and meaning), and the cruel-world scale (which measures the tendency to regard the world as cold and indifferent) point up some of the problems of the poorly educated individual. Clearly, these individuals feel estranged, bewildered, and overwhelmed by a complex world and seek simple explanations of this world.

A hostile, dangerous, or indifferent world can be explained most easily as the consequence of a conspiracy; and lower-class movements are typically concentrated upon a scapegoat. In the generations before a permanent Cold War ideology took shape, the scapegoat for lower-class

Table 5–3
Democratic and Antidemocratic Attitudes among Elites and Masses (Percent Scoring High)

	Leaders	General Public	
		High Education	Low Education
	(N = 3,020)	(N = 787)	(N = 697)
Democratic commitment	49%	36%	13%
Elitism-inequalitarianism	23	31	47
Faith in democracy	40	24	13
Faith in direct action	26	32	53
Faith in freedom	63	53	43
Faith in procedural right	58	32	15
Tolerance	61	55	30
Political cynicism	10	23	41
Sense of political futility	4	22	39
Political suspiciousness	9	20	34
Left wing	7	16	41
Right wing	17	22	46
Populism	13	24	50
Totalitarianism	10	22	47
Authoritarianism	15	21	48
Rigidity	28	33	52
Alienation	17	26	43
Anomie	8	21	51
Cruel, indifferent world	10	16	35
Intellectuality	57	47	23
We-they (general)	23	24	44
We-they (specific)	12	24	49
Chauvinism	13	16	47
Ethnocentrism	17	22	39
Anti-Semitism	28	36	54
Segregation-integration	29	28	49
Pro-business attitudes	50	40	42
Classical conservatism	17	23	53
Economic conservatism	42	23	16
Opposition to government welfare	57	41	25

Source: Adapted from Herbert McClosky, "Personality and Attitude Correlates of Foreign Policy Orientation," in James N. Rosenau (ed.), *Domestic Sources of Foreign Policy* (New York: Free Press, 1967), pp. 51–110.

lack of purpose, identity, rootlessness

movements seemed to alternate between Catholics and "Wall Street," but in present-day America, the scapegoat for all the world's evils is communism or "radicalism" or militant blacks. Scapegoating is linked with intellectuality, since prejudice declines with information about the "out-group." The undereducated strata do not read and are poorly informed about public matters. For example, a Gallup poll indicated that whereas 41 percent of the college graduates had read a book in the past month, only 9 percent with a grade-school education had done so.

Social Class, "Liberalism," and Political Alienation

We are accustomed to associating conservatism with the upper classes, but the facts are not that simple. While the poorly educated masses may be more "liberal" with respect to *economic* matters—they favor more welfare measures and more government intervention in economic life than do the upper strata—they are in fact more "conservative" than elites when conservatism is defined as an emphasis on tradition, order, status hierarchy, duty, obligation, obedience, and authority. Commitment to order and authority is much more a characteristic of poorly educated masses (see Table 5–3).

On the other hand, notice that both elites and masses share a relatively probusiness attitude. The economic liberalism of the poorly educated might be assumed to dispose them against the business system; but actually the ideology of business seems to be shared by *all* strata of

© 1977 Jules Feiffer. Dist. Field Newspaper Syndicate.

Elites and Masses: The Shaky Foundations of Democracy 131

society. The idea of starting a business with one's savings, for instance, prompts literally millions of American workers to establish a business of their own. In an Oakland labor mobility study by Lipset and Reinhard Bendix, two-thirds of the manual workers interviewed had considered going into business for themselves, and about two-fifths of them had actually tried to do so. Although most of these businesses ultimately fail, many Americans regard self-employment as desirable.[17] However, in spite of the commitment of all sections of the system to a business ideology, this ideology is *more* characteristic of the elite than of the masses.

Morris Janowitz has found an exception that proves the rule in respect to the distribution of liberalism among elites and masses.[18] Janowitz describes the military elite as conservative (his measure of conservatism, however, is limited to the respondent's evaluation). He notes that although military elites are well educated, they share an ideology comparable to that of the masses: military ideology is concerned with a respect for authority and shows little respect for the compromises inherent in the political process—the same kind of impatience toward democracy and politics that characterizes the poorly educated.

Rejection of politics and politicians is basic to the rejection of democracy itself; in the minds of the poorly educated masses, politics in a democracy is "all talk and no action." Moreover, the poorly educated view the government as a manipulating "they." Of course, feelings of helplessness are not necessarily all in the mind, and indeed might be a rational and accurate evaluation of the real situation: the poorly educated have no faith in the system because the system has not rewarded them.

Those who feel helpless are not likely to be politically active. However, given the appropriate provocation, they may initiate more radical types of activities, such as rioting. The blacks who led the riots in the urban ghettos, for example, were much more inclined than nonrioters to think that the country is not worth fighting for and were substantially less trusting of the city government. Whites of similar socioeconomic status were reacting similarly to their feelings of helplessness when they attacked court-ordered busing for racial balance in South Boston. Political behavior of the disadvantaged segments of the society, then, is likely to be violent and illegal and outside the normal framework of democratic decision making.

Political Socialization of the Masses

If education is the key to commitment to a democratic system, then we need to know something about the quality of the educational experience. The evidence presented so far has suggested, tentatively, that there is a fundamental difference between the college educated and noncollege educated population.

This distinction is generally blurred and needs to be sharpened. If the association between education and a variety of attitudes typical of the political elite is measured, commitment to democratic rules of the game becomes apparent only after substantial exposure to a college education. At least through high school, learning how to be a good citizen does not necessarily include respect for the rights of minorities.[19]

The liberalizing effects of education are, in large measure, reserved for the potential elite who enter college. For those who go no further than high school, the learning process is better characterized as "schooling." As Lane and Sears put it: "The home, and, to some extent, early formal education, encapsulate the past; higher education subjects it to scrutiny in the light of different ideas."[20] High school merely reinforces attitudes acquired in the home. In Table 5–4, we can see that the only appreciable impact of education upon attitudes occurs after high school.

	Grade School	High School	College
Believe Negroes are treated the same as whites	71%	75%	71%
Believe Negroes are more to blame for present condition than whites	56	58	42
Believe that businesses discriminate against Negroes in hiring	17	19	30
Believe that labor unions discriminate against Negroes in membership practices	15	13	30
Believe that looters should be shot on sight	54	55	45

Source: *Gallup Opinion Index* (July 1968), pp. 15–22.

Table 5–4
Attitudes of Various Educational Groups Toward Racial Problems (Percentages)

Of course, insulation of the masses from critical thinking is not necessarily a *sufficient* explanation for their unrealistic attitudes. For instance, one study reveals that high school students who intend to go to college are more tolerant than those who do not.[21] Nevertheless, it is clear that primary and secondary education do not provide the opportunity for critical thinking required of decision makers. As an agent of political socialization, formal instruction generally does not affect students' values. This is the case primarily because the instructional efforts in public schools are redundant; they are largely symbolic reinforcements of the "democratic creed"—a litany heard by most students so many times that sheer boredom would allow for, at the most, slight increments in loyalty, patriotism, and other virtues presumed to be the goal of civics and social studies courses.

We can get some general notion of what students are told in social studies courses from the texts they use and from the attitudes of those who teach. The chief conclusion of such an examination is that controversy is to be avoided. An exhaustive survey of public school texts found that:

Textbooks generally present an unrealistic picture of American society and government. Many social problems that exist today are not discussed. In statements about democracy and the good life textbooks often do not separate prescriptions from descriptions. Thus the persuasive usage of concepts are not distinguishable from descriptive and explanatory ones. America is presented as the champion of freedom, good will, and rationality, while all other nations are depicted as aggressors or "second raters." . . . Many authors assume naively that the political system functions in accordance with the fundamental laws of the land. . . . Controversial issues are not dealt with in an ethically or intellectually responsible manner. Nowhere do authors outline a defensible model for dealing with social cleavages and value incompatibility.[22]

Race relations are regarded as a "controversial social issue" that is treated with extreme caution. While some texts are more realistic than others, the following quotation is typical.

In 1954, the United States Supreme Court made a decision stating that separate schools for Negro children were unconstitutional. This decision caused much controversy, but there has been general agreement, however, that some system must be developed to provide equal educational opportunity for all children—regardless of race, nationality, religion or whether they live in cities or rural areas.[23]

Of course, this statement is patently false. There is no discussion of the vigor with which southern states resisted the order. Presumably, students were given no explanation for the fact that race relations remain America's most divisive problem.

Patriotism, which is characteristic of the study of American government in the public schools, may be less jingoistic than it once was. However, texts carefully intersperse discussion of government structure (considered in purely legalistic terms) with appropriate exhortations such as: "No other country has more nearly approached the goals of true democracy as [sic] our United States. . . . No doubt many of the early settlers were inspired men . . .,"[24] and, "because the nations of the world have not yet learned to live permanently at peace, the United States today must maintain large defensive forces."[25]

Surely there are some social studies teachers who can contradict the pap of textbooks and produce an element of realism, but they are rare. Few are trained to distinguish facts from values and, in any case, probably find the anticommunism and ethnocentrism of texts quite compatible with their own values. Therefore, little contrary information filters into the classroom. Further, since such unreal descriptions are reinforced by other sources of information (such as the family), we should expect attitudes to change little during formal schooling.

Schools teach loyalty and, to some extent, a belief in the efficacy of individual political participation; overwhelming majorities of students defined being a "good citizen" in these two dimensions: loyalty and participation. There is, however, an additional irony. For blacks, loyalty rather than participation is dominant.[26] Similar perceptions of citizenship are found among lower-class whites. Only in the upper-class school is politics viewed as a feasible process for the resolution of conflict.[27] Thus, for both blacks and lower-class whites, civic education encourages obedience and conformity to elite values. The college-educated future elites are given a somewhat more realistic appraisal of the use of the political process.

Clearly, then, the public educational process operates not to change beliefs, but to reinforce established values; to encourage not diversity but conformity. Public education serves established elites quite well: It denies political skills and knowledge to the masses. As Lane and Sears aptly put it: "The Platonic Code (only the 'guardians' to be educated for leadership) here, in fact, had its modern incarnation."[28]

How Does Democracy Survive?

It is the irony of democracy that democratic ideals survive because authoritarian masses are also generally apathetic and inactive. Thus, the capacity for intolerance, authoritarianism, scapegoatism, racism, and violence of the American lower classes is seldom translated into organized, sustained political movements.

The survival of democracy is not based upon mass support for democratic ideals. It is apparently not necessary that most people commit themselves to a democracy; all that is necessary is that they fail to commit themselves actively to an antidemocratic system. American democracy might, then, seem to be on shaky foundations. However, it is important to keep in mind that although the masses may have antidemocratic attitudes, they are also inclined to avoid political activity. And those with the most dangerous attitudes are the least involved in politics.[29]

Conditions for Mass Activism

Occasionally, however, mass apathy gives way to mass activism. Reflecting the masses' antidemocratic, extremist, hateful, and violence-prone sentiments, this activism seriously threatens democratic values.

Mass activism tends to occur in crises—defeat or humiliation in war, economic depression and unemployment, or threat to public safety. William Kornhauser correctly observes:

There appears to be a close relation between the severity of crises and the extent of mass movements in Western societies. The more severe the depression in industrial societies, the greater the social atomization, and the more widespread are mass movements (for example, there is a high [inverse] association between level of employment and increase in the extremist electorate). The stronger a country's sense of national humiliation and defeat in war, the greater the social atomization, and the greater the mass action (for example, there is a close association between military defeat and the rise of strong mass movements). [30]

Defeat in war, or even failure to achieve any notable victories in a protracted military effort, reduces mass confidence in established leadership and makes the masses vulnerable to the appeals of counterelites. Both fascism in Germany and communism in Russia followed on the heels of national humiliation and defeat in war. The current antiestablishment culture in America owes a great deal to the mistakes and failures of the nation's leadership in Vietnam.

Mass anxiety and vulnerability to counterelites are also increased by economic dislocation—depression, unemployment, or technological change—which threatens financial security. Poverty itself is less a source of anxiety than change or threat of change in the level of affluence. Another source of anxiety among the masses is their perceived level of personal safety. Crime, street violence, and terrorism can produce disproportionately strong anxieties about personal safety. Historically, when they believe their personal safety is threatened, masses in America have turned to vigilantes, the Ku Klux Klan, and "law and order" movements.

The masses are most vulnerable to extremism when they are alienated from group and community life and when they feel their own lives are without direction or purpose. According to William Kornhauser:

People become available for mobilization by [counter] elites when they lack or lose an independent group life. The term masses *applies only where we deal with people who . . . cannot be integrated into any organization based on common interest, into political parties or municipal governments or professional organizations or trade unions. The lack of autonomous relations generates widespread social alienation. Alienation heightens responsiveness to the appeal of mass movements because they provide occasions for expressing resentment against what is, as well as promises of a vitally different world. In short,* people who are atomized readily become mobilized. *Since totalitarianism is a state of total mobilization, mass society is highly vulnerable to totalitarian movements and regimes.* [31]

Counterelites: The Demagogue as Voice of the People

Threats to established elite values occur periodically, from both left and right. The counterelite pattern is similar, no matter which ideological direction it moves from. Both left and right counterelite movements base their appeal upon the desire of those who perceive themselves as powerless to overthrow the established elite.

Though "left" counterelites in America are just as antidemocratic, extremist, intolerant, and violence-prone as "right" counterelites, their appeal is currently limited to small numbers of alienated blacks, intellectuals, and college students. "Left" counterelites have no mass following among workers, farmers, or middle-class Americans. In contrast, "right" counterelites have been more native to American life, and have mobilized broad mass followings. Many changes in American society have contributed to the popular appeal of "right" counterelites: shifts in power and prestige from the farms to the cities, from agriculture to industry, from the South to the North; shifts away from individual enterprise toward collective action; shifts away from racial segregation toward special emphasis on opportunities for blacks; shifts from old values to new, from religion to secularism, from work to leisure; shifts in scale from small to large, from personal to impersonal, from individual to bureaucratic; increases in crime, racial disorder, and threats to personal safety. Any genuine "people's" revolution in America would undoubtedly take the form of a right-wing nationalist, patriotic, religious-fundamentalist, antiblack, anti-intellectual, antistudent, "law and order" movement.[32]

Counterelite movements may employ equalitarian rhetoric but (like all political activity) are well in control of the articulate few. Rarely, of course, do counterelites accumulate sufficient resources to put any portion of their values into practice. They can, however, threaten established elites, which, in hopes of reducing the anxieties expressed in the counterelite movement, provide symbolic satisfaction. Nixon's "Southern strategy," for instance, was certainly partially generated by his fear of George C. Wallace. Similarly, during the 1930s, Roosevelt's economic policies were partially inspired by a desire to defuse the more radically left political movements of the time.

The early career of George C. Wallace was typical of many counterelites in its populism, extremism, antielitism, and equalitarianism. But Wallace was atypical in the breadth of his mass base: In the 1968 presidential election, 14 percent of the American electorate completely abandoned the two-party system to support Wallace's independent candidacy. Given the historic, institutional role of the two-party system in America and the strength of traditional party loyalties, family ties, and socialization patterns, the fact that so many people would abandon both parties for an independent candidate is truly astounding.

Both North and South, Wallace appealed to *racial sentiments*—a mass characteristic of whites that Wallace successfully exploited.* But it is a mistake to dismiss Wallace as merely a racist. He appealed to "little people" throughout the nation by expressing a wide variety of mass sentiments.

Wallace spoke in *populist* terms about the role of "the people":

The Wallace for President movement is a movement of the people and it doesn't make any difference whether top leading politicians endorse this movement or not. I think that if the politicians get in the way in 1968, a lot of them are gonna get run over by this average man in the steel mill, this barber, this beautician, the policeman on the beat, they're the ones—and the little businessman—I think those are the mass of people that are going to support a change on the domestic scene in this country. [33]

Wallace was *equalitarian* on everything but race. He attacked the "Eastern money interests" and "the over-educated ivory-tower folks with pointed heads looking down their nose at us." He identified communism with wealth: "I don't believe in all this talk about poor folks turning Communist! It's the damn rich who turn Communist. You ever seen a poor Communist?"[34] Republicans were attacked as "bankers and big money people" who exploit "us ordinary folks." Wallace welfare and public-works programs, when he was governor of Alabama, were the most liberal in the state's history, and he was regarded as a threat to conservative business interests in that state.

Mass fears about personal safety were just as influential as racial prejudice in stimulating Wallace support. Wallace frequently referred to demonstrators as "the scum of the earth"; he pledged that if a demonstrator ever tried to lie down in front of a Wallace motorcade "it would be the last car he ever lies down in front of." Wallace's simplistic solu-

---

*Whether Wallace is personally a racist is open to question. In his first run for Governor of Alabama in 1958, Wallace shunned KKK support and ran as a Southern "moderate," against strong segregationist John Patterson. Wallace was badly beaten, and was widely quoted as saying "They out-niggered me that time but they'll never do it again." One Wallace observer says, "I would term the Governor a pseudo-demagogue, because he doesn't really believe what he says about the race question. He uses it only as a technique to get the vote of the nonsophisticated white man." But another observer adds, "He used to be anything but a racist, but with all his chattering he managed to talk himself into it." See Robert Sherrill, *Gothic Politics in the Deep South* (New York: Grossman, 1968), p. 283.

tion to rioting was "to let the police run this country for a year or two and there wouldn't be any riots."[35] Wallace correctly judged that this mass audience would welcome a police state in order to insure their personal safety. Opinion surveys consistently reported that "crime and violence," "riots," and "law and order" were rated as the most important issues by Wallace's mass following.[36]

Wallace frequently expressed contempt for established institutions and procedures, and an undercurrent of violence is easily detectable in his speeches. He symbolized popular resistance to court-decreed de-segregation by "standing in the schoolhouse door in person" at the University of Alabama when he personally interposed his body between federal marshals and the entrance to the registrar's office. Wallace expressed very little tolerance of diverse views. Intellectual critics of the Vietnam War were "long-hairs who ought to be treated as traitors, which they are." As for courts and constitutional rights of defendants: "Of course if I did what I'd like to do I'd pick up something and smash one of these federal judges in the head and then burn the courthouse down. But I'm too genteel."

It is not unusual—indeed it is normal—for major parties to absorb, and de-radicalize, the protest of third-party movements. For they are, indeed, "movements." Wallace was *initially* concerned more about the articulation of protest than with immediate electoral success; an uprising against established elites is not likely to propel its leaders into national office. Jimmy Carter, Richard Nixon, George Meany, and Edward Kennedy made overtures to Wallace, and the Democrats accommodated Wallace's followers within the party. Wallace supporters are represented on the Democratic National Committee and on all other party commissions. In return, Wallace himself moved appreciably away from the ideological postures of his early populism. In the 1976 Democratic presidential primaries, Jimmy Carter won over most of Wallace's followers. Carter's views were acceptable to many Wallace supporters, as were his southern background and his pretended remoteness from the eastern establishment and circles of power in Washington, D.C. Wallace himself, crippled for life in a 1972 assassination attempt, had not campaigned with his earlier vigor and volatility. The Wallace movement died. No longer would Wallace represent any significant threat to established liberal values or to the two-party system.

Summary

Elite theory suggests that elites are distinguished from the masses not only by their socioeconomic background but also by their attitudes and values. Elites give greater support to the principles and beliefs underlying the political system. Our analysis of elite and mass attitudes suggests the following propositions:

1. Elites give greater support to democratic values than masses. Elites are also more consistent than masses in applying general principles of democracy to specific individuals, groups, and events.

2. Extremist and intolerant movements in modern society are likelier to be based in lower classes than in middle and upper classes. The poor may be more liberal on economic issues, but on noneconomic issues—support for civil liberties, for example—the upper classes are more liberal and the lower classes more conservative. Masses demonstrate antidemocratic attitudes more often than elites. The masses are less committed to democratic rules of the game than elites and more likely to go outside these rules, to engage in violence. Mass movements exploit the alienation and hostility of lower classes by concentrating on scapegoats.

3. The survival of democracy depends on elite rather than mass commitment to democratic ideals.

4. Political apathy and nonparticipation among the masses contribute to the survival of democracy. Fortunately for democracy, the antidemocratic masses are generally more apathetic than elites. Only an unusual demagogue or counterelite can arouse the masses from their apathy and create a threat to the established system.

5. Occasionally mass apathy is replaced by mass activism, which is generally extremist, intolerant, antidemocratic, and violence-prone. Conditions which encourage mass activism include defeat or humiliation in war, economic dislocation, or perceived threats to personal safety.

6. Counterelites appeal to mass sentiments and express hostility toward the established order and its values. Both "left" and "right" counterelites are antidemocratic, extremist, impatient with due process, contemptuous of law and authority, and violence-prone. Counterelites express racial prejudices, populism, equalitarianism, anti-intellectualism, and simplistic solutions to social problems.

7. Although "left" counterelites are just as antidemocratic as "right" counterelites, their appeal is limited to small numbers of alienated blacks, college students, and intellectuals. In contrast, "right" counterelites have mobilized mass support among large numbers of farmers, workers, and middle-class Americans. George C. Wallace was a typical mass counterelite, not only in his appeal to racial sentiments but in his appeal to other mass values.

8. Although more committed to democratic values than masses, elites may abandon these values in crises. When war or revolution threatens the existing order, elites themselves may deviate from democratic values to maintain the system. Dissent is no longer tolerated—the mass media are censored, free speech curtailed, counterelites jailed, police and security forces strengthened.

9. Elite-mass communication is very difficult. Most of the communication received by decision makers is from other elite members rather than the masses. Because the decision maker's perceptions of mass attitudes are likely to be affected by elite values, public opinion is interpreted as supporting the decision maker's position.

10. Although elites are relatively free of mass influence, this freedom varies with the issue. The masses are ignorant about most political issues and consequently cannot convey any message about them to decision makers. But on issues of race and civil rights mass attitudes are well-formed. Decision

makers have a reasonably accurate perception of mass attitudes on civil rights and are more likely to vote their perception of mass attitudes than their own feelings on civil rights questions.

11. The masses believe that elected decision makers should behave as instructed delegates, but very few decision makers consider themselves delegates. Instead decision makers believe they are free agents who should follow the dictates of their own conscience.

12. Efforts by elites to change mass attitudes are not uniformly successful, although elites believe that they are very influential. Television serves as an example.

References

[1]*Fortune* (June 1940).

[2]Herbert H. Hyman and Paul B. Sheatsley, "Trends in Public Opinion on Civil Liberties," *Journal of Social Issues*, 9 (1953), 6–16.

[3]Samuel A. Stouffer, *Communism, Conformity and Civil Liberties* (New York: John Wiley, 1966). Originally published in 1955.

[4]J. Allen Williams, "Communism, Conformity, and Civil Liberty: Highlights of a 1973 Replication of Stouffer's 1954 Study." Paper presented at the Southwestern Sociological Association Convention, Dallas, March 1974.

[5]Hazel Erskine, "The Polls: Freedom of Speech," *Public Opinion Quarterly*, 34 (February 1970), 484.

[6]Williams, "Communism, Conformity, and Civil Liberty," p. 6

[7] William Fulbright, *The Arrogance of Power* (New York: Vintage, 1966), p. 27.

[8]Herbert McClosky, "Consensus and Ideology in American Politics," *American Political Science Review*, 58 (June 1964), 361–382.

[9]Seymour Martin Lipset, *Political Man* (Garden City, N.Y.: Doubleday & Co., 1963), p. 87.

[10]*Ibid.*, p. 92

[11]Lewis Lipsitz, "Work Life and Political Attitudes: A Study of Manual Workers," *American Political Science Review*, 58:4 (December 1964), 959.

[12]Lipset, *Political Man*, p. 114.

[13]*Ibid.*, p. 110.

[14]Lewis Lipsitz, "Working-class Authoritarianism: A Reevaluation," *American Sociological Review* 30 (1965), 108–109.

[15]David G. Lawrence, "Procedural Norms and Tolerance: A Measurement." APSA, LXX (March 1976), p. 89.

[16]Herbert McClosky, "Personality and Attitude Correlates of Foreign Policy Orientation," Publication A-48, Survey Research Center, University of California at Berkeley, in J. Rosenau (ed), *Domestic Sources of Foreign Policy* (New York: Free Press, 1967), pp. 51–110.

[17]Seymour Lipset and Reinhard Bendix, *Social Mobility in Industrial Society* (Berkeley: University of California Press, 1960), p. 103.

[18]Morris Janowitz, *The Professional Soldier: A Social and Political Portrait* (New York: Free Press, 1970), p. 238.

[19]This section draws heavily upon Harmon Zeigler and Wayne Peak, "The Political Functions of the Educational System," *Sociology of Education*, 43 (Spring 1970), 115–142.

[20]Robert E. Lane and David O. Sears, *Public Opinion* (Englewood Cliffs, N.J.: Prentice-Hall, Inc., 1964), p. 25.

[21]Kenneth P. Langton, *Political Socialization* (New York: Oxford University Press, 1969), p. 18.

[22]Byron G. Massialas, "American Government: We Are the Greatest!", in C. Benjamin Cox and Byron G. Massialas, *Social Studies in the United States* (New York: Harcourt, Brace and World, 1967), pp. 191–192.

[23]Cited in Mark N. Krug, *History and the Social Sciences* (Waltham, Mass.: Blaisdell Publishing Co., 1967), p. 202.

[24]Cole and Montgomery, *op. cit.*, pp. 341–342. Cited in Girault, *op. cit.*, p. 227.

[25]Robert P. Ludlum, *et al.*, *American Government* (Boston: Houghton, Mifflin, 1965), p. 2. Cited in Massialas, *op. cit.*, p. 180.

[26]Kenneth P. Langton and M. Kent Jennings, "Political Socialization and the High School Civics Curriculum," *American Political Science Review*, 62 (September 1968), 864.

[27]Edgar Litt, "Civic Education, Community Norms, and Political Indoctrination," *American Sociological Review*, 28 (Feb. 1963), 69–75.

[28]Lane and Sears, *op. cit.*, p. 27.

[29]Herbert H. Hyman, "England and America: Climates of Tolerance and Intolerance, 1962," In Daniel Bell (ed.), *The Radical Right* (Garden City, N.Y.: Doubleday & Co., 1963), p. 229. Although England went through the same postwar stress as America, English investigations of suspected subversives were more limited. Hyman concludes that "when millions of individuals . . . are brought under official scrutiny as possible security risks, it validates the belief that everyone ought to be regarded with suspicion. . . . It thus encourages in the public at large a climate of intolerance toward those who may exhibit nonconformist opinions."

[30]William Kornhauser, *The Politics of Mass Society* (New York: Free Press, 1959), p. 174.

[31]Kornhauser, p. 33.

[32]Seymour Martin Lipset and Earl Raab, *The Politics of Unreason* (New York: Harper and Row, 1970), p. 348.

[33]*Ibid.*, p. 349.

[34]*Ibid.*, p. 350.

[35]*Newsweek*, September 16, 1968, p. 27.

[36]Lipset and Raab, *Politics of Unreason*, p. 406.

Elite-Mass Communication: Television, the Press, and the Pollsters

6

Communication in the American political system flows downward from elites to masses. Television and the press are the means by which elites communicate to the masses not only information but also values, attitudes, and emotions. Professional pollsters in turn try to measure mass response to these elite communications. But elite-mass communication often fails. Masses may misinterpret elite messages to them, and elites may not change mass opinion as they want; and just as frequently, elites, guided by their own biases, misinterpret mass opinion.

In this chapter we will examine the concentration of power in the mass media and document the emergence of a new and powerful segment of the nation's elite—the newsmakers. We will also examine "establishment" bias in the news, particularly television news. We will also examine why elite communications are sometimes misinterpreted by the masses—the problem of "selective perception." Finally, we will examine how elites try to learn about mass attitudes and what effect, if any, mass attitudes have on elite behavior.

The Newsmakers

Elites instruct masses about politics and social values chiefly through television, the major source of information for the vast majority of Americans. Those who control this flow of information are among the most powerful persons in the nation. In 1972 virtually every family in America (99.8 percent) had a TV set, compared to only 19.8 percent in 1952. Thus, it is only recently that TV newsmakers rose to power. Newspapers have always reported on wars, politics, crime, and scandal, just as they do today; but the masses of Americans did not read them. Instead, they quickly passed over the headlines to the sports and comics, pausing perhaps at the latest scandals and violent crimes. But television is the first really *mass* communication form. Nearly everyone, including children, watches the evening news. And over two-thirds of the public testify that television provides "most of my views about what is going on in the world today."[1] But TV has its greatest impact because it is visual: it can convey emotions as well as information. Police dogs attacking blacks, sacks of dead American GIs being loaded on helicopters, scenes of burning and looting in cities, all convey emotions as well as information.

The power to determine what Americans will see and hear about the world is vested in just three private corporations—the American Broadcasting Company (ABC), the Columbia Broadcasting System (CBS), and the National Broadcasting Corporation (NBC), a division of RCA. Contrary to public belief, there is no public regulation whatsoever of network broadcasting. Each television station is privately owned and licensed to use broadcast channels by a government regulatory agency, the Federal Communications Commission (FCC). But because of the high costs of producing news and entertainment at the station level, virtually all stations are forced to receive some news and programming from the three networks. The top officials of these corporate networks are indeed "a tiny, enclosed fraternity of privileged men."*

What news and entertainment will be seen is decided by the top network executives—presidents, vice-presidents, directors, and producers—not by Walter Cronkite, John Chancellor, David Brinkley, Harry Reasoner, or Barbara Walters; these reporters simply read what is put in front of them.[2] But the network executives exchange views with the editors of the *New York Times*, the *Washington Post* and *Newsweek*, *Time* magazine, and a few of the largest newspaper chains.** These TV

---

*So called by former Vice-President Spiro T. Agnew, who also described them more colorfully as "super-sensitive, self-anointed, supercilious electronic barons of opinion." See *Newsweek* (November 9, 1970), p. 22.

**Ten newspaper chains control over one-third of the daily newspaper circulation in America: Tribune, Newhouse, Scripps-Howard, Knight, Hearst, Gannett, Times-Mirror, Dow-Jones, Ridder, and Cox.

executives and producers and print editors and publishers can be considered collectively as "the newsmakers."

The newsmakers frequently make contradictory remarks about their own power. On the one hand, they sometimes claim that they do no more than "mirror" reality. The "mirror" myth is nonsense, of course. A mirror makes no choices about what images it reflects, but television executives have the power to create some national issues and ignore others; to elevate obscure people to national prominence; to reward politicians they favor and punish those they disfavor. Indeed, at times the newsmakers proudly credit themselves with the success of the civil rights movement, ending the Vietnam War, and forcing two presidents —Johnson and Nixon—out of office. These claims contradict the "mirror" image, but they more accurately reflect the power of the mass media.

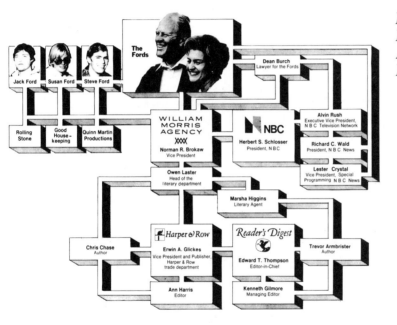

Figure 6–1
Publishing and Television
Arrangements for the
Ford Family

Source: © 1977 by The New York Times Company. Reprinted by permission.

Far less diversity of views is permitted on television than in the press. Conventionally "liberal" and "conservative" views can be found in newspapers and magazines; for example the *New York Times* versus the *Wall Street Journal; Newsweek* versus *U.S. News and World Report; Harper's* magazine versus the *National Review*. But a conventional liberal position is presented on all three major television networks—ABC, NBC, and CBS. (Only William F. Buckley's "Firing Line," on public, educational

Establishment Bias in TV News

TV stations, represents the "conservative" viewpoint of network television.) This liberal "bias" has several sources.

The first source of bias are the values of the newsmakers themselves. TV newsmakers may be perfectly sincere when they insist that they are impartial, objective, and unbiased, because in their world—the New York and Washington world of reporters, writers, and intellectuals—the liberal point of view is so uniformly held. Network entertainment programming, newscasts, and news specials are designed to communicate to the masses liberal values: a concern for social reform, a public-regarding attitude, an interest in the problems of the poor and the black, a concern for ecology and the quality of life, and a willingness to use government power to "do good."

Another source of bias in television is the need to capture and keep mass-audience interest. Television must entertain, even in newscasts and news specials. News must be selected that involves emotionally charged rhetoric, shocking incidents, or dramatic conflict. Violence, sex, and government corruption are favorite topics because they draw popular interest. More complex problems—inflation, government deficits, foreign policy—must either be simplified and dramatized, or ignored.

The television networks' concentration on scandal and corruption in government, however, has not always produced the desired liberal, reformist attitudes in the masses. Contrary to the expectations of the network executives, the emphasis given government scandals—Watergate, CIA investigations, FBI abuses, congressional sex scandals, etc.—produces political distrust and cynicism among the masses.

Indeed, much of the political apathy among the mass public today can be attributed to "television malaise," a combination of social distrust, political cynicism, feelings of powerlessness, and dissociation from established parties, caused by television's emphasis on the negative aspects of American life.[3] Network executives do not intend to produce television malaise among the masses; but because scandal, sex, violence, and corruption attract large audiences, stories about them are given prominence in the telecast, usually with some vivid visual aids. Negative television journalism in America ". . . is concerned with what is *wrong* with our government structure, our leaders, our prisons, schools, roads, automobiles, race relations, traffic systems, pollution laws, every facet of our society. In Europe there is much less emphasis on exposing what is wrong, much more satisfaction with the status quo."[4] The effect of these unpleasantries on the American public is to "turn them off" politics and government.

A third source of bias in the news is the technological requirement to decide well in advance of broadcast time what will be "news." Television executives and producers must select topics that will be presented as "news" weeks and months in advance of scheduled broadcasts.[5] This is because network television crews must be sent on location to obtain videotapes, which must be transported, processed, and edited; a script must be prepared with a "lead in," a "voice over," and a "recapitulation." All of this takes time and requires advanced decision making about what will be "news"; executives and producers must rely on their own (liberal) values.

"And here to bend the news a little is Jim Cravanaugh."

Drawing by H. Martin. © 1977 The New Yorker Magazine Inc.

Outright falsification of the "news" as a source of bias is less frequent; but it does occur. One of the most impressive "news specials" ever produced by CBS was "Hunger in America"—a 1968 production designed to increase popular support for the Food Stamp Program. The film began with a close-up shot of a dying baby, pitifully thin and malformed, being given resuscitation in a hospital. The narrator, Charles Kuralt, said: "Hunger is easy to recognize when it looks like this. The baby is dying of starvation. He was an American. Now he is dead."[6] Of course, viewers assumed the baby died of starvation. But in a subsequent congressional investigation it was disclosed that the dying baby was born three months premature, weighed less than three pounds at birth with parents who were neither poor nor starving. In defending the falsification, CBS president Richard Salant said he believed that babies were dying of starvation in America, although CBS could not find any to televise, and that a starving baby would look like the one pictured.[7]

Elite-Mass Communication: Television, the Press, and the Pollsters 147

Mass attitudes—particularly deeply held hatreds or fears—are not easily changed. The liberal-establishment bias of the mass media runs into strong resistance in the masses "selective perception": viewers mentally screen out information or images with which they disagree, and they see only what they want to see on the tube.

Masses do not always respond to the liberal messages of the media executives. Consider, for example, the rise of the "law and order" movement of the late 1960s and the election of Richard M. Nixon as president. For several years in the mid-60s, the networks had provided extensive coverage of urban ghetto riots, campus disruption, and civil disorder in America. The media chiefs believed this coverage would help bring the civil rights movement to northern urban areas and to end U.S. involvement in the Vietnam War. (Until late 1967 media coverage was in support of the war, but then elite groups deserted the Johnson administration effort.) Televised ghetto riots and campus disorders generally gave legitimacy to them; "voice overs" cited the social evils of the ghetto and the concern for peace among America's "kids." But the strategy backfired. White working-class Americans saw the image of black rioting and campus violence, and ignored the words of explanation. Mass hostilities against militant blacks and radical students were reinforced by the broadcasts. In such a television environment, a new "law and order" movement was born, and the principal benefactors in 1968 were George C. Wallace and Richard M. Nixon.

For a long time there were two basic issues in National politics: foreign policies, a traditional advantage to the Republicans, and economics, a plus for the Democrats. Now there is a third: law and order's shorthand for street crime, race, protest tactics, and "revolution." It has been forty years since American politics generated an issue so intense that it could change partisan loyalties for vast numbers of citizens. Law and Order may be such an issue. Where did it come from?

We suggest that the essential midwives in birth of the issue were Messrs. Cronkite, Brinkley, and their brethren—television's newsmen who, we hasten to add, are probably as strongly revolted by the appearance of Law and Order as any group in America. [8]

Another example of "selective perception" is found in mass response to the popular CBS show "All In The Family." The producer, Norman Lear, and the leadership of CBS believed that the crude, bumbling, working-class, superpatriotic, conservative, racist, Archie Bunker would be an effective weapon against prejudice. Bigotry would be made to appear ridiculous. Archie would end up in each episode as a victim of his own bigotry; and the masses would be instructed in liberal values.

But after the show was introduced, evidence soon developed that many viewers agreed with Archie's bigotry, believing that he was "telling it like it is."[9]

The mass audience missed the intended lessons of the show altogether. Sixty percent of the viewers liked and admired the bigoted Archie more than his liberal son-in-law, Mike ("Meathead"). More importantly, it turned out that highly prejudiced people enjoyed and watched the show *more* than less-prejudiced people.[10] When these trends in public opinion became apparent, the show was sharply attacked by the *New York Times*.[11] But by that time, "All In The Family" had become the top-rated show on television. CBS executives optimistically predicted that in the long run the humor of the program would help destroy bigotry.[12] Nevertheless, the media elite had misjudged their mass audiences, as they occasionally do. Selective perception had once again intervened to muddle up elite communication with the masses.

Elites and Public Opinion

Like values, opinions flow downward from elites to masses. Public opinion rarely affects elite behavior; instead, elite behavior shapes public opinion. There are several reasons why elites are relatively unconstrained by public opinion: (1) First, few people among the masses have opinions on the great bulk of policy questions confronting the nation's decision makers. (2) Second, public opinion is very unstable; it can change in a matter of weeks in response to "news" events precipitated by elites. (3) Third, elites do not have a clear perception of mass opinion. Most communications received by decision makers are from other elites—newsmakers, interest-group leaders, those influential in a community, etc.—and not by ordinary citizens.

There is little evidence that public opinion ever directly influences elite behavior. We must not assume that the opinions expressed in the news media *are* public opinion. Frequently, this is a source of confusion. Newspersons believe *they* are the public, often confusing their own opinions with public opinion. They even tell the mass public what its opinion is, thus actually helping to mold it to conform to their own beliefs. Elites, then, may act in response to news stories or the opinions of influential newsmakers in the mistaken belief that they are responding to "public opinion."

Absence of Public Opinion

Masses do not have opinions on most policy issues. Public opinion polls frequently create opinions by asking questions that respondents never thought about until they were asked.[13] Few respondents are willing to say they have no opinion; they believe they should provide some sort of answer, even if their opinion is weakly held or was nonexistent before the question was asked. Thus they produce "doorstep" opinions. But it is unlikely that many Americans have seriously thought about, or gathered much information on, such specific issues as government reorganization, zero based budgeting, the B-1 bomber, investment tax credits, municipal bond interest exemption, and similar specific questions; nor have many Americans information about these topics.

Instability of Public Opinion

Public opinion is very unstable. Mass opinion on a particular issue is often very weakly held. Asked the same question at a later date, many respondents fail to remember their earlier answers and give the pollster the opposite reply. These are not real changes in opinion, yet they register as such. One study estimates that less than 20 percent of the public holds meaningful, consistent opinions on most issues, even though two-thirds or more will respond to questions asked in a survey.[14]

Opinions also vary according to the wording of questions. It is relatively easy to word almost any public policy question in such a way as to elicit mass approval or disapproval. Thus, differently worded questions on the same issue can produce contradictory results. For example, in a California poll about academic freedom,[15] a majority of respondents (52-39) agreed with the statement: "Professors in state supported institutions should have freedom to speak and teach the truth as they see it." However, a majority of respondents (by the same 52-39 ratio) also agreed with the statement: "Professors who advocate controversial ideas or speak out against official policy have no place in a state supported college or university."

Opinion polls that ask the exact same question over time are more reliable indicators of public opinion than one-shot polls. Respondents in a one-shot poll may be responding to the wording of the question. But if the same wording is used over time the bias in the wording remains constant and changes in opinion can be observed. This is why only the exact same wording used continuously over time produces reasonably accurate information about the public mood, and why it is a mistake for elites to rely on one-shot polls.

Bias in Communication

Elites can easily misinterpret public opinion because most of the communications they receive have an upper-class bias. Members of the masses seldom call or write their senators or representatives, much less converse with them at dinners, cocktail parties, or other social occasions. Most of the communications received by decision makers are *intra-elite* communications—communications from newspersons, organized group leaders, influential constituents, wealthy political contributors, and personal friends—people who for the most part share the same views. It is not surprising, therefore, that legislators say that most of their mail is in agreement with their own position; their world of public opinion is self-reinforcing. Moreover, persons who *initiate* communication with decision makers, by writing or calling or visiting their representatives, are decidedly more educated and affluent than the average citizen.

Elite Response to Mass Opinion

Do elites respond to public opinion, or, instead, do they shape public opinion to conform to their own attitudes? When government policy and public opinion are in agreement, is it because the policy was fitted to prevailing opinion, or because opinion was molded to accept predetermined policy? These are difficult questions to answer, yet so often are policies enacted in the face of widespread public opposition, which eventually melts away into acquiescence, that public opinion seems to follow elite decisions, rather than the other way around. Consider national policy on civil rights—one of the few areas in which Americans demonstrably have opinions. The decisions of courts, Congress, and executive bureaucracies in this field have consistently run contrary to public opinion.

When the Supreme Court decided in *Brown* v. *Topeka*, in 1954, that segregation of the races in public schools violated the equal-protection clause of the Fourteenth Amendment of the Constitution, a majority of Americans opposed sending their children to integrated schools. Not until several years after this historic decision did a majority of Americans come to favor school integration. In 1967, a public referendum in California resulted in an overwhelming defeat of a "fair housing" proposal, which would have forbidden discrimination in the sale or rental of housing. One year later, Congress passed the Civil Rights Act of 1968, which, among other things, outlawed discrimination in the sale or rental of housing. Several states have held referenda on busing—the assignment and transportation of children to public schools to achieve racial balance in the classroom. Busing has been voted down in every such referendum, sometimes by margins of 75 to 80 percent; yet the Supreme Court has held that busing may be required where there is evidence of past or present racial segregation in the schools; the Court's policy is based on the requirements of the Constitution and not on public opinion. In short, elite support for civil rights at the national level is *not* a response to mass opinion.

Any congruence between public policy and public opinion is likely to be accidental. Political scientists Ronald E. Weber and William Shaffer estimated public opinion in each of the fifty states on five important policy areas: (1) discrimination in public accommodations, (2) public aid for church-related schools, (3) right-to-work laws, (4) teacher unionization laws, (5) firearms-control laws. Then they attempted to match public opinion in each state with its laws in these fields. In four of the five fields there was no relation between public opinion in the states and their laws. (Only in the area of state antidiscrimination laws was there any congruence between public opinion and state laws.)[16] Indeed, in an earlier study using the same technique, political scientist Frank Munger concluded that the probability that a state law matched the preferences of its citizens was only slightly better than the fifty-fifty ratio generated purely by chance.[17]

War, Elites, and Public Opinion

When political scientist V. O. Key, Jr., wrestled with the same problem—What impact, if any, does mass opinion have on public policy?—he concluded that the "missing piece of the puzzle" was "that thin stratum of persons referred to variously as the political elite, the political activists, the leadership echelons, or the influentials."[18] In other words, it is not mass opinion but rather elite opinion that shapes public policy. Elite preferences are more likely to be in accord with public policy than mass preferences. Of course, this does not prove that policies are determined by elite preferences. It may be that policy makers are acting rationally in response to events and conditions, and well-educated, informed elites understand and approve of government actions more than masses do.

Consider, for example, the relationships between elite and mass opinion and America's involvement in the Korean and Vietnam wars.[19] Despite the greater vocal opposition to the Vietnam War, "both wars were supported to much the same degree and largely by the same segments of the population."[20] In the early stages of both wars, there was great public support for the fighting, especially among college-educated groups, from which elites are drawn. The masses supported both wars at their outset, but not as strongly as the better-informed and better-educated groups. It was elites who supported the policies of Truman and Johnson during the escalation of both wars. Note, in Figure 6–2, that college-educated groups gave significantly greater support for Vietnam in its initial phases.

Nothing arouses patriotism more than decisive military victory; and nothing loses support for war efforts more than military defeat. When the United States was forced to retreat from North Korea after the

Chinese invaded it in December 1950, popular support for the war plunged. Likewise, after the successful communist "Tet" offensive in 1968 support of the Vietnam War by college-educated Americans declined and President Lyndon Johnson announced that he would not seek reelection and would open peace negotiations in Paris with the North Vietnamese. Support for both wars lasted a little over two years after the introduction of American combat ground troops. Analysis reveals that support for these wars declined in direct relationship to the numbers of casualties and the length of the war. "To summarize, then, when one takes support or opposition for the wars in Korea or Vietnam and correlates them with (1) the casualties suffered at the time of the poll or (2) the direction of the war at the time of the poll, one gets a reasonably good fit."[21] The initial support of all population groups for the military action indicates that the masses will support the military adventures of the leadership. This support will evaporate only when military action fails to bring a speedy victory.

Perhaps more importantly, policy making in both wars followed elite, not mass, opinion. Mass opinion never supported the Vietnam War. When elites supported these wars in their early stages, the United States "escalated" its participation—despite less than enthusiastic support by less-educated groups. The United States withdrew from both

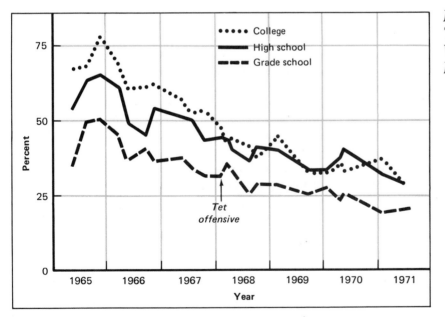

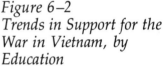

Figure 6–2
Trends in Support for the War in Vietnam, by Education

Source: From John E. Mueller, *War, Presidents and Public Opinion* (1973), p. 125. Used with permission of John Wiley & Sons, Inc.

wars and sought negotiated settlements after elites, not masses, made a dramatic shift in opinion. Elites agreed on escalation in the early phases of the Vietnam War, and they agreed on withdrawal in its later phases. The only disagreements occurred over how quickly we should withdraw. The student antiwar protestors had no significant effect on the course of the war. Indeed, if anything, the protestors strengthened the war effort. After a careful analysis of change in elite and mass opinion on the war, John E. Mueller concludes: ". . . the protest against the war in Vietnam may have been counterproductive in its impact on public opinion: that is, the war might have been somewhat *more* unpopular if protest had not existed."[22] Disagreement over the speed of withdrawal occurred within elite circles. Elites were not responding to mass opinion in their decision to withdraw.

Finally, elites can initiate events that profoundly shape public opinion. Any successful use of force will win widespread public approval in its initial phases. Indeed, even a crisis will strengthen the support of national leaders. Polls showed dramatic increases in support for Truman after the beginning of the Korean War, for Eisenhower after the invasion of Lebanon, for Johnson after committing U.S. combat troops to Vietnam, for Nixon after the Cambodian invasion, and for Ford after the Mayaguez attack. Thus, the president's ability to "make something happen" is an important tool in shaping mass opinion.

Mass Opinion and Elite Interaction

Pluralists argue that competition among elites enhances the power of the masses: Because elites try to win mass support by favoring their preferences, mass support becomes a source of power in intra-elite struggles. We have already challenged this notion with three objections: (1) Masses have no clear, consistent policy positions on most issues; (2) public opinion is very unstable and responds to elite behavior; and (3) public policy does not reflect mass opinion as it is reported in public opinion polls. A fourth objection can be added: Mass popularity does *not* increase the policy-making influence of any particular segment of the nation's elite.

It is widely assumed that mass popularity is a source of power for presidents in their relations with Congress.[23] But systematic studies over time show little relationship between presidential popularity in Gallup polls and support for that president's programs in Congress.[24] (See Table 6–1.) For many years Gallup pollsters have asked the identical question: "Do you approve of the way President _____ is handling his job?" It is clear that presidential popularity among the masses changes rapidly and significantly over time with media coverage of scandal, recession, war, and international crisis. (See Figure 6–3.) How-

	Overall Policy	Domestic Policy	Foreign Policy
Congressmen	1953–72	1955–70	1955–70
All	.12	−.03	.40
Democrats	.10	.03	.32
Republicans	−.07	−.08	.12

*Figures are simple correlation coefficients: 1.00 would be a perfect positive relationship; zero or near-zero coefficients indicate no relationship.

Source: Derived from figures in George C. Edwards, "Presidential Influence in the House: Presidential Prestige as a Source of Presidential Power," *American Political Science Review,* 70 (March 1976), pp. 101–113.

Table 6–1
*Relationships Between Presidential Approval Ratings by the Public and Support for Presidential Programs in Congress on Roll Call Votes**

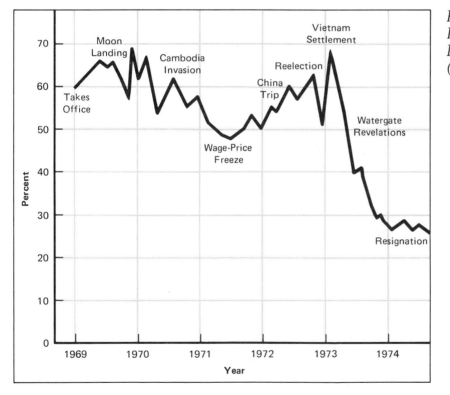

*Figure 6–3
President Nixon's Popularity Ratings (Percentage of Approval)*

Source: Data from *Gallup Opinion Index,* Sept. 1974, p. 12.

ever, these changes in presidential popularity among the masses corre-late little with presidential influence over policy making. As Table 6–1 indicates, in the administrations of Eisenhower, Kennedy, Johnson, and Nixon there was hardly any relationship between presidential popular-ity and congressional voting. Such relationships are near zero in overall policy and domestic policy. Only in foreign policy does presidential popularity seem to help in winning congressional support; but even here presidential popularity accounts for very little—only 16 percent. Thus, mass opinion has relatively little to do with elite interaction in policy making.

Communication, then, between elites and masses is chiefly one-way—downward. Members of the elite, with general success, use the mass media to communicate values and opinions to the public. The masses, on the other hand, hold few strong or stable opinions. Partly for this reason, and partly because members of the elite often mistake intra-elite communication for expressions of "public opinion," policy making often shows little congruence with the mass opinion of the time.

Summary

Communications in the American political system flow downward from elites to masses. Elites are generally isolated from public opinion—not only because the masses do not have opinions on most issues but also because of the many barriers to accurate assessment of public opinion. Our analysis fits the elitist notion that elites are subject to relatively little direct influence from masses. Elites influence mass opinion more than masses influence elite opinion.

1. Television is the principal means by which elites communicate to masses. Control of the flow of information to the masses is highly concentrated. Three television networks and a handful of prestigious news organizations decide what will be the "news."

2. Bias in the news arises from the liberal establishment views of the newsmak-ers themselves, together with the need to dramatize and sensationalize the news. However, the newsmakers' recent concentration on scandal and cor-ruption in government has produced "television malaise"—social distrust, political cynicism, and feelings of powerlessness—instead of reform.

3. Mass attitudes are frequently resistant to elite indoctrination through the mass media; principally through "selective perception"—the tendency to mentally screen out information with which one disagrees. Frequently, the masses see violence, disorder, or war on television, but ignore the elite mes-sages attached to it.

4. Masses seldom have opinions on specific issues. Pollsters may create "doorstep" opinions by asking questions which respondents never thought of before answering. Moreover, public opinion is unstable—it changes over time and with the wording of the question.

5. Most communications received by elites come from other elites. This intra-elite communication usually reinforces elite views.

6. There is no evidence that public policy reflects mass opinion. Civil rights laws came about despite majority opposition. Moreover, laws in the states do not correspond to public opinion in the states.

7. Public policy changes when there are shifts in elite, not mass, opinion. Elites initially gave greater support than the masses to the war in Vietnam. But by 1968 elite opinion had shifted dramatically against the war, and the United States began its withdrawal from Southeast Asia. Mass opinion, and even the much-publicized antiwar protests, had little to do with United States policy shifts.

8. Mass support for the president has little to do with the president's successes or failures in Congress. In other words, a president cannot use mass support very effectively to impose administration views or policies on the Congress.

References

[1]The Roper Organization, *Most People Think of Television and Other Mass Media* (New York: Television Information Office, 1973), p. 3.

[2]Edward J. Epstein, *News from Nowhere* (New York: Random House, 1973), pp. 27–28.

[3]See Michael J. Robinson, "Public Affairs Television and the Growth of Political Malaise," *American Political Science Review*, 70 (June 1976): 409–432.

[4]Merrill Panitt, "America Out of Focus," *TV Guide* (January 15, 1972), p. 6; also cited by Robinson, *op. cit.*, p. 428.

[5]Epstein, *News from Nowhere*, p. XX.

[6]*Ibid.*, p. 21.

[7]*Ibid.*, p. XX.

[8]Byron Shafer and Richard Larson, "Did TV Create the Social Issue?" *Columbia Journalism Review* (September-October 1972), p. 10. See also Richard Scammon and Ben Wattenberg, *The Real Majority* (New York: Coward, McCann, 1970), p. 162.

[9]See Neil Vidmar and Milton Rokeach, "Archie Bunker's Bigotry: A Study in Selective Perception," *Journal of Communications* (Winter 1974), pp. 36–47.

[10]*Ibid.*

[11]L. Z. Hobson, "As I Listened to Archie Say 'Hebe,'" *New York Times*, September 12, 1972.

[12]Norman Lear, "As I Read How Laura Saw Archie," *New York Times*, October 10, 1972.

[13]Robert S. Erikson and Norman R. Luttberg, *American Public Opinion*, (New York: John Wiley, 1973).

[14]Phillip Converse, "Attitudes and Non-Attitudes," Edward R. Tufte (ed.), *Quantitative Analysis of Social Problems* (Reading, Mass.: Addison-Wesley, 1970), pp. 168–189.

[15]Erikson and Luttberg, *American Public Opinion*, p. 38.

[16]Ronald E. Weber and William R. Schaffer, "Public Opinion and American State Policy-Making." *Midwest Journal of Political Science*, 16 (November 1972): 683–699. See also Anne H. Hopkins, "Opinion Publics and Support for Public Policy in the American States," *American Journal of Political Science*, 18 (February 1974): 167–178.

[17]Frank J. Munger, "Opinions, Elections, Parties, and Policies," paper delivered at the Annual Meeting of the American Political Science Association, New York, 1969.

[18]V. O. Key, Jr., *Public Opinion and American Democracy* (New York: Alfred Knopf, 1967), p. 537.

[19]The following discussion relies on the important book by political scientist John Mueller, *War, Presidents and Public Opinion* (New York: John Wiley, 1973).

[20]*Ibid.*, p. 266.

[21]*Ibid.*, pp. 61–62.

[22]*Ibid.*, p. 164.

[23]See particularly Richard Neustadt, *Presidential Power* (New York: New American Library, 1964), Chapter 5.

[24]George C. Edwards, "Presidential Influence in the House: Presidential Prestige as a Source of Presidential Power," *American Political Science Review*, 70 (March 1976), pp. 101–113.

Elections: Imperfect Instruments of Accountability

7

Traditional "pluralist" textbooks in American government tell us that elections are a means by which masses can hold elites responsible for their policy decisions. In this theory (which we call the "policy mandate" theory of elections), elections enable masses to direct future public policy by voting for one candidate or another on election day.

We shall argue that elections do *not* serve as "policy mandates." Instead, elections serve as "symbolic reassurance" to the masses. Enabling the masses to participate in a political activity contributes to the legitimacy of government. What elections allow the masses to help choose is personnel for public office, but *not* future public policy.

For elections to serve as "policy mandates," and for voters to exercise influence over public policy through elections, four conditions would have to be fulfilled: (1) Competing candidates would offer clear policy alternatives; (2) voters would be concerned with policy questions; (3) majority preferences on these questions could be ascertained in election results; (4) elected officials would be bound by the positions they assumed during the campaign.

Elections—Evidence Against the Myth

In this chapter and the next, we shall contend that *none* of these conditions is fulfilled in American politics and that voters consequently cannot directly control public policy for several reasons:

1. The parties do not offer clear policy alternatives. Because both parties agree on the major direction of public policy (see Chapter 8), the voters cannot influence it by choosing between the parties.

2. Voter decisions are not motivated primarily by policy considerations. For a mandate to be valid, the electorate must make informed, policy-oriented choices; but traditional party ties and candidate personalities influence voters more than policy questions do. Thus, party loyalty dilutes the voters' influence over policy.

3. Even if the voters were primarily concerned with policy questions, it would be difficult to ascertain majority preferences on these questions from the election results. Victory for a candidate's party need not mean that the voters support its programs. First, voters are inconsistent in their policy preferences. Second, they often misinterpret or pay little attention to a candidate's policy preferences. Third, among the voters for a given candidate there are often not only advocates of the candidate's position but also opponents (as well as some who are indifferent to positions). Fourth, a popular majority may really be composed of many policy minorities. How is a candidate to know which (if any) policy positions brought electoral victory?—not, surely, all of them.

4. For voters to exercise control over public officials, elected officials would have to be bound by their campaign pledges. Needless to say, campaign pledges are frequently ignored by elected officials.

The Ignorance of the Electorate

If elections are to be a means of popular control over public policy, voters must be reasonably well informed about policy issues and must hold opinions on them. Yet large numbers of the electorate are politically uninformed and inarticulate. Some years ago, public-opinion analysts reported what is now a typical finding about the low level of political information among adult Americans. (See Table 7–1.) Only about one-half of the public knew the elementary fact that each state has two United States senators; fewer still knew the length of the terms of congressmen or the number of Supreme Court justices.[1]

It is often claimed that voters are becoming more sophisticated, but evidence of their ignorance remains high. For instance, a recent poll (Table 7–2) reveals results roughly comparable to earlier evidence. Although most people could identify at least one visible public figure, such as the governor of their state, few understood the workings and structure of Congress. Elites view such ignorance with astonishment because, to them, the cost of information is cheap. But the average person, given the opportunity to acquire political information, implicitly decides that the costs of acquiring information outweigh its benefits. For active and influential elites, however, the stakes of competition in politics are high; their careers, self-esteem, and prestige are directly and often daily, affected by political decisions.

Although a tiny fraction of the total fraction of the total electorate, there are among the masses numerous *grass-roots* activists for whom

	Percentage of Correct Responses
How many senators are there in Washington from your state?	55
When a man is elected to the United States House of Representatives, how many years does he serve in one term of office?	47
Do you happen to know whether all United States Senators come up for re-election this fall?	46
Can you tell me how many justices there are normally on the United States Supreme Court, including the Chief Justice?	40
Do you happen to know whether federal or state governments make the laws about who can vote in a presidential election?	33
What do you know about the Bill of Rights? Do you know anything it says?	23

Source: Fred I. Greenstein, *The American Party System and the American People* (Englewood Cliffs, N.J.: Prentice-Hall, 1963).

Table 7–1
Proportion of Adult Americans Informed about Aspects of the American Political System

	Governor		1st Senator		2nd Senator		Representative	
	Name	Party	Name	Party	Name	Party	Name	Party
Total	89%	77%	59%	53%	39%	36%	46%	41%
18 to 29 years	84	68	50	42	30	28	30	25
30 to 40 years	90	79	62	56	42	40	53	45
50 years and over	91	81	63	58	42	40	53	48
Men	90	81	64	58	44	41	51	44
Women	87	73	54	48	33	32	42	37
8th grade	76	66	45	42	28	26	35	31
High School	90	76	53	47	32	30	44	37
College	93	83	74	66	52	50	55	49
Under $5,000	80	68	46	42	29	28	38	34
$5,000–$9,999	87	74	55	48	34	32	40	34
$10,000–$14,999	92	79	61	54	39	36	49	40
$15,000 and over	95	87	74	69	53	50	60	55
Republican	89	80	61	57	39	36	49	46
Democrat	89	79	58	52	39	37	49	42
Independent	90	75	64	57	42	40	45	38

Source: U.S. Senate, Committee on Governmental Operations, *Confidence and Concern: Citizens View American Government* (Washington D.C.: Government Printing Office, 1973), p. 244.

Table 7–2
People Who Correctly Identified Name and Party of Their Elected Leaders

politics involves important emotional stakes and substantial perceived benefits (although the actual benefits are insignificant). These minorities are unable to understand why others cannot acquire information as easily as they do. Moreover, if one vote in millions is infinitesimally influential, it must seem quite reasonable to remain ignorant about politics. Thus, the average voter systematically tunes out political information. The more information one already has, the easier it is to acquire new information and to sort it into meaningful categories. Those most informed about political issues are usually among better educated.[2] (See Table 7–3.) (Perhaps it is a truism to observe this relationship; for the purpose of education is, of course, to increase knowledge.) Hearing a surprising statement about the Secretary of Defense, for example, informed voters will pay close attention. They relate this information to what they already know about recent defense policy and to the relationship between the secretary and the president. Uninformed voters hearing the same statement, however, may not even know who the secretary of defense is and will find the report of little consequence or interest, for they have no way of fitting the information into a larger scheme of understanding. Furthermore, the decisions at issue in the typical presidential election are of little personal significance to the average voter; such decisions are not whether to have a draft, to increase or cut taxes, or to borrow against social security. Presidential campaign issues are rarely so specific.

As Converse puts it, "For many people, politics does not compete in interest with sports, local gossip, and television dramas." Thus, many people simply have no opinion about political issues that are the subject of heated debate in the mass media. No more than a third of the public recognizes legislative proposals that have been the center of public debate for months, and sometimes years. Further, even among that third, few could describe the proposal accurately or in detail, and fewer still could describe the intricacies and alternatives available to policy makers.

Table 7–3
Education and
Familiarity with
Policy Issues

Familiarity with Issues	Less Than 8 Years of School	High School	College
High	21%	31%	50%
Medium	37	47	44
Low	42	22	6
Total	100	100	100

Source: A. Campbell, P. Converse, W. Miller, and D. Stokes, *The American Voter* (1960), p. 175. Used with permission of John Wiley & Sons, Inc.

As ill-informed as the masses generally are, they show a congruent inability to sort out and relate information that they do possess. Frequently the same public will offer simultaneous approval to candidates with fundamentally different positions. They do so partly because they are poorly informed about the candidates' positions, but also partly, it seems, because broad segments of the public hold opinions that are contradictory.

Except for those issues that are unusually visible to large numbers of people (for example, civil rights), mass attitudes are very inconsistent. For example, those who support an enlargement of public services do not necessarily support taxes to pay for them; in fact, many who support a tax cut also favor expansion of federal welfare spending.

Persons who hold inconsistent positions are most likely to come from the lower social strata. And although they demand expanded federal services and a reduced federal budget, they show extreme disfavor toward the worth of the services they want. Obviously, self-interest makes simultaneous support for tax reduction and expansion of federal welfare quite compatible. However, for the political system as a whole, the combination is irrational. Even if the elite tried, it could not satisfy both demands.

A possible reason for these inconsistencies is that the opinions of the masses are frequently created by public opinion polls. Because the questions asked in opinion polls are meaningless to a substantial portion of the population, so are the answers. Many people have never thought about the question before it is asked and will never think about it again. As one moves down the socioeconomic ladder from elites to masses, consistent political beliefs rapidly fade away. As consistency declines, objects of beliefs shift from abstract principles to simple, concrete goals.[3]

To estimate the ability of the electorate to conceptualize (to think abstractly), the University of Michigan Survey Research Center, in 1956, examined the responses of a sample to questions concerning the good and bad points of the two major parties.[4] The following categorization was derived. *Idealogues* are those respondents who are either "liberal" or "conservative" and are likely to rely on abstract principles in evaluating candidates and issues. *Near idealogues* are those who mentioned an abstract principle, but clearly did not rely on it as much as the ideologues did. Near ideologues used ideology in a fashion that raised doubts about their understanding of the terms employed. At the next level of respondents, the *group benefits* class, were those who did not exhibit any overriding ideological dimension in their thinking, but were able to evaluate parties and candidates by expected favorable or unfavorable treatment for social groups. A favored candidate was seen as "for" a group with which the subject was identified. A fourth level of conceptualization defines respondents whose judgment is based upon their perception of the *"goodness"* or *"badness" of the times.* They blame or praise parties and candidates because of their association with conditions of war or peace, prosperity or depression. The last level includes those respondents whose evaluations of the political scene hold *no relationship whatever to policy,* even in the broadest and most symbolic use of the term. Some of these profess a loyalty to one of the two parties but have no idea about the positions advocated by that party.

When the entire electorate was examined, in 1956, ideological commitments were seen to be significant in the political decisions of only a tiny fraction. (See Table 7–4.) Three percent of the total electorate were ideologues, 10 percent were near ideologues, and the remainder displayed no ideological content in their evaluations.

It is clear, therefore, that the majority of the public does not conceptualize politics in the manner of the highly educated. Thus, except for a small educated portion of the electorate, the ideological debate between the elites has very little meaning. Since the masses lack the interest and level of conceptualization of the educated, they cannot be expected to possess an ideology.

Recent replications of the SRC study show only modest increases in ideological thinking among the masses. By 1972, the percentage of the population classified as ideologues was 7 percent; the percentage of those classified as near ideologues was 20 percent. The increase in the

Table 7–4
Levels of Political
Conceptualization in the
United States: 1956,
1968, 1972

	1956 Percentage (Survey Research Center coding)	1968 Percentage (Klingemann-Wright coding)	1972 Percentage (Arthur Miller coding)
A. Ideology			
I. Ideology	3	5.9	7
II. Near ideology	10	17.1	20
B. Group benefits	15	9.	—
I. Perception of conflict Single-group interest	18	18.6	—
II. Shallow group benefit responses	11	5.2	—
C. Nature of the times	25	24.6	—
D. No issue content			
I. Party orientation	4	7.8	—
II. Candidate orientation	9	6.8	—
III. No content	5	4.9	—
Total	100	100.0	—

Source: Adapted from Philip Converse, "Public Opinion and Voting Behavior," in Fred I. Greenstein and Nelson W. Polsby, eds., *Handbook of Political Science*, Vol. 4 (Reading, Mass.: Addison-Wesley, 1975), p. 102; and from Arthur Miller and Warren A. Miller, "Ideology in the 1972 Election: Myth or Reality—A Rejoinder," *American Political Science Review*, 70 (September 1976), p. 844.

percentage of ideologues and near ideologues is explained almost solely by an upward movement from those who were previously classified as voting on the basis of group benefits. Those in the lower SRC categories moved hardly at all. (Note also that the rate of increase in ideology tapered off after the crises of the 1960s.)

At best, one-third of the electorate can be classified as having an ideology or near ideology. Again, as in 1956, ideology is associated most with education; the increase in the ideological sophistication of those with grade school education was modest and was much greater among the college educated. (See Table 7–5.) Since 1964, the turnout among the less educated has been declining, while the turnout among the college educated has been increasing. Thus, by 1972, 37 percent of the electorate had at least some college education, compared to 26 percent in 1964.

Between 1968 and 1976, the level of ideology and the educational composition of the electorate stabilized. Thus, it appears that with an educated electorate voting in an extremely issue-oriented decade (as the 1960s surely were) the maximum pool of ideologically sophisticated voters is one-third. But the ideologically sophisticated voter is very unlikely ever to become a majority of the electorate.

Members of the elite often make the mistake of confusing the educated minority with the mass of uninformed voters. As Warren Miller concludes: "Levels of conceptualization have not altered much in recent years, but it remains difficult to convey to politically interested and active citizens the lack of complexity or sophistication in the ways most Americans talk and apparently think about politics."[5]

Table 7–5 Proportions of Ideologues* at Three Educational Levels, 1956–1972.

	1956	1968	1972
Grade School	5	10	11
High School	10	13	21
College	32	47	47

*Combines ideologues and near ideologues.

This table provided through the courtesy of Arthur Miller, Survey Research Center, University of Michigan.

Instability of Mass Attitudes

Mass influence over public policy is nullified also by the instability of mass opinions. An extended study of public opinion on various issues showed that only about thirteen out of twenty people took the same side that they had taken four years earlier on the same issues (ten out of twenty would have done so by chance alone). Indeed, an examination of opinion consistency over time indicates that with the exception of party identification (a .70 correlation over time), there is a remarkable instability.[6] This instability suggests once again that issues and ideology are simply not relevant to the mass electorate. Furthermore, the most consistent attitudes relate to clearly identifiable groups, such as blacks. Attitudes about school desegregation are substantially more stable (.50) than attitudes toward foreign policy (.35). Evidently, the mass electorate thinks about race relations, but does not think about foreign policy unless someone happens to ask the question. Hence, the answers to questions about foreign policy vary randomly through time. Looking at the instability of mass attitudes, Converse concludes that "large portions of the electorate do not have meaningful beliefs, even on those issues that have formed the basis for intense political controversy among elites for substantial periods of time."[7]

The average voter's attitudes are unstable over time largely because the voter acquires little information. In addition, consistency of attitudes—the holding of consistent "liberal" or "conservative" attitudes on a range of policy questions—is dependent upon the behavior of elites. The greatest increase in attitude consistency occurred in the early 1960s, a period climaxed by Barry Goldwater's unsuccessful quest for the presidency in 1964. Between 1964 and 1972, attitude consistency actually suffered a modest decline,[8] then plunged sharply in 1976. This leads us to conclude that consistency is to some extent a response to the behavior of elites. When Goldwater pronounced consistent "conservative" opinions in 1964, the electorate became more conscious of the difference between "liberal" and "conservative" positions on many issues. Voter consistency on issues declined somewhat through 1972, even though McGovern was a self-professed "liberal." But consistency declined sharply in 1976 when neither presidential candidate, Ford or Carter, took clearly defined "liberal" or "conservative" positions. As Niemi and Weissberg argue,

An important ingredient in the level of voter sophistication appears to be elite behavior. If elites consciously use ideological terms in election campaigns, if they interpret issues in terms of larger questions and in terms of

© 1976 Jules Feiffer. Dist. Field Newspaper Syndicate.

the relationships between various political matters, and if presidential candidates take stands that are reasonably clear and differentiated, then the voters will react by making the appropriate ideological distinctions. If these conditions are absent, the voters will appear to be, and may in fact be, disorganized and non-ideological in their approach to politics. Elites, then, play a role not only determined by which particular issues attract attention at a given time, but determining the way in which voters organize and structure their political thinking. [9]

Long-Hairs and Hard Hats

Despite recent declines in attitude consistency, the 1960s were a period of political history that did produce two disparate ideological groups and sharply polarized the American population. At one extreme was a group of individuals whom Miller and Levitin call the "silent minority." (We might call them the "hard hats.") This group is unequivocally opposed to protest and hostile to the counterculture, and places a high priority on maintaining law and order. [10] Approximately 17 percent of the population can be categorized as "hard hats." At the other extreme were people—let us call them "long hairs"—who consistently differed from the "hard hats" in their responses to all the symbols and sentiments associated with the new politics; they were uniformly sympathetic to political protest and to counterculture values, and gave lowest priority to law and order. This group, called by Miller and Livitin the "new liberals," constituted 14 percent of the voting population in 1972. Between these two extremes can be found the vast majority (69 percent) of voters who made up the middle ground. As might be expected, the long-hairs were young and highly educated, whereas the hard hats were older and poorly educated. Radically different in attitudes and social composition, the two groups had one thing in common: they were substantially more consistent in their attitudes than the majority of voters who occupied the center. The long-hairs may have been more consistent because of their education. The hard hats, although educationally deprived, reacted consistently because of their vigorous hostility to the goals of the counterculture. But this attitude consistency is not characteristic of the electorate, only of its two extremes.

We have considered three measures of ideological sophistication: information level, ideological conceptualization, and degree of attitude consistency. Most of the increased sophistication in the first two measures is a consequence of increases in education; but most of the increases and decreases in attitude consistency are caused by mass response to elites. Attitude consistency is, therefore, less stable than levels of information or ideological sophistication. The 1960s appear to be rather exceptional in that they produced at least some increase in the level of attitude consistency among the masses. While in the future we may expect information and ideological sophistication to increase slowly with increases in education, we can probably expect that attitude consistency will decrease if political crises decline.

Election Choices in Relation to Issues

Given the ignorance of the masses, what is actually decided through elections? In congressional elections, the incumbent is usually reelected. This tendency, and the voters' lack of awareness of the challengers' policies, is related to the relatively low-keyed nature of congressional elections, especially in off-years. In presidential elections there is greater awareness of the candidates, but this does not necessarily mean that the issues are more completely discussed.

The ideal model of democracy requires that the two major parties offer the electorate policy alternatives and compete for votes on the basis of their contrasting programs. This competition helps keep the elite responsible. Therefore, the masses, although not necessarily completely informed about the programs advocated by the elites, should at least be aware of their broad outlines.

For this model to work, the voters must perceive alternatives and determine which most closely match their own ideological positions. However, most evidence suggests that voters are not capable of doing so. For example, in examining the responses of the electorate in the 1952 and 1956 elections, Campbell, Converse, Miller, and Stokes concluded that only about one-third had an opinion, were aware of what the government was doing, and perceived a difference between the parties. This one-third is the *maximum* pool of issue-oriented people. While it is true that the nature of the election to some extent influences the size of the issue-oriented portion of the electorate, it is probable that two-thirds of the electorate make a choice unrelated to the issues raised by the competing candidates or parties.

It is important to recognize that these blurred perceptions may be caused by the behavior of elites as much as by the ignorance of masses. If the parties do not, in fact, provide clear alternatives, then failure to perceive alternatives cannot be blamed on the electorate. Party activists are separated by a wide ideological gulf, but party followers are not. For example, the leaders of the Democratic party are "liberal," and the leaders of the Republican party are "conservative" (when conservatism is measured in terms of economic policy). However, how much these differences are translated into clear statements by either party is questionable, and most Democratic and Republican voters hold fairly similar opinions on most issues.

Since few voters make a clear distinction between the parties on the issues, or even necessarily share the attitudes of party leaders, it seems that American national elections are not high in their ideological or issue content and that successful candidates are therefore not directed by mass opinion. This is not to suggest that voters are fools who are easily manipulated by clever use of the mass media and other instruments of persuasion. The stability of party identification and the operation of such faculties as selective perception considerably reduce the manipulative possibilities of campaigns.

Party identification is remarkably stable, while opinions are quite unstable. Ironically, the party is substantially more central to the belief system of mass electorates than are the policies it pursues. Short-term forces, such as a candidate's religion, smile, or TV image, can deflect voters away from choosing their party's candidate, but these short-term forces are, in many cases, unrelated to issues.

Our discussion does not deny that some voters are issue-oriented and informed. (Recall that we described about one-third of the electorate as having an opinion, being informed, and perceiving a difference between parties.) Political scientist V. O. Key has chosen to characterize the electorate as "responsible," but his conclusion is based solely upon those who switch from one party to another.[11] However, relatively few voters—one-fifth to one-eighth, depending upon the election—actually switch parties. Nevertheless, Key does tend to portray the electorate in more flattering terms than we have. He asserts, for instance, that "From our analyses the voter emerges as a person who appraises the actions of the government, who has policy preferences, and who relates his vote to those appraisals and preferences."[12] Granted that in close elections a few switching voters might be crucial; but to describe "the voter" as Key does, is to ignore the fact that only a tiny fraction of voters can be properly called "responsible."*

1972: An "Ideological" Election?

The McGovern candidacy in 1972 helped to develop a more discernible ideological difference between the candidates of the two major parties. McGovern appealed to an ideologically committed core of liberals, leaving the rest of the electorate to Nixon. The landslide for Nixon was the result. In carrying every state except Massachusetts (and Washington, D.C., with its black majority), Nixon gained 61 percent of the vote, roughly equal to the margin by which Johnson in 1964 defeated another ideological candidate, Barry Goldwater. McGovern's 38 percent was the lowest proportion by a major party candidate in recent presidential elec-

---

*Since Key's book was published after his death, it is doubtful whether he wrote the sentence quoted. Two years before he died, he wrote: "...the more I study elections the more disposed I am to believe that they have within themselves more than a trace of the lottery. . . . Even when the public in manifest anger and disillusionment throws an administration from office, it does not express its policy preferences with precision."

tions. Not only did Nixon receive 94 percent of the vote among Republicans and 66 percent among Independents, he also captured 42 percent of the vote among Democrats.

The American voters obviously found some differences between McGovern and Nixon, regarding McGovern as too far out of the ideological mainstream. It was not so much the *what* of McGovern, but rather the *how* and *when*. On the eve of the election, a Harris poll reported that, by a margin of two to one, the electorate felt McGovern wanted to "change things too much." (See Table 7–6.) Thus, Nixon and McGovern supporters disagreed over the speed of change rather than its content. Actually, there was substantial agreement between McGovern and Nixon supporters on the issues. As Table 7–6 reveals, of fourteen issues, in only one (decreasing defense spending) did a majority of McGovern supporters take a position in opposition to a majority of Nixon supporters. This is not, of course, to deny a difference. What we are asserting is that the differences occur *within a basic consensus*. Speaking of the electorate, Lipset and Raab conclude:

What they resist is change that takes place in a non-traditional manner . . . the basic threat perceived by the electorate in the McGovern candidacy was not so much to existing social arrangements as to the social order itself. And especially to due process. That is the "extremism" which the voters finally rejected, not any liberal social or economic policy per se. [13]

Table 7–6
Ideological Differences among 1972 Voters

	% More Likely to Vote for Candidate Who Favored:	
	Nixon Supporters	McGovern Supporters
Ending U.S. involvement in Vietnam	74%	93%
Busing School Children to Achieve Racial Balance	10	37
Stricter Control on Firearms	57	74
Greater Equality—More Opportunity for Women	60	79
Checking the Rising Cost of Living	91	95
Removing Wage and Price Controls	28	38
Increasing Aid to Parochial Schools	42	49
Allowing Men Who Left the Country to Avoid Draft to Return Without Punishment	15	39
Decreasing Defense Spending	45	66
Tougher Sentences for Lawbreakers	87	72
Improving Opportunities for Blacks & Other Minority Groups	60	82
Providing National Health Insurance for All Americans	60	82
Lessening Penalties for Marijuana Possession	23	40
Increasing Spending to Control Air & Water Pollution	79	85

Source: Gallup Opinion Index (September 1972), pp. 5–12.

McGovern supporters were appreciably more "left" (or liberal) than Nixon's supporters. However, on those issues that strike at the heart of the counterculture (amnesty, marijuana, busing), a majority of both Nixon and McGovern supporters took a "right" perspective. The majority of McGovern supporters did not want to legalize marijuana, grant amnesty to draft resisters, or bus children out of neighborhoods. Nevertheless, *half* of McGovern's supporters had an ideology stressing social change; *half* of Nixon's supporters were opposed to social change. Such a split is hardly indicative of the widely portrayed "either-or" election (half of McGovern's supporters did not support social change; half of Nixon's did not oppose it). Actually, the Democrats were more divided in opinion within their ranks than Democrats were divided from Republicans.[14]

Massive defections of Democrats and Independents left McGovern with a relatively tight, ideologically intense following. Issues, as distinguished from partisan identification or candidate perception, clearly had an exceptional impact on the 1972 vote. In some respects, this election was the most ideological in modern history. A portion of the electorate was responding in a relatively sophisticated manner. We refer here again to the notion of consistency, the ability of an individual to organize "liberal" and "conservative" beliefs and relate these beliefs to voting.

It is one thing, of course, to develop a consistent ideology; it is quite another to translate it into a vote. Even though attitude consistency increased somewhat in 1972, we still need to know how much of it was translated into "issue voting." The 1972 election strongly suggests that for the *majority* of the voters ideological concerns are trivial compared to personal assessments of candidates (irrespective of their policy positions). Translating issue attitudes into a voting decision is much easier for those with a college education; they are better informed politically, generally more aware of policy differences between the candidates, and therefore more likely than the less educated to make a decision on the basis of policy preferences.* Consequently, for the sophisticated minority, ideology is translated into a vote. As can be seen in Table 7–7, for most voters, ideology was irrelevant to the vote. The table reveals the "variance" in vote attributable to ideology and to candidate assessment

---

*The role of ideology increases dramatically with education. The college educated is the only group that casts an ideological vote. It may be, therefore, that the "issue voting" of 1972 was a consequence of a *shift* in the electoral participation of the various educational groups. Turnout among the less educated declined from 68 percent in 1964 to 58 percent in 1972; turnout among the college-educated group has remained constant (88–89 percent). Thus while the college-educated population contributed 25 percent to the electorate in 1964, in 1972 it contributed 37 percent. As interest in politics declines, elections assume more elitist characteristics.

Table 7–7
Percent of Vote Related to
Candidate Perception and
Ideology

	Candidate Ratings		Liberal-Conservative Ideology
	Nixon	McGovern	
Grade School	45%	15%	1%
High School	37	16	7
College	12	6	45
Total Population	41	14	5

Source: Miller *et al.,* "A Majority Party in Disarray," p. 68.

(the higher the percentage, the greater the contribution of each factor to the vote).

What did such sophistication—normally associated with the educated minority—mean in 1972? Specifically, did the educated minority translate its issue orientation into a vote? In Table 7–7, the percentage of variance in the vote (the higher the percentage, the greater the contribution of each factor to the vote) is related to candidate perception and ideology for college and noncollege groups.

In short, McGovern lost because he was the least-popular Democratic candidate in twenty years. Issues were more important than usual, but the most important factor was McGovern himself. Nixon, by contrast, was clearly a popular candidate, receiving positive ratings from voters of all ideological leanings.

1976: A Return to "Normalcy"

Jimmy Carter's narrow victory over Gerald Ford heralded a return to party loyalty. The massive defection of the Democrats in 1972 was reversed; 92 percent of those with a strong Democratic identification voted for Carter (as compared to a 73 percent Democratic vote in 1972), and 71 percent of those with a weak Democratic identification voted for Carter (as compared to a 48 percent Democratic vote in 1972). The return of the Democrats is the single most important political event of 1976; if they had not returned, Carter would have lost.

From the beginning of his primary campaign to his final victory, Carter sought to solidify his position with the "vital center" of the electorate. During the primaries he was not, until the final weeks, the choice of rank and file Democrats (Hubert Humphrey was their choice). Carter's primary victories improved his image, but he was clearly second choice. His strategy was to avoid the bitter polarization of 1972 and, if possible, gain the support of all Democratic factions (right, left, and center). The effort was largely successful. Many Democrats viewed him as left of center, while many others thought he was right of center. Unlike McGovern whose primary campaign was viewed as a challenge by the left wing of the Democratic party, Carter was himself challenged by the left (Harris and, later, Udall).

After the nomination, Carter solidified his support with the major urban political machines, organized labor, and blacks. However, despite his best efforts during his campaign, he could not avoid a liberal image. The mass public, perhaps because of eight years of Republican administration, had acquired a distinctly conservative self-image. At best, one-third of the electorate identified themselves as "left" whereas a majority were "middle" or "right." Heeding the lesson of 1972, Carter tried, unsuccessfully, to project himself as a center candidate. Carter's liberalism became more visible to the electorate as the campaign focused increased attention on him. Carter lost his wide early lead over Ford in the polls. (See Table 7–8.) Moreover, Carter was under constant pressure from media representatives to take a clear liberal position. Finally, the "new left" of 1972 was least enthusiastic in support for Carter during the primaries, and their opinion leaders joined with the liberal columnists in pressuring Carter. Carter's resistance to this pressure contributed to an unflattering portrait—that of a "waffler," one who avoided clarity in public statements. As Arthur Miller explains: "In the campaign, Carter did an excellent job of obfuscating the issues. If he had pushed clear-cut, liberal Democratic issues, the outcome would have paralleled 1972 because of the set of Conservative Democrats willing to defect on the basis of the issues."[15]

While Carter's image shifted, Ford's remained essentially unchanged; hence he sought to make a major theme of Carter's "waffling." Ironically, as Miller suggests, had Carter "waffled" less, he would have lost. Before the campaign, the public's perception of Carter's position was a good match with its self-perception. By September, Carter had moved while Ford had not.

A more careful analysis reveals how much voters overlooked the disparity between their own conservatism and Carter's liberalism, illustrating again the wisdom of Carter's covert decision to obfuscate as much as possible. The only voters with whom Carter had any ideological commonality were the Democrats who had voted for McGovern in 1972. Republicans, by contrast, identified ideologically with their candidate. Democrats who defected to Nixon in 1972 were substantially closer to Ford ideologically in 1976, yet they voted for Carter.

	Perceptions of Carter		Perceptions of Ford		Electorate's self-perceptions	
	March	Sept.	March	Sept.	March	Sept.
"Left"	30%	48%	23%	19%	31%	31%
"Middle"	5	7	7	3	10	10
"Right"	30	26	55	59	49	42
Unsure	35	19	15	19	10	17

Source: Gallup Opinion Index (December 1976), p. 41.

Table 7–8
Ideological Position and Choice of Candidate, 1976

The conservatism of the electorate is made even more apparent in the response to the question, "Should government assure a job and good standard of living for all, or let each person get ahead on his own?" On this issue, McGovern Democrats were to the right of Carter, and all others were to the right of both candidates. Exacerbating Carter's ideological mismatch with Democratic voters was the issue of "trust." Naturally, Republicans were more inclined to trust Ford and Democrats, Carter. However, just as Republicans regarded Ford as more compatible ideologically, they also trusted Ford more than Democrats trusted Carter.

Beyond trust, the entire campaign appeared to center upon other personal characteristics. Unlike 1972, there was no single set of polarizing issues. The war was over, protests were a distant memory. While Carter was imploring voters to "trust him," he was also projecting the image of a person of ability, an intriguing style, and a colorful personality. Thus, the following adjectives were volunteered by voters about Carter: "bright, intelligent," a "colorful, interesting personality." Ford was described as a "person of average abilities" and as "predictable." Overall candidate ratings thus favored Carter, even though he was regarded as a "waffler" and was not really trusted by his own partisans.* He won as a "personality." Forty-two percent gave him a "highly favorable" rating, compared to 28 percent for Ford. Significantly, Ford's rating remained unchanged while Carter's improved substantially (from 20 percent in March). Thus, while Ford enjoyed the advantage of being more compatible ideologically and was regarded as equally trustworthy, he was also dull.

However, *party identification*, Carter's major advantage, gave him a final, narrow victory. As we have seen, a return of Democrats to their party's nominee occurred. The votes of the party's normal affiliates illustrate the point well: among voters with less than high school education, the Democratic percentage improved from 40 percent in 1972 to 69 percent in 1976; the Democratic black vote improved from 73 to 93 percent; the vote among union members increased from 43 to 64 percent.

Thus Carter, like McGovern, was viewed as liberal and untrustworthy; but unlike McGovern, he was not an "extremist" and he held the Democratic voters in their party. The Democratic party had an advantage on the issues. The 1972 election was fought largely on the "social issues" (crime in the streets, permissive treatment of radicals, etc.). By 1976, these issues had been replaced by the economic issue: unemploy-

---

*In response to the question: "Would you trust Ford (Carter) as President?" the following categorization by party identification is generated:

Democrats	Independents	Republicans
Ford +18	Ford +49	Ford +84
Carter +58	Carter +23	Carter +16

Source: University of Michigan, Survey Research Center.

ment and a stagnating economy. The percentages of voters identifying either inflation or unemployment as the nation's major problem rose from 62 to 78 percent during the campaign.

Elections as Symbolic Reassurance

If elections do not enable voters to directly control public policy, what are the purposes of elections? Elections are a symbolic exercise to help tie the masses to the established order by giving them the feeling that they play a role. Political scientist Murray Edelman agrees that voters have little effect on public policy and contends that elections are primarily "symbolic reassurance." According to Edelman, elections serve to "quiet resentments and doubts about particular political acts, reaffirm belief in the fundamental rationality and democratic character of the system, and thus fix conforming habits of future behavior."[16]

Virtually all modern political systems—whether authoritarian or democratic, capitalist or communist—hold elections. Indeed, communist dictatorships take elections very seriously and strive to achieve 90 to 100 percent voter turnout rates—and this is despite there being only one candidate (the Communist party's) for each office! Why do these nations bother to hold elections when the outcome has already been determined? All political regimes seek to tie the masses to the system by holding symbolic exercises in political participation to give the

© 1968 Jules Feiffer. Dist. Field Newspaper Syndicate.

ruling regime an aura of legitimacy. Of course, democratic governments gain even greater legitimacy from elections; democratically elected officeholders can claim that their activities in office are legitimate, and that their laws ought to be obeyed, because "the people" participated in elections.

Elections Choose Personnel, Not Policy

In democratic nations, elections serve a second function—choosing personnel to hold public office. In 1976, the American voters decided that Jimmy Carter and not Gerald Ford would occupy "the nation's highest office" for the next four years. (The vast majority of people in the world today have never had the opportunity to participate in such a choice.) However, this is a choice of personnel, not policy: Parties do not offer clear policy alternatives in election campaigns; voters do not have their choice as to policy positions of the candidates; and candidates are not bound by their campaign pledges anyway.

Elections Allow for Retrospective Judgments

The third function of elections is to give the masses an opportunity to express themselves about the conduct of the public officials who have been in power. Elections do not permit the masses to direct *future* events, but they do permit the masses to render retrospective judgment about *past* political conduct. For example, in 1968, voters could not choose a specific policy by voting for Nixon. They had no way of knowing what specific policies Nixon would follow in Vietnam, because he set none forth. But the voters *were* able to express their discontent with Johnson's handling of the war by voting against a continuation of the Democratic administration. As political scientist Gerald Pomper explains:

The voters employ their powerful sanction retrospectively. They judge the politician after he has acted, finding personal satisfactions or discontents as the results of these actions. . . . The issue of Viet Nam is illustrative. . . . For their part, critics of the war did not emphasize their own alternative policies, but instead concentrated on retrospective and adverse judgments. . . . Declining public support of the war brought all major candidates to promise its end. The Republican Party, and particularly Richard Nixon, joined in this pledge, but provided no specific programs, instead seeking the support of all voters inclined to criticize past actions.[17]

The voters' retrospective judgment on past administrations may affect the behavior of current and future elected officials. Pomper contends, rather optimistically, that even though the voters have no *power* over government, they nonetheless have an *influence* on government. Pomper contends that because "politicians might be affected by the voters in the next election, they regulate their conduct appropriately."[18]

But Pomper fails to say how elected officials are supposed to know the sentiments of voters on policy questions in order to "regulate their conduct appropriately." As we have seen, most voters do not have an opinion that can be communicated to elected officials; and elected officials have no way of interpreting voters' policy preferences from electoral results. By ousting the Democratic administration from power in 1968, were the voters saying they wanted a military victory in Vietnam? Or that they wanted a negotiated peace and compromise with the Viet Cong?

Perhaps all that we can really say is that the retrospective judgment that voters can render in an election helps to make governing elites sensitive to mass welfare. Elections do not permit masses to decide what should be done in their interests, but they do encourage governing elites to consider the welfare of the masses. Knowing that a day of reckoning will come on election day, elected officials strive to make a good impression on the voters in the meantime.

The existence of the vote does not make politicians better as individuals; it simply forces them to give greater consideration to demands of enfranchised and sizeable groups, who hold a weapon of potentially great force. . . . The ability to punish politicians is probably the most important weapon available to citizens. It is direct, authoritative, and free from official control.[19]

Elections Provide Protection Against Official Abuse

It has been argued that elections have a fourth function—that of protecting individuals and groups from official abuse. John Stuart Mill wrote: "Men, as well as women, do not need political rights in order that they might govern, but in order that they not be misgoverned."[20] He went on:

Rulers in ruling classes are under a necessity of considering the interests of those who have the suffrage; but of those who are excluded, it is in their option whether they will do so or not, and however honestly disposed, they are in general too fully occupied with things they must attend to, to have much room in their thoughts for anything which they can with impunity disregard.[21]

Certainly the long history of efforts to insure black voting rights in the South suggests that many concerned Americans believed that if blacks could secure access to the polls, they could better protect themselves from official discrimination. Some major steps in the struggle for voting rights were the abolishment of the "white primary" in 1944; the Civil Rights Acts of 1957, 1960, 1964, and 1965, all of which contained provisions guaranteeing free access to the polls; and the Twenty-fourth Amendment to the Constitution, which eliminated poll taxes. But the high hopes stirred by the development of new law were often followed by frustration and disillusionment when blacks realized that their problems could not be solved through the electoral process alone. No doubt William R. Keech is correct when he asserts that the vote is a symbol of full citizenship and equal rights, which may contribute to black self-respect.[22] But it is still open to question how much blacks can gain through the exercise of their vote. In the North, blacks have voted freely for decades, but conditions in the urban ghettos have not been measurably improved through political action. In signing the Voting Rights Act of 1965, President Johnson said:

The right to vote is the most basic right, without which all others are meaningless. It gives people—people as individuals—control over their own destinies. . . . The vote is the most powerful instrument ever devised by man for breaking down injustice and destroying the terrible walls which imprison men because they are different from other men.

But the black experience in both the North and the South suggests that the ballot cannot eliminate discrimination, much less enable men to "control their own destinies." It is probably true that people can *better* protect themselves from government abuse when they possess and exercise their voting rights, but the right to vote is not a guarantee against discrimination.

Electoral Participation and Nonparticipation

Another problem with the theory of popular control over public policy through elections is the fact that nearly half the adult population fails to vote, even in presidential elections.

Since the 1960 presidential race between John F. Kennedy and Richard Nixon, voter turnout has steadily slipped from 64 percent of the eligible voters, to 63 percent in the Johnson-Goldwater race in 1964, to 60 percent in the Nixon-Humphrey-Wallace race in 1968, to 56 percent in 1972, and to 53 percent in the Carter-Ford race. Off-year (nonpresidential) elections bring out fewer than half the eligible voters. Yet in these off-year contests the nation chooses all of its U.S. representatives, one-third of its senators, and about one-half of its governors. (See Figure 7–1.)

Lester Milbrath listed six forms of "legitimate" political participation.[23] Individuals may run for public office, become active in party and campaign work, make financial contributions to political candidates or causes, belong to organizations that support or oppose candidates, take stands on political issues, attempt to influence friends while discussing candidates or issues, and vote in elections. Activities at the top of this list require greater expenditure of time, money, and energy than those activities at the bottom, and they involve only a tiny minority of the population. Less than 1 percent of the American adult population ever runs for public office. Only about 5 percent are ever active in parties and campaigns, and only about 10 percent make financial contributions. About one-third of the population belongs to organizations that could be classified as political interest groups, and only a few more ever try to persuade their friends to vote a certain way. And finally, about 60 to 65 percent of the American people will vote in a hard-fought presidential campaign.

Participation does not occur uniformly throughout all segments of the population. U.S. census data (Table 7–9) show the percentages of voter turnout for the 1964 and 1968 elections. High voter turnout is related to college education; to professional, managerial, or other white-collar occupations (indicated by salary range, $10,000 or more); to living in the North or West; to being white; and so on. While these figures pertain only to voting, other forms of participation follow substantially the same pattern. White, middle-class, college-educated, white-collar Americans participate more in all forms of political activity than nonwhite, lower-class grade school-educated Americans. Marches and

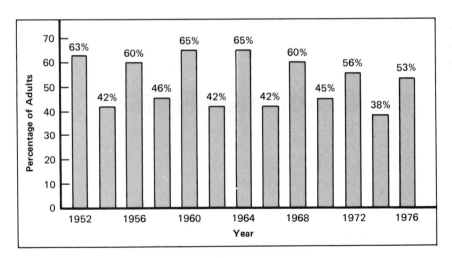

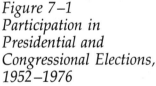

Figure 7–1
Participation in
Presidential and
Congressional Elections,
1952–1976

Source: From *Statistical Abstract of the United States,* (Washington, D.C.: U.S. Government Printing Office.) Composite of data from annual editions.

demonstrations, which are special tactics of minority groups, are excepted.

Election turnout figures in the United States are lower than those of several other democracies. The turnout in recent elections has been 74 percent in Japan, 77 percent in Great Britain, 83 percent in Israel, 88 percent in West Germany, and 93 percent in Italy. Of course, our lower turnouts may be explained by our stricter residence and registration requirements and by our greater frequency of elections. But it may also be that Americans are less "political" than citizens of other democracies, less likely to care about the outcome of elections, and less likely to feel that government has much effect on their lives. This lack of interest in politics may be a product of an underlying consensus in America that brings opposing parties and candidates so close to each other on major political issues that it matters little which party or candidate wins.[24]

Voter participation is highly valued in American political theory; popular control of government, control of leaders by followers, is supposed to be effected through the electoral process. The majority of Americans do vote, and by so doing they indicate they have some stake in the outcome of elections, but a sizeable group of Americans never vote or participate in politics in any accepted fashion. This nonvoting

Table 7–9
Percent of Different
Groups Voting in
Presidential Elections*

Voters	Percentage voting			
	25	50	75	
More than 12 years education				81%
Family income: $10,000 and over				80
Age: 45–64 years			75	
Family income: $7500–9999			73	
Employed			71	
Residence in North or West			71	
Age: 35–44 years			71	
Male			70	
White			69	
Education: 9–12 years			69	
Residence in metropolitan area			68	
Residence in nonmetropolitan area			67	
Female			66	
Age: 65 years and over			66	
Family income: $5000–7499			66	
Age: 25–34 years			63	
Residence in the South			60	
Family income: $3000–4999			58	
Black			58	
Education: 8 years or less			55	
Family income: under $3000			54	
Unemployed			52	
Age: 21–24 years			51	
Age: 18–20 years		33		

*These figures are from the 1964 and 1968 elections. Breakdowns of voting records for more recent elections do not exist.
Source: U.S. Census, 1970.

might reflect "alienation" from the political system: a feeling that voting and other forms of participation are useless, that nothing is really decided by an election, and that the individual cannot personally influence the outcome of political events. The higher frequency of nonvoting among those at the bottom of the income, occupation, education, and status ladder tends to confirm this view; alienation *should* occur more frequently in groups who have not shared in the general affluence of society. However, this interpretation is discouraging for those who wish well for the democratic ideal, because it suggests that not all groups in society place a high value on democratic institutions.

Of increasing concern to those who value popular participation is the *expansion* of the alienated, coupled with a decline in participation. As distrust in government soars, the alienated tend to be more evenly distributed among *all* population groups, rather than concentrating among the traditional have-nots.

The growing disillusionment and distrust of government—and attendant feelings of helplessness and lack of influence—began about 1964 and has continued virtually unabated. In 1964, about one-third of the electorate was classified as cynical, compared to about half in 1972; in 1964, about one-fourth thought government operated more to the benefit of special interests than to that of the general public, compared to nearly 60 percent in 1973. Not only are cynicism and alienation becoming less class-linked; they are also reaching across generations. Figure 7–2, tracing the rise of distrust in two separate generations, dramatically indicates how pervasive the feeling of distrust has become.

The alienation of Americans from government goes beyond dissatisfaction or opposition to particular politicians or parties. A national survey conducted by pollster Louis Harris in 1973 revealed that a *majority* of Americans give alienated replies to general questions about American society. Few people believe that government improves their lives. The federal government is the worst culprit—a plurality of Americans believe that it makes their lives *worse*. State and local governments fare better—most Americans believe they do no great harm. (See Table 7–10.)

How Has Government Changed Your Life?			
	Improved It	Made It Worse	No Change
Federal Government	23%	37%	34%
State Government	27	14	52
Local Government	28	11	54
			Undecided omitted

Table 7–10
Mass Feelings Toward
Government

Source: U.S. Senate, Committee on Government Operations, Subcommittee on Intergovernmental Relations, *Confidence and Concern: Citizens View American Government* (Washington: Government Printing Office, 1973), pp. 42–43.

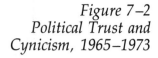

*Figure 7–2
Political Trust and
Cynicism, 1965–1973*

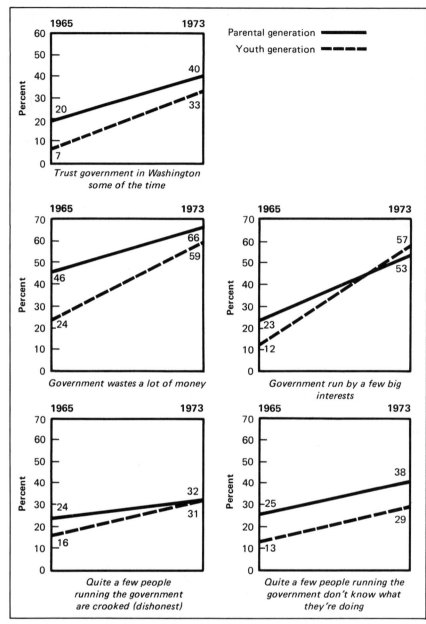

Source: From M. Kent Jennings and Richard G. Niemi, "Continuity and Change in Political Orientation: A Longitudinal Study of Two Generations." Paper presented to the 1973 meeting of the American Political Science Association, New Orleans, p. 25.

Has the Quality of Life Improved Since 1963?			
	Improved	*Become Worse*	*Stayed Same*
Total Public	35	46	15
Selected Leaders	61	20	16

Source: U.S. Senate, Committee on Government Operations, Subcommittee on Intergovernmental Relations, *Confidence and Concern: Citizens View American Government* (Washington: Government Printing Office, 1973), p. 231.

Table 7–11
Elite and Mass Attitudes on the Quality of Life

Perhaps even more disturbing is the widespread feeling that the quality of life in America is declining. Nearly half (46 percent) the public believe that the quality of their life has *declined* in the last decade; 15 percent believe it has stayed the same; and 35 percent believe it has improved. (See Table 7–11.) Interestingly, *elites* think the quality of life is improving—61 percent of a national leadership sample believed life had improved over the decade, and only 20 percent believed it had grown worse. Thus, elites and masses are clearly differentiated in their respective notions of whether things are getting better or worse in this nation.

Mass distrust of a democratic government is an invitation to tyranny. When asked what they thought were the nation's biggest problems, Americans listed inflation, lack of integrity in government, crime, welfare, federal spending, taxes, pollution, and overpopulation well ahead of racial justice, health care, or housing. This suggests that there is no widespread mass demand for traditional liberal reforms. More ominous, perhaps, is the fact that, presented with the statement, "It's about time we had a strong federal government to get this country moving again," fully 67 percent of the American people agreed (this despite the plurality of those who think the federal government has worsened their lives). Some may interpret this reply as a demand for greater integrity, honesty, etc.; but a more realistic interpretation is that the nation would welcome a strong leader—perhaps even an authoritarian figure. Democracy is at its weakest when the citizenry loses confidence in its governing elites.

The trend toward mass discontent continued through 1976, and indeed the spread of distrust accelerated. Having used the same questions over a twelve-year span, political scientist Warren Miller estimates that 1976 produced the most cynical and distrustful electorate in history. A glance at Table 7–12 indicates the massive erosion of trust: In 1964, more trusting than cynical responses were provided to all five questions; in 1976, more cynical than trusting responses were given. The majority thought the government in Washington was run by incompetent, wasteful crooks who were beholden to powerful interest groups.

Table 7–12
Mass Attitudes Toward
Government, 1964–1976

	1964	1972	1976
Trust government in Washington some of the time.	+54*	+ 8	−63
Government is run by a few big interests.	+35	−16	−45
Government wastes a lot of money.	+ 5	−33	−73
Quite a few people running the government are crooked.	+38	+23	−30
Quite a few people running the government don't know what they are doing.	+41	+15	− 7

*Entries are the differences between trusting and cynical responses.
Source: University of Michigan, Survey Research Center.

There was no counterelite, however, to channel this surge of discontent. The 1976 election (which produced a turnout even smaller than the 1972) again offered no targets of opportunity for the rising number of cynical voters with both parties nominating from the mainstream and Wallace eliminated. As issues become more complex and major candidates remain equivocal, the opportuni.ies for the simplistic appeal of the demagogue may be enhanced.

Violence as an Alternative to Elections

There is a strong relationship between status deprivation and political violence. Perhaps this deprivation explains why many blacks, rather than taking their hostility to the ballot box, had increasingly participated in violence in the 1960s and early '70s. As Table 7–13 shows, the rioters in disorders of the recent past were better educated than the nonrioters, but were likely to hold menial jobs, and the affront to their racial pride was intensified by the discrepancy between their education and their occupation. For these people, conventional political participation lost its meaning, and violence became a device to communicate intense dissatisfaction. The rioters were not vagrants or criminals; they were long-time

Table 7–13
Education, Occupation,
and Participation
in Riots

	Newark		Detroit	
	Rioters	Nonrioters	Rioters	Nonrioters
Education				
Grade school	1.9%	14.3%	7.0%	27.9%
Some high school	63.2	46.8	53.5	33.8
High school graduate	29.2	31.0	23.3	26.1
Some college or college graduate	5.7	7.9	16.2	12.2
Occupation				
Unskilled	50.0	39.6		
Semiskilled or better	50.0	60.4		

Source: Report of the National Advisory Commission on Civil Disorders (Washington, D.C., 1968).

residents of the city and were, in fact, cited among the more intellectually oriented and politically sophisticated of the black community.[25]

Furthermore, actions of the militant rioters are supported by substantial portions of blacks who did not participate directly in the riots.
Postriot survey information indicated that roughly 20 percent of the
blacks in the Watts area participated actively in the riot of 1964, and
more than half the residents supported the activities of the rioters. Inter-
viewers found that 58 percent of the Watts residents felt that the long-
run effects of the riots would be favorable; 84 percent said that whites
were now more aware of black problems; 62 percent said that the riot
was a black protest. In summary, the riots are looked upon favorably by
a large proportion of the ghetto residents.

Rioting and political violence are not considered political participation by most political scientists. Perhaps this is because we wish to
regard political violence as an atypical temporary aberration. Actually,
the American political system is not as stable as we like to assume.[26]
Although most whites regard the system as legitimate, a substantial
proportion of blacks do not, because they believe that it has not provided adequate rewards for their conventional political participation.
Middle- and upper-class whites tend to view our system of government
as extremely satisfactory and find it difficult to understand why a minority group communicates its dissatisfaction violently. In Milbrath's
hierarchy of political involvement (discussed on p. 179) violence is
excluded, because the hierarchy of participation does not apply to behavior "designed to disrupt the normal operation of democratic political
processes."[27] But violence is a continuing threat to any political system.
To be sure, this form of political participation is a criminal one. And it
may be irrational and self-defeating, for the great majority of the casualties of the riots—the dead, the injured, and the arrested—were rioters
themselves, and much of the property destroyed belonged to ghetto
residents. Moreover, the riots may have changed the attitudes of many
whites toward the black community and toward the civil rights movement from sympathy or indifference to opposition. Nonetheless, violence must be recognized as a form of political participation by the
masses.

Summary

Elite theory contends that the masses do not participate in policy making, and that the elites who do are subject to little direct influence from
apathetic masses. But many scholars who acknowledge that even
"democratic" societies are governed by elites seek to reaffirm democratic
values by contending that voters can influence elite behavior by choosing between competing elites in elections. In other words, elitism is
sometimes challenged by modern pluralists on the grounds that elec-

tions give the masses a voice in policy making by holding governing elites accountable to the people.

Our analysis suggests that elections are imperfect instruments of accountability. But even if the people can hold *government* elites accountable through elections, how can corporate elites, financial elites, union leaders, and other private leadership be held accountable? The accountability argument usually dodges the problem of *private* decision making and focuses exclusive attention on *public* decision making by elected elites. But certainly men's lives are vitally affected by the decisions of private institutions and organizations. So the first problem with the accountability thesis is that, at best, it applies only to elected government elites. However, our analysis of elections also suggests that it is difficult for the voters to hold even *government* elites accountable.

1. Competing candidates in elections do not usually offer clear policy alternatives; hence it is seldom possible for the voter to affect policy by selecting a particular candidate for public office.
2. Voters are not well-informed about the policy stands of candidates, and relatively few voters are concerned with policy questions. The masses cast their votes in elections on the basis of traditional party ties, personality of the candidates, group affiliations, and a host of other factors having little relation to public policy.
3. Mass opinion on public policy is inconsistent and unstable. Relatively few voters (generally well-educated, upper-class voters from whom elites are drawn) hold reasonably consistent political ideologies. Mass opinion is unguided by principle, unstable, and subject to change.
4. Available evidence suggests that elites influence the opinions of masses more than masses influence the opinion of elites. Mass publics respond to political symbols manipulated by elites, not to facts or political principles.
5. The only reasonably stable aspect of mass politics is party identification. But party identification in the mass electorate is unaccompanied by any wide policy gaps between Democrats and Republicans. Democratic and Republican voters hold fairly similar opinions on most issues.
6. It is difficult to use election results to ascertain majority preferences on policy questions because (a) campaigns generally stress the presentation of political ideologies rather than the *content* of the ideologies; (b) victory for a party or a candidate does not necessarily mean that the voters support any particular policy position of the candidate; (c) voters frequently misinterpret the policy preferences of a candidate; (d) often a candidate's voters include not only advocates of the stated position, but some who oppose it and some who vote for the candidate for other reasons; (e) a candidate may take positions on many different issues, so it cannot be known which of the policy positions resulted in his election; (f) for voters to influence policy through elections, winning candidates would be bound to follow their campaign pledges.
7. Elections are primarily a symbolic exercise that helps tie the masses to the established order. Elections offer the masses an opportunity to participate in the political system, but electoral participation does not enable them to determine public policy.

8. Elections are means for selecting personnel, not policy. Voters choose on the basis of a candidate's personal style, filtered through partisan commitment. A candidate's election does not imply a policy choice by the electorate.

9. At best, elections provide the masses with an opportunity to express themselves favorably or unfavorably about the conduct of past administrations, but not to direct the course of future events. A vote against the party or candidate in power, however, does not identify the particular policy being censured. And there is no guarantee that an ousted official's replacement will pursue any specific policy alternatives.

10. Few individuals participate in any political activity other than voting. One-third of the adult population fails to vote even in presidential elections.

11. Riots and other forms of political violence are clear signs that some members or groups within the masses no longer consider the system legitimate because it withholds from them what they believe should be the rewards of conventional participation.

References

[1] Fred I. Greenstein, *The American Party System and the American People* (Englewood Cliffs, N.J.: Prentice-Hall, 1963), p. 12.

[2] A. Campbell, P. Converse, W. Miller, and D. Stokes, *The American Voter* (New York: John Wiley, 1960), p. 175.

[3] Philip E. Converse, "The Nature of Belief Systems in Mass Publics," in David E. Apter (ed.), *Ideology and Discontent* (New York: Free Press, 1964), pp. 213–230.

[4] Campbell *et al.*, *The American Voter*, p. 227.

[5] Warren E. Miller and Teresa E. Levitin, *Leadership and Change: The New Politics and the American Electorate* (Cambridge: Winthrop Publishers, Inc. 1976), p. 15.

[6] Converse, "The Nature of Belief Systems," p. 240.

[7] *Ibid.*, p. 245.

[8] Norman E. Nie, Sidney Verba, and John R. Petrocik, *The Changing American Voter* (Cambridge: Harvard University Press, 1976), p. 129.

[9] Richard Niemi and Herbert Weissberg, *Controversies in American Voting Behavior* (San Francisco: W. H. Freeman & Co., 1976), p. 83.

[10] Miller and Levitin, *Leadership and Change*, p. 70.

[11] V. O. Key, Jr., *The Responsible Electorate* (Cambridge: Harvard University Press, 1966).

[12] *Ibid.*, pp. 58–59.

[13] Seymour Martin Lipset and Earl Raab, "The Election and the National Mood," *Commentary*, 55 (January 1973), p. 44.

[14] Arthur H. Miller, Warren E. Miller, Alden S. Raine, and Thad A. Brown, "A Majority Party in Disarray: Political Polarization in the 1972 Election," paper presented to the 1973 annual meeting of the American Political Science Association, p. 12.

[15] Arthur Miller, *ISR Newsletter*, Institute for Social Research, University of Michigan, Winter, 1977, pp. 4–5 (for tables).

[16] Murray Edelman, *The Symbolic Uses of Politics* (Urbana: University of Illinois Press, 1964), p. 17.

[17] Gerald Pomper, *Elections in America: Control and Influence in Democratic Politics* (New York: Dodd, Mead, & Co., 1968), pp. 255–256.

[18] *Ibid.*, p. 254.

[19] *Ibid.*, pp. 254–255.

[20] John Stuart Mill, *Considerations on Representative Government* (Chicago: Henry Regnery, Gateway edition, 1962), p. 144.

[21]*Ibid.*, pp. 130–131.

[22]William R. Keech, *The Impact of Negro Voting: The Role of the Vote in the Quest for Equality* (Chicago: Rand McNally, 1968), p. 3.

[23]Lester Milbrath, *Political Participation* (Chicago: Rand McNally, 1965), pp. 23–29.

[24]Robert E. Lane, "The Politics of Consensus in an Age of Affluence," *American Political Science Review*, 61:4 (December 1965), 880.

[25]*Report of the National Advisory Commission on Civil Disorders* (Washington, D.C., 1968), pp. 111–112; pp. 128–135.

[26]See Ted Gurr, "Urban Disorder: Perspectives from the Comparative Study of Civil Strife," *American Behavioral Scientist*, 4 (March–April 1968), 50–55; Ivo K. Feierabend and Rosalind L. Feierabend, "Aggressive Behaviors."

[27]Milbrath, *Political Participation*, p. 18.

The American Party System: A Shrinking Consensus 8

There is a great deal of truth to the "Tweedledum and Tweedledee" image of American political parties; they do in fact share the same fundamental political ideology. Both the Democratic and the Republican parties have reflected prevailing elite consensus on basic democratic values: the sanctity of private property, a free-enterprise economy, individual liberty, limited government, majority rule, and due process of law. Moreover, since the 1930s both parties have supported the public-oriented, mass-welfare domestic programs of the "liberal establishment": social security, fair labor standards, unemployment compensation, a graduated income tax, a national highway program, a federally aided welfare system, counter-cyclical fiscal and monetary policies, and government regulation of public utilities. Finally, both parties have supported the basic outlines of American foreign and military policy since World War II: international involvement, anticommunism, the Cold War, European recovery, NATO, military preparedness, selective service, and even the Korean and Vietnam wars. Rather than promoting competition over national goals and programs, the parties reinforce social consensus and limit the area of legitimate political conflict.[1]

The Two Parties—Nuances within Consensus

The major parties are not, of course, *identical* in ideology; there are nuances of difference. For instance, Republican leaders are "conservative" on domestic policy, while Democratic leaders are "liberal." Moreover, the social bases of the parties are slightly different. Both parties draw their support from all social groups in America, but the Democrats draw disproportionately from labor, urban workers, Jews, Catholics, and blacks, while the Republicans draw disproportionately from rural, small-town, and suburban Protestants, businessmen, and professionals. (See Table 8–1.) To the extent that the aspirations of these two broad groups of supporters differ, the thrust of party ideology also differs. This difference, however, is not very great. Democratic identifiers are only slightly more "left" than Republicans. (See Table 8–2.) The more active partisans, however, are more ideologically distinct. Active Republicans and Democratic activists are more conservative and more liberal, respectively, than their less active colleagues. Still, all roads lead to the center; active partisans who fail to heed this lesson suffer the electoral consequences. However, since even active partisans cluster toward the center of the political spectrum (Figure 8–1), only occasional aberrations, such as Goldwater in 1964 and McGovern in 1972, are likely to occur.

Both party's nominees, then, if they are to succeed, must appeal to the center, with Republicans safely offering somewhat more conservative alternatives on the various issues of the campaign. Since there are only two parties and an overwhelmingly nonideological electorate, "consumer" demand (as perceived by leadership) requires that party ideologies be ambiguous and moderate. Therefore, we cannot expect the parties, who wish to alienate the minimum number of voters and attract the maximum number, to take up a cause supported by only a minority of the population.

Since parties seek political office, strong ideology and innovation are virtually out of the question. Firmer, more precise statements of ideologies by the political parties would probably create new lines of cleavage and eventually fragment the parties. The development of a clear "liberal" or "conservative" ideology by either party would cost it votes unless the electorate, stimulated by elites, became more ideologically oriented. Even so, it is doubtful that the country could divide itself into two warring liberal and conservative camps.

Both the 1964 and 1972 presidential elections showed that a strong ideological stance will *not* win elections in America. In 1964, the Republicans came as close to offering a clear ideological alternative to the majority party as has occurred in recent American political history. Goldwater, the Republican presidential candidate, specifically rejected moderation ("moderation in defense of liberty is no virtue") and defended extremism ("extremism in defense of liberty is no vice"). He rejected the

Table 8–1
Vote by Groups in Presidential Elections, 1952–1976

	1952 Stevenson %	1952 Ike %	1956 Stevenson %	1956 Ike %	1960 JFK %	1960 Nixon %	1964 LBJ %	1964 Goldwater %	1968 HHH %	1968 Nixon %	1968 Wallace %	1972 McGovern %	1972 Nixon %	1976 Carter %	1976 Ford %	1976 McCarthy %
National	44.6	55.4	42.2	57.8	50.1	49.9	61.3	38.7	43.0	43.4	13.6	38	62	50	48	1
Sex																
Male	47	53	45	55	52	48	60	40	41	43	16	37	63	53	45	1
Female	42	58	39	61	49	51	62	38	45	43	12	38	62	48	51	*
Race																
White	43	57	41	59	49	51	59	41	38	47	15	32	68	46	52	1
Non-White	79	21	61	39	68	32	94	6	85	12	3	87	13	85	15	*
Education																
College	34	66	31	69	39	61	52	48	37	54	9	37	63	42	55	2
High School	45	55	42	58	52	48	62	38	42	43	15	34	66	54	46	*
Grade School	52	48	50	50	55	45	66	34	52	33	15	49	51	58	41	1
Occupation																
Prof. & Business	36	64	32	68	42	58	54	46	34	56	10	31	69	42	56	1
White Collar	40	60	37	63	48	52	57	43	41	47	12	36	64	50	48	2
Manual	55	45	50	50	60	40	71	29	50	35	15	43	57	58	41	1
Age																
Under 30 years	51	49	43	57	54	46	64	36	47	38	15	48	52	53	45	1
30–49 years	47	53	45	55	54	46	63	37	44	41	15	33	67	48	49	2
50 years & older	39	61	39	61	46	54	59	41	41	47	12	36	64	52	48	*
Religion																
Protestants	37	63	37	63	38	62	55	45	35	49	16	30	70	46	53	*
Catholics	56	44	51	49	78	22	76	24	59	33	8	48	52	57	42	1
Politics																
Republicans	8	92	4	96	5	95	20	80	9	86	5	5	95	9	91	*
Democrats	77	23	85	15	84	16	87	13	74	12	14	67	33	82	18	*
Independents	35	65	30	70	43	57	56	44	31	44	25	31	69	38	57	4
Region																
East	45	55	40	60	53	47	68	32	50	43	7	42	58	51	47	1
Midwest	42	58	41	59	48	52	61	39	44	47	9	40	60	48	50	1
South	51	49	49	51	51	49	52	48	31	36	33	29	71	54	45	*
West	42	58	43	57	49	51	60	40	44	49	7	41	59	46	51	1
Members of Labor Union Families	61	39	57	43	65	35	73	27	56	29	15	46	54	63	36	1

*Less than 1 percent.
Source: Gallup Opinion Index (December 1976), pp. 16–17.

Table 8–2
Ideological
Self-Identification
by Party

	Republicans	Democrats	Independents
Far Left	—	3%	4%
Substantially Left	2%	4	4
Moderately Left	7	11	11
Middle of the Road	46	43	49
Moderately Right	19	13	13
Substantially Right	6	3	2
Far Right	5	4	4
No Opinion	15	19	13
	100%	100%	100%

Source: Gallup Opinion Index (November–December 1975), p. 6.

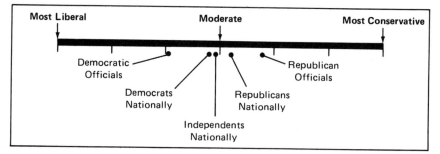

Source: Adapted from the *Washington Post* (September 27, 1976)

"peace" image of Eisenhower in favor of an aggressive, military-oriented stance on foreign policy.

The overwhelming 1964 defeat of the "pure" conservative position (which drew only 33 percent of the vote) reveals the fallacy of the argument that the nonideological two-party system suppresses basic ideological cleavages within the masses: there were in fact few ideologues to rally to the call. A party can suffer the same disastrous defeat by adopting a "pure" liberal position. In 1972 McGovern seriously overestimated the liberal change-orientation of the electorate, particularly among the younger voters (McGovern won only 38 percent of the vote). Given the widely publicized youth movement and the great potential for support in the newly enfranchised eighteen-year-olds, McGovern's belief in a "new politics" majority appeared justified. Indeed, he counted on a three-to-one advantage among eighteen-year-olds, particularly among the college students who participated so enthusiastically in the primaries and the convention. But his supposed advantage was largely unsupported by empirical information; not only was no distinction made between college and noncollege youth, but the "liberalism" of the college population was also overestimated, especially among those living at home or attending junior colleges or church-affiliated schools.[2] Assessing the implications of such findings, Kent Jennings and Richard Niemi are struck by the similarity between the younger and older generations, especially in view of "open efforts to pit the young against the middle-aged." As intergenerational antagonisms have diminished, the lesson of 1964 and 1972 has become even more apparent: the party strategy is to attract voters from the center of the political spectrum, for here lies the majority and the way to victory.

If young, poor, and black are what most voters aren't, let us consider the electorate for what it largely is: white, median family income of [$14,000]; median age of about forty-seven. In short, middle aged, middle-class whites. . . . There are no two strategies for victory—they are the same strategy with different rhetoric. This single strategy involves a drive to the center of the electorate . . . this moving attitudinal center involves progressivism on economic issues and toughness on the social issue . . . the winning coalition in America is the one that holds the center group on an attitudinal battleground. . . . For the seventies, the battlefield shows signs of splitting into two battlefields: the old economic one and the new social one that deals with crime, drugs, racial pressure, and disruption. To the extent that this transformation occurs, then the party and the candidate that can best occupy the center ground of the two battlefields will win the election.[3]

Mass Perceptions of the Parties

In the 1960s, a period of intense intellectual combat among elites, the majority of voters perceived no difference between the two major parties on most issues. Furthermore, after a modest increase in the 1960s, perception of differences between them disappeared in the 1970s. Failure to perceive a difference between the parties cannot be laid entirely to voter ignorance; the party elites themselves articulated no clear differences. Such a strategy is rational, since the majority of voters are not issue-oriented, and, when they are, lean toward the center of the political spectrum anyway. Moreover, voters may have had no clear opinion on the issue, and therefore had no idea where the parties stood.

Another approach to discovering perceptions of parties is to avoid issues as conceived by elites, and to ask respondents among the masses to volunteer issues that are "on their mind a lot" or cause "them extreme worry." If we ask which party is likely to do what "the people want" on the most important issue identified by the individual, the results are hardly more encouraging. In 1964 and in 1968, bare majorities of the voters perceived a difference between Democrats and Republicans on their most important problem, but by 1972 less than half did so. Further, the percentage of voters believing that there is no difference nearly doubled between 1964 and 1972. (See Table 8–3.) Correctly or incorrectly, most people do not believe the parties offer realistic alternatives, and therefore cannot relate policy or issue differences to their vote.

Reflecting on the belief systems of masses, political scientist Murray Edelman concludes that rather than communicating demands to elites, masses absorb a crude and simplified version of elite attitudes.

The basic thesis is that mass publics respond to currently conspicuous political symbols: not to "facts," and not to moral codes embedded in the character or soul, but to the gestures and speeches that make up the drama of the state. . . . It is therefore political actions that chiefly shape men's political wants and "knowledge," not the other way around. The common assumption that what democratic government does is somehow always a response to the moral codes, desires, and knowledge embedded inside people is as inverted as it is reassuring. This model, avidly taught and ritualistically repeated, cannot explain what happens; but it may persist in our folklore because it so effectively sanctifies prevailing policies and permits us to avoid worrying about them. . . . The public is not in touch with the situation, and it "knows" the situation only through the symbols that engage it. [4]

Political Parties as Organizations

Unlike European mass-membership parties, American parties are not "organizations" in the normal sense of that term. To be a "Democrat" or a "Republican" involves no greater commitment to the organization than occasionally supporting the nominees of that party.

Table 8–3
Most Important Problem Government Should Take Care of: Which Party Has Best Position

	1964	1968	1972
Democrats	35%	21%	23%
Republicans	19	30	24
No difference	21	35	41
DK	7	10	8
Wallace	—	2	1
No problem	18	3	3
(Numbers	1565	1547	1066)

Source: Inter-University Corsortium for Political Research: Survey Research Center; CPS American National Election Studies.

There is, of course, a party organization, consisting of the formally chosen leadership, informal powerholders (who do not hold government or party office), and the party activists who contribute their time and money and consequently acquire the right to make decisions in the name of the party. However, neither political party is structurally hierarchical. Both are decentralized to the extent that no chain of command from national through state to local levels can be said to exist. But the structure of power within the activist group in each party is not especially relevant to our concern. Rather, we are interested in interaction *between* this group and the overwhelming majority of Democrats and Republicans, who do not involve themselves in formulation of party objectives or the selection of candidates (except in primaries) but merely accept or reject the product offered to them by the party activists. All but a tiny portion of the participants in the political system are consumers. The association with the party is entirely passive.

"From the way he talks, I can't tell whether he's a Texas Democrat, a New York Republican, or an Iowa Independent."

Leo Garel

The American Party System: A Shrinking Consensus   195

It is somewhat of an irony that the parties, as the agents of democratic decision making, are not themselves democratic in their structures. One of the most sweeping indictments of political parties on this count comes from Roberto Michels, whose "iron law of oligarchy" leads him to conclude that "every party . . . becomes divided into a minority of directors and a majority of directed."[5] However, the organizational characteristics of American parties supply few relevant data to either support or refute Michels's assertion. There is, indeed, an active minority, but there is no passive majority because the party in the electorate, the masses, are not really members of the party. The party as an organization is composed of those persons who exercise varied degrees of influence within the activists' cadre. Sorauf describes American parties in this way:

Despite recent trends, the American parties remain largely skeletal, "cadre" party organizations, manned generally by small numbers of activists and involving the great masses of their supporters scarcely at all. . . . By the standards of the parties of much of the rest of the world, American party organization continues to be characterized by its unusual fluidity and evanescence, by its failure to generate activity at non-election times, and by the ease by which a handful of activists and public officeholders dominate it.[6]

In essence, power in American parties tends to rest in the hands of those who have the time and the money to make it a full-time, or nearly full-time, occupation. Party activists—consisting of no more than 3 or 4 percent of the adult population—can decide what product is to be offered to political consumers (the party in the electorate). Beyond this, there is little interaction between the party in the electorate and the party activists. The crucial question is, therefore, who are the party activists? We know, from research cited in previous chapters, that the activists are strongly ideological and committed to the norms of the democratic decision-making process. Since these characteristics describe the upper socioeconomic groups, it is not surprising to discover that party activists are of relatively high socioeconomic status, and come from families with a history of party activity. The highest socioeconomic levels are found in the highest echelons of the party organization. As Sorauf notes, "the parties . . . attract men and women with the time and financial resources to be able to afford politics, with the information and knowledge to understand it, and with the skills to be useful in it."[7]

It is, of course, true that—reflecting the basis of support among the party in the electorate—Democratic activists are of somewhat lower socioeconomic status than their Republican counterparts. The activists of both parties are somewhat representative of their clientele. Nevertheless, the socioeconomic status of both Democratic and Republican activists is above the average for the area they represent. This distinction between elite and mass, then, is especially characteristic of American political parties.

But what does it matter whether or not the parties are democratic in structure? If the competition between parties is similar to the competition between businesses, the structural characteristics of each group of producers are not very important. Competitors, democratic or not, have the primary function of satisfying their customers. Yet the political alternatives offered by parties are much more constricted than those offered in business. The voter cannot choose from a number of competing products, but is limited to a choice between two. A voter who finds the product of one competitor unsatisfactory must either accept the single alternative or decline to become a consumer. Given the consensual nature of American parties, the range of alternatives is quite narrow.[8]

Further, it is difficult for consumers to force the producers to change their product. At first glance, it would seem easy to become an activist in a party and change the agenda-setting personnel. At most levels of political participation, this is superficially quite simple. State legislatures generally require that the party machinery be "open," so anyone can become an activist. Indeed, thousands of party positions are unfilled. However, gaining control of the political party apparatus takes longer than the normally short-term commitment that even more active portions of the citizenry are willing to make. Also, challenges to the dominant group of activists are generally focused on a candidate such as Eugene McCarthy or George McGovern. Thus, relatively few party leaders can control the decisions of a large proportion of the delegates to the national conventions. The choice of a nominating convention will be, therefore, the choice of the party activists who have long-term commitments to the party, rather than the choice of those activists who are occasionally mobilized by a particular candidate. Only on the rare occasions when temporarily mobilized activists encounter the power of the permanent activists are we able to see how much the parties are the property of the small cadre willing to commit themselves to politics as an avocation.

Attempts at Party Reform

The debacle of the 1968 Democratic Convention, with huge television audiences observing total anarchy, led to an effort to reform the delegate-selection process. In 1969 the Commission on Party Structure and Delegate Selection (the "McGovern Commission") proposed to maximize rank and file participation, so that the nominee of the Democratic Convention would accurately reflect the views of the Democratic electorate. The commission, chaired by McGovern and dominated by his supporters, proposed a quota system (whereby "blacks, youth and women" would achieve representation in "reasonable relationship" to the group's presence in the population of a state). Further, delegate selection in state conventions and local caucuses was to be opened to participation by nonregulars. The goal here was to reduce, if not eliminate, the traditional dominance of party activists. Consequently, many local party machines decided to use primary elections for the election of delegates to state conventions (which, in turn, named delegates to the national convention). In 1976, *thirty* states had presidential primary elections.

At the Democratic party's 1972 convention, the McGovern reform had an immediate impact on the nature of the representation. As Table 8–4 shows, the quota system gave blacks, women, and youth a solid block, whereas in 1968 these groups had been virtually excluded. In addition to these demographic representational changes, delegates in 1972 (as compared with 1968) were substantially less likely to have attended a previous convention, or to have a strong identification with the Democratic party. Only the delegates supporting the center candidates were strong party identifiers with previous convention experience.

Given the distinctly amateur characteristics of the 1972 convention, and the visible replacement of party regulars, it is not surprising that McGovern and Wallace delegates (as distinguished from mainstream delegates) adopted a "purist" position. That is, they viewed their mission as a crusade, with compromise to be avoided.[9]

McGovern's supporters asserted that the reform rules, and the expulsion of the "bosses," would make the 1972 convention "the most representative group ever gathered in one spot in one party's history." From the point of view of issues, Democratic elites have always been more liberal than Democratic masses. Therefore, to achieve the desired congruence, either the 1972 convention would have had to be more conservative, or the masses more liberal, than in previous years. Such was clearly not the case in 1972. The gap between elites and masses was *wider* than usual. Seventy percent of the Democratic rank and file opposed busing, compared with 21 percent of the delegates; 69 percent of the Democratic rank and file opposed amnesty, compared with 18 percent of the delegates; 57 percent of the Democratic masses opposed a guaranteed annual income, compared with 26 percent of the delegates. The Democratic party platform, which reflected the views of the delegates, was thus in opposition to the views of the masses. It is probable, then, that McGovern's insurgency provided the *least* representative convention in the history of the party. However, the center had not been obliterated. It would reappear in November to bury the Democratic can-

Table 8–4
Representation at
Democratic Conventions

	1968	1972	1976
Blacks	6%	15%	11%
Youth	2%	21%	n.a.*
Women	14%	40%	34%

*Not available.

Source: Denis G. Sullivan, Jeffrey C. Pressman, Benjamin I. Page, and John J. Lyons, *The Politics of Representation: The Democratic Convention of 1972* (New York: St. Martin's Press, 1974), p. 23.

didate, who represented a new elite—the amateurs—which was extraordinarily unrepresentative.

After Nixon's landslide victory in 1972, the Democratic party took prompt steps to return control to the traditional party activists. A Commission on Delegate Selection was appointed, with much greater representation given to party regulars, to undo as quickly and quietly as possible the quota system. A new Charter Commission was created to present a new scheme to an extraordinary 1974 convention. Most significantly, McGovern's personal choice as party chairman, Jean Westwood, was replaced by Robert Strauss, Dallas lawyer and Treasurer of the Democratic National Committee. Described by McGovern forces as a symbol of old-guard Democrats, Strauss was supported by organized labor, supporters of the centrist candidates, and a newly formed Coalition for a Democratic Majority (an organization designed to reconstruct the old traditional liberal-organized labor alliance). So it ended, as had Goldwater's insurgency in 1964, with the summary removal of the amateurs and the return of the old guard to positions of influence.

The Rise of the Independent Voter

Large numbers of people on both the left and right in American politics are deserting the Democratic and Republican parties. To be sure, there is substantial evidence that the poor and the blacks were never wholly within the two-party system in the first place. (Figures on nonvoting indicate that a majority of blacks and a majority of poor—families earning less than $5,000 per year—do not participate in American party politics.)

Several trends indicate that the established parties have decayed. But the chief sign is decline in voter participation (again, in 1976, slightly more than half those eligible voted). The decline of political parties reflects a continuing deterioration of partisan loyalty—along with trust—which began before Watergate, probably during the turbulent confrontation politics of the 1960s. The percentage of voters identifying themselves with neither party is increasing, as Table 8–5 shows for a twenty-four-year period. By 1976, the proportion of Independents had increased to 36 percent; Democratic identifiers had stabilized at 39 percent; and Republican identifiers had declined to 24 percent. It is occasionally argued that the growth of independence is symptomatic of alienation with political institutions. Clearly, such alienation has occurred. It is not clear, however, that such alienation is so rationally translated into an independent attitude. As we suggested in Chapter 7, partisan identifications are stable, and deflections away from party identification are accounted for by short-term factors (principally candidate appeal).

A more reasonable explanation of the growth of Independents, then, is the replacement of older, more partisan voters by younger,

Table 8–5
Voters'
Self-Identifications,
1952–1976

	1952	1976	% Change 1952–1976
Democrat			
Strong	22	15	−7%
Weak	25	24	−1
Independent*			
Democrat	10	12	+2
Independent	5	15	+10
Republican	7	9	+2
Republican			
Weak	14	15	+1
Strong	13	9	−4

*Party names in this entry indicate the major party the respondent most identified with.

Source: University of Michigan, Survey Research Center.

Table 8–6
Age Composition of
Independent Voters
(1974)

Age	% Independent
18–22	56%
23–34	42
35–39	38
40–46	39
47–56	33
57–61	26
62–68	32
69–78	25
79–83	12
84+	25

Source: University of Michigan, Survey Research Center.

weaker partisans, due chiefly to lowering of the minimum voting age to eighteen. The age composition of Independents makes this clear. (See Table 8–6.) What about the ultimate, long-term partisan commitment of the Independents? Each election year, first-time voters have been progressively more independent. But will they lose their independence as they age? The political parties must face the possibility that their respective strengths can be much altered, more because the electorate changes in composition than because individuals change partisan identification. As Miller and Levitin observe, "If the young Independents, and the Independents who follow them into the electorate, are never persuaded to establish party ties, the future of the Republican and even the Democratic party may become problematic."[10]

Jimmy Carter's nomination and election by the Democratic party may turn out to effectively solve the problem of Democratic party disintegration. By concentrating on the center, Carter reversed the 1972 defection from the party. As president, Carter can use his position to continue to move the Democratic party closer to center.

Political Campaigns and Party Voting

If most voters cannot perceive the alternative policy positions of political parties, what do campaigns accomplish? Candidates confer extensively with their advisors, plan elaborate political statements, and make public appearances to discuss the issues that they perceive as relevant to the election. The presentation of their ideologies actually produces more voter support than do the ideologies themselves; the candidate's image, not his proposed policies, affects voter choice.

Why, then, do candidates travel about the nation speaking mostly to audiences who already support them? They do so to insure that their supporters turn out to vote on election day. Since more than two-thirds of the potential voters have already made up their minds before the campaign begins, this mobilization of the faithful becomes the most important strategy of the political campaign. To understand why, we look at the concept of the "normal vote." The normal vote is simply the division of the vote that would occur if party identification were unaffected by such short-term forces as issue orientation and candidate identification.[11] For example, if there were no "image" impact of the Democratic and Republican candidates, and if the issues were of no relevance, and if the predicted percentage of turnout for each party occurred, the Democrats would receive 54 percent of the vote—that is the normal vote for the Democrats. The normal vote is a model, not a real-world occurrence. But like any model, it enables us to better understand the real world. In this case it provides a guideline for assessing the impact of a campaign, specifically for measuring how well the candidates were able to mobilize their supporters. The normal vote model is able to do this because it takes into account predicted voter turnout. Thus, the normal vote for any party is not the same thing as party identification.

For Democratic candidates, the campaign strategy is simply to guarantee that Democratic identifiers maintain their preferences. Since there are more Democratic than Republican identifiers, barring short-term forces, Democrats will win. For Republican candidates, the strategy is to deflect Independents and weak Democrats from their partisan affiliation, getting them to vote more on issues or on perception of candidates. Thus, a presidential candidate's strategy can begin with a simple calculus. Approximately 39 percent of the population identify with the Democratic party, 24 percent identify with the Republican party, and 36 percent regard themselves as Independents. (See Table 8–7.) However, the dominance of Democratic identifiers is complicated by two factors: first, the question of the stability and reliability of partisan attitudes; second, turnout.

Partisan attitudes are generally stable: Individual voters rarely change their party affiliation. Although the percentage of independents is increasing, and that of party identifiers decreasing, it is because the new, younger voters have poorly developed party affiliations, not because older voters are converting from one party to another. Such conversion is extremely rare.

The increased role of the independent voters adds an element of volatility in presidential elections. During such elections Independents, who are not tied to parties and who respond primarily to short-term forces such as candidate image and issues, contribute to the surge and decline in the distribution of votes.

Finally, although the individual's party identification remains stable, individual Democratic and Republican identifiers have nevertheless

Question:	"Generally speaking, do you usually think of yourself as a Republican, a Democrat, an Independent, or what? (IF REPUBLICAN OR DEMOCRAT) Would you call yourself a strong (R) (D) or a not very strong (R) (D)? (IF INDEPENDENT) Do you think of yourself as closer to the Republican or Democratic Party?"

	Oct. 1952	Oct. 1956	Oct. 1960	Oct. 1964	Nov. 1968	Nov. 1972	Oct. 1976	% Change 1952–1976
Democrat								
Strong	22%	21%	21%	26%	20%	15%	15%	– 7%
Weak	25	23	25	25	25	25	24	– 1
Independent								
Democrat	10	7	8	9	10	11	12	+ 2
Independent	5	9	8	8	11	13	15	+10
Republican	7	8	7	6	9	11	9	+ 2
Republican								
Weak	14	14	13	13	14	13	15	+ 1
Strong	13	15	14	11	10	10	9	– 4
Apolitical,								
Don't Know	4	3	4	2	1	2	1	
Total	100%	100%	100%	100%	100%	100%	100%	

Source: University of Michigan, Survey Research Center.

increasingly tended to vote for an opposing party's candidate. Since 1960 there has been a gradual weakening of the correlation between party identification and party voting. Table 8–8 shows the varying impact of party identification on the vote in three recent elections: in 1964, when the Republicans nominated Barry Goldwater from the most conservative wing of the party; in 1972, when the Democrats nominated George McGovern from the most liberal wing of the party; and in 1976, when each party nominated from its mainstream. In 1964, Lyndon Johnson gained the votes of virtually all Democrats (strong, weak, and independent Democrats), and three-fourths of the Independents. Goldwater fared differently. Whereas 90 percent of the strong Republican identifiers supported Goldwater, a mere 57 percent of the weak Republican identifiers and 75 percent of the independent Republicans did so. Thus, his extremism provoked a substantial switch among Republican partisans. Likewise, in 1972, substantially fewer strong Demo-

Table 8–8
Party Identification
and Voter Choices

	1964		1972		1976	
Strong Democrat	95 ⎫	%	73 ⎫	%	92 ⎫	%
Weak Democrat	82 ⎬	Voted	48 ⎬	Voted	71 ⎬	Voted
Independent Democrat	90 ⎭	Democratic	61 ⎭	Democratic	84 ⎭	Democratic
Independent	77	% Voted Demo.	30	% Voted Demo.	42	% Voted Demo.
Independent Republican	75 ⎫	%	87 ⎫	%	83 ⎫	%
Weak Republican	57 ⎬	Voted	91 ⎬	Voted	86 ⎬	Voted
Strong Republican	90 ⎭	Republican	97 ⎭	Republican	96 ⎭	Republican

Source: University of Michigan, Survey Research Center.

crats supported McGovern than supported Johnson in 1964; a minority of weak Democratic identifiers voted for McGovern, as did fewer independent Democrats. Among Republicans, however, party loyalties held firm in 1972 and Nixon gained the support of virtually all party identifiers. The two elections were said to demonstate the decaying impact of party loyalty on the vote.* Such was indeed the case—until 1976, when party loyalties resumed their normal role. Carter substantially increased the support of all Democratic identifiers, and improved the performance of the Democratic party among Independents. Ford, like Nixon, did extremely well among Republican partisans. In the 1976 election, the long-term force of partisan identification overcame the short-term impact of issues and candidate evaluations.

Strategic considerations must take into account the second complicating factor of partisan identification: turnout. Despite the preponderance of Democratic identifiers, variations in turnout can favor Republican candidates. Since Republican voters typically are of higher socioeconomic status than are Democratic voters, their turnout rates are substantially higher. Hence, "getting out the vote" is a Democratic strategy, while stimulating short-term deflection against party affiliation is a Republican strategy.

Creating a Favorable Image

Candidates seek to create a positive image of themselves or a negative image of their opponents. Hence, most campaign energy is directed to image-making, not issue-making. This choice is further enhanced by the rise of television as the most important source of campaign information—which it is for more than two-thirds of the voters, especially among the less educated, for whom it is the only source of information about candidates. Thus, the shift has occurred among passive media users. More-educated voters supplement television viewing with the reading of newspapers and magazines, sources of more thorough analyses of candidates' positions. Just as candidates favor images rather than issues, so do TV newscasters in their competitive bids for higher ratings. The campaign role of television is well illustrated by the 1976 election. From the start, both President Ford and his challenger chose to avoid issues and instead to articulate "themes"—Carter's that of the "outsider" untainted by Watergate; Ford's that of the competent, well-experienced manager. The televised debates between the two candidates simply heightened their inclination to avoid issues (there was no discussion of energy policy, the disintegration of urban areas, etc.) and to stress images.

*In 1968, substantial defection from the party among Democrats also occurred, while the Republicans held firm.

Had the election been decided ideologically, Ford would have won. Like Nixon in 1972, he was more conservative than his Democratic challenger, and thus better aligned with most of the electorate. But Carter was elected in 1976 largely because he was a Democrat. Party loyalty once again became the crucial factor, because issues were downplayed.

Money and Politics

Political campaigns cost money—usually far more than candidates themselves are willing or able to spend. In 1976, Ford and Carter each spent $22 million on the general election. Earlier, Ford spent an additional $14 million in the Republican primaries (Reagan, his opponent, spent nearly $18 million), and Carter an additional $13 million in the Democratic primaries. But in 1972 Richard Nixon spent $60 million in his reelection campaign, and his "poor" opponent McGovern spent $30 million. Few candidates can even begin a political career for state or local

"Carter: 'I'll be JFK. Who do you want to be?'"

© Szep, *The Boston Globe*

office without first securing financial support from wealthy "angels." The far-sighted among the wealthy may choose to back a promising young politician in early career and continue this support for many years.* Few representatives or senators have no wealthy sponsors.

Prior to 1976, the spiraling costs of political campaigns (and of television advertising in particular) forced candidates and would-be candidates to find large financial contributors. For example, in 1972, Richard Nixon's top financial backers included: W. Clement Stone, centi-millionaire chairman of Combined Insurance Company of America (donation: $2 million); Richard Mellon Scalfe, director of Mellon National Bank and Trust and Gulf Oil Corporation, and centi-millionaire heir to the Mellon fortune (donation: $1 million); and Arthur K. Watson, former chairman of the board of IBM (donation: $300 thousand). There were several other large contributors as well.

Democrats usually receive less money than Republicans from the corporate world, although about half of Democratic funds come from this source—from the Xerox Corporation, for example. Traditionally, Democrats have turned for support to big labor, notably to the Committee on Political Education (COPE) of the AFL-CIO and the larger international unions like the United Auto Workers and United Steel Workers. Liberal Democrats have also been supported by upper-class liberal philanthropists. These "limousine liberals" provided much of the financial support for the civil rights and antiwar movements and other liberal causes. For example, in 1972, George McGovern was supported by Stewart Mott (heir to a fortune in General Motors stock), Max Palevsky (former chairman of the board of the Xerox Corporation), Nicholas and Daniel Noyes (wealthy students who are heirs to the Eli Lilly Pharmaceutical fortune), Richard Saloman (president, Charles of the Ritz, Inc.).

Nevertheless, chronic Democratic campaign deficits were a stimulus to campaign "reform," especially when Democrats overwhelmingly controlled both houses of Congress with a close presidential election approaching. In 1974, Congress passed a comprehensive Campaign Spending Law with the following provisions:

A Presidential Election Campaign Fund was created from voluntary one dollar per person check-offs from individual income taxes.

A Federal Election Commission was created (two members selected by the

---

*Richard Nixon was long supported by Chicago insurance tycoon W. Clement Stone. George McGovern was backed for many years by Stewart Mott, heir to the General Motors fortune. Jimmy Carter was backed in his early races in Georgia by J. Paul Austin, chairman of the board of Coca Cola; Charles Kirbo, Atlanta attorney; and Thomas B. (Bert) Lance, former president of the National Bank of Georgia and Director of the Office of Management and Budget.

House, two by the Senate, and two by the president) to oversee federal election spending.

The Commission would distribute campaign monies from the fund (1) to candidates in the primaries (in 1976 up to $5 million to those who could raise themselves $5,000 in each of 20 states); (2) to the Democratic and Republican parties for their national conventions (in 1976 $2 million each); (3) and to the Republican and Democratic candidates in the general election (in 1976, $20 million each).

Individuals are limited to making a $1,000 contribution in any election, and organizations are limited to $5,000. All contributions must be reported to the Federal Elections Commission.

The Supreme Court modified these provisions by declaring that, as an exercise of First-Amendment rights, an individual can spend unlimited personal wealth on that person's own election campaign. Moreover, also as an exercise of First-Amendment rights, any amount of personal wealth may be spent to advertise the individual's own political views. As long as these independent expenditures are not tied directly to a political campaign, no legal limits apply. While the campaign spending law, as modified by the Supreme Court, reduces the role of the large financial "angels," it permits wealthy persons to spend large amounts on their own campaigns, thus keeping direct exercises of political power, as well as control of the parties, in the hands of the elites.

Summary

Elitism asserts that elites share a consensus about the fundamental values of the political system. This elite consensus does not mean that elite members never disagree or never compete with each other for preeminence. But elitism implies that competition centers on a narrow range of issues and that elites agree on more matters than they disagree. The single elite model suggests that parties agree about the direction of public policy and disagree only on minor details. Our analysis of the American party system suggests the following propositions:

1. American parties share consensus both on basic democratic values and on major directions of American policy. They believe in the sanctity of private property, the free enterprise economy, individual liberty, and limited government. Moreover, both parties have supported the same general domestic and foreign policy—including social security, a graduated income tax, counter-cyclical fiscal and monetary policies, anticommunism, the Cold War, and the Korean and Vietnam wars.

2. The American parties do not present clear ideological alternatives to the American voter. Both American parties are overwhelmingly middle class in organization, values, and goals. Deviation from the shared consensus by either party ("a choice not an echo") is more likely to lose than attract voters.

3. Both parties draw support from all social groups in America, but the Democrats draw disproportionately from labor, workers, Jews, Catholics, and

blacks, and the Republicans draw disproportionate support from rural, small-town, and suburban Protestants, businessmen, and professionals.

4. Democratic and Republican party leaders differ over public policy more than Democratic or Republican mass followers. The consensus about welfare economics extends to Democratic leaders, Democratic followers, and Republican followers; only the Republican leadership is outside this consensus, with a more laissez-faire position. However, all party differences observed fall well within the range of elite consensus on the values of individualism, capitalism, and limited government.

5. American parties are dominated by small groups of activists who formulate party objectives and select candidates for public office. The masses play a passive role in party affairs. They are not really "members" of the party; they are "consumers."

6. Among party activists, power is generally diffused, not centralized. Power within parties is not in the hands of a single elite, but rather a "stratarchy" of elites. The exceptions to this rule are the few large city machines, particularly in the Democratic party.

7. Party activists differ from the masses, because they have the time and financial resources to be able to "afford" politics, the information and knowledge to understand it, and the organization and public relations skills to be successful in it.

8. The choice of party nominees is a choice of party activists, not a choice of the masses of party members.

9. Political party identification is reasonably stable. However, there has been a rapid growth of Independents is recent years, particularly among younger voters.

10. Political campaigns are designed to focus on images of candidates, not issues. They are also designed to increase the turnout of a candidate's supporters.

11. The "normal vote" in America today is Democratic. Republicans must stress image rather than party identification in a campaign. Democrats must stress "getting out the vote" among their more numerous party loyalists.

12. Congress has reduced the role of large campaign contributors in presidential elections through a system of public financing of elections.

References

[1] See Walter Dean Burnham, "The Changing Shape of the American Political Universe," *American Political Science Review*, 59 (March 1965), 28; and Walter Dean Burnham, "Party Systems and the Political Process," in William Nisbet Chambers and Walter Dean Burnham (eds.) *The American Party Systems: Stages of Political Development* (New York: Oxford University Press, 1967), pp. 305–307.

[2] M. Kent Jennings and Richard G. Niemi, "Continuity and Change in Political Orientations: A Longitudinal Study of Two Generations," paper presented to the 1973 Annual Meeting of the American Political Science Association, New Orleans, p. 15.

[3] Richard M. Scammon and Ben J. Wattenberg, *The Real Majority* (New York: Coward-McCann, 1970), pp. 59, 78, 80.

[4] Murray Edelman, *The Symbolic Uses of Politics* (Urbana: University of Illinois Press, 1964), p. 172.

[5]Roberto Michels, *Political Parties: A Sociological Study of the Oligarchical Tendencies of Modern Democracy* (New York: Dover Publications, 1959; originally published in English in 1915), p. 32.

[6]Frank J. Sorauf, *Party Politics in America* (Boston: Little, Brown and Co., 1968), pp. 79–80.

[7]Sorauf, *Party Politics in America*, p. 94.

[8]See the consideration of the party-voter-as-business-firm-customer relationship in Robert A. Dahl, *Pluralist Democracy in the United States: Conflict and Consent* (Chicago: Rand-McNally, 1967), pp. 247–252.

[9]Denis G. Sullivan, Jeffrey C. Pressman, Benjamin I. Page, and John J. Lyons, *The Politics of Representation: The Democratic Convention of 1972* (New York: St. Martin's Press, 1974), p. 124.

[10]Warren E. Miller and Teresa E. Levitin, *Leadership and Change: The New Politics and the American Electorate* (Cambridge, Mass.: Winthrop, 1976), p. 200.

[11]*Ibid.*, p. 37.

The Organized Interests: Defenders of the Status Quo

9

Active membership in interest groups—private, nongovernment organizations—should be a more effective method of political participation than individual voting. Presumably, a combination of voices is more effective than a single one; the "interests" with their better organization achieve more tangible benefits than do the unorganized "people" (voters). In fact, studies of the policy-making process indicate that cohesion and organization do contribute disproportionately to political success.

But what are the real functions of interest groups? Why are some groups powerful and others not? Why are some issues vulnerable to group influence and others not? Do organized groups contribute to social change or social stability?

PTQ

Contemporary pluralists contend that interest groups perform several important functions for their members and for a democratic society. First, the organized group is said to link the individual and the government. Political scientists Gabriel Almond and Sidney Verba state:

The Premises of Interest-Group Theory

Voluntary associations are the prime means by which the function of mediating between the individual and the state is performed. Through them the individual is able to relate himself effectively and meaningfully to the political system. [1]

But is the organized group mediating between individual and government any more efficient than a direct citizen-government interaction? Why do we need a "middleman"?

It is also argued that interest groups enhance individual well-being. In a mass society, with primary associations (small groups, such as the family) diminishing in importance, secondary associations (less intimate but more goal-oriented) may help the individual overcome the sense of powerlessness characteristic of mass societies. Groups help integrate the individual with society.

Finally, interest groups are said to help reduce potentially divisive conflicts. According to the theory of overlapping group memberships, all citizens are members of groups (unorganized and organized).[2] Each person can be summed up as a product of group affiliations; a person may be, for example, a lawyer, a Southerner, a military veteran, and a Protestant, each of these affiliations imposing separate values. No single group affiliation would be able to claim the individual's total, undivided loyalty. Hence, group demands are modified and societal conflict reduced. However, there is a problem with this theory. Because it is difficult to measure affiliation with unorganized groups, the conflict-reducing function of interest groups is also difficult to test.

To sum up, the "old" theory that interest groups are "bad" because they are opposed to the "public interest" has been replaced. Interest groups are now considered "good" because (1) they provide a more effective voice for citizens competing for the allocation of resources; (2) they reduce the anxiety produced by a feeling of powerlessness; and (3) they provide an element of stability for the society. This new theory subtly but significantly transforms democratic theory. No longer is the emphasis on individual participation; individuals who want something from a government must pool their resources in organized group activity and get it. Indeed, thousands of organizations make their demands on Congress, various administrative agencies, state legislatures, city councils, and even school boards. A glance at the list of registered lobbyists in Washington and in various state capitals gives credence to the argument. Each group, or potential group, is free to organize. Consequently, organization produces counterorganization. In the process of resolving group demands, each interest is given a voice, and public policy is formed in response to these competitive demands. Interest groups, then, serve pluralistic democracy well by insuring that government decision makers respond to the claims of the various groups. It is in the competition among the varieties of competitive groups that pluralism finds its most frequently stated defense. Pluralistic interest-group theory does not deny the existence of elites, but rather contends that each elite is specialized, representative of a set of mass demands, and counterbalanced by a set of opposing demands.

For the pluralist interest-group theory to be judged correct, a series of assumptions must be verified:

1. Membership in organizations is widespread and thus broadly represents all individual interests.
2. Organized groups efficiently translate members' expectations into political demands; nothing is lost in the translation, and a great deal is gained by presenting demands through a representative association.
3. Although interest groups are not always and uniformly successful (some win and some lose), each group, whatever its demands, has equal access to the political resources necessary for success.
4. By representing individuals organizations help make them politically effective; thus, they strengthen the social fabric.

We shall refute the first three of these assumptions; and, although the final assumption has empirical evidence in its behalf, we will argue that *because* of their integrative function, organizations help to guide their members toward an acceptance of the *status quo*. We suggest that interest groups, rather than articulating the demands of masses, serve to protect the values of established elites, as George McGovern, who is neither a pluralist nor an elite theorist, implied:

Pluralism, the "politics of interest," describes governmental decision making essentially as a competition among interest groups. The result of the competition—whether one side, or another wins, or a compromise is reached—then defines the public interest.

The politics of interest is a flawed method for making national decisions and an incomplete description of how they actually are made. There is a public good which must be defined independently of political pressures or organized interests. Political leaders have an obligation to advance such qualities as morality and decency—to distinguish between right and wrong—regardless of how the interest groups balance those values. [3]

It is widely believed that "Americans are joiners," and a majority of the population in fact belongs to at least one formal organization. Yet, membership in organized interest groups is clearly linked to socioeconomic status. Membership is greatest among the professional and managerial classes, college-educated (Table 9–1), and high-income persons. Or-

How Widespread Is Interest-Group Affiliation?

Table 9–1
Percentage of
Respondents Who Belong
to Some Organization by
Nation and Education

	Total		Primary or Less		Some Secondary		Some University	
	(%)	(no.)*	(%)	(no.)	(%)	(no.)	(%)	(no.)
United States	57	(970)	46	(339)	55	(443)	80	(188)
Great Britain	47	(963)	41	(593)	55	(322)	92	(24)
Germany	44	(955)	41	(792)	63	(124)	62	(26)
Italy	30	(995)	25	(692)	37	(245)	46	(54)
Mexico	24	(1,007)	21	(877)	39	(103)	68	(24)

*Numbers in parentheses refer to the bases upon which percentages are calculated.

Source: Gabriel A. Almond and Sidney Verba, *The Civic Culture: Political Attitudes and Democracy in Five Nations* (Boston: Little, Brown and Co. 1965), p. 249.

ganized group membership is primarily an upper-middle-class to upper-class phenomenon.[4]

Of course, the upper-class bias of organized groups varies according to the organization. Unions (which frequently are not voluntary), civil rights organizations, and the Ku Klux Klan recruit from the lower strata. However, even within the civil rights movement, the masses of blacks are uninvolved. Civil rights organizations are lower class in comparison to white organizations, but within the black community, participation and social status are still related. For example, the National Association for the Advancement of Colored People represents the moderate black "establishment," not the blacks in urban ghettos who take direct and violent action. Liberal causes, such as the women's movement and Common Cause, are likely to attract a disproportionate element of the university "liberal establishment," and rarely appeal to the lower classes. At any rate, the social bias in association membership, whether or not the association is "political," is complemented by the high social origins of lobbyists and the predominance of business organizations in *effective* lobbying.

This bias has obvious implications for the functions of interest groups. Whatever they do is done mostly for the upper-middle and upper classes, not for the total population. Even if interest groups are an effective link between the citizen and government, many citizens do not avail themselves of this benefit. For example, 87 percent of farmworkers belong to no organization, compared to 58 percent of farm owners. Even if the formal organization reduces anxiety or increases feelings of power, it does not serve the poor and the uneducated, whose alienation from the society is the greatest and whose need for such services is most extreme.[5]

Further, among members of organizations, active participation—and holding formal office—is directly related to social status. Whereas the majority of Americans are members in organizations, only a minority of members are active. All organizations are typically controlled by a small elite. The "iron law of oligarchy" describes the fact that even the most democratically inclined organizations gradually evolve into oligarchies. The oligarchs, who help to shape the goals of the organization, are drawn disproportionately from the upper social classes.[6]

Here again, the oligarchy's social status may vary according to the nature of the organization. Cesar Chavez, leader of the Mexican-American farmworkers' movement, can hardly be thought of as an aristocrat. True, his early life was above average for Chicanos: He is a native-born American citizen whose parents were prosperous farmers until the depression forced his family to live the grim life of the migrant laborer. As leader of the National United Farm Workers, however, Chavez is typically autocratic—indeed, authoritarian.[7] Work assignments are handled by the union; any worker who fails to report to a job assigned by the union gets to the bottom of the list. (Chavez has opposed placing farmers under the jurisdiction of the National Labor Relations Board, since they would make this practice illegal.) Within the union, there are no bylaws, and no election of officers. Union dues may be raised or lowered by Chavez without approval from the members. In brief, an organization which is, in Chavez's words, dedicated to the dissolution of "the existing social order" is as dictatorial as any in the country—certainly as autocratic as the Teamsters Union with which Chavez struggles for power. (Whereas the degree of oligarchical control can vary among organizations, Chavez's power is to some extent necessary; a democratic organizational structure and organizational affectiveness are frequently incompatible.)

Participation in organizations is also related to satisfaction with one's life situation. The more satisfying a worker's job, for example, the more likely the worker is to participate in union affairs. Hence, those who have the least to complain about are most likely to guide the affairs of formal organizations. Naturally, the higher one's social status, the less one has to complain about.

Thus, our first empirical test of contemporary pluralist interest-group theory fails to corroborate one of its basic assumptions. Those who are active in interest groups constitute only a small portion of the populace; moreover, they tend to be from a higher socioeconomic status than those who are not active. In short, it is the elites who are the most active in interest groups in America.

Given the clan bias of organizations, it is not surprising that business associations are the largest lobbying groups, both in the nation as a whole and in the states. (See Table 9–2.) Common Cause, the so-called people's lobby,

Table 9–2
Top Twenty-Five
Reported Spenders
for Lobbying

Organization	1973
Common Cause	$934,835
International Union, United Automobile, Aerospace and Agricultural Implement Workers	460,992
American Postal Workers Union (AFL-CIO)	393,399
American Federation of Labor-Congress of Industrial Organizations (AFL-CIO)	240,800
American Trucking Associations Inc.	226,157
American Nurses Association Inc.	218,354
U.S. Savings and Loan League	204,221
Gas Supply Committee	195,537
Disabled American Veterans	193,168
The Committee of Publicly Owned Companies	180,493
American Farm Bureau Federation	170,472
National Education Association	162,755
National Association of Letter Carriers	160,597
National Association of Home Builders of the United States	152,177
Recording Industry Association of America Inc.	141,111
National Council of Farmer Cooperatives	140,560
American Insurance Association	139,395
The Farmers' Educational and Co-operative Union of America	138,403
Committee of Copyright Owners	135,095
National Housing Conference Inc.	125,726
American Petroleum Institute	121,276
American Medical Association	114,859
Citizens for Control of Federal Spending	113,659
American Civil Liberties Union	102,595
National Association of Insurance Agents Inc.	87,422

Source: Congressional Quarterly Weekly, July 27, 1974.

is a model of elitism. Its membership . . . comprises one-tenth of one percent of the American public . . . less than one-tenth of those members do more than write their annual dues check . . . Common Cause has largely been an expression of the personal values of its founder and chairman, John Gardner, a classic American aristocrat. [8]

Hence, as E. E. Schattschneider concludes:

The business or upper-class bias of the pressure system shows up everywhere. . . . The data raise a serious question about the validity of the proposition that special interest groups are a universal form of political organization reflecting all interests. [9]

Interest-group conflict, then, reflects merely the most visible disputes between factions within the established elite. Business and labor may contest over the raising of the minimum wage, but both unite to keep demands for radical reform out of the pressure system. The game of pressure-group politics has rules that exclude the masses.

The next test of pluralist group theory is how well—or whether—member demands are translated into political action. Since we have seen in the previous section that membership demands are rarely made, we can hardly expect that organizational leadership is merely a transmitter. Still, group leaders *do* lobby and, to the extent that they are successful, protect their membership (even though the membership may not know or care) in most cases.

The size of the group is an important variable in its leadership's effectiveness. Since elected officials are sensitive to numbers, access to legislators is enhanced by a large membership. However, large groups find it difficult to commit themselves to an explicit position, since their membership is so heterogeneous. The policy positions of mass membership organizations must be vague and broad, devoid of specific content—and thus harmless. The Chamber of Commerce, for example, seeks to represent "businessmen," without regard for the nature of the business. Since intrabusiness disputes are often as bitter as labor-management disputes, the Chamber cannot take a position on many of the legislative and administrative details that involve the economic health of various portions of the business community.

Generally, mass membership groups achieve symbolic success, while smaller, more cohesive groups are able to persist in the pursuit of limited objectives and gradually exhaust their enemy. Tangible benefits are rarely distributed by legislatures, the arena of the large groups; rather, they are distributed in the *administration* of legislation, an activity in which small groups have the advantage. Numbers are not as important to administrators, who are only indirectly concerned with election results. When administrative action reverses legislative intent, "deprived groups often display little tendency to protest or to assert their awareness of the deprivation. . . . The most intensive dissemination of symbols commonly attends the enactment of legislation, which is most meaningless in its effects upon resource allocation."[10]

Among the groups most active in the legislative process are large, well-organized labor unions. Still, many of their achievements are symbolic. Much the same can be said of those civil rights organizations that seek to achieve political results through established democratic procedures. In spite of the turmoil since the 1954 Supreme Court decision outlawing segregation in public schools, the economic condition of blacks has changed very little.

In contrast to these large groups, small and highly organized groups have achieved very tangible benefits. Small groups with narrow interests can achieve cohesion more readily and concentrate their resources on a limited, tangible objective. They can act decisively and persistently, on the basis of precise information. Such organizations are most frequently business, professional, or industrial; these groups employ the majority of lobbyists at the state and national level. Many business people are organized into trade associations representing varieties of industrial and commercial activity. Because their membership is limited to a specific form of business activity—for example, insurance—many trade associations are quite small, some with as few as 25 members. They have disproportionate power with regard to the specific values they advocate, while the business community as a whole fights symbolic battles.

The "businessmen in politics" movement, in which the United States Chamber of Commerce distributed a "practical politics" package to be used in company classes for junior executives, shows how symbolic are the struggles of the larger, undifferentiated business community. Executives spoke of labor's "domination of Congress," alleging business to be "powerless."[11] These practical politics seminars were profitable for those who organized and staffed them and were perhaps symbolically meaningful. Tangibly, however, they were valueless. But business is not powerless with regard to the allocation of tangible rewards to specific kinds of business.

Lobbying

Lobbying is any communication directed at a legislator with the hope of influencing the decisions made. But communications flow both ways; a legislator learns about the interest of nongovernment elites, and these elites are influenced to support the legislator. The lobbyist presents demands on the legislative system from organized interests, participates in negotiations leading to resolution of conflicts, and helps to facilitate elite support for public policy through the lobbyist's involvement in these decisions.

The Federal Regulation of Lobbying Act of 1946 requires the registration of names and spending reports of anyone who "solicits, collects or receives money or any other thing of value to be used principally to aid in . . . the passage and defeat on any legislation by the Congress of the United States." However, enforcement of this law is quite lax, and many of the larger lobby groups—for example, the National Association of Manufacturers, the National Bankers Association, the Americans for Constitutional Action—have never registered as lobbyists. Only about three hundred groups register as lobbyists each year, and only about $4 million per year is reported as having been spent for lobbying activities. These figures grossly underestimate the extent of lobbying in Congress; because the law only requires reports on money spent on direct lobbying before Congress, not money spent for public relations or for campaign contributions. Further, many hundreds of lobbyists do not register on the pretext that they are not really lobbyists, but lawyers, researchers, or educational people. (More restrictive legislation on lobbying might in fact violate the First Amendment freedom to "petition the government for a redress of grievances.")

Political scientists examining the political activity of a group's elite tend to infer the values of the group's followers from the group's lobbying actions, when in fact lobbyists and other organization leaders have much the same function in relation to members as do societal elites to masses in general. They make opinions more often than they follow them.

Whatever its goals, an organization is dominated by its active minority. An organization is composed of formal leaders, active followers, and (the majority of members) passive followers. A "realistic" theory would have leaders (including lobbyists) representing "virtually"—by means of shared values—the aspirations of their followers. Actually, leaders accommodate only those factions represented by active members, whose values do not necessarily reflect those of most members. Since rarely are the followers especially interested in political activities, lack of accurate representation is not crucial to their continued

"Could you hurry and find a cure for cancer? That would be so much easier than prevention."

Copyright © 1977 by Herblock in the *Washington Post*.

The Organized Interests: Defenders of the Status Quo   217

membership. Only when the leaders go beyond the limits of acceptable behavior, and thus become highly visible, will they encounter much opposition.

The discrepancy between leaders' and followers' beliefs is greater than leaders perceive it to be. Interest-group leaders pride themselves on their ability to intuit the followers' feelings. However, like all elites, they are inclined to attribute to followers ideologies that the followers do not possess.

For example, although labor union leaders support civil rights legislation, not many union members do. However, although there is no clear chain of communication between leaders and followers, leaders can still exert lobbying pressure based on the number of their followers. Legislators may *assume* that these numbers are convertible into a deliverable vote. In Oregon, for example, the Oregon Education Association is regarded as powerful by legislators primarily because it has a large membership. The inference is that these members can be turned out to vote in a block; actually, few of the members can correctly identify the position of the organization, and fewer still are likely to follow the advice of group leaders. Therefore, power is less a function of *actual* resources than of *perceived* resources.

However, the surest way to dissipate such a resource is to allow it to be put to the test. An inexperienced lobbyist might threaten to defeat a legislator at the polls, but most skilled lobbyists never mention electoral defeat, because they know that the threat is an empty one. Threats can also produce negative reactions. If directly threatened, a legislator may take an adamant position to prove independence, a highly valued trait in American political lore. Legislators are reluctant to contradict their image of themselves, so unless the threat is capable of being enforced immediately, it is usually ineffective.[12] However, if the threat is only implied, and thus no one has seen evidence that the threat is ineffective, it retains its influence.

Lobbyists' political resources are not immediately convertible into power. The legislator, however, possesses a resource that is highly valued by the lobbyist: the vote. Therefore, the lobbyist seeks to create goods desired by the legislator so that the legislator's resource will be used to the benefit of the lobbyist's organization. The key resource that a lobbyist may develop is *information*. It may be technical, dealing with the details of legislation, or it may be political, concerning the impact of legislation upon the attitudes and behavior of a public. How much a lobbyist can use information as a resource depends on whether there are competing sources of information. In state legislatures, the informational role of the lobbyist is more important because legislators do not have personal or committee staffs. National legislators, on the other hand, are difficult for lobbyists to see, because their other sources of information are usually adequate for their tasks. Thus, there are recent estimates that the efforts of lobbyists in Congress have been highly exaggerated by popular commentators.[13]

Lobbyists can be more effective in state politics because state legislators are comparative amateurs. The turnover in state legislatures is very high; in any given session, a substantial proportion of the legislators are "freshmen." This inexperience makes it difficult for them to acquire an "in group" identification with their colleagues. The institutional life of the state legislature is consequently more easily influenced.

Successful lobbying has little to do with "pressure." In fact, successful lobbying is *negatively* related to the application of pressure. Groups perceived by legislators to be the most pressure-oriented are least likely to achieve satisfactory results. The smaller, persistent groups that concern themselves with tangible rewards have no resources for the application of pressure; yet they are successful, especially at the administrative level, because their personnel gradually identify with the day-to-day problems of a particular industry. This identification results in the desire to protect the group from nonindustry attackers. Agencies originally designed by legislation (in victories won by larger groups) to regulate an industry in the "public interest" frequently are converted to agencies defending the industry against its competition. The members of the agency come to share the values of the regulated industry. This type of interest group's success, while less visible than symbolic victories, is more meaningful, being an allocation of tangible resources.

The Oil Industry and the Energy Crisis: A Case Study

The activities of the oil industry in the energy crisis of 1973–74 present an almost classic example of how a well-organized lobbying group with a near monopoly on critical information can influence government policy making and acquire a beachhead for its interest within the institutional framework of government. The oil industry has always enjoyed special benefits from government in the way of tax benefits and easy access to both elected and appointed officials. However, environmental and international setbacks caused profits of the major companies to dip in the early '70s. The industry responded with massive contributions to the 1972 reelection campaign of Richard Nixon. On January 1, 1974, Representative Les Aspin (D-Wisc.) released a 58-page report on oil industry contributions to the President's 1972 reelection, showing that 413 company officers and principal stockholders contributed a total of almost $5 million to the campaign.

When in the fall of 1973, the oil-producing Arab nations of the Middle East announced an embargo on oil exports to the United States, there was a great deal of publicity about possible shortages of petroleum products. The oil industry had been predicting the currect shortage increasingly since the spring of 1970, and given the fact that it was the only source of industry-wide statistics, few people disputed the industry's story. Although the Arab nations accounted for only a fraction of the oil supply used by the nation, and although later evidence seemed to dispute the effectiveness of the embargo in actually reducing supplies of crude oil, the industry urged the government to institute a rationing system for oil products and offered its assistance.

At the same time the Arabs announced the embargo, they also quadrupled the price of their oil. This led to an enormous jump in oil company profits as the crude oil price increases were used to justify increased retail prices. Again, given the complex nature of the multinational oil companies and the lack of independent cost data, few people were in a position to dispute the industry argument that higher prices and record profits were unavoidable in a time of oil-product shortages to consumers.

The oil industry waged an intensive publicity campaign in the newspapers and on television defending its increased profits and urging the government to institute a rationing system to allocate scarce oil supplies. The industry claimed high profits were necessary to provide an incentive for individual companies to develop new sources of energy. The *Oil and Gas Journal*, a trade publication reflecting the views of the American Petroleum Institute (API), the industry lobbying organization, editorialized that the "profit gains such as those being shown this year must become commonplace. . . . oil companies can make higher profits palatable to the public and government, only as they translate them into investments that will produce more fuel." The *Journal* urged the government to call upon the industry for "assistance" in instituting a rationing system and said that Department of Interior officials "confirm they are looking into the legal aspects of enlisting industry executives on a large scale in a formal operational capacity (to install mandatory allocation of oil) as well as in an advisory role."[14] Industry confirmation of the push for formal, widespread participation of oilmen came from Frank N. Ikard, president of API. Ikard, a former congressman from Texas who served on the tax-writing House Ways and Means Committee, noted that petroleum supply and distribution operations are tremendously complex:

In view of this the government should promptly recruit knowledgeable experts from the private sector in the day-to-day implementation of its program. Simply creating an industry advisory group won't do the job. Oil executives must be able to talk with one another and with top government officials to act quickly to minimize disruption of essential public services and economic activity. [15]

The following week the National Petroleum Council (NPC), an industry organization made up of oil company executives, with quasi-official advisory capacity to the Department of Interior, and responsible for developing statistics used to project U.S. energy needs and resources, said that "mandatory rationing of all petroleum fuels—gasoline, distillates, and heavy fuels—should be undertaken in the U.S. on a national scale immediately." The NPC argued that the nation must establish priorities and determine where cuts in demand should be made. "The general public would undoubtedly prefer some discomforts and inconveniences to idle plants and high unemployment," concluded the NPC.[16] In an editorial entitled, "Rationing is the Answer only if Experts Operate It," the *Oil and Gas Journal* developed the point:

[Rationing involves] a complex producing, processing, and distribution system demanding immediate and accurate decisions by knowledgeable experts. An intricate intelligence system must be maintained to spot critical areas and anticipate needs. Constant product exchanges and transportation shifts must be effected to keep the system in balance. Unless the administration enlists the services of hundreds of experienced oil-operating people, fuel rationing will only compound the shortages into chaos. There just are not enough career government people knowledgeable in operations of the energy system to man the 12 regional and 50 state offices administering the program. There's no time to train them. The only sensible approach is to call in those already trained. Legislation is needed to give emergency antitrust and conflict of interest clearances to free the pool of talent in the petroleum industry for public service. Congress and the Nixon administration should clear these obstacles quickly.[17]

What benefits did the industry hope to gain in return for assuming responsibility for allocating the nation's energy supplies? Another *Oil and Gas Journal* editorial answered the question by stating that "new supplies and not rationing are the ultimate energy solution," and outlined a program for the future:

What is involved are assurances to private industry of free price and reasonable environmental regulations that will not outpace technological capability to comply. . . . Operators must know they can market their coal, oil, or gas over a time frame and at a price that will justify the investment of large sums on a new supply venture. . . . It's too easy for price regulators to pull the rug from under prices.

Coal operators also need market assurances—for instance, that relaxed regulations on sulphur will continue until stock-gas equipment will permit compliance with cleaner, stricter standards.

Other decisions on the environment likewise are overdue: New drilling offshore. Low rating of nuclear-power plants. Ban on strip-mining. In short, nuclear energy and coal eventually must share with petroleum the burden of supplying the nation's needs. And the need to increase supply must not be obscured by the hue and cry over rationing, allocation, shifting refinery yields, Sunday closings, car pools, 50-m.p.h. speed limits, cool houses in winter, or turning off display lights all over the country. The country doesn't have to settle for this kind of future life style. It still has the possibility for energy growth if it adroitly manages its resources. [18]

The editorial went on to applaud a Department of Interior plan to call up 250 "executive reservists" from the industry, saying this "will bring oilmen and gasmen into the government in a major way."

On November 8, 1973, representatives of 20 major oil companies met with State Department officials at the Interior Department and agreed to establish a task force in New York City for pooling information about the location and destination of crude oil in the world. The meeting was held under the auspices of Duke Ligon, a former executive of Continental Oil Company, now serving as director of the Office of Oil and Gas at the Interior Department. The companies represented were members of the Emergency Petroleum Supply Committee, an industry group which meets with government representatives present. Industry sources argued that what was needed to help alleviate the fuel shortages was a policy that would enable oil companies to work together within the United States on pipeline construction, the building of deepwater ports, and exchanges of fuels in different parts of the country. Such cartelization of the industry would require such sweeping waivers of the antitrust laws as had not been given for domestic operations since World War II, but industry sources reported that government officials at State and Interior were "completely receptive" to the idea.

Not all government officials were so sympathetic to the industry, however. Senator Thomas J. McIntyre (D-N.H.) asked the Federal Trade Commission (FTC) to stop the six-month-old "massive advertising campaign" designed to convince the American people that the oil industry is "relatively blameless" for the current shortages:

We are being told that the shortages are the result of misguided government policies and the uncontrolled consumer appetite for petroleum prod-

Arnoldo Franchioni

ucts. *The companies have even suggested the environmental controls have been a major contributing factor to our present crisis. . . . This mass media assault is not only disgusting but blatantly false and deceptive. The firms fail to tell consumers that it was the industry which urged that the quota system be adopted to limit imports into this country and that the government granted the industry a number of incentives such as oil depletion allowance, intangible drilling cost tax deductions, foreign investment credits, and others which the industry said would protect this country's domestic oil supply. The energy crisis will require a tremendous sacrifice by each American and it is a tragedy that a number of major oil companies have attempted to turn this energy crisis into a vehicle to improve their tarnished public image, destroy competition, implement enormous price increases, and radically alter national public policy.* [19]

The Office of Petroleum Allocation was established in the Interior Department in late November 1973, with retired Vice Admiral Eli T. Reich as its head. Reich immediately announced that he planned to draw in 225 oil industry persons within six months to run the program. At the same time, Secretary of Interior Rogers C. B. Morton revealed that 250 oil executives would be recruited by the government to run the various fuel allocation programs. An Interior Department spokesman said, "there is no antitrust or conflict of interest involved" in bringing the executives into government positions. However, President Nixon informally asked the Senate to exempt the oil companies from antitrust laws and other conflict of interest regulations, but he was turned down.

In early December President Nixon established the Federal Energy Administration to coordinate national energy policy, with William H. Simon as head. Simon's appointment was seen as a "plus" by the oil industry. The *Oil and Gas Journal* noted that "incentives to develop domestic resources, and access to them, will have a most articulate and able advocate in . . . Simon."[20] White House energy advisor John Love again asked Congress to grant exemptions from the antitrust laws to oil and other energy companies because "they will be forced to cooperate and plan for mutual action" to implement the proposed emergency energy act.

At the same time Senator Lee Metcalf (D-Mont.) charged that oil companies and a few banks dominate federal energy policy through an "interlocked apparatus" that virtually excludes other concerned segments. Metcalf supported his charge of an "interlocked apparatus" with detailed examples:

1. The White House had recently partially activated the Emergency Petroleum and Gas Administration Executive Reserve, which in event of national emergency is to direct the petroleum industry in the government's behalf. In key positions were twenty-four officials from ARCO, twelve from Sun Oil, eleven from Northern National Gas, and ten from Gulf. The Emergency Petroleum Supply Committee, an advisory committee required to include members from all segments of the oil industry, was completely dominated by the major companies.
2. Other government advisory committees had fifty-four representatives from Standard Oil of Indiana and Socol, forty-six from Exxon, thirty-three from Mobil, twenty from Texaco, twenty from Gulf, seventeen from Citgo and twenty-one from Phillips.[21]

A Senate committee investigating the causes of fuel shortages focused on the Office of Emergency Preparedness, whose function was to regulate oil imports. The committee reported that "the agency's director, retired Army General George A. Lincoln relied for guidance upon executives of major oil companies that stood to benefit from tight restrictions on imports."[22] The investigating committee concluded that the OEP provided "a classic case of a bureaucracy setting a course of action not in response to the nation's needs but to secure its own comfort."

Although the Emergency Energy Act was voted down in December, and Congress failed to waive antitrust and conflict of interest provisions to allow formal appointment of oil executives to government agencies dealing with energy, the *Oil and Gas Journal* announced that "Simon Finds Roundabout Means of Using Oilmen's Expertise." The "roundabout means" was the establishment by Simon of "citizen advisory committees" to provide "expert counsel and information." Simon said that "a prime objective in establishing the committees would be to ensure that the great diversity of interests and talents in our society are considered in the decision-making process and fully utilized." The committees were made up of over 100 oil executives who would act as advisors to Simon in Washington and on six regional committees throughout the country.[23]

An investigation by Representative Benjamin S. Rosenthal (D-N.Y.) showed that within three months of its formation, fifty-eight former oil executives held key FEO jobs, including an assistant administrator, two deputy assistant administrators, two acting division directors, two fuel distribution specialists, three economists, two office directors, sixteen industrial specialists, three case resolution officers, and assorted technical experts and advisors. The list also showed fourteen former oil company people holding jobs in the FEO's key Office of Policy, Planning and Regulation, which acts on pricing matters, draws up regulations, and considers general policy questions.

The FEO defended its position by denying that it had a "deliberate policy of hiring professionals from the oil industry . . . although where such people are available and can be utilized to assist us, we have not declined to employ them." The FEO said its policy was "to employ those persons most qualified to assist in moving in an expeditious and knowledgeable manner to deal with the current national energy emergency." Congressman Rosenthal called the policy an "incestuous game of musical chairs that is played so frequently by industry and government."[24]

It seems clear that the oil industry is in a firm position to strongly influence, if not control, the development and implementation of future energy legislation, bearing out our argument that the groups most effective as mediators between their members and government are small, cohesive groups that represent finite, well-articulated interests. These elite groups are best able to concentrate their resources and activities where they can attain tangible rewards for their members. Government administrators tend to be the targets for such groups. Large groups, on the other hand, are characterized by broad, hazily defined goals, and their activities tend to be directed at legislators rather than at administrators. What rewards such groups receive tend to be symbolic.

How Well Do Groups Integrate the Individual?

What are the effects of group membership on the individual and on society? Belonging to an organization has beneficial consequences for the individual, and therefore, indirectly, for the society, if we assume that social stability is desirable. Although membership in organized groups is highly related to social status (which, as we know, contributes to feelings of political effectiveness), membership in a group contributes to the effectiveness of an individual of any social status. In measuring "subjective competence" (feelings of personal power with respect to government), Almond and Verba found that members of political organizations believed themselves to be more competent than people who did not belong to an organization.[25]

Members of any organizations are more active and interested in political affairs, and are more committed to, and satisfied with, "the system." For instance, members of organizations are more in accord than are nonmembers with community preferences. Community influences are mediated through organizations, contributing to a general commitment by their members to the concept of the community.[26]

Many political scientists believe that groups help stabilize the individual because overlapping memberships create conflicting demands, and thus moderate the effects of each group on the individual. But membership in voluntary associations is stabilizing, not through overlapping of membership, but in itself. Few people belong to more than one organization. Even among those who do, memberships are likely to have a cumulative effect rather than be in conflict. People associate with reinforcing groups; most political discussion takes place among partisans rather than among adversaries.

Further, because people are able to compartmentalize conflicting values, and also because they desire to avoid disagreement, people can be loyal to two conflicting sets of values—and to the organizations that reflect these values. As we noted earlier, mass beliefs may be very inconsistent. Presumably, a Catholic member of a communist-dominated labor union would have a difficult conflict to resolve, provided there was a strong commitment to both ideologies. A study of just such a conflict reached the following conclusions: "Perhaps the most important finding in this study of cross pressures is the small number of individuals who evidenced awareness of conflicting influences."[27]

The Conservative Influence of Organizations

Organizations perform a conservative, stabilizing function for the society. Formal organizations seldom cause social change. Of course, the goals of associations vary, some being more radical than others. But in general, organizations gradually become more moderate as the goal of organizational perpetuation takes priority over the original goal:

> . . . the running of an organization creates problems not related to original goals. These goals of internal relevance assume an increasing proportion of time and may gradually be substituted for externally directed goals. The day-to-day behavior of the permanent staff and active participants (a minority of the membership) becomes centered around proximate goals of primary internal importance, modifying or "displacing" the stated goals of the organization.[28]

In other words, as organizations grow older, they shift from trying to implement their original values to maintaining their structure as such, even if they thereby sacrifice the organization's central mission.[29] Organizations thus come to be dominated by people who have the greatest stake in the existing social system. This is not to suggest that organizations seek no change, but that the extent of change they seek is minimal. If they achieve even a portion of what they wish to achieve, then they have established a stake in the ongoing system and have a rational basis for moderate politics. Social stability is apparently a product of the organizational system, not necessarily because of overlapping affiliations, but because of the intrinsic nature of organizations. Associations that begin with a radical ideology must modify their views to attract the sustained membership necessary for organizational health.

Since groups serve society by cementing their members to the established social system, those who seek to alter this system find organizations an unsatisfactory mechanism. True, some groups are created with radical change in mind, but the process of bureaucratization and the evolution of the membership from "have-nots" to "haves" gradually reduces any organization's commitment to substantial change. Impoverished people and blacks have gained little from groups, because the group structure is dominated by people with a favored position in society. For segments of society effectively barred from other forms of participation, violent protest is the most effective method of entry into the political process. Ironically, if deprived peoples succeed in organizing and achieving a more equitable distribution of rewards, violence will probably decline, to be replaced by organizational activity. In time, the new organizations (for example, the "new left" groups) will develop their own commitment to the *status quo*, thus making the development of more radical groups likely.

As agents of stability, then, groups function quite effectively. Not only do group members tend to feel effective, but they are also more active and interested in political affairs, are more satisfied with the political system, and identify more readily with the community. Because they contribute to the social integration of their members, organized interest groups have a conservative, stabilizing influence on society.

Summary

Pluralism asserts that organized interest groups provide an effective means of participation in the political system for the individual. It contends that the individual can make his voice heard through membership in the organized groups that reflect his views on public affairs. Pluralists further contend that competition among organized interests provides a balance of power to protect the interests of the individual. Interest groups divide power among themselves and hence protect the individual from rule by a single oppressive elite.

Earlier we pointed out that pluralism diverges from classical democratic theory. Even if the plural elite model accurately portrays the reality of American politics, it does not guarantee the implementation of democratic values. Our analysis of interest groups produced the following propositions:

1. Interest-group membership is drawn disproportionately from middle- and upper-class segments of the population. The pressure-group system is not representative of the entire community.

2. Leadership of interest groups is recruited from the middle- and upper-class population.

3. Business and professional organizations predominate among organized interest groups.

4. Generally mass membership groups achieve only symbolic success and smaller, more cohesive groups are able to achieve more tangible results.

5. There is a great deal of inequality among organized interest groups. Business and producer groups with narrow membership but cohesive organization are able to achieve their tangible goals at the expense of broad, unorganized groups seeking less tangible goals.

6. Organized interest groups are governed by small elites whose values do not necessarily reflect the values of most members.

7. Business groups and associations are the most highly organized and active lobbyists in Washington and in the state capitals.

8. Organizations tend to become conservative as they acquire a stake in the existing social order. Therefore, pressures for substantial social change must generally come from forces outside the structure of organized interest groups.

References

[1] Gabriel A. Almond and Sidney Verba, *The Civic Culture: Political Attitudes and Democracy in Five Nations* (Boston: Little, Brown and Co., 1965), p. 245.

[2] David B. Truman, *The Governmental Process* (New York: Alfred A. Knopf, 1951).

[3] George McGovern, "Pluralistic Structures or Interest Groups?" *Society*, vol. 14, no. 2 (Jan.–Feb., 1977): 13–15.

[4] Almond and Verba, *The Civic Culture*, p. 249.

[5] Sidney Verba and Norman H. Nie, *Participation in America* (New York: Harper and Row, 1972), p. 208.

[6] Roberto Michels, *Political Parties: A Sociological Study of the Oligarchical Tendencies of Modern Democracy* (New York: Dover, 1959; originally published in English in 1915), esp. p. 248.

[7] See Robert Hargreaves, *Superpower* (New York: St. Martin's Press, Inc., 1973), pp. 85–90.

[8] David S. Broder, the *Boston Globe*, April 24, 1977, p. A7.

[9] E. E. Schattschneider, *The Semisovereign People: A Realist's View of Democracy in America* (New York: Holt, Rinehart and Winston, 1960), pp. 31–34.

[10] Murray Edelman, *The Symbolic Uses of Politics* (Urbana: University of Illinois Press, 1964), pp. 24–26.

[11] Andrew Hacker and Joel D. Aberbach, "Businessmen in Politics," *Law and Contemporary Problems*, 27 (Spring 1962), 266–279.

[12] Harmon Zeigler and Michael A. Baer, *Lobbying: Interaction and Influence in American State Legislatures* (Belmont, Calif.: Wadsworth Publishing Co., 1969), pp. 120–121.

[13] See, for example, Lester W. Milbrath, *The Washington Lobbyist* (Chicago: Rand McNally, 1963).

[14]*The Oil and Gas Journal* (November 12, 1973), p. 85

[15]*Ibid.*, p. 101.

[16]*Ibid.*, p. 33.

[17]*The Oil and Gas Journal* (November 19, 1973), p. 17.

[18]*Ibid.*, p. 11.

[19]The *Washington Post*, November 23, 1973, p. 10

[20]*The Oil and Gas Journal* (December 10, 1973), p. 30.

[21]The *Washington Post*, December 6, 1973, p. A-11.

[22]The *Washington Post*, December 14, 1973, p. 1.

[23] *The Oil and Gas Journal*, (December 24, 1973), p. 15.

[24]The *Washington Post*, March 6, 1974, p. 12.

[25]Almond and Verba, *The Civic Culture*, p. 253.

[26]Robert D. Putnam, "Political Attitudes and the Local Community," *American Political Science Review*, 60 (September 1966), pp. 646–648.

[27]Martin Kriesberg, "Cross-Pressures and Attitudes: A Study of the Influence of Conflicting Propaganda on Opinions Regarding American-Soviet Relations," *Public Opinion Quarterly*, 13 (Spring 1949), p. 8.

[28]Harmon Zeigler, *Interest Groups in American Society* (Englewood Cliffs, N.J.: Prentice-Hall, 1964), p. 81.

[29]Sheldon L. Messinger, "Organizational Transformation: A Case Study of a Declining Social Movement," *American Sociological Review*, 20 (February 1955), p. 10.

The Presidency in Crisis 10

Government elites in America do not command; they seek consensus with other elites. Decision making by government elites is a process of bargaining, accommodation, and compromise among the dominant interests in American society. Government elites act essentially as go-betweens, mediating, seeking policies that are mutually beneficial to the major interests—industrial, financial, labor, farm, military, bureaucratic, and so on.

Accommodation and compromise, the prevailing style of American politics, are made possible by a consensus that includes fundamental agreement among the nation's elite groups on the worth of the system itself. Compromise is possible because elites do not perceive their interests as irreconcilable. If elite differences in America were fundamental, it would be difficult to find acceptable accommodations, bargains, or compromises.

Bargaining among elites need not be explicit, particularly when elites already understand the interests of other elites. Of course, explicit contracts, by formalizing agreements among elites, minimize the chance of misunderstanding. In international politics, these contracts take the form of treaties; in domestic politics, wage contracts, government defense contracts, and so on. (Probably the most famous explicit agreement or contract among the elites is the Constitution of the United States itself.) But most bargaining occurs as implicit or tacit understandings, in which elites agree to support each other in exchange for "good will" and expectations of future support. "You scratch my back and I'll scratch yours" is the traditional style of policy making in America.

Separation of Powers—Ambition to Counteract Ambition

The potential power of government officials worried the Founding Fathers. They were not so much concerned that a *minority* might seize control of the national government as that the *majority* of people might gain access to the legitimate use of force and threaten the established men of principle and property. There was a real fear that, even under the republican and federal structure of the American government, a majority might still be able to "outnumber and oppress the rest." The Founding Fathers, therefore, sought to place additional obstacles in the way of "an unjust and interested majority."

To provide some "precautions" against mass movements that might threaten the rights of property, the Founding Fathers devised two different but related arrangements—separation of powers, and checks and balances. These arrangements had two goals: first, to make it more difficult for the masses to capture control of the entire government; and second, to prevent government elites from abusing their power and threatening the interests of nongovernment elites.

The idea of a *separation of powers*—that is, the dividing of power among the three branches of national government—was derived from the writings of a French political scientist, Baron Montesquieu, whose two volumes on *The Spirit of the Laws* appeared about 1748. Montesquieu wrote:

In every government there are three sources of power: the legislative, the executive and the judiciary power. . . . When the legislative and executive powers are united in the same person, or in the same body of magistrates, there can be no liberty. . . . Again, there is not liberty if the judiciary be not separated from the legislative and executive. [1]

The separation of powers concept is expressed in the opening sentence of the first three articles of the Constitution, which establishes separate legislative, executive, and judicial branches of government. To further separate these powers, each of the major decision-making bodies in the national government is chosen by a different constituency—the House by voters in the several legislative districts, the Senate by the state legislatures and later by the voters of whole states, the president by "electors" chosen by the voters in whole states, and the judiciary by the president with the consent of the Senate. A sharp differentiation is also made in the terms of office of each of these decision-making bodies, so that the government cannot possibly be completely replaced by popular majority at one stroke. The House is chosen for two years, and the Senate for six; but the entire Senate is not chosen in one election, for one-third of the senators go out every two years. The president is chosen every four years, and the judges of the Supreme Court hold office for life. Thus the people are restrained from bringing about immediate changes in government policy.

The idea of *checks and balances* supplemented the notion of separating power. "Ambition must be made to counteract ambition."[2] Not only did the Founding Fathers want separate branches of government to be responsive to different constituencies, they also wanted to give each branch of the national government some control over the other two. The separate branches of the American government are not independent but, rather, interdependent. They really share power rather than holding separate powers; for each branch participates in the activities of every other branch.

Thus, an elaborate system of overlapping powers and responsibilities was established. The president shares the legislative powers through the veto and through the responsibility to make recommendations to Congress about legislation the president believes to be necessary and expedient. The president can also convene special sessions of Congress. But the appointing power of the president is shared by the Senate, as is the treaty-making power; and Congress can override effective presidential vetoes. The president must execute the laws, but to do so must rely on executive departments, which can be created only by Congress. Moreover, the executive branch cannot spend money that has not been appropriated by Congress. The president appoints judges of the Supreme Court, but only with the consent of the Senate. And the Supreme Court can determine when the president has acted outside the Constitution or the laws of Congress and can even invalidate laws of Congress that are contrary to the Constitution. Finally, Congress possesses the ultimate check on the president and the Supreme Court through its powers of impeachment and removal from office.

Those who criticize the United States government for its slow, unwieldy processes should realize that this characteristic was deliberately built into the government by its founders. These cumbersome arrangements—the checks and balances and the fragmentation of authority that make it difficult for government to realize its potential power over private interests (business, industry, banks, and labor)—were designed by the Founding Fathers to protect the private interests from government interference and to shield the government from an unjust and self-seeking majority. If the system handcuffs government and makes it easy for established groups to oppose change, then the system is working as the Founding Fathers intended.

The Founding Fathers planned well. The system of intermingled powers and conflicting loyalties that they established is still alive today. Of course, some things have changed: Senators are now directly elected by the voters, and the president is more directly responsible to the voters than was originally envisioned. But the basic arrangement of checks and balances endures. Presidents, senators, representatives, and judges are chosen by different constituencies; their terms of office vary, and their responsibilities and loyalties differ. This system makes majority rule virtually impossible.

Sources of Presidential Power

The presidency's real power does not depend on formal authority, but on the president's abilities at persuasion. The president does not command American elites, but stands in a central position in the elite structure. Responsibility for the initiation of public policy falls principally on the president and the presidential staff and executive departments. The president has a strong incentive to fulfill this responsibility; for a large segment of the American public holds the president responsible for everything that happens in the nation during that term of office, whether or not there is presidential authority or capacity to do anything about it. At the very least, there is a general public expectation that every president, even a president committed to a "caretaker" role, will put forth some sort of policy program.

Through the power of policy initiation alone, the president's impact on the nation is considerable. The president sets the agenda for public decision making. The president's programs are presented to Congress in various presidential messages and in the budget, and the president thereby largely determines what the business of Congress will be in any session. Few major undertakings ever get off the ground without presidential initiation; the president frames the issues, determines their context, and decides their timing.

The powers of the presidency and the importance of this office in the American political system vary with political circumstances and with the personalities of those who occupy the office. In debates about the real extent of executive power, the contrasting views of presidents William Howard Taft and Theodore Roosevelt are often quoted as examples of the different approaches individuals take to the presidency. Taft once said:

The true view of the executive function is, as I conceive it, that the president can exercise no power which cannot be fairly and reasonably traced to some specific grant of power or justly implied and included within such express grant as proper and necessary to its exercise. Such specific grants must be either in the federal constitution or in the pursuance thereof. There is no undefined residuum of power which can be exercised which seems to him to be in the public interest. [3]

The alternative view was held by Theodore Roosevelt:

I decline to adopt the view that what was imperatively necessary for the nation could not be done by the president unless he could find some specific authorization to do it. My belief was that it was not only his right but his duty to do anything that the needs of the nation demanded, unless such action was forbidden by the Constitution or by the laws. Under this interpretation of executive power I did and caused to be done many things not previously done by the president and the heads of departments. I did not usurp the power, but I did greatly broaden the use of executive power. [4]

Most evaluations of presidential performance favor the more activist approach to the office. Taft, Herbert Hoover, and Dwight Eisenhower, who took more restricted views of the presidency, are usually downgraded in comparison with Woodrow Wilson, Theodore and Franklin Roosevelt, and Harry Truman, who were much more active presidents.

It is sometimes argued that the presidency has grown more powerful in the twentieth century, but few presidents have been more powerful than Abraham Lincoln, as Wilfred Binkley comments:

Unquestionably, the highwater mark of the exercise of the executive power in the United States is found in the administration of Abraham Lincoln. No President before or since has pushed about the degrees of executive power so far into the legislative sphere. . . . Under the war power he proclaimed the slaves of those in rebellion emancipated. He devised and put into execution his peculiar plan of reconstruction. With disregard of law he increased the army and navy beyond the limits set by statute. The privilege of the writ of habeas corpus was suspended wholesale and martial law declared. Public money in the sum of millions was deliberately spent without Congressional appropriation. Nor was any of this done innocently. Lincoln understood his constitution. He knew, in many cases, just how he was transgressing, and his infractions were consequently deliberate. It is all the more astonishing that this audacity was the work of a minority president performed in the presence of a bitter congressional opposition even in his own party.[5]

Yet, on the whole, presidents of the twentieth century have exercised greater power and initiative than those of the nineteenth century. This increase in power has occurred for several reasons. First, because of America's greater involvement in world affairs and the resulting *increase in the importance of military and foreign policy.* In foreign and military affairs, the Constitution gives the president unmistakable and far-reaching powers: to send and receive ambassadors, to make treaties (with the advice and consent of the Senate), and to direct the armed forces as commander-in-chief. In effect, these powers give the president almost exclusive authority over foreign and military policy in the nation.

A second contributor to a twentieth-century president's power has been *the growth of the executive branch.* The federal bureaucracy has grown into a giant elite structure, and the Constitution places the chief executive at the top of this structure. The Constitution gives the president broad, albeit vague, powers to "take care that the laws be faithfully executed" and to "require the opinion in writing of the principal officer of each of the executive departments upon any subject relating to the duties of their respective offices." This clause gives the president general executive authority over the 2.5 million civilian employees of the federal bureaucracy. Moreover, the president has the right to appoint (and the right to remove) the principal officers of the executive branch of government. The Senate must consent to appointments, but not removals. A major addition to the president's constitutional authority over the executive branch came in the Budget and Accounting Act of 1921, in which Congress vested in the president the control of the initiation and execution of the federal budget. Budgetary control is a major weapon in the hands of the president, for it can mean the life or death of an administrative agency. While it is true that Congress must appropriate all monies spent by executive departments, nonetheless, the president has responsibility for formulating the budget. Congress may cut a presidential budget request and even appropriate more than the president asks for a particular agency or program, but by far the greatest portion of the president's budget is accepted by Congress.

The third reason for the importance of the presidency in the twentieth century can be traced to technological improvements in the mass media and *the strengthening of the role of the president as party leader and molder of mass opinion.* Television brings the president directly in contact with the masses, and the masses' attachment to the president is unlike their attachment to any other public official or symbol of government. Fred I. Greenstein has classified the "psychological functions of the presidency."[6] The president:

1. "simplifies perception of government and politics" by serving as "the main cognitive 'handle' for providing busy citizens with some sense of what their government is doing";
2. provides "an outlet for emotional expression" through public interest in his and his family's private and public life;
3. is a "symbol of unity" and of nationhood (as the national shock and grief over the death of a president clearly reveals);
4. provides the masses with a "vicarious means of taking political action" in that the president can act decisively and effectively while they cannot do so;
5. is a "symbol of social stability" in providing the masses with a feeling of security and guidance. Thus, for the masses, the president is the most visible elite member.

The president has many sources of formal power (see Table 10–1), being chief administrator, chief diplomat, commander-in-chief, chief of state, party leader, and voice of the people. But despite the great powers of the office, no president can monopolize policy making. The president functions within an established elite system, and can exercise power only within the framework of the elite system. The choices available to the president are limited to those alternatives for which elite support can be mobilized. He cannot act outside existing elite consensus—outside the "rules of the game." The president must be sensitive to the interests of major elites—business, agriculture, military, education, bureaucratic, and so on.

Table 10–1
Formal Presidential
Powers

Chief administrator
  Implement policy—"Take care that laws be faithfully executed."
  Supervise executive branch of government.
  Appoint and remove policy officials.
  Prepare executive budget.
Chief legislator
  Initiate policy—"Give to the Congress information of the State of the Union and recommend to their consideration such measures as he shall judge necessary and expedient."
  Veto legislation passed by Congress.
  Convene special session of Congress "on extraordinary occasions."
Party leader
  Control national party organization.
  Control federal patronage.
  Influence (not control) state and local parties through prestige.
Chief diplomat
  Make treaties ("with the advice and consent of Senate").
  Make executive agreements.
  Power of diplomatic recognition—"to send and receive ambassadors."
  Represent the nation as chief of state.
Commander-in-chief
  Command U.S. Armed Forces—"the President shall be Commander-in-chief of the army and the navy."
  Appoint military officials.
  Initiate war.
  Broad war powers.

Of course, on some issues the president may have greater opportunity for mobility and a larger number of alternatives for which elite support can be found. But on many questions of domestic and foreign policy, the president is hedged in by other government elites—Congress, the Supreme Court, and party leaders—and by the demands of influential business, financial, agricultural, and military elites. The Congress can clearly frustrate the president when it chooses to do so, particularly on budgetary questions. Similarly, the Supreme Court may restrict presidential actions. For example, in 1952, within three months after President Truman ordered the government to seize the steel industry to end a strike during the Korean War, the Supreme Court held his action unconstitutional, and the steel mills were returned at once to the owners. President Truman also encountered strong opposition from government, military, and private elites when he dismissed General Douglas MacArthur from his command in Korea for failure to carry out presidential orders. Because of the great following that the distinguished general had in Washington and the country, this action led to cries of impeachment in the Congress. Many presidents have been forced to discard or modify policies because of negative responses from industry, farmers, doctors, union leaders, and so on.

Issues in Presidential Power

For decades, the liberal intellectuals in America praised the presidency and scorned the Congress. Textbooks taught students that the hope of the nation rested with a powerful president; the Congress was viewed as unprogressive, dilatory, even reactionary. Strong presidents—Lincoln, Roosevelt, Truman—were eulogized; weak presidents—Coolidge, Hoover, Eisenhower—were ridiculed. Leading establishment scholars—for example, Harvard political scientist Richard Neustadt—taught that presidents should conduct themselves in ways which would maximize their power.[7] Americans were led to believe that because the president is the only official elected by *all* of the people, the presidential powers would be used to "do good."

But then came two successive presidents—Johnson and Nixon—who were distrusted by most of the nation's intellectuals. The result has been an abrupt reversal of establishment views regarding the presidency. The Vietnam War and Watergate convinced liberal intellectuals that the presidency was too powerful and that the Congress must be prepared to check the actions of unruly presidents. Today most commentators, journalists, intellectuals, and, of course, senators and representatives argue the importance of curtailing the president's war-making powers, overseeing the activities of the White House, and protecting the nation from the abuses of presidential power.

From time to time in America's political history, both liberals and conservatives, responding to the current political situation, have jumped from one side of the argument about presidential power to the other. The lesson to be learned is that arguments over presidential power can never be removed from their political context.

The War-Making Controversy

The American colonists who declared their independence from Britain in 1776 were deeply suspicious of standing armies, and of a king who would send British troops to the colonies. This distrust carried over after independence, contributing to a determination among the Founding Fathers to subject military affairs to civilian control. The Second Continental Congress had general oversight over the conduct of the military during the Revolutionary War. It commissioned George Washington to be commander-in-chief but instructed him "punctually to observe and follow such orders and directions . . . from this or a future Congress." But George Washington himself chaired the Constitutional Convention of 1787, and he recognized the need for a strong chief executive who could respond quickly to threats to the nation. Moreover, he was aware of the weaknesses of civilian militia, and he favored the establishment of a national army and navy.

The Constitutional Convention of 1787 *divided* the war power between Congress and the president. Article I Section 8 says: "The Congress shall have the power to . . . provide for the common defense . . . to declare war . . . to raise and support armies . . . to provide and maintain a navy . . . to make rules for the government and regulation of the land and naval forces. . . ." Article II Section 2 says: "The President shall be Commander-in-Chief of the army and navy of the United States. . . . " In defending the newly written Constitution, *The Federalist* papers construed the president's war powers narrowly, implying that the war-making power of the president was little more than the power to defend against imminent invasion when Congress was not in session. But historically the president has exercised much more than strictly defensive war-making powers. Since 1789 U.S. forces participated in military actions overseas on more than 150 occasions, but Congress has declared war only five times: the War of 1812, the Mexican War, the Spanish-American War, World War I, and World War II. Supreme Court Justice William H. Rehnquist wrote before he was elevated to the Court:

It has been recognized from the earliest days of the Republic, by the President, by Congress and by the Supreme Court, that the United States may lawfully engage in armed hostilities with a foreign power without Congressional declaration of war. Our history is replete with instances of "undeclared wars" from the war with France in 1789–1800 to the Vietnamese War.[8]

The Supreme Court has generally refused to take jurisdiction in cases involving the war powers of the president and Congress.

Thus, while Congress retains the formal power to "declare war," in modern times wars are seldom "declared." Instead, they are begun by direct military actions, and the president, as commander-in-chief of the armed forces, determines what military actions will be undertaken by the United States. Over the years Congress had generally acceded to the supremacy of the president in military affairs. Not until the Vietnam War has there been serious congressional debate over who shall have the power to commit the nation to war. In the past, Congress tended to accept the fact that under modern conditions of war only the president has the information-gathering facilities, the speed, and the secrecy for reaching quick military decisions during periods of crisis.

The war in Vietnam was not an unprecedented use of the president's war-making powers. John Adams fought a war against the French without a congressional declaration; Thomas Jefferson fought the Barbary pirates; every president in the nineteenth century fought the Indians; Abraham Lincoln carried presidential war-making powers beyond anything attempted by any president before or since; Woodrow Wilson sent troops to Mexico and a dozen Latin American nations; Franklin D. Roosevelt sent U.S. destroyers to protect British convoys in the North Atlantic before Pearl Harbor; and Harry Truman committed American forces to a major war in Korea. So when President Johnson initiated bombing attacks on North Vietnam in 1965 and eventually committed more than half a million men to the battle, he was not really assuming any powers that had not been assumed by presidents before him. Perhaps his greatest mistake was his failure to achieve either a military or diplomatic solution to the war.

In the early days of the Vietnam War there was strong support for the war effort among the liberal leadership of the nation, and no one really questioned the president's power to commit the nation to war. However, by 1969 most of the liberal leadership in Congress who had supported the war in its early stages now rushed to assume the image of doves. Indeed, senators argued over who had been the first to change his mind about the war. Moreover, now there was a *Republican* president and a *Democratic* Congress, and congressional attacks on presidential policy became much more partisan. Thus, as opposition to the Vietnam War grew in public opinion, and with different parties in control of the presidency and Congress, the members of Congress now sought to reassert the role of Congress in making decisions leading to war.

A series of attempts was made in Congress to curtail the president's war-making powers by cutting off money for U.S. military activity in Southeast Asia. It was generally recognized that Congress did not have the authority to end the Vietnam War by congressional declaration. However, Congress could set a date after which it would not permit any government funds to be spent in the support of U.S. troops in Southeast Asia. Nonetheless, antiwar legislators were unable to get their colleagues to cut off funds for the war until after President Nixon announced a peace agreement in 1973. Congress then cut off funds for continued bombing in Cambodia. But it is important to note that Congress has never voted to cut off funds to support armies in the field.

In 1973, the Congress passed a War Powers Act that was designed to restrict presidential war-making powers. The President vetoed the bill, but the Watergate affair appeared to undermine his support in this struggle with Congress, and Congress overrode his veto. The act provides an interesting example of the continuing struggle over checks and balances in the American government. It provides that:

I.   In the absence of a declaration of war by Congress, armed forces could be committed to hostilities or to "situations where imminent involvement in hostilities is clearly indicated by the circumstances" only:
   1. To repel an armed attack on the United States or to forestall the "direct and imminent threat of such an attack."
   2. To repel an armed attack against U.S. armed forces outside the United States or to forestall the threat of such attack.
   3. To protect and evacuate U.S. citizens and nationals in another country if their lives were threatened.
   4. Pursuant to specific statutory authorization by Congress, not to be inferred from any existing or future law or treaty unless specific authorization was provided.
II. Required the president to promptly report to Congress the commitment of forces for such purposes.
III. Limited to 60 days the length of involvement of U.S. forces unless Congress by specific legislation authorized their continued use.
IV. Authorized Congress to end a presidential commitment by a concurrent resolution—an action which does not require the president's signature.

The combination of executive failures in Vietnam and executive abuses in Watergate has encouraged Congress to reassert its powers relative to the executive branch. The War Powers Act may be more symbolic than instrumental in times of real crisis: the Congress has supported the president in the initial stages of every U.S. overseas military involvement, including Vietnam. Hence, a real constitutional confrontation between the president and Congress over its implementation is unlikely. However, the War Powers Act is a reminder that the president is a member of a larger elite group. Even presidential command of America's military depends on broad elite consensus.

The Impoundment Controversy

The Constitution grants to the Congress the power to appropriate money for public purposes: "No money shall be drawn from the Treasury, but in consequence of appropriations made by law." There is no doubt that the president cannot spend money that has not been appropriated by Congress. But can the president decline to spend money which *has* been appropriated? Over the years, many presidents have impounded—that is, refused to spend—funds appropriated by Congress. In the early 1970s impoundment involved billions of dollars and became a major irritant in presidential-congressional relations.

Historically, the practice of impoundment arose when presidents confronted changing conditions that eliminated the need to spend money already approved by Congress, or when presidents achieved a program's purposes while spending less than anticipated. Generally, Congress welcomed the return of the money to the Treasury.

In recent years, however, presidents have impounded funds because they disagreed with the objectives of the appropriations, or because they placed a low priority on the programs and a high priority on cutting government spending. Some appropriations were impounded by a president after a presidential veto of the appropriation measure had been overridden by Congress. Indeed, in some cases, Congress has specifically directed the president to spend monies for designated purposes, incorporating anti-impoundment language into law. Conflict over impoundment, of course, was worse when there was a liberal Democratic Congress and a more conservative Republican president. Although the impoundment controversy antedated it, the Watergate scandal certainly contributed to an awakening congressional desire to curtail Nixon's powers.

Presidents have argued that the "executive power" includes the power to control expenditures of executive agencies. Presidents have historically withheld funds from programs that were not working properly. In contrast, congressional members have contended that the president is constitutionally required to "faithfully execute" the laws of Congress, including appropriation measures. The president cannot frustrate the laws of Congress by refusing to spend money for programs established by Congress, simply because the president does not agree with the purposes of the programs. To date, lower federal courts have generally upheld the Congress on this point, particularly where the law specifically mandates the president to spend money for the purposes of an act. But the Supreme Court has not yet produced a definitive decision in the matter, and presidential impoundment continues.

The Executive Privilege Controversy

Executive privilege is an assertion of the right of the president to withhold information, documents, or testimony from either the Congress or the courts if, in the president's opinion, national security or the proper functioning of the executive makes it necessary to do so. The notion of "executive privilege" is derived from the constitutional separation of legislative, executive, and judicial branches of government: the presidency is a popularly elected and constitutionally independent office; neither the Congress nor the courts can compel presidential action or interfere with the functioning of the Executive. The claim of executive privilege is made not only relative to information affecting national security and international diplomacy; it has been claimed on *all* communications between presidents and their own advisors and cabinet members. This is to insure that advisors can be completely candid in their conversations with the president. The legislative branch enjoys a specific constitutional protection of privilege: Article I Section 6 provides that "for any Speech or Debate in either House, they shall not be questioned in any other Place." Presidents have asserted the same privilege, but there is no specific language in the Constitution granting it.

Executive privilege was first invoked *against Congress* by President George Washington in 1796, when he refused a request by the House of Representatives for documents relating to the controversial Jay Treaty with Great Britain. According to Washington, "a just regard to the Constitution and to the duty of my office . . . forbids a compliance with your request." Since Washington's days, every president has invoked executive privilege.[9] However, Congress has never sanctioned the notion of executive privilege, and it has always been a sensitive topic in presidential-congressional relations. Congressional critics of executive privilege argue that it can be used to frustrate congressional oversight of executive actions and to cover up fraud and corruption in office.

Executive privilege was first invoked *against the courts* by President Thomas Jefferson in 1807. Supreme Court Chief Justice John Marshall, then presiding over the trial of former Vice President Aaron Burr for treason, issued a subpoena to President Thomas Jefferson to appear at the trial and bring certain documents from his files bearing on the case. Marshall argued: "That the President of the United States may be subpoenaed, and examined as a witness, and required to produce any paper in his possession, is not controverted." The president, Marshall argued, was subject to law like any other person; the English principle that the King could do no wrong did not apply to the president. But Jefferson saw things differently. He sent the documents to the trial in Richmond, but declined to appear in person. He argued that the Constitution placed higher obligations on him than answering court subpoenas, which would "withdraw him entirely from his constitutional duties" and "leave the nation without an executive branch." More importantly, if the president were obliged to honor court orders, then the doctrine of separation of powers would be destroyed.

The second president ever to be served a court subpoena was Richard Nixon. He was served subpoenas in the Watergate affair from both the Senate Watergate Committee and from the first Special Prosecutor, Archibald Cox. Nixon invoked executive privilege against both the Congress and the Special Prosecutor:

I must decline to obey the command of that subpoena. In doing so I follow the example of a long line of my predecessors as President of the United States who have consistently adhered to the position that the President is not subject to compulsory process from the courts.

The independence of the three branches of our government is at the very heart of our constitutional system. It would be wholly inadmissible for the President to compel some particular action by the courts. It is equally inadmissible for the courts to seek to compel some particular action from the President.[10]

The issue finally reached the Supreme Court in *United States* v. *Richard M. Nixon,* when the second Watergate Special Prosecutor, Leon Jaworski, subpoenaed the President for tapes of presidential conversations with his aides in the White House. A unanimous Supreme Court recognized the legitimacy of executive privilege, but held that such privilege did *not* extend to criminal cases, where the public interest in a fair trial outweighed the public interest in presidential confidentiality. Chief Justice Warren Burger cited the landmark case of *Marbury* v. *Madison* in holding that the president is not above the rule of law nor insulated from orders of the judicial branch. The Court said that executive privilege was not absolute, but limited to "military, diplomatic, or sensitive national security secrets" and other areas "essential to the effective discharge of the President's powers." Even in criminal cases, the Court said that judges must carefully weigh the competing claims of the president, the prosecution, and the defendants; and that judges must screen presidential material themselves to make sure that only relevant criminal evidence is given out.

It is clear that the Supreme Court was trying to assert judicial supremacy over the executive branch while trying to prevent constant harassment of the president from four hundred federal court judges seeking presidential material. President Nixon agreed to abide by the Supreme Court's decision in this case. Since he was facing imminent impeachment, he was in too weak a position to offer further resistance. But the question of executive privilege is likely to be raised again in the future, and President Nixon's case may be cited by both prosecutors and defendants.

Watergate and the Resignation of Richard Nixon

The president must govern the nation within the boundaries of elite consensus. Mass opinion can be manipulated, but elite opinion is a powerful restraint on executive action. Voters may elect the president, but elites determine what is done in office.

The forced resignation of President Nixon is one of the most dramatic illustrations of the president's dependence on elite support in the nation's history. A president who was reelected by an overwhelming majority of the nation's voters found himself obliged to resign his office less than two years after his landslide victory. It is our contention that Nixon's threatened impeachment and subsequent resignation were more than a product of specific misdeeds or improprieties in office. Instead, Nixon's demise was a result of (1) his general isolation from established elites, (2) his failure to adopt an accommodationist style of politics, and (3) his frequent disregard of traditional "rules of the game."

Impeachment as a Political Process

The Constitution defines an impeachable offense as "treason, bribery, or other high crimes and misdemeanors." But impeachment is not really a *legal* process—it is a political process. And Nixon's offenses were political, perhaps more than criminal.* Congressman Robert Drinan, of the House Judiciary Committee that recommended impeachment, explained it directly: "The first illusion we have to break is that you have to prove a criminal offense to impeach the President. This is a political offense."[11] Nixon's former Attorney General Richard Kliendienst put it succinctly, if somewhat cynically: "To impeach the President, you don't need facts, you don't need evidence—all you need is votes."[12]

*The only precedent for a presidential impeachment—the impeachment and trial of Andrew Johnson in 1868—was also political. There was no evidence of President Johnson's personal involvement in a crime for which he could be indicted and found guilty in a court of law. Johnson was a Southern Democrat, a U.S. senator from a seceding state (Tennessee) who had remained loyal to the Union. Lincoln chose him as Vice President in 1864 as a gesture of national unity. When Johnson acceded to the presidency after Lincoln's assassination, he resisted attempts by "radical" Republicans in Congress to restructure Southern society by force. When Johnson dismissed some federal officials who opposed his conciliatory policies, Congress passed a Tenure of Office Act over Johnson's veto, forbidding executive removals without Senate consent. Johnson contended that the act was an unconstitutional infringement of his powers as chief executive. (Years later the Supreme Court agreed, holding that the power of removal is an executive power, and specifically declaring that the Tenure of Office Act had been unconstitutional.) When Johnson dismissed his "radical" Republican Secretary of War, Edwin M. Stanton, Congress was enraged. The House impeached Johnson on a party line vote, charging that Johnson had violated the Tenure of Office Act. The Civil War had left a legacy of bitterness against Johnson as a Southerner and a Democrat. But following a month-long trial in the Senate, the result was thirty-five guilty, nineteen not guilty—one vote short of the necessary two-thirds vote for removal. Seven Republicans joined the twelve Democrats in supporting the President. John F. Kennedy, in his book *Profiles in Courage,* praised the strength and courage of those senators who resisted popular emotions and prevented the President's removal. See Michael Les Benedict, *The Impeachment and Trial of Andrew Johnson* (New York: W. W. Norton, 1973).

The House Judiciary Committee voted in early August 1974 to recommend to the full House of Representatives "the impeachment and trial and removal from office" of President Richard M. Nixon. The Committee charged that the President:

. . . using the powers of his high office, engaged personally and through his close subordinates and agents, in a course of conduct or plan designed to delay, impede, and obstruct the investigation of such unlawful entry; to cover up, conceal, and protect those responsible; and to conceal the existence and scope of other unlawful activities. [13]

Democrats on the committee were united against the President, but Republicans were split, with a majority supporting him. Shortly after the formal vote, however, newly subpoenaed court tapes tended to support the charge that Nixon himself, although he had no knowledge of the original break-in at Watergate, did in fact order the FBI to restrict its investigation of this offense and implied to investigators that the break-in was a CIA operation, which it was not. [14] Following this revelation, pro-Nixon Republicans on the committee announced that they had changed their minds and would vote to impeach when the vote was taken by the full House of Representatives. Senator Hugh Scott, Senate Republican leader, Representative John Rhodes, House Republican leader, and Senator Barry Goldwater, former GOP presidential candidate, met with the President to inform him he could expect to be impeached by the full House, and removed from office by a two-thirds vote of the Senate. In a dramatic nationwide television speech on August 8, 1974, Richard Nixon announced his resignation—the first president in the history of the nation to resign this high office.

The formal charges against the President were serious, but they were not the real cause of his ouster. Nixon's demise was not a result of the fact that the Democratic national headquarters was wiretapped and burglarized; that the president's top White House staff and the president himself attempted to cover up the Watergate affair with illegal payments to defendants and promises of executive clemency; that the president withheld taped conversations and documents bearing on the Watergate investigation from prosecutors, courts, and Congress.

Nor was Nixon's resignation a result of mass demands for his removal. He was reelected with a landslide 62 percent of the vote five months *after* the initial Watergate arrests. He achieved an all-time high approval rating in the public opinion polls *after* initial reports of a cover-up. (See Figure 6–3, p. 155.)

Isolation from Established Elites

Nixon's ouster was chiefly a result of his isolation from established elites and the suspicion, distrust, and hostility generated by his isolation.

Nixon was never fully accepted by established eastern elites. Despite his apprenticeship in a top Wall Street law firm, he was always regarded as opportunistic, uncultured, and middle class by the eastern corporate and financial leaders he served, by influential segments of news media, and by intellectuals in prestigious universities and foundations. Nixon was upwardly mobile, competitive, self-conscious, boorish; he stood in marked contrast to the wealthy, cool, self-assured, aristocratic John F. Kennedy. Nixon fought his way up from rooms over his father's grocery store, through the local, unprestigious Whittier College (California), to Duke Law School (North Carolina), by self-sacrifice and hard work, long hours of studying, and postponement of pleasures and luxuries. In 1952, when the dominant eastern Republicans nominated Eisenhower over the Ohio Senator Robert Taft, they chose Richard Nixon as Eisenhower's running mate in a gesture to the losing western and midwestern interests. Even so, shortly thereafter, they nearly dumped him from the ticket when it became known that his early career was financed by a "slush fund" set up by wealthy Californians. Nixon resorted to a "dirty trick": he appealed for *mass* support in his famous nationally televised "Checkers" speech. His appeal was effective, and it drowned the Republican headquarters in a sea of letters and telegrams from sympathetic viewers. The eastern leadership kept Nixon on the ticket, but they never forgot this resort to demagoguery.

Nixon always stood closer to the new-rich southern and western elites than to the eastern establishment. Nixon was a self-made man in the political world who shared with self-made men of the business world an aggressive instinct, a sense of competition, and a belief in traditional, individualistic values. Yet Nixon tried to straddle both factions in America's elite structure. He served humbly as vice president under Eisenhower; he courted the favors of Nelson Rockefeller; he went to work on Wall Street; and he frequently voiced support of liberal and moderate programs and policies. Indeed, his vacillation between factions led to cynical references to the "New Nixon," the "New New Nixon," and "Tricky Dick." But his personal friends were sunbelt Cowboys such as Charles "Bebe" Rebozo (who started his career as a gas station attendant, opened a successful tire recapping business, expanded into Florida real estate, and later established the Key Biscayne Bank), and Robert Abplanalp (inventor of the spray valve used on aerosol cans and co-owner of Nixon's Key Biscayne Florida and San Clemente California properties). And Nixon's admiration of Texan John Connally was undisguised.

When Nixon came to the presidency, he found a giant Washington bureaucracy, overwhelmingly liberal in its politics, and more responsive to the news media, influential interest groups, and key senators and representatives than to the chief executive. This is how it has always been in Washington. But Nixon sought to gather up the reins of power over the bureaucracy by adding to the size and powers of his own White

"Ask not what your king can do for you . . . but what you can do for my country."

© Szep, *The Boston Globe*

House staff. He attempted to centralize decision making in the White House—his national security advisor Henry Kissinger became more powerful than the secretary of state (which he himself was later to become) or secretary of defense; his domestic affairs advisor John Ehrlichman became more powerful than the secretaries who headed the domestic departments, and his chief of staff H. R. Haldeman became more powerful than anyone else, determining what information the President received and implementing presidential orders. Not only did this style of administration win the President the lasting enmity of the Washington bureaucracy, but it also contributed to his isolation from other elites. Unlike Roosevelt and Kennedy, who deliberately encouraged multiple and often competitive channels of information, Nixon became a prisoner of a single information system.

Nixon's long-standing hostility toward the press, a hostility that was more than reciprocated, contributed immeasurably to his isolation. But it was Nixon himself who, in reaction to a hostile press, cut himself off from the dialogue with influential publics.

James David Barber writes:

Progressively, Nixon isolated himself not only from legislative and executive powers that be, but from his own aides, setting his assistant H. R. Haldeman to the task of keeping the horde at a distance. [15]

Failure at Accommodation

Nixon's personality made it difficult for him to engage in the friendly, hand-shaking, back-slapping politics that his predecessor Lyndon Johnson had developed into a fine art. As a consequence Nixon never really fit comfortably into the accommodationist style of elite interaction. Nixon did not really enjoy politics. He was by nature a "loner." His major decisions were not made in White House gatherings of top officials and advisors, but alone in the presidential retreat at Camp David or at his San Clemente or Key Biscayne homes far from the hubbub of Washington.

Nixon also cut himself off from other elites—representatives and senators could not reach the President, phone calls were shifted to aides, and key influential persons outside the government were seldom if ever consulted. Only the "Germans" at the White House—Haldeman, Ehrlichman, Ziegler, and Kissinger—had direct access to the President. They stood as a "Berlin Wall" isolating the President from other elites—because the President wanted it that way. Those who directed the influential news media (such as CBS News, the *Washington Post*, and the *New York Times*), who Nixon (correctly) perceived as his enemies, were aggressively shut out; Nixon held fewer press conferences than any president since Herbert Hoover.

Nixon complained that his critics blew up a petty incident—the Watergate break-in—out of all proportion to its importance. And indeed the burglary of a party headquarters was trivial compared to ending the Vietnam War, or the trip to China, or the Middle-Eastern crisis. But Watergate's importance grew as the President escalated his defense, challenged the powers of other elites, asserted his own authority, and offended the Congress, the courts, and the press. Liberal writer Arthur Schlesinger, Jr., condemns Nixon in highly partisan terms, but acknowledges that:

Despite Senator McGovern's efforts to rouse the conscience of the electorate, most Americans regarded "the Watergate caper" with indifference if not with complacency till well into 1973, and they began to react only after the issue had changed from the original depredation to the subsequent obstruction of justice. . . . The expansion and abuse of Presidential power constituted the underlying issue, the issue that, as we have seen, Watergate raised to the surface, dramatized and made politically accessible. [16]

It was the President's style to confront crisis directly, to avoid surrender, to test his own strength of character against adversity. His gut instinct in a crisis was to "fight like hell" rather than to bargain, accommodate, and compromise. Nixon viewed "politics" as a burden to be borne, rather than an art to enjoy. James David Barber believes that such political figures eventually become rigid:

Such a President will, eventually, freeze around some adamant stand—as did Wilson in the League of Nations fight, Hoover in refusing relief to Americans during the Depression, and Johnson in the Vietnam escalation. Increasingly, as his stance rigidifies, he will see compromise as surrender, justify his cause as sacred, plunge into intense and lonely effort, and concentrate his enmity on specific enemies he thinks are conspiring against him. [17]

As the Watergate affair broadened and intensified, Nixon increasingly viewed it as a test of his strength and character. He perceived a conspiracy of liberal opponents in Congress and the news media to reverse the 1972 election outcome. He became rigid in his stance on executive privilege, withholding tapes and documents. He came to believe he was defending the presidency itself.

Violating Rules of the Game

The Watergate bugging and burglary of Democratic national headquarters violated established "rules of the game." Elites and masses in America have generally condoned repressive acts against communists, subversives, and "radicals." But when these tactics are turned against established political opposition—Democrats, liberals, and assorted presidential critics—then elite consensus is clearly violated.

Yet despite all of the revelations by the media—the Watergate cover-up, the activities of the Plumbers, the ITT case, the dairy industry case, the President's tax returns and home improvements—Nixon would *not* have been forced to resign if he had publicly repented and cooperated with Congress, the news media, and representatives of the eastern establishment in cleansing his administration.

The direct stimulus to Nixon's impeachment was his firing of Attorney General Elliot Richardson and Special Prosecutor Archibald Cox in October 1973. The story of Richardson and Cox illustrates very clearly the necessity of the president's accommodating established elites. As the Watergate scandal broadened in early 1973, and evidence of a cover-up was exposed, the President's top two White House advisors—Chief of Staff H. R. Haldeman and Domestic Advisor John Ehrlichman—were dismissed. Attorney General Richard G. Kliendienst resigned because, he said, he would be uncomfortable in prosecuting so many close associates. At this point, the President and key elites in Congress appeared to reach an understanding. The President would appoint an eastern establishment representative, Elliot Richardson, as Attorney General, who would appoint a Harvard professor, Archibald Cox, as Special Prosecutor. Cox would have complete independence in conducting his investigations of Watergate. This pledge was made to the Senate during confirmation hearings on Richardson's appointment as Attorney General.

But when Cox was installed in office, he recruited a highly partisan staff of liberal attorneys, and expanded his own investigative activities well beyond the Watergate break-in and cover-up. Later, Nixon began to suspect a conspiracy to destroy him. When Nixon appeared to reach an agreement with the Senate Watergate Committee's chairman and vice-chairman, Senators Sam Ervin (D) and Howard Baker (R), to allow Senator Stennis to listen to certain taped conversations in lieu of turning over the tapes to the courts, Cox objected and insisted on hearing the tapes himself. Cox cited the original promise to give him full independence in pursuing his investigation. Attorney General Richardson backed up his former Harvard Law School professor. Nixon acted abruptly in the "Saturday Night Massacre" to dismiss both Cox and Richardson.

In firing Cox and Richardson, President Nixon made his most serious error. He not only broke a solemn pledge made to the Congress, but more importantly he cut his last ties with the eastern establishment. (Former Harvard professor and Rockefeller Foundation scholar Henry Kissinger would remain as secretary of state to conduct crucial foreign affairs, but the President was now stripped of establishment support in his efforts to avoid impeachment.) Richardson and Cox represented a good-faith effort on the part of the eastern establishment to correct the errors of the Nixon administration. In rejecting these efforts, the President further isolated himself from established elites.

Yet no one in the news media, the Congress, the Democratic party, or the intellectual community could seriously consider impeaching Richard Nixon as long as Vice President Spiro Agnew was next in line of succession. Agnew was even more isolated from established elites than Nixon; indeed, Agnew publicly attacked the "effete intellectual snobs" of the eastern establishment and openly criticized the news media—"a tiny enclosed fraternity of privileged men." So removing Agnew was a prerequisite to any serious impeachment movement.

Agnew was extremely vulnerable to attack; the task of removing him was relatively easy. Agnew had served his political apprenticeship as Baltimore county manager before moving on to the governorship of Maryland and the vice presidency. It was widely known that Baltimore was one of the nation's most corrupt city and county governments. Indeed, for years Washington cocktail parties had been spiced by stories of scandal implicating the Vice President. So all that was required was a thorough investigation—one which revealed that Agnew received cash payments from Maryland contractors as county manager and governor, and, more importantly, continued to receive such payments as vice president.* Agnew resigned after his indictment, pleaded no contest to the charge of income tax fraud (failure to report the payments as income for tax purposes), was convicted and given a suspended sentence. Nixon was now open to direct frontal attack.

Nixon's final line of defense was legal and technical—a feeble plea to abide by the constitutional definition of impeachment, "high crimes and misdemeanors." But the President was really forced to resign because of political acts—his isolation from establishment elites, his failures in accommodationist politics, and his misunderstanding of the rules of elite interaction. As Barber explains:

If this country is to avoid more presidential crises, we need to elect Presidents who enjoy the politics of persuasion—the process of evoking consent, rather than commanding or coercing it. Further, our chief executives should be people committed to working within the balance of institutional roles we have inherited from the Constitutional Tradition. [18]

The Irony of Richard Nixon

It is ironic that Richard Nixon saw himself as a tribune of the people—"the great silent majority"—pitting himself against a liberal establishment that was not popularly elected and did not reflect grass-roots sentiments. Nixon believed he understood "Middle America," and he probably did, since he was Middle American himself. But in the end, established elites were able to turn Middle America against him. Public opinion is unstable, changeable, and susceptible to manipulation by the mass media. In six months in 1973, Nixon suffered the steepest plunge in public opinion approval ratings ever recorded.

Richard Nixon failed to understand that without elite support, even landslide victories at the polls are meaningless. Popular majorities elect a president, but they are not what permits a president to govern. A president can govern only with the support of the nation's elite—a costly lesson Nixon learned in his "final crisis." [19]

---

*There are few senators, representatives, or governors who have *not* accepted contributions from highway and building contractors. This industry is a major source of political campaign financing. However, most politicians place the money received in separate campaign finance accounts and use this money for campaign purposes rather than personal living expenses. If the money is used for personal living expenses, it becomes taxable income under federal tax laws, and it is more likely to be regarded as a "bribe" than a "campaign contribution."

Pluralist writers usually present Nixon's forced resignation as an illustration of the working of American pluralism—executive wrongdoing that was corrected by the operation of our system of checks and balances, competitive parties, and a free press. Such an interpretation fits the prevailing ideology of multiple competitive centers of power, checking each other and protecting against the abuse of power.

But complacency about the survival of democratic values is unwarranted. The White House "horrors" are typical of the behavior of elites when they feel threatened by crisis situations. Nixon was an "outsider" to the liberal establishment. He rejected many opportunities to accommodate with his liberal opposition. Would Watergate-type abuses have been uncovered in a liberal administration? Would Watergate abuses have been uncovered except for the chance occurrence of the capture of the original Watergate burglars? Will future periods of mass unrest be treated any differently by elites because of Watergate?

Jimmy Carter: A New Smile on the Face of the Establishment

James Earl Carter, Jr., is a political "outsider" who was catapulted in less than two years from a Plains, Georgia, peanut farmer to president of the United States. At first glance, Carter's meteoric rise from rustic obscurity to the nation's most powerful office would seem to demolish the elitist notion that leaders are selected from upper-class backgrounds or from the ranks of seasoned officeholders. But a closer examination of elite concerns in 1976—especially concern over declining public confidence in established elites themselves—together with Carter's reassuring, smiling, "we're-okay" style of politics—provides a better understanding of how and when an "outsider" will be selected for national leadership. Specifically, we shall argue that: (1) established elites were concerned in 1976 with declining public trust in national institutions and national leaders; (2) established elites realized that many "old" faces had to be replaced to give a "new look" to the national leadership structure; (3) the "new look" would be cosmetic only, and would include no fundamental changes in policies, programs, or values.

One year before he was elected president, three-quarters of the American people had never heard of Jimmy Carter. He had served only one lackluster term as governor of Georgia. He had never served in Congress, and except for seven years in the Navy, he had never worked for the federal government. He was not even a lawyer. His family's four million dollar holdings in Sumter County, Georgia, may have made them persons of *local* influence, but few *national* leaders had ever heard of Sumter County, Georgia. Carter, however, judged correctly in early 1974 that these political disadvantages could be turned to his favor in an era of popular discontent with national leadership over Watergate, inflation and unemployment, and defeat and humiliation in Vietnam.

The national news media paid little attention to Carter's December 1974 announcement of his presidential candidacy. Media executives and political observers everywhere expected that established leaders—Hubert H. Humphrey or Edward M. Kennedy—would win the presidency in 1976. (Only the *New York Times* argued in early 1975 that a "new face" was needed in the White House; but their choice was Walter Mondale, not Jimmy Carter.) However, Carter knew that the first two presidential primaries were in New Hampshire and Florida. The first was a small state where he had two years to engage in face-to-face campaigning, and the second was a neighboring southern state. These two early primary victories brought Carter the recognition that he needed. In the spring of 1976, discussion within national elite circles turned to the question of whether Humphrey or Kennedy could dispel public doubts about national leadership, or whether these men had been tarnished by past scandals, errors, and humiliations.

Carter defeated weaker candidates in the early primaries—Morris Udall, Henry Jackson, George Wallace, Sargent Shriver, Fred Harris, Milton Schapp, Lloyd Bentson—although he lost to Gerry Brown and Frank Church in later primaries. Throughout early 1976 the real question, however, was whether either of the heavyweights, Humphrey or Kennedy, would enter the race and take the prize away from Carter. In the end, consultations with other top leaders persuaded both men not to run and to allow Carter to become president.

Carter was careful not to offend the established liberal leadership. He supported standard liberal policies, avoided specifics on issues, and campaigned on charm, decency, and brotherly love. He described himself as "a farmer, an engineer, a businessman, a planner, a scientist, a governor, and a Christian." No one campaigned harder, worked more zealously, or hungered more obsessively for the presidency than Jimmy Carter. He was a conservative before conservative groups, a liberal before liberal groups, a farmer in the farm belt, a businessman before the local chamber of commerce, a born-again Christian, a Navy man for the hawks, a friend of prominent blacks, and "good ole boy" to southern whites. His choice of Mondale as vice presidential running mate reassured liberals that he was not a southern populist, and that his values were consistent with those of the leadership of his party and the nation.

Jimmy Carter is in the great log cabin tradition of American politics. Like Andrew Jackson, Abraham Lincoln, and many others before him, he emphasizes his humble beginnings. Carter reminisces about a childhood without electricity; but before rural electrification in the 1930s, no one outside of the large cities in the South enjoyed electricity. The Carter "peanut farm" consisted of over 4,000 acres and a processing warehouse. But his barnyard boyhood, his Annapolis training, his years in the Navy, his rebuilding of the family peanut business, his years as a

Georgia legislator (1962–67), his two campaigns for the Georgia governorship (1966, when he lost to conservative Lester Maddox, and 1970, when he defeated liberal Carl Sanders), and his service as governor (1971–75), all contributed to the development of a tough-minded yet flexible politician. In 1970, running against a liberal opponent, Carter proudly proclaimed himself "an ignorant and bigoted redneck,"[20] but after his election he charmed the black leaders of Georgia by ceremoniously placing a portrait of Martin Luther King, Jr., in the state capitol. He correctly calculated that in 1976 both elites and masses in America would be searching for a new face, an original style, a high moral tone.

Carter brought a new down-home, God-fearing, peanut farmer image into national politics. But he stuck closely to established liberal remedies for society's problems: social programs for the poor and the aged; civil rights commitments for blacks; jobs for the unemployed; a strong national defense; federal aid for cities; support for large labor unions; and even government reorganization, tax "reform," and a balanced budget.

Carter had been introduced to the "political and economic elite" several years before he began his race for the presidency. The Coca Cola Company is the largest industrial corporation headquartered in Atlanta. J. Paul Austin, its chairman of the board and a friend and supporter of Jimmy Carter, nominated the Georgia governor to serve as a U.S. representative on the international Trilateral Commission. The Trilateral Commission, established in 1972 by David Rockefeller (chairman of the board of Chase Manhattan Bank) with the assistance of the Council on Foreign Relations and the Rockefeller Foundation, is a group of officials of multinational corporations and of the governments of several industrial nations, who meet periodically to coordinate economic policy among the United States, Western Europe, and Japan.* Carter's appointment was made by Rockefeller himself and came with the support of Coca Cola and Lockheed, both Atlanta-based multinational corporations. The executive director of the Commission was Columbia University professor Zbigniew Brzezinski (now Carter's national security advisor). The Commission's membership is a compendium of power and prestige; it included Cal Tech president Harold Brown (now secretary of defense); Coca Cola's J. Paul Austin; *Time* magazine editor Hedley Donovan; Paul Warnke, senior partner in Averell Harriman's Wall Street investment firm; Alden Clausen, president of Bank of America, the nation's largest bank; United Auto Workers president Leonard Woodcock;

*Or as Jane Fonda's husband, unsuccessful Senate aspirant Tom Hayden, put it, "The Commission is just another form of colonialism. The basic idea is to act in concert to make the underdeveloped nations of the world economically dependent on the West," *San Francisco Examiner*, December 12, 1976, p. 14.

Bendix Corporation president Werner M. Blumenthal (now secretary of the treasury); Cyrus Vance, senior Wall Street lawyer (now secretary of state); and U.S. Senator Walter Mondale (now vice president of the United States).

Thus, Carter as an "outsider" provides the new face, the smile, the reassuring manner, that a worried establishment perceives as essential in winning back mass confidence in national leadership. At the same time, Carter reinforces established programs and policies; he personifies traditional American values—humble beginnings; hard work; success in business and politics; deep roots in the soil, the family, and the community; and pronounced Christian morals and principles. He is welcomed into top elite circles as a man who can restore mass confidence in public institutions and national leadership, and do so without changing things much.

It is interesting that many "old" faces in American politics disappeared from the national scene in 1976. Senate Democratic Majority Leader Mike Mansfield retired; Speaker of the House Carl Albert retired; Nelson Rockefeller, four-term governor of New York and former vice president, finally shelved his life-long ambition to become president and went into semiretirement. The old Democratic party warhorse Hubert Humphrey not only kept out of the presidential race, but was also defeated by Senator Robert Byrd for the vacant Senate Majority Leadership. Even Senator Edward M. Kennedy kept a "low profile," waiting for a new era in American politics to reassert his national dominance.

Jimmy Carter's rapid rise to national leadership, and his welcome into top elite circles, represents still another tactic available to an embattled elite—replace the old faces associated with past defeats and humiliations with smiling new faces promising honesty, compassion, and good times.

Carter and the Establishment

At the height of the campaign, Carter's campaign director Hamilton Jordan said, "If, after the inauguration you find a Cy Vance as Secretary of State and Zbigniew Brzezinski as head of National Security, then I would say we failed. And I'd quit. But that's not going to happen. You're going to see new faces, new ideas. The government is going to be run by people you have never heard of." Mr. Jordan's faith in Carter's populism was clearly misplaced: Cyrus Vance was named secretary of state and Zbigniew Brzezinski as national security advisor a few weeks after the election. (Jordan did *not* quit.)

The popular misconception that Carter would reach outside of the establishment for men to govern the nation was quickly put to rest when Carter announced his key cabinet selections:

Jimmy Carter's Reorganization.

© Szep, *The Boston Globe.*

Secretary of State.   Cyrus Vance, senior partner, Wall Street law firm of Simpson, Thatcher and Bartlett; a director of IBM and Pan American World Airways; a trustee of Yale University and chairman of the board of trustees of the Rockefeller Foundation; and a member of the Council on Foreign Relations. Vance had served as U.S. negotiator at the Paris Peace Conference on Vietnam, and as secretary of the Army and undersecretary of defense under President Lyndon Johnson. He is closely associated with Rockefeller-supported organizations, including the Trilateral Commission of which he is a member.

Secretary of Defense.   Harold Brown, president of the California Institute of Technology; a director of IBM and the Times-Mirror Corporation; a physicist and defense intellectual, credited with the development of the Polaris missile nuclear warhead; served as secretary of the Air Force under President Lyndon Johnson and helped direct the bombing of North Vietnam; appointed by President Nixon as a U.S. representative to the SALT (Strategic Arms Limitation) talks that resulted in the first strategic nuclear arms agreement between the U.S. and USSR.

Secretary of Treasury.   Werner Michael Blumenthal, president of the Bendix Corporation, one of America's one hundred largest industrial corporations; a naturalized U.S. citizen whose parents fled Nazi Germany in 1938; an earned Ph.D. in international economics from Princeton; former vice president of Crown Cork Co. and special presidential representative on trade negotiations under President John F. Kennedy; a trustee of Princeton and a member of the Council on Foreign Relations.

Chairman of the Council of Economic Advisors. Charles L. Schultze, former director of the Office of Management and Budget (OMB) under President Lyndon Johnson; an earned Ph.D. in economics from the University of Maryland; after leaving OMB, was supported for eight years by the Brookings Institution to develop alternatives to Republican economic policies.

National Security Advisor. Zbigniew Brzezinski, son of a Polish diplomat with an earned Ph.D. in government from Harvard; as a professor of government at Columbia University, was a professional rival of Henry Kissinger's, although both agreed on the fundamental directions of U.S. foreign policy; a member of the Council on Foreign Relations; was named by David Rockefeller in 1974 as executive director of the Trilateral Commission.

Attorney General. Griffin B. Bell, senior partner in the top Atlanta law firm of King and Spaulding; a former partner of President Carter's personal attorney, Charles Kirbo; appointed U.S. Circuit Court of Appeals judge in 1961 by President John F. Kennedy (after he served as Georgia campaign manager for Kennedy in 1960); served on the Fifth Circuit Court until 1976 and heard many civil rights cases during his fifteen years on the bench.

To the Cabinet Carter named two women (one more than President Gerald Ford), one of these women is black (President Ford also had one black on the Cabinet): Patricia Roberts Harris, a well-known Washington attorney and former dean of predominantly black Howard University Law School, was named secretary of housing and urban development. Ms. Harris is also a director of IBM, Chase Manhattan Bank, Scott Paper Co., and a member of the Council on Foreign Relations. Her law partner is Sargent Shriver, brother-in-law of Edward M. Kennedy. She was U.S. Ambassador to Luxembourg under President Lyndon Johnson. Juanita M. Kreps, vice president of Duke University, was named secretary of commerce. She has an earned Ph.D. in economics from Duke. She is a director of J. C. Penney Co., Western Electric, Eastman Kodak, Blue Cross-Blue Shield, R. J. Reynolds Tobacco, and North Carolina National Bank. She was also a director of the New York Stock Exchange. Thus, "minorities" are no better represented in the Carter Cabinet than are "new faces."

Carter's early association with the Rockefeller-supported Trilateral Commission appeared to influence his Cabinet selections. Among the Commission's eighty members are Secretary of State Cyrus Vance, Secretary of Defense Harold Brown, National Security Advisor Zbigniew Brzezinski, and Secretary of the Treasury Werner Michael Blumenthal.

Carter also named James R. Schlesinger as a Cabinet-level energy advisor, with a view toward creating a new department to deal with energy policy. This is the same Schlesinger who served as secretary of defense under President Nixon and was former director of the CIA. Carter's appointment of Georgia Representative Andrew Young as ambassador to the United Nations was widely heralded as a major breakthrough for blacks. Young was an early member of the Southern Christian Leadership Conference, directed by Martin Luther King, Jr.; Young was beaten and jailed in Birmingham in 1963 with King. Young helped to bring King's father and widow into Carter's camp during the campaign, and helped Carter survive the "ethnic purity" remark that might have alienated his black political support. But the UN ambassadorship is a traditional dumping ground for political figures who are too important to be ignored but who carry little influence with the president (for example, Adlai Stevenson, Daniel Patrick Moynihan, William Scranton). The surprise is that the handsome, articulate Young accepted this largely ceremonial position.

Other Executive Elites

The presidency is not one person, but more than five thousand permanent employees in the executive office of the president (Figure 10–1), which is composed of the White House Office, the Bureau of the Budget, the Council of Economic Advisers, the National Security Council, the National Aeronautics and Space Council, the Office of Emergency Planning, and the Office of Science and Technology. In addition, there is the presidential Cabinet, consisting of heads of twelve major executive departments. Finally, there are more than forty independent agencies that function outside the regular departmental organization of the executive branch, including the Interstate Commerce Commission, the Federal Reserve Board, the Federal Trade Commission, the Federal Power Commission, the Federal Communications Commission, the Securities and Exchange Commission, the National Labor Relations Board, the Civil Aeronautics Board, and the Atomic Energy Commission.

The White House Staff

Closest to the president is a group of aides and assistants who work with the chief executive in the White House Office, which is organized as the president sees fit. These aides and assistants perform whatever duties the president assigns them. There is usually a chief of staff, a press secretary, an appointment secretary, and one or more special assistants for liaison with Congress. Some of the president's assistants have ad hoc

Figure 10–1
The Government
Organization of the
United States

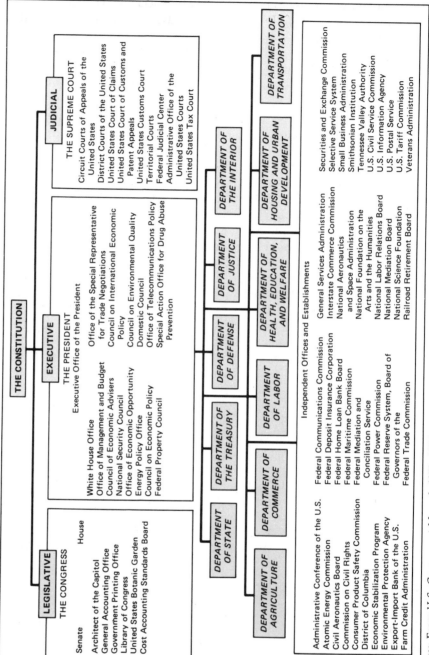

THE CONSTITUTION

LEGISLATIVE

THE CONGRESS

Senate   House

Architect of the Capitol
General Accounting Office
Government Printing Office
Library of Congress
United States Botanic Garden
Cost Accounting Standards Board

EXECUTIVE

THE PRESIDENT
Executive Office of the President

White House Office
Office of Management and Budget
Council of Economic Advisers
National Security Council
Office of Economic Opportunity
Energy Policy Office
Council on Economic Policy
Federal Property Council

Office of the Special Representative
  for Trade Negotiations
Council on International Economic
  Policy
Council on Environmental Quality
Domestic Council
Office of Telecommunications Policy
Special Action Office for Drug Abuse
  Prevention

JUDICIAL

THE SUPREME COURT

Circuit Courts of Appeals of the
  United States
District Courts of the United States
United States Court of Claims
United States Court of Customs and
  Patent Appeals
United States Customs Court
Territorial Courts
Federal Judicial Center
Administrative Office of the
  United States Courts
United States Tax Court

DEPARTMENT OF AGRICULTURE
DEPARTMENT OF COMMERCE
DEPARTMENT OF STATE
DEPARTMENT OF THE TREASURY
DEPARTMENT OF DEFENSE
DEPARTMENT OF LABOR
DEPARTMENT OF HEALTH, EDUCATION, AND WELFARE
DEPARTMENT OF JUSTICE
DEPARTMENT OF THE INTERIOR
DEPARTMENT OF HOUSING AND URBAN DEVELOPMENT
DEPARTMENT OF TRANSPORTATION

Independent Offices and Establishments

Administrative Conference of the U.S.
Atomic Energy Commission
Civil Aeronautics Board
Commission on Civil Rights
Consumer Product Safety Commission
District of Columbia
Economic Stabilization Program
Environmental Protection Agency
Export-Import Bank of the U.S.
Farm Credit Administration

Federal Communications Commission
Federal Deposit Insurance Corporation
Federal Home Loan Bank Board
Federal Maritime Commission
Federal Mediation and
  Conciliation Service
Federal Power Commission
Federal Reserve System, Board of
  Governors of the
Federal Trade Commission

General Services Administration
Interstate Commerce Commission
National Aeronautics
  and Space Administration
National Foundation on the
  Arts and the Humanities
National Labor Relations Board
National Mediation Board
National Science Foundation
Railroad Retirement Board

Securities and Exchange Commission
Selective Service System
Small Business Administration
Smithsonian Institution
Tennessee Valley Authority
U.S. Civil Service Commission
U.S. Information Agency
U.S. Postal Service
U.S. Tariff Commission
Veterans Administration

Source: From *U.S. Government Manual, 1973–1974.*

assignments, while others have a particular specialty. Theodore Sorensen, special assistant to President Kennedy, defined the role of the White House staff as the auxiliary eyes and ears of the president, with responsibilities as broad as those of the president.[21]

Increasingly, White House staff personnel have come to exercise great power in the name of the president. They frequently direct affairs in the name of the president ("The president has asked me to tell you. . . ." "The president wants you to. . . ." etc.), but the president may have little direct oversight of their activities. Even more serious is the fact that staffers come into power with little preparation or experience for elite membership. Often their training consists of nothing more than serving as "advance guard" in presidential election campaigns—scheduling presidential appearances, handling campaign advertising, and fetching coffee and doughnuts. Staffers are valued not for their independent contributions to policy but rather for their personal loyalty to the president. When, for example, President Johnson praised his staff, it was in terms like these:

[Domestic advisor Jack Valenti] is about the best fellow with me. He gets up with me every morning. He stays with me until I go to bed at night, around midnight, and he is the only one who can really take it. The rest of these fellows are sissies. [22]

Frequently, in recent presidential administrations, these men have embarrassed the president: Truman's personal secretary went to jail for fixing a tax case; Eisenhower's "Assistant to the President," Sherman Adams, retired in disgrace for accepting expensive gifts; Johnson's White House advisor, Walter Jenkins, was convicted of a homosexual assault; and Nixon's original White House staff were nearly all indicted in the Watergate scandal.

Executive Agencies

The Office of Management and Budget (OMB) is the largest agency in the executive office of the president. The function of OMB is to prepare the budget of the United States for the president to submit to Congress. No money may be spent by the federal government without appropriations by Congress, and all requests for congressional appropriations must be cleared through OMB. This gives OMB great power over the executive branch of government. Since all agencies request more money than they can receive, the primary responsibility for reducing budget requests rests with the bureau. The bureau reviews, reduces, and approves estimates submitted by departments and agencies (subject, of course, to their appeal to the president), and it also continuously scrutinizes the organization and operations of executive agencies so that changes promoting efficiency and economy can be recommended. Like members of the White House staff, the top officials of OMB are solely responsible to the president, and they are supposed to reflect the president's goals and priorities in their decision making.

The Council of Economic Advisers, created by the Employment Act of 1946, is composed of three professional economists of high standing, appointed by the president with the consent of the Senate. The functions of the council are to analyze trends in the economy and to recommend to the president the fiscal and monetary policies necessary to avoid both depression and inflation. In addition, the council prepares the Economic Report that the Employment Act of 1946 requires the president to submit to Congress each year. The Economic Report, together with the annual budget message to Congress, gives the president the opportunity to present broadly the major policies of that administration.

The National Security Council resembles a cabinet; it is composed of the president as chairman, the vice president, the secretary of state, the secretary of defense, and the director of the Office of Emergency Planning (a minor unit in the executive office). The chairman of the Joint Chiefs of Staff and the director of the Central Intelligence Agency are advisors to the Security Council. The staff of the council is headed by a special assistant to the president for national security affairs. The purposes of the National Security Council are to advise the president on security policy and to coordinate foreign, military, and domestic policies. However, presidents do not rely exclusively on the National Security Council for direction in major foreign and military decisions.

Cabinet officers in the United States are powerful because they sit at the heads of giant administrative organizations. The secretary of state, the secretary of defense, the secretary of the treasury, the attorney general, and to a lesser extent, the other departmental secretaries are all men of power and prestige in America. But the Cabinet, as a council, rarely makes policy.[23] Seldom does a strong president hold a Cabinet meeting to decide important policy questions. More frequently, he knows what he wants and is inclined to hold Cabinet meetings to help him sell his views.

There are forty independent executive agencies that function outside the departmental organization. Some are small and obscure, while others are large and powerful. The independent regulatory commissions are usually headed by boards or commissions of five to eleven members appointed by the president but free from direct responsibility to the White House. Members are appointed for fixed overlapping terms and are not easily removed from office. The first regulatory agency was the Interstate Commerce Commission, created in 1887; it was followed by the Federal Reserve Board (1913), the Federal Trade Commission (1915), the Federal Power Commission (1920), the Federal Communications Commission (1934), the Securities and Exchange Commission (1934), the National Labor Relations Board (1935), the Civil Aeronautics Board (1938), and the Atomic Energy Commission (1946). All of these regulatory commissions engage in policy making, regulation, and quasi-judicial activities, mostly in the economic sphere. These commissions exercise tremendous power in transportation (railroads, buses, trucks, pipelines, the merchant marine, and airlines); communications (telephone, telegraph, radio, and television); power and natural resources (electricity, water and flood control, and natural gas); unfair trade practices in industry and commerce; unfair labor practices in labor-

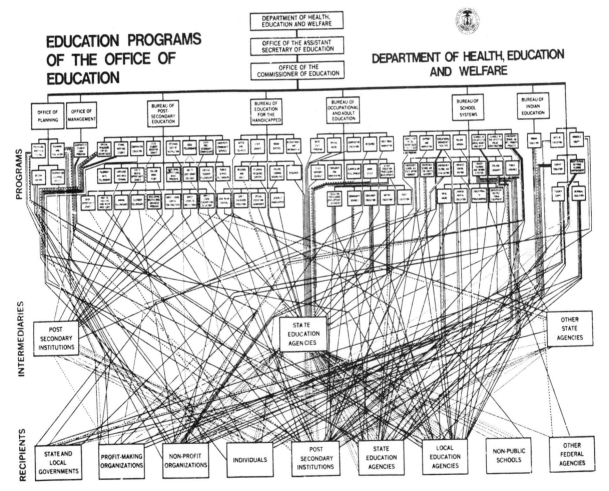

Chart from Department of Health, Education, and Welfare.

management relations; and banking practices, credit policies, issuance of securities, and trading in national stock markets.

The Regulatory Bureaucracy

The regulatory commissions generally represent the industry they are supposed to regulate, rather than "the people." One reason is that commission members are usually selected from the industry that they are supposed to regulate. As Marver Bernstein points out, "Expertness plays into the hands of regulated interest."[24] The commissions usually regard the industries they are supposed to regulate as clients who need to be promoted and protected. While the commissions may act against wayward members of an industry, they seldom do anything that is not clearly acceptable to industry leaders.

The close relationship between regulatory bureaucracies and their clientele groups is based on a common resource: expertise. The Department of Health, Education and Welfare looks to schools of medicine, education, and social work for its personnel. The Department of Defense finds the armed services convenient recruiting grounds, and the Federal Energy Administration is heavily staffed with oil company executives. Sharing a common background, they share a common understanding of "their" problems. Each agency, and its supporting clientele group, views "outsiders" with suspicion and is hostile toward their attempts at participation, for the problems that each agency administers in the interests of its clientele group are technical and complex. As a new agency is created (as, for example, the Federal Energy Agency was in 1974), the enabling legislation encourages (or occasionally mandates) "maximum feasible participation." How is such participation to be achieved? Expertise, an essential political resource in administrative politics, can only be acquired by those few whose lives are spent in active personal pursuit of professionalism.

Expertise is not, of course, neutral, nor is expertise necessarily better than common sense. President Kennedy relied on CIA experts about Cuban military strength, and President Johnson was continually deceived by Pentagon estimates of North Vietnamese military strength. More recently, federal energy experts, supported by oil companies, assured Congress (and the president) that the Alaska pipeline was essential if we were to become less dependent upon foreign oil. Unfortunately, no experts (either public or private) revealed that, once the oil arrived on the West Coast it could not be refined (because the oil companies had not expanded their refinery capacity).

Yet, right or wrong, expertise is a growing resource as we grope continuously, and as yet unsuccessfully, for a national energy policy. Both presidents Ford and Carter recommended the creation of a new Cabinet-level energy office, which will, of necessity, be staffed by experts provided by client groups. The trend toward regulation of energy at the expense of nonexpert influence follows a typical pattern. Agencies created to "regulate" an industry in the "public interest" soon become that industry's mouthpiece within the government. Presidents Kennedy, Johnson, Nixon, Ford, and Carter recognized the close relationship between bureaucracies and client groups and all supported deregulation (that is, "free enterprise"). Proposals to reduce the control of the Interstate Commerce Commission and Civil Aeronautics Board over railroads, interstate trucking, and airlines have met with substantial and unified opposition by the "regulating" agencies and the "regulated" industries, which have argued that they would be placed "in jeopardy" by free competition.

A probable model for the sharing of information between technological elites is the Federal Reserve Board, which has substantial control over the availability of capital for credit. The Federal Reserve Board (FRB) is composed of seven persons appointed by the president with the consent of the Senate for staggered terms of fourteen years; a chairman is designated by the president from among its members. The Federal Reserve Board is essentially the governing board of the nation's banking system. However, Federal Reserve Board members are generally bankers themselves, and financial support for the Federal Reserve System comes from payments made by banks that are members of the system (while only half the nation's banks are members of the Federal Reserve System, this half possesses over 85 percent of all deposits). The policies of the FRB toward the supplies of money and credit in the nation, which profoundly affect the state of the economy, generally reflect the views of bankers in economic matters. Neither the president nor Congress has direct control over the activities of the FRB.

Summary

Government elites in America do not command; they seek consensus. Government decision making involves bargaining, accommodation, and compromise among government and nongovernment elites. Our examination of the crisis of the presidency provides clear evidence of the consensual nature of elite interaction, and the heavy price a president must pay for failure to pursue accommodationist policies.

1. The "separation of powers" system was designed to make it difficult for masses to capture control of the entire government, and to prevent government elites from abusing their power and threatening the interests of private elites. Not only did the Founding Fathers want separate branches of government to be responsive to different interests, they also wanted to give each branch of the national government some opportunity to control and check the activities of the others. In other words, the system was designed to insure bargaining and compromise.

2. The president is the first among equals of America's elites. Presidential power depends not on formal authority but on personal abilities of persuasion. Moreover, the president must still function within the established elite system. The choices available to the president are limited to alternatives for which elite support can be mobilized. Despite access to mass opinion, the president can be effectively checked by other public and private elites.

3. Traditionally, most presidential decisions were made in consultation with key elite members inside and outside of government. These decisions reflect elite consensus, and, moreover, are incremental—they involve marginal shifts in public policy rather than radical changes in national purposes or objectives.

4. In the twentieth century, presidential power has increased as a result of the increased importance of military and foreign policy in national life—areas in which the president has greatest constitutional powers. The growth of the executive branch of government, and the increased visibility of the president in the mass media, also contribute to the growth of presidential power.

5. Controversies over presidential power can never be removed from their political context. Recently Congress has sought to curtail presidential powers over war-making, impoundment of appropriated funds, and "executive privilege."

6. The forced resignation of President Nixon was a dramatic illustration of the president's dependence on elite support. A president must govern within the boundaries of elite consensus or face removal from office. The president can be removed not only for "high crimes and misdemeanors," but also for *political* offenses—violating elite consensus.

7. The resignation of Nixon was a product not only of specific improprieties in office, but also of his isolation from established elites, his failure to adopt an accommodationist style of politics, and his disregard of traditional rules of the game.

8. Popular majorities may select the president, but they do not permit a president to govern. A president with an overwhelming electoral majority in November might be fighting to hold onto the office the next year. A president can only govern with the support of the nation's elite.

9. Established elites who are concerned with declining public trust and confidence frequently turn to "new faces" to provide the appearance of change. But the change is cosmetic only and does not include fundamental change in programs, policies, or values. Jimmy Carter's rapid rise to the presidency may be attributed to the need to find a "new face" to reassure the masses.

References

[1]Baron de Montesquieu, *The Spirit of the Laws.*

[2]James Madison, Alexander Hamilton, and John Jay, *The Federalist* No. 51 (New York: Modern Library, 1937).

[3]William Howard Taft, *Our Chief Magistrate and His Powers* (New York: Columbia University Press, 1938), p. 138. Reprinted in John P. Roche and L. W. Levy (eds.) *The Presidency* (New York: Harcourt Brace Jovanovich, Inc., 1964), p. 23.

[4]From Arthur B. Tourtellot, *President on the Presidency* (Garden City, N.Y.: Doubleday & Co., 1964), pp. 55–56.

[5]Wilfred E. Binkley, *President and Congress* (New York: Alfred A. Knopf, 1947), p. 127.

[6]Fred I. Greenstein, "The Psychological Functions of the Presidency for Citizens," in Elmer E. Cornwell (ed.), *The American Presidency: Vital Center* (Chicago: Scott, Foresman and Co., 1966), pp. 30–36.

[7]Richard Neustadt, *Presidential Power* (New York: John Wiley, 1960).

[8]Quoted in *Congressional Quarterly*, "The Power of the Pentagon" (Washington: Congressional Quarterly, Inc., 1972), p. 42.

[9]*Congressional Quarterly* (February 10, 1973), p. 295.

[10]*Congressional Quarterly* (July 28, 1973), p. 2032.

[11]*Congressional Quarterly* (January 26, 1974), p. 159.

[12]*Ibid.*, p. 127.

[13]House Judiciary Committee, Bill of Impeachment Against Richard M. Nixon, reprinted in *Newsweek*, August 5, 1974.

[14]Transcript of subpoenaed conversations between President Richard M. Nixon and H. R. Haldeman on June 23, 1972 (six days after the break-in), reprinted in *Time*, August 19, 1974.

[15]James David Barber, *The Presidential Character* (Englewood Cliffs, N.J.: Prentice-Hall, Inc., 1972), pp. 423–424.

[16]Arthur Schlesinger, Jr., *The Imperial Presidency* (Boston: Houghton Mifflin, 1973), p. 265.

[17]James David Barber, "Tone-Deaf in the Oval Office," *Saturday Review* (January 12, 1974), p. 14.

[18]*Ibid.*, p. 11.

[19]For further information on Richard M. Nixon's career, see his partial autobiography, *Six Crises* (Garden City, N.Y.: Doubleday, 1962).

[20]*Congressional Quarterly Weekly Report*, July 24, 1976.

[21]See Theodore C. Sorensen, *Decision Making in the White House* (New York: Columbia University Press, 1963).

[22]Quoted in Barber, p. 81.

[23]See Richard F. Fenno, Jr., *The President's Cabinet* (Cambridge, Mass.: Harvard University Press, 1959).

[24]Marver H. Bernstein, *Regulating Business by Independent Commissions* (Princeton, N.J.: Princeton University Press, 1965), p. 118.

Congress: The Legislative Elite

11

Congress was established to represent the people in policy making. But how does Congress "represent" the people, and who are "the people"? Because of the way congressmen are elected, Congress tends to represent local elites in America and thereby injects a strong parochial influence into national decision making. Legislators are part of local elite structures; they retain their local businesses, club memberships, and religious affiliations. They are also recruited by local elites rather than national elites. They are not responsible to national political leaders but rather to leaders within their home constituency. Thus, congressional members represent many small segments of the nation rather than the nation as a whole.

The "representational bias" of Congress begins with recruitment. Senators and representatives are seldom recruited from the masses, but from the well-educated, prestigiously employed, affluent upper and upper-middle classes.[1] Only a small minority come from families of wage earners or salaried workers.

Their own occupations also show that congressional members are generally of higher social standing than their constituents; professional

The Social Backgrounds of Congress: The Class Bias

and business occupations dominate the halls of Congress. One reason for this is, of course, that candidates for Congress are more likely to be successful if their occupations are socially "respectable" and provide opportunities for extensive public contacts. The lawyer, insurance broker, farm implement dealer, and realtor establish in their business the wide circle of friends necessary for political success. Another, more subtle reason is that successful candidates must have occupations with flexible work responsibilities. The lawyer, landowner, or business owner can adjust work responsibilities to the campaign and then the legislative schedule, but the office manager cannot.

The overrepresentation of lawyers as an occupational group in Congress and other public offices is particularly marked, since lawyers constitute no more than two-tenths of 1 percent of the labor force.[2] Lawyers have always played a prominent role in the American political system. Twenty-five of the fifty-two signers of the Declaration of Independence and thirty-one of the fifty-five members of the Continental Congress were lawyers. The legal profession has also provided 70 percent of the presidents, vice presidents, and Cabinet officers of the United States; 50 percent of the U.S. senators from 1947 to 1957; and 56 percent of the members of the House of Representatives from 1949 to 1951. In 1973, 63 percent of the senators and 48 percent of the representatives were lawyers. Lawyers are in a reasonably high-prestige occupation, but so are physicians, businessmen, and scientists. Why, then, do lawyers dominate Congress?

It is sometimes argued that the lawyer brings a special kind of skill to Congress. The lawyer's occupation is the representation of clients; therefore, no great change in occupation occurs when representing clients in private practice gives way to representing constituents in Congress. Also, the lawyer, trained to deal with public policy as it is reflected in the statute books, may be reasonably familiar with public policy before entering Congress. But professional skills alone cannot explain the dominance of lawyers in public office. Of all the high-prestige occupations, only lawyers can really afford to neglect their careers for political activities. The physician, the corporate manager, and the scientist find the neglect of their vocation for political activity very costly. But political activity can be a positive advantage to the occupational advancement of a lawyer—free public advertising and opportunities to make contacts with potential clients are two important benefits. Moreover, lawyers have a natural monopoly on public offices in the law and the court system, and the offices of judge or prosecuting attorney often provide lawyers with steppingstones to higher public office, including Congress.

To sum up, information on the occupational background of congressional members indicates that more than high social status is necessary for election to Congress. It is also helpful to have experience in personal relations and public contacts, easy access to politics, and a great deal of free time to devote to political activity.[3]

Congressional members are among the most-educated occupational groups in the United States. They are much better educated than the populations they represent. Of course, their education reflects their occupational background and their middle- and upper-class origins. White Anglo-Saxon Protestants (WASPs) are substantially overrepresented in Congress. About two-thirds of the House and three-fourths of the Senate are Protestant. The main minority groups—blacks, Catholics, Jews, and foreign-born—have disproportionately fewer seats in Congress. Religious denominations of high social status, such as Episcopalians and Presbyterians, are regularly overrepresented in Congress. About one-third of the United States senators and representatives are affiliated with the Congregational, Presbyterian, Episcopalian, or Unitarian churches. Although the representation of Catholics and Jews has been increasing in recent years, evidence indicates that these minorities can win representation in Congress only in districts in which they constitute a majority or near majority. Nearly all Catholic and Jewish members are elected from northern and industrial states, notably from major cities; Mississippi, Georgia, and South Carolina send congressional delegations composed largely of Baptists and Methodists; whereas New York City sends delegations almost solidly Catholic and Jewish. Apparently congressional members must be of the religious and ethnic backgrounds dominant in their districts.

If blacks were to have representation in Congress equal to their proportion of the population, there would be forty-three blacks in the House of Representatives and ten in the Senate. However, not until 1966 was the first black, Republican Edward Brooke of Massachusetts, popularly elected to the Senate; in the Ninety-Fourth Congress (1974–1975), there were sixteen blacks in the House of Representatives. Their districts were chiefly the black ghetto areas of large cities—Chicago, New York, Philadelphia, Los Angeles, Cleveland, and Baltimore. All were Democrats.

Larger Constituencies Give Legislators More Freedom

Congressional members must be concerned with the interests of local elites; they are not as free as the president or the executive elites to direct themselves to national problems or concerns. Moreover, congressional members represent a more homogeneous constituency than the president; a congressional constituency is usually well defined—rural or urban, mining or manufacturing or agricultural, defense-oriented or cotton-producing or citrus-growing. A president, on the other hand, must please a much wider and more heterogeneous constituency. No

Elite-Mass Interaction: Legislators and the Folks Back Home

single interest need dominate his judgment; he is freer to seek bargains, accommodations, and compromises among separate elites. He is freer to be concerned about the general welfare, and he can take a more cosmopolitan view of national affairs. Similarly, senators, who represent larger constituencies than representatives, are somewhat less parochial and are freer to be concerned about the general public welfare. Lewis A. Froman presents evidence that senators support "liberal" measures more often than do representatives, and he suggests that this difference in political behavior may result from the narrower constituencies of representatives and the localism of their political orientation.[4]

The inference here is not that larger constituencies are more liberal, but rather that they are more heterogeneous. There is more of an opportunity to pick and choose from among the various demands. The comparative liberalism of the Senate appears to be remarkably stable. A study of all employment, housing, health care, education, and welfare measures from 1955 through 1970 reveals the Senate to be consistently more inclined than the House toward spending for such legislation.[5] What does such a phenomenon tell us about the representation of constituents by legislators? Between the Senate and the House of Representatives, which is "right," that is, more reflective of the opinions of its constituents?

Take, for example, a variety of the most politically "hot" topics discussed widely in the media during the 1970s. A CBS poll revealed that, as expected, the Senate was more "liberal" than the House, but that *both* were more "liberal" than the mass public. (See Table 11–1.) Such a finding is in keeping with our argument that elites (in this case, representatives) are typically more committed to the principles of democratic government than are masses. Here we find the elites also more accepting of new ideas. Note, however, that members of the House of Representatives are more nearly in agreement with the public than senators are.

Table 11–1
Comparison of Public and Congressional Opinion on Key Policy Issues, 1970

	Public	U.S. House Members	U.S. Senators
1. Vietnam: Percent say "speed up our withdrawal"	27	30	45
2. Defense: Percent say "place less emphasis" on military weapons programs	30	37	45
3. Guaranteed Income: Percent approve at least "$1600 for a family of four or more"	48	65	76
4. Civil Rights: Percent say government should go farther to improve blacks' conditions	53	58	76
5. Supreme Court: Percent deny it gives "too much consideration to rights of people suspected of crimes"	29	36	56

Source: Robert S. Erikson and Norman Luttbeg, *American Public Opinion* (1973), p. 257. Used with permission of John Wiley and Sons, Inc.

Elites: The Relevant Constituents

Who are a congressional member's *real* constituents? The relevant political constituency is not the general population of the district, but the elite of the district. We should think of a constituency not as an aggregate body of people, but as a relatively small group of political activists. Such activists are those with the time, interest, and skill to communicate about political events. Consequently, they are of a disproportionately high social status, as high as (or higher than) their representatives. For the great mass of the people, Congress is simply an institution with very low visibility. A study commissioned by the Senate Subcommittee on Intergovernmental Relations discovered some grim facts about the public's awareness of Congress: Only 59 percent of a national sample of Americans could identify one senator from their state, and barely half could name his party. Only a paltry 39 percent could name *both* senators. Members of the House of Representatives, allegedly closer to their constituents, fared even worse. Only 46 percent could identify their representative; only 41 percent, political affiliation. Further, impressive minorities were ignorant of even the most rudimentary institutional arrangements. For example, 20 percent thought that Congress included the Supreme Court![6] People thus confused cannot assess performance, even in the most general terms. We know, for instance, that party identification colors perception of government performance. Thus, Democrats should be expected to rate Democratic-controlled Congresses more favorably. However, individual party identification operates in such a way as to inflate estimation of congressional performance when the White House, rather than Congress, is controlled by the party of individual preference. The "government," rather than its components, is being assessed.

It is important to realize that the poll was taken in the midst of the Watergate investigation, a time when attention was probably at its sharpest focus! Even the most tumultuous events apparently fail to stimulate the mass of the population to acquire the most elementary knowledge about Congress. One cannot expect the "man on the street" to write a congressional member whose name he does not know.

An excellent example is provided by the debate upon, and ultimate defeat of, the funding for the Supersonic Transport (SST) in 1970 and 1971. Heavily lobbied against by environmental groups, vigorously supported by the president, viewed as necessary for economic survival by a depressed aircraft industry, extensively covered by the media, the target of a Senate filibuster of two weeks, the SST became a symbol of the struggle of environmentalists against unchecked industrial expansion. In this particularly bitter contest, Common Cause, the latest in a series of "citizen lobbies," led the fight against a strong coalition of business and labor groups, guided by the administration. Here, then, are "the people"* defeating the "establishment." Soon after Congress voted to terminate funds to the SST, a poll of selected congressional districts revealed more than two-thirds of the respondents were uncertain of their representative's position. Among those claiming to know, about half were wrong. As Erikson and Luttbeg explain: "Thus, the voters were almost totally unaware of how their Congressman voted on an issue that had commanded a major share of newspaper headlines for a period of months."[7]

Even when a congressional member's name is known, few constituents know the member's specific policy positions, or for that matter, overall political position. Hence, Miller and Stokes found that, among those who offered a reason for candidate choice, only 7 percent indicated that their choice had any "discernible issue content."

By this general definition of issue content (for example, the congressman is "for the working man"), only a tiny fraction of the population can qualify as an attentive public. If more stringent standards are imposed, such as detailed information about policy stands, only a "chemical trace" of the population qualifies as attentive.

But surely legislators are not totally free of input from their districts. *Somebody* communicates, on some issues. Approximately only 15 percent of the population has *ever* written a letter to their senators or representative, and 3 percent of the population accounts for over two-thirds of congressional mail. During periods of turmoil the flow of letters becomes more urgent. Thus, about one-third of the public claims to have written in regard to the Watergate scandal. Even if we disallow the normal tendency to inflate, and assume the figure to be accurate, one can hardly regard one-third of the population as indicative of a veritable flood, except by comparison with "normal" times. Yet it is generally assumed that the Watergate scandal involved widespread popular response. However, even in situations approaching a state of siege, the flow of communication is unrepresentative. As Miller and Stokes put it:

The communication most Congressmen have with their districts inevitably puts them in touch with organized groups and individuals who are relatively well informed about politics . . . as a result, his sample of contacts with a constituency . . . is heavily biased.[8]

The relevant constituents of a legislator, then, are the home district's active, interested, and resourceful elites. Usually these are the key economic elites of that district. In an agricultural district, they are the leaders of the American Farm Bureau Federation and the major agricul-

*Common Cause, like all organizations, is disproportionately representative of the middle to upper social classes.

tural producers—cotton producers, wheat growers, and so on; in the Southwest, oil producers or ranchers; in the mountain states, the copper, lead, and silver mining interests; in upper New England, the lumber, granite, and fishing interests; in central Pennsylvania and West Virginia, the coal interests and leaders of the United Mine Workers. In more heterogeneous urban constituencies, there may be a variety of influential constituents—bankers and financial leaders, real estate owners and developers, owners and managers of large industrial and commercial enterprises, top labor leaders, and the owners and editors of newspapers and radio and television facilities. In certain big city districts with strong, disciplined party organizations, the key congressional constituents may be the city's political and government elites—the city or county party chairpersons or the mayor. And, of course, anyone who makes major financial contributions to a congressional candidate's campaign is always considered an important constituent, for such money is hard to come by.

Sending the Message to Legislators

The messages that are transmitted from the elite of the constituency to its representative tend, in most cases, to be in *agreement* with the representative's known policy preferences.[9] Representatives, like most people, tend to associate with people with whom they agree. Contacts with the constituency will then be maintained largely through those who were acquaintances before the legislator's election to office. Two-thirds of the representative's information about constituency preferences are gained through such personal contact, with another 25 percent obtained by mail. Thus, representatives, in effect, hear what they want to hear. Perhaps this selective perception helps explain why conflicting reports of public opinion are so common. Barry Goldwater, for example, was allegedly perplexed about his presidential aspirations in 1964: on the one hand, his mail offered considerable encouragement; on the other hand, poll data suggested that his chances were slim. In an ingenious examination of the Goldwater campaign, the Survey Research Center of the University of Michigan found an explanation. Among the tiny minority of active communicators, Goldwater held a clear lead over Johnson. Further, in Goldwater's "public," those with whom he communicated, his position against the growth of bureaucracy in federal government was supported by a 3 to 1 ratio. However, the vast majority of less-active constituents did not show this concern, nor did they support the Goldwater candidacy.[10] Small wonder that Goldwater was perplexed! Similarly, during the height of the Vietnam War, congressional mail (originating from less than 3 percent of the population), was nearly twice as hawkish as was the population.

Constituency communications, then, are sources of encouragement. Consider the ebb and flow of communication surrounding the investigation of Watergate. At various junctures, most usually when President Nixon made a public statement, we learned that his mail was quite favorable. Simultaneously, Senator Ervin's committee indicated *its* mail was equally favorable. As V. O. Key notes:

Those who write letters to the White House tend to write in support or approbation rather than in criticism. . . . The tendency to write letters of approval doubtless gives Presidents, Senators, Congressmen, and other officials a distorted notion of the nature of public response to their actions and positions. [11]

Two legislators from the same constituency, who take opposing points of view on a particular issue, are therefore probably speaking the truth when they claim (as they usually do) that an overwhelming majority of their mail supports their position.

As we have seen, communication of legislators with local *elites* is relatively intense. Since elite opinions are not those of the masses, a general lack of congruence between what the masses want and what the legislator actually does is hardly surprising. On particularly visible issues, those which minimize the distortion in communication, the agreement between legislative performance and constituency demand can be relatively high. On civil rights issues, for instance, congressional voting and constituency opinion is highly correlated. On most other issues, however, the correlation is low. That is to say, if the constituents knew what their representative was doing, they would not be particularly happy (or unhappy, since Congress is of such low salience). Except for the few major issues—such as civil rights—the "average" constituent would say of the representative's behavior: "I don't like it; I don't dislike it; I just don't think about it very much."

While we cannot say with assurance what the representative process *is*, we certainly know what it is *not*. It is not the representation of the will of "the people." At best, representation is intra-elite communication.

The Reelection of Incumbents

There are, of course, elections. The ultimate reprisal for a congressional member who fails to keep his ear to the ground is to be sent home. Legislators, of course, subscribe to the popular theory of representative government, summarized by Charles O. Jones: "[Election time] is the period of accounting: either the representative is instructed further, or he is defeated for malrepresentation, or he is warned, or he is encouraged."[12]

Actually, very little such accounting takes place. In brief, incumbents rarely lose. Indeed, if we accept the standard theory of election, Americans are ecstatic over the performance of Congress. Roughly 81 percent of the senators who seek reelection win; and a whopping 93 percent of House members who seek reelection win.

A glance at Table 11–2 will bring us back to our earlier point from another perspective. Popular support for Congress is diminishing; criticism is increasing. But are the rascals to be thrown out? Clearly not. Not only are incumbents routinely returned to their seats; the postwar trend is toward even greater safety for incumbents. Notice the continuation of the trend in 1974, the year of an alleged revulsion against incumbents as a consequence of a general negative reaction to politics.

The relatively large-scale rejection of Senate incumbents in 1976 contrasts sharply with 1974, when alleged anti-incumbent feeling was running high, yet few incumbents were defeated. (In the House, however, incumbents enjoyed an unusually high rate of success in 1976.) Such a finding should not be surprising. We know that the electorate has a marked inability to identify their representatives in Congress. We can imagine how many voters can identify the challenger. Name familiarity—in the absence of any knowledge of issues—can be a powerful advantage. The average voters, if even aware of the incumbents, are likely to perceive them favorably and vote for them.

	% of Public Expressing Positive Rating of Congress	% Senatorial Incumbents Reelected	% House Incumbents Reelected
1948		65%	
1950		80	
1952		74	
1954		85	95%
1956		86	96
1958		65	91
1960		96	94
1962		90	96
1964		93	88
1965	64%		
1966	49	96	90
1967	38		
1968	46	83	96
1969	34		
1970	34	88	95
1971	26		
1972	24	84	93
1974	29	92	90
1976	33	61	96

Table 11–2
Popular Support for
Congress and Reelection
of Incumbents

Additionally, incumbents are likely to have developed a more effective political organization and a stable network of communication with local elites. Assiduous incumbents can use their franking privilege for mailing newsletters, polls, and other information; they can appear at various public events, call news conferences, address organizational meetings, and, in general, make themselves as visible as possible with a minimum of expense.

By developing such ties with local elites, and because the "smart money" will back a winner, incumbents have more to spend, thus maximizing exposure. Incumbents are generally able to raise almost twice as much as challengers. Regardless of party, Senate incumbents in 1972 spent an average of $480,000 to get reelected, while their challengers spent, on the average, $244,000. In the House, the cost is less, but the discrepancy equal. Incumbents spent roughly $50,000, their challengers, $30,000.

The growing influence of incumbency upon electoral success calls our attention again to the discussion of the constituency-legislator linkage. The cue for voters is incumbency (name familiarity), rather than issue position or even party affiliation (as the role of incumbency grows, the role of party identification is weakened). Clearly, then, Congress is an institution that can generally operate free of mass reprisals: "We have neither a Democratic nor a Republican party. Rather, we have an incumbency party which operates a monopoly."[13]

Congress and the President: An Unstable Balance of Power

How do the roles of Congress and other elites differ? Policy proposals are initiated outside Congress; Congress's role is to respond to proposals from the president, executive and military elites, and interested nongovernment elites. Congress does not merely ratify or "rubber stamp" decisions, it plays an independent role in the policy-making process. But this role is essentially deliberative; Congress accepts, modifies, or rejects the policies initiated by others. For example, the national budget, perhaps the single most important policy document, is written by executive and military elites and modified by the president before it is submitted to Congress. Congress may make further modifications, but it does not formulate the budget. Of course, Congress is a critical conduit through which appropriations and revenue measures must pass. But sophisticated lawmakers are aware that they function as arbiters rather than initiators of public policy.

The relationship between Congress and other policy-making elites is not necessarily stable. Whether Congress operates merely to ratify the decisions of others or to assert its voice independently depends on many factors: the aggressiveness and skill of the president, the strength of congressional leadership, and so on. Nevertheless, except in cases of unusually passive presidents (such as Eisenhower), Congress—however tenacious it appears in rejecting policy—rarely *initiates* policy.

Of course, the potential *constitutional* power in Congress is very great. Article I empowers Congress to levy taxes, borrow and spend money, regulate interstate and foreign commerce, coin money, declare war, maintain armies and navies, and a number of other important functions, including the passing of all laws "necessary and proper" to carry out these powers.

The Historical Perspective

The pendulum swings back and forth between congressional and executive power, but the general trend since Franklin D. Roosevelt has been toward the president. A key event in the power struggle between Congress and the president was the depression of the 1930s and the creation of the massive New Deal federal programs. In response to economic crisis, Congress, with its cumbersome decision-making process, simply gave up. Roosevelt's first act was to close all banks by executive order, explaining that he intended to use executive power to wage war against depression just as he would do in the event of foreign invasion. In the early days of the New Deal, senators and congressmen voted for bills they had never even read.

Granted that these were exceptional events, it is nevertheless true that Roosevelt's "revolution" remained intact. While Congress recovered more of an active role in domestic affairs (confined, however, to modifying executive-sponsored legislation), its role in foreign affairs remains minimal. Under the pressure of cold-war ideology, the president frequently assumed that information should be withheld; that "national security" made it imperative to minimize congressional participation. Huge military appropriations bills routinely passed both houses with only a single day of debate, and usually without amendment. Thus, the decision to commit troops to Korea was made with only the most cursory communication; the decision to escalate in Vietnam—the famous Tonkin Resolution, of 1965—was technically approved, with two days' debate, and two dissenting votes.

Foreign Affairs

The disappointments of the Vietnam War led to a congressional resurgence, which became apparent when Congress amended a foreign-aid bill to prohibit the use of ground forces in Southeast Asia, and ultimately imposed upon President Nixon a deadline for all military activity in Vietnam. The culmination of the process of renewed congressional vigor was the passage—over presidential veto—of the War Powers Act of 1973, limiting presidential power to commit troops to combat without congressional approval. (Ironically, the president was given two months of unchecked war power before congressional approval was required. (See Chapter 10.)

When put to the test, however, the War Powers Act proved a feeble restraint on the president. With the Cambodian seizure of the freighter *Mayaguez*, President Ford authorized an air assault and troop commitment to secure the crew's release. Although the War Powers Act requires the president to consult "in every possible instance" before the use of armed forces, President Ford did no such thing. He informed a *few* senators and representatives *after* he had decided upon his course of action. The decision to commit ground troops was made at 4 PM, Wednesday, May 14, 1975. The order was sent to the Defense Department at 4:45 PM. The assault began at 5:14. Seventeen members of Congress were informed at 6:40. Not only did Congress not demand prior consultations as required by the War Power Act, it quickly (through the Senate Foreign Relations Committee) endorsed President Ford's action. Clearly, another precedent for future military adventures was created, and, to demonstrate American military prowess, another merely symbolic piece of legislation was disregarded. The abandonment of congressional responsibility in the *Mayaquez* incident was a natural consequence of (1) the traditional dominance of the executive branch in foreign and military policy, (2) the desire to reestablish a coercive military posture after the humiliation of defeat in Vietnam.

Whether Congress, as an institution, is capable of regaining the initiative is very much in doubt. Congress, as we have seen, is accustomed to responding to presidential initiative. It is not accustomed to developing separate legislative programs.

Domestic Affairs

Domestic policy is another matter: No threats from other nations are involved; nobody has to be punished; "commitments" do not have to be honored. Yet Congress has been less assertive in domestic affairs than might be expected. The establishment of a federal budget was the exclusive domain of the president—until 1974 when, with the presidency disgraced by Watergate and tarnished by conspicuous failure in foreign policy, Congress seized an opportunity for policy making by passing the Budget and Impoundment Control Act of 1974. As can be seen by its title, the Act had two goals: to assert congressional responsibility in budgeting, and to prevent future presidents from impounding appropriated funds, as Nixon had.

The Act created budget committees in the House and Senate and a joint Congressional Budget Office with a staff of fiscal experts. By creating a single staff, Congress intended to provide an unprecedented cohesive budget philosophy. Formerly, the president's unified budget was presented to separate Appropriations committees in the Senate and the House, making a unified response impossible. The president, with access to the expertise of the executive branch, could argue persuasively that only he was capable of budgetary coordination. The new congressional budget procedures require that by April 15 the House and Senate Budget Committees are to report an initial resolution setting a ceiling on spending and specifying the maximum to be spent in each area (for example, defense, housing, education, etc.). A month later, both houses of Congress must pass the resolution. Only then do the Appropriations committees report their regular appropriations bills—limited, of course, by the ceilings imposed by the resolution. By September 15, Congress must adopt a final, binding resolution, setting budgetary ceilings in all areas. Thereafter, neither the House nor the Senate can consider legislation which exceeds these established amounts. The new fiscal year begins October 1st, and major appropriations bills should pass Congress before that date.

In practice, the goals of the legislators appear to be only partially realized: The system allows Congress to establish overall ceilings, yet there are provisions for exceeding spending limits if there are unforeseen rises in "uncontrollable" parts of the federal budget. The 1975 Congress missed its budget deadline by three months, and major conflict developed between the new House and Senate Budget committees and the established Appropriations committees; in the House, the budget resolution was approved by a margin of only two votes. Moreover, between the initial and final resolutions, ceilings were raised by $8 billion. Nevertheless, the new process does reveal the emergence of congressional priorities. Clearly, the success of the budget process will depend on whether congressional leadership can centralize a traditionally decentralized process, and convince established committees and their allies (interest groups) of the desirability of cooperation.

The restrictions on presidential impoundment also reflect an effort to reestablish congressional control of spending. This part of the Act was appended to the original budget control act and specified the process whereby appropriated funds could be withheld by the executive branch: Impoundment, whether deferral (delaying spending) or recission (refusal to spend), requires special executive justification. Deferrals can be overturned by a simple majority of either house. Recissions require approval by both houses within 45 days. While appearing to restrict executive authority, the Act actually *legitimized* impoundment. Although President Nixon asserted that impoundment was his constitutional right, the courts generally disagreed. However, the new legislation was interpreted by President Ford as legitimate authorization for withholding funds. Thus, when the congressional guidelines exceed a president's budget, the excess can be returned in the form of recissions and deferrals. Congress must then respond to force the president to spend the money which it originally appropriated.

The Elaborate Procedures of Legislative Elites

The rules and procedures of Congress are elaborate but important to the functioning of legislative elites. Much legislative debate concerns rules and procedures; and many policy questions turn on the question of proper procedure. Legislative procedures and rules make the legislative process fair and orderly; without established customs, rules, and procedures, it would be impossible for 435 men to arrive at collective decisions about the thousands of items submitted to them during a congressional session. Yet the same rules also delay or obstruct proposed changes in the *status quo;* they strengthen Congress's conservative role in policy making. In congressional procedures legislation faces many opportunities for defeat and many obstacles to passage. Of course, it is not surprising that an elite that functions as an arbiter of public policy should operate under rules and procedures that maximize deliberation and grant advantages to those who oppose change.

Congress follows a fairly standard pattern in the formal process of making laws; Table 11–3 describes briefly some of the more important procedural steps. Bills are generally drafted in the president's office, in executive departments, or in the offices of interested elites, but they must be formally introduced into Congress by members of the House or Senate. A bill may be introduced in either the House or the Senate, except that bills for raising revenue are required by the Constitution to begin in the House. Upon introduction, a bill is referred to one of the standing committees of the House or the Senate, which may: (1) recommend it for adoption with only minor changes; (2) virtually rewrite it into a new policy proposal; (3) ignore it and prevent its passage through inaction; (4) kill it by majority vote. The full House or Senate *may* overrule the decision of its committees, but this is a rare occurrence. Most members of Congress are reluctant to upset the prerogatives of the committees and the desires of recognized leaders. Therefore, committees have virtual power of life or death over every legislative measure.

The Standing Congressional Committees and Subcommittees

Committee work is essential to the legislative process; Congress as a body could never hope to review all the measures put before it. As early as 1885, Woodrow Wilson described the American political process as "government by the standing committees of Congress." But while reducing legislative work to manageable proportions, the committees

Table 11–3
How a Bill Becomes a Law

1. *Introduction.* Most bills can be introduced in either house. (In this table, the bill is first introduced in the Senate.) It is given a number and referred to the proper committee.
2. *Hearings.* The committee may hold public hearings on the bill.
3. *Committee action.* The full committee meets in executive (closed) session. It may kill the bill, approve it with or without amendments, or draft a new bill.
4. *Calendar.* If the committee recommends the bill for passage, it is listed on the calendar.
5. *Debate, amendment, vote.* The bill goes to the floor for debate. Amendments may be added. The bill is voted on.
6. *Introduction to the second house.* If the bill passes, it goes to the House of Representatives, where it is referred to the proper committee.
7. *Hearings.* Hearings may be held again.
8. *Committee action.* The committee rejects the bill, prepares a new one, or accepts the bill with or without amendments.
9. *Rules Committee consideration.* If the committee recommends the bill, it is listed on the calendar and sent to the Rules Committee. The Rules Committee can block a bill or clear it for debate before the entire House.
10. *Debate, amendment, vote.* The bill goes before the entire body, is debated and voted upon.
11. *Conference Committee.* If the bill as passed by the second house contains major changes, either house may request a conference committee. The conferees—five persons from each house, representing both parties—meet and try to reconcile their differences.
12. *Vote on conference report.* When they reach an agreement, they report back to their respective houses. Their report is accepted or rejected.
13. *Submission to the president.* If the report is accepted by both houses, the bill is signed by the speaker of the House and the president of the Senate and is sent to the president of the United States.
14. *Presidential action.* The president may sign or veto the bill within ten days. If he does not sign and Congress is still in session, the bill automatically becomes a law. If Congress adjourns before the ten days have elapsed, it does not become a law. (This is called the "pocket veto.") If the president returns the bill with a veto message, it may still become a law if passed by a two-thirds majority in each house.

exercise considerable influence over the outcome of legislation. A minority of the legislators, sometimes a single committee chairman, can delay and obstruct the legislative process.

In the Senate, the most prestigious committees are Foreign Relations, Appropriations, and Finance; in the House, the most powerful are the Rules Committee, Appropriations, and Ways and Means. (The twenty-one standing committees of the House and the eighteen of the Senate are listed in Table 11–4.) To expedite business, most standing committees create subcommittees to handle particular matters falling within their jurisdiction. This practice further concentrates power over particular subject matter in the hands of a very few congressional members. A great deal of power lies in the hands of subcommittee members, especially the chairmen; interested elites cultivate the favor of powerful subcommittee chairmen as well as committee chairmen.

In examining legislation, a committee or subcommittee generally holds public hearings on bills deemed worthy by the chairman or, in some cases, by the majority of the committee. Influenced by the legal

Table 11–4
The Standing Committees
of Congress

Senate Committees	House Committees
Foreign Relations	Appropriations
Appropriations	Ways & Means
Finance	Armed Services
Budget	Banking, Financing, & Urban Affairs
Agriculture & Forestry	Agriculture
Armed Services	Education & Labor
Judiciary	Government Operations
Commerce	Judiciary
Banking	(Budget) Interstate
Rules	Foreign Commerce
Interior	International Relations
Public Works	Interior & Insular
Government Operations	Science & Technology
D.C.	Post Office Civil Service
Labor and Public Welfare	Stds. of Official Conduct
Aeronautics & Space Science	(Small Business)
Post Office	House Administration
Veterans Affairs	Merchant Marine and Fisheries
	Veterans Affairs
	D.C.
	Rules

profession, from which a majority of congressmen are drawn, the committees tend to look upon public hearings as trials in which contestants present their side of the argument to the committee members, the judges. Presumably, during this trial the skillful judges will sift facts on which to base their decisions. In practice, however, committees use public hearings primarily to influence public opinion or executive action, or, occasionally, to discover the position of major elite groups on the measure under consideration. Major decisions are made in executive session in secret.

The membership of the standing committees on agriculture, labor, interior and insular affairs, and judiciary generally reflects the interest of particular elite groups in the nation. Farm interests are represented on the agricultural committees; land, water, and natural resource interests are represented on interior and insular affairs; congressmen with labor ties and urban industrial constituencies gravitate toward the labor committee; and lawyers dominate the judicial committees of both houses.

In view of the power of congressional committees, the assignment of members to committees is one of the most significant activities of Congress. In the House of Representatives, the Republicans assign their members to committees through a Committee on Committees that consists of one representative from each state sending a Republican to Congress. Each representative votes with the strength of his state delegation. But the real business of this committee is conducted by a subcommittee appointed by the Republican party leader. The subcommittee fills committee vacancies with freshman members and those who request transfer from other committees. The Committee on Committees considers the career backgrounds of members, their seniority, and their reputation for "soundness," which usually means adherence to conservative policy positions. Often, the chairman of a standing committee tells the Committee on Committees whom he prefers to have on his committee. Democrats in the House are assigned by a Steering and Policy Committee. In the Senate, Republican committee positions are filled by a Committee on Committees, and Democratic committee positions are selected by a steering committee appointed by the Democratic floor leader. Usually, only senators with seniority are eligible for major committee positions in the Senate, such as Foreign Relations, Armed Services, and Appropriations.

Until recently, House Democrats were given committee assignments by the Ways and Means Committee. But in 1975, Ways and Means—staggered by the erratic behavior of its chairman, Wilbur Mills—was stripped of this authority. The House Democratic Caucus (discussed below), viewed as a vehicle for reform by the younger, more liberal Democrats, transferred responsibility for committee assignments to the Steering and Policy Committee. Created in 1973, this committee is comprised of the party leadership, twelve members elected by the Caucus to represent geographic regions, and nine members appointed by the Speaker.

This new use of the Steering and Policy Committee substantially increased the party leadership's power, especially that of the Speaker (who was given the additional authority to name members of the Rules Committee). Clearly, the Democrats' aim was (as was true of budget reform) to centralize and coordinate congressional policy power. To achieve this goal, they were willing to elevate the Speaker to a position of great influence.

Committee and subcommittee chairmen are very powerful. They usually determine which bills will be considered by the committee, whether or not public hearings will be held, and what the agenda of the committee will be. The chairman of the committee is officially consulted on all questions relating to that committee; this procedure confers status with the executive branch and with interested nongovernment elites. Only occasionally is the chairman's decision about a committee matter overruled by a majority within the committee–subcommittee "baronage."

The Growing Power of Subcommittees

The chairman's power has been eroded somewhat by successful House Democratic Caucus challenges of the seniority system, and by the growth in the power of subcommittees. Indeed, the move to strengthen the autonomy of subcommittees may be the most significant structural change to occur in Congress in the last decade, eclipsing the more publicized modification of seniority. By 1976, many subcommittee chairmen had eclipsed full committee chairmen in influence and autonomy. Those leading the drive to establish subcommittee autonomy were the younger Democrats, who gained more influence than they would have had without reforms. Again, the Democratic Caucus was the instrument of change. By 1974, each member of Congress was virtually assured of a personal feudal kingdom. No House member could be chairman of more than one subcommittee: Thus, younger members gained access to key chairmanships. A subcommittee "bill of rights" gave the Democrats on each committee (rather than the committee chairman) the authority to select subcommittee chairmen, guaranteed all members adequate assignments, and provided adequate subcommittee budgets. Finally, all committees with more than twenty members were required to have at least four subcommittees.

Thus, subcommittee chairmen assumed influence equal to committee chairmen, decentralizing decisions to a degree surely uncontemplated by the reformers. The growth of subcommittees, and the attendant fragmentation of authority, is at odds with the centralizing impact of budget reform and the increasing influence of the Democratic Caucus and leadership. Once acquired, power is not readily relinquished. Thus, Caucus activists' efforts to reorganize existing committees were defeated.

The Seniority System

The practice of awarding chairmanships according to seniority is another guarantee of conservatism in the legislative process. The member of the majority party having the longest continuous service on the committee becomes chairman; the member of the minority party with the longest continuous service on the committee is the ranking minority member. Therefore chairmen are not chosen by their own committees, by their own party, or by the House and Senate as a whole. They are chosen by the voters of noncompetitive congressional districts, whose representatives are likely to stay in office the longest. Thus, the major decisions in Congress are made by those from areas where party competition and voter participation are low; in the past, these areas have been southern and rural and big-city machine constituencies. In both houses, the seniority system works against the competitive urban and suburban districts. In 1971, both parties modified seniority to allow review and ratification by the party caucus. Occasionally a committee chairman is displaced by the Democratic Caucus, but most senior members remain at the top of the capitol hierarchy.

In recent years, the position of southerners has been weakened by strengthening of the Democratic party nationally; about half the Democrats in Congress were once southerners; whereas now only one-fourth are. As young southerners replace old, and as Democrats from other regions build seniority, southern domination of committee chairs has been reduced. Thus in 1977, southerners held 23 and 33 percent of the chairmanships in the House and Senate respectively compared to 40 and 47 percent in 1973. Nevertheless, the seniority system still lends a rather conservative cast to committee leadership. The most prestigious committees in the Senate—with the exception of the newly created Budget Committee—are chaired by southerners, all with conservative voting records: Sparkman (Ala.), McClellan (Ark.), Long (La.), Talmadge (Ga.), Stennis (Mississippi), and Eastland (Mississippi). They are conspicuous supporters of the "conservative coalition" (discussed below). Thus, although the Senate is more liberal than the House and the general public, conservative interests are overrepresented when it is Democratically controlled.

Conspicuous by their absence in key committee assignments are legislators from the most populous states in the country—New York, California, and Illinois. Also notably absent are senators whose public visibility far exceeds their influence: Goldwater, Kennedy, Humphrey, McGovern, and Muskie. In the world of the Senate, their power is considerably less than that of, say, Senator Eastland of Mississippi, whose influence over the appointment of Supreme Court justices is legend. Eastland came to the Senate in 1942, when Edward Kennedy was ten years old.

As their influence *within* Congress grows, so does the tendency of high-seniority legislators to identify with Congress as an institution, to the detriment of possible constituency influences. Two factors are at work here. Legislators get to know each other well (they see each other more regularly than they see constituents); and older legislators probably have learned from experience that the expected vigorous constituency response to a perceived "unpopular" vote simply does not materialize. Having learned this, the experienced legislator may develop a more realistic view of the electorate: ". . . after several terms, I don't give a damn any more. I'm pretty safe now and I don't have to worry about reaction in the district."[14] Also, legislators develop expertise, specializing in certain kinds of legislation, and are viewed by their colleagues as credible sources of information. As one put it: "That's the beauty of the seniority system—there are informed, experienced people on each Committee you can consult."[15] Indeed, when congressional members need advice, they usually turn to someone of higher seniority.

Initial committee assignment is, of course, not strictly made according to seniority. But once assigned, the legislator can remain, building up seniority. First, though, each party must make its selection. Since control of Congress depends upon reelection, efforts are made to place party members where they can do the most good, and are most likely to be reelected. Thus, as we noted, the major interests in a constituency are represented on the appropriate committee.

The seniority system has its critics and its defenders. Its most active critics are: (1) those with low seniority, (2) those without formal leadership positions, (3) those from urban districts, and (4) those with a more liberal voting record.[16] Supporters of seniority (those whose characteristics contrast with those reformers on the four points listed above) talk more of the rewards of experience, the development of expertise, and the nurturing of stability in relationships. The maintenance of the "subsystem" is greatly enhanced by seniority: without it, the established network of relationships among interest groups, executive agencies, and committees would flounder.

The Democratic Caucus

The most serious challenge to the seniority system occurred in the House as a consequence of the continued strengthening of the Democratic Caucus and the liberal faction of the Democratic party. By 1974, 82 of the House members had been elected since 1960. Because the seniority system denied them influence, these members had a personal interest in changing it. In 1974, a secret-ballot Caucus vote was required for the approval of all committee chairmanships. As a consequence, three conservative southerners were unseated chairmen of Armed Services; Banking, Financing, and Urban Affairs; and Agriculture. While much has been made of these defeats, little mention is made of action the Caucus refused to take: it declined to make subcommittee chairmen (except for those of the Appropriations Committee) subject to Caucus approval. Thus, subcommittee chairmen are assuming the privileges and freedom once held solely by committee chairmen. Significantly, as the newer members moved into positions of authority, no additional challenges to seniority occurred. Because, in 1977, the newest members proved to be more conservative than their previous freshman class, further challenges seem unlikely. The storm passed with moderate damage to the system.

Lobbyists, Committees, and Committee Reform

Lobbyists try to focus their activities as narrowly as possible, thus enabling them to develop strong ties with relevant congressional committees and administrative agencies. Such a "subsystem" can develop to the benefit of all participants. Legislators benefit from campaign contributions by interest groups; lobbyists benefit by a personal working relationship with committees and their staffs; administrative agencies benefit by the support of interest groups and congressional committees of their budget requests. For example, the largest campaign contribution made by organized Labor in 1976 ($125,000) was to the Chairman of the Senate Labor and Public Welfare Committee.

Such established networks of elites are threatened occasionally, when Congress proposes to reorganize the committee structure and jurisdiction. In 1974, a bipartisan select committee proposed a radical realignment of House committee jurisdiction. Labor vigorously lobbied, especially against a proposal to split the Education and Labor Committee. The plan was replaced by a far milder reorganization that left existing subsystems intact. In 1977, the Senate undertook a similar effort—a reform intended to abolish or absorb several committees: Veterans Affairs; Joint Economic; Post Office and Civil Service; Select Committee on Small Business; and the Special Committee on Aging. Although nominally unaffected, labor opposed the abolition of Post Office and Civil Service committees because it would have reduced the lobbying influence of government employees. Small-business and veterans organizations were equally opposed. Each group focused on its own special interest, in collaboration with the senator most clearly aligned with that interest. In the end, a modest adjustment was made, leaving each subsystem of interest groups and committees intact.

Legislative Procedure

In the House of Representatives, after a standing committee reports a bill (step 8 in Table 11–3), a special rule or order must be issued by the Rules Committee before the bill can be considered by the membership of the House. This means that in the House of Representatives bills must be approved by the Rules Committee as well as the standing committee. (The only exceptions are bills reported by the House Appropriations and the Ways and Means committees; their bills may be considered at any time as "privileged motions.") The Rules Committee can kill a bill by shelving it indefinitely. It can insist that the bill be amended as the price of permitting it on the floor and can even substitute a new bill for the one framed by another committee. The Rules Committee determines how much debate will be permitted on the floor of the House on any bill, and the number and kind of amendments that may be offered from the floor. The only formal limits on Rules Committee authority are the "discharge petition" (which is rarely used and hardly ever successful) and "calendar Wednesday," a cumbersome procedure that permits standing committees to call up bills that have been blocked by the Rules Committee. The Rules Committee, clearly the most powerful single committee in

Congress, is dominated by senior members elected from noncompetitive districts.

In the Senate, control of floor debate rests with the majority leader. But the majority leader does not have the power to limit debate; a senator who has the floor may talk without limit and may choose to whom the floor is yielded. If enough senators wish to talk a bill to death (filibuster), they may do so. This device permits a small minority to tie up the business of the Senate and prevent it from voting on a bill. Under Rule 22 of the Senate, debate can be limited only by cloture. When 16 members sign a petition for a cloture, cloture must be voted upon, and a three-fifths vote of the full Senate ends the filibuster. But cloture has been successful only six times in the history of the Senate. It has been a major weapon in civil rights legislation; the Civil Rights Act of 1964 passed the Senate through a cloture petition. But generally senators agree to protect each other's right of unlimited debate. Like the Rules Committee in the House, the filibuster is a means by which a small elite can defend itself against majority preferences.

Of the 10,000 bills introduced into Congress every year only about 1,000, or one in ten, become law. After a bill has been approved by the standing committee in the Senate or by the standing committee and the Rules Committee in the House, it is reported to the floor for a vote. Usually the most crucial votes come on the amendments to the bill that are offered to the floor (however, amendments may be prevented in the

"Just between us, Forbes—how does a bill become a law?"

Sidney Harris.

House by the Rules Committee). Once major amendments have either been defeated or incorporated into the bill, the bill usually picks up broad support, and the vote on final passage is usually a lopsided one in favor of the bill.

One of the most conservative features of American government is its bicameralism; the complicated path that a bill follows in one house must be repeated in the other. A bill must pass both branches of Congress in identical form before it can be sent to the president for his signature. However, the Senate often amends a House bill, and the House usually amends Senate bills. This means that even after a bill has passed both houses, it must be resubmitted to the originating house for concurrence with the changes made by the other. If either house declines to accept changes in the bill, specific differences must be ironed out by an ad hoc joint committee, called a conference committee. Disagreements between the houses are so frequent that from one-third to one-half of all public bills, including virtually all important ones, must be referred to conference committees after passage by both houses.

Conference committee members, appointed by the presiding officers of each house, are usually drawn from the two standing committees that handled the bill in each house. Since the final bill produced by the conference committee is generally accepted by both houses, conference committees have tremendous power in determining the final form of legislation. Reports of conference committees must be accepted or rejected as a whole; they cannot be further amended. Most conference committee meetings are closed and unrecorded; they hold no hearings and listen to no outside testimony. The bill that emerges from their deliberations may not represent the view of either house and may contain items never considered by either house. Conference committees have sometimes been characterized as a "third house" of Congress, whose members are not elected by the people, keep no record of their work, and usually operate behind closed doors—and there can be no debate about their product.

Elites within Elites—The Congressional Establishment

Among federal government elites there is a power hierarchy, supported by protocol, by the distribution of formal constitutional powers, by the powers associated with party office, by the committee and seniority systems of Congress, and by the "informal folkways" of Washington. According to the protocol of Washington society, the highest social rank is held by the president, followed by former presidents and their widows, the vice president, the Speaker of the House, members of the Supreme Court, foreign ambassadors and ministers, the Cabinet, United States senators, governors of states, former vice presidents, and finally congressmen.

The Constitution grants greater formal powers to senators than to representatives. There are only 100 senators; therefore, each senator is more visible than a representative in the social and political life of Washington, as well as in his home state. Also, senators have a special authority in foreign affairs not accorded to representatives, for the Senate must advise and consent by a two-thirds vote to all treaties entered into by the United States. The threat of Senate repudiation of a treaty makes it desirable for the president to solicit Senate views on foreign affairs; generally the secretary of state works closely with the Foreign Relations Committee of the Senate. Influential senators undertake personal missions abroad and serve on delegations to international bodies. Another constitutional power afforded senators is to advise and consent on executive appointments, including Supreme Court justices, Cabinet members, federal judges, ambassadors, and other high executive officials. Although the Senate generally approves the presidential nominations, the added potential for power contributes to the difference between the influence of senators and of House members. Finally, senators are elected for a six-year term and from a broader and more heterogeneous constituency. Thus, they have a longer guaranteed tenure in Washington, more prestige, and greater freedom from minor shifts in opinion among nongovernment elites in their home states.

Senators can also enhance their power through their political roles; they often wield great power in state parties and can usually control federal patronage dispensed in their state. The power of the Senate to confirm nominations has given rise to the important political custom of "senatorial courtesy": Senators of the same party as the president are given a virtual veto power over major appointments—federal judges, postmasters, customs collectors, and so on—in their state.When presidential nominations are received in the Senate, they are referred to the senator or senators from the state involved. If the senator declares the nominee "personally obnoxious" to him, the Senate usually respects this declaration and rejects the appointment. Thus, before the president submits a nomination to the Senate, he usually makes sure that the nominee will be acceptable to his party's senator or senators from the state involved.

Party leadership roles in the House and the Senate are major sources of power in Washington. (See Table 11–5 for a list of Senate and House leaders for the 96th Congress.) The Speaker of the House of Representatives, who is elected by the majority party of the House, exercises more power over public policy than any other member of either house. Before 1910 the Speaker appointed all standing committees and their chairmen, possessed unlimited discretion to recognize members on the floor, and served as chairman of the Rules Committee. But in 1910, a group of progressives, led by George Norris, severely curtailed the authority of the Speaker, who today shares power over the appointment of committees with the Committee on Committees; committee chairmen are selected by seniority, not by the Speaker; and the Speaker no longer serves as chairman of the Rules Committee. However, the Speaker retains considerable authority: referring bills to committees, appointing all conference committees, ruling on all matters of House procedure, recognizing those who wish to speak, and generally directing the business of the floor. More importantly, the Speaker is the principal figure in House policy formulation, leadership, and responsibility; although sharing these tasks with standing committee chairmen, he is generally "first among equals" in his relationship with them.

Next to the Speaker, the most influential party leaders in the House are the majority and minority floor leaders and the party whips. These party leaders are chosen by their respective party caucuses, which are held at the beginning of each congressional session. The party caucus, composed of all the party's members in the House, usually does little more than elect these officers; it makes no major policy decisions. The floor leaders and whips have little formal authority; their role is to influence legislation through persuasion. Party floor leaders are supposed to combine parliamentary skill with persuasion, good personal relationships with party members, and close ties with the president and administration. They cannot deny party renomination to members who are disloyal to the party, but because they can control committee assignments and many small favors in Washington, a maverick will have a difficult time becoming an effective legislator. The whips, or assistant floor leaders, keep members informed about legislative business, see that members are present for important floor votes, and communicate party strategy and position on particular issues. They also serve as the eyes and ears of the leadership, counting noses before important votes are taken. Party whips should know how many votes a particular measure has, and they should be able to get the votes to the floor when the roll is called.

The vice president of the United States, who serves as president of

Table 11–5
Party Leadership in the Congress

	Senator	State		Representative	State
President Pro Tempore	Eastland	Miss.	Speaker	O'Neill	Mass.
Deputy Pres. Pro Tempore	Humphrey	Minn.	Majority Leader	Wright	Texas
Majority Leader	Byrd	W. Va.	Majority Whip	Brademas	Ind.
Majority Whip	Cranston	Cal.	Minority Leader	Rhodes	Ariz.
Dem. Conf. Secretary	Inouye	Hawaii	Minority Whip	Michel	Ill.
Minority Leader	Baker	Tenn.	Dem. Caucus Chairman	Foley	Wash.
Minority Whip	Stevens	Alaska	Rep. Conf. Chairman	Anderson	Ill.
Rep. Policy Com. Chmn.	Tower	Texas			
Rep. Conference Chmn.	Curtis	Neb.			
Rep. Conf. Secretary	Hansen	Wyo.			

the Senate, has less control over Senate affairs than the Speaker of the House has over House affairs. The vice president votes only in case of a tie, and must recognize senators in the order in which they rise. The majority party in the Senate also elects from its membership a president pro tempore who presides in the absence of the vice president.

The key power figures in the Senate are the majority and minority leaders. The majority leader usually has great personal influence within the Senate and is a powerful figure in national affairs. The majority leader, when of the same party as the president, is in charge of getting the president's legislative program through the Senate. Although having somewhat less formal authority than the Speaker of the House, the majority leader has the right to be the first senator to be heard on the floor, and, with the minority floor leader, determines the Senate's agenda. He can greatly influence committee assignments for members of his own party. But on the whole, his influence rests on his powers of persuasion. It is widely recognized that the most effective majority leader in recent times, 1953–1960, was Lyndon Johnson.

The committee system and the seniority rule also create powerful congressional figures: the chairmen of the most powerful standing committees—particularly the Senate Foreign Relations, Appropriations, and Finance Committees, and the House Rules, Appropriations, and Ways and Means Committees. Chairmen of the standing committees in both houses have become powerful through the respect the members have for the authority of their committees. The standing committee system is self-sustaining because an attack on the authority of one committee or committee chairman tends to be regarded as a threat to all; if one committee or committee chairman can be by-passed on a particular measure, so could others on other measures. Hence, committee chairmen and ranking committee members tend to stand by each other and support each other's authority over legislation assigned to their respective committees. Committee chairmen or ranking committee members are also respected because of their seniority and experience in the legislative process. Committee chairmen are often experts in parliamentary process as well as in the substantive area covered by their committees. Finally, and perhaps most importantly, committee chairmen and ranking committee members acquire power through their relationships with executive and private elites who are involved in the policy area within the jurisdiction of the committee. "Policy clusters"—alliances of leaders from executive agencies, congressional committees, and private business and industry—tend to emerge in Washington. Through their control over legislation in Congress, committee chairmen are key members of these policy clusters. One policy cluster might include the chairmen of the House and Senate committees on agriculture, the secretary of agriculture and other key officials of the Department of Agriculture, and the leaders of the American Farm Bureau Federation. Another vital policy cluster would include the chairmen of the House and Senate Armed Services Committees; the Secretary and Undersecretaries of Defense; key military leaders, including the Joint Chiefs of Staff; and the leadership of defense industries such as Lockheed and General Dynamics. These alliances of congressional, executive, and private elites determine most public policy within their area of concern.

Power also accrues to key senators and congressmen by virtue of custom and informal folkways. Professor David B. Truman writes that Congress "has its standards and conventions, its largely unwritten system of obligations and privileges. . . . The neophyte must conform, at least in some measure, if he hopes to make effective use of his position."[17] A new member of Congress who wishes to "get along" should expect to "go along" with its customs. These informal folkways appear more important in the Senate, where there are fewer formal controls over members than in the House. Donald Matthews has described some of the folkways of the Senate as: respect for the seniority system; good behavior in floor debate; humility in freshmen senators; a willingness to perform cheerfully many thankless tasks, such as presiding over floor debate; deference to senior members; making speeches only on subjects on which you are expert or which concern your committee assignment or your state; doing favors for other senators; keeping your word when you make an agreement; remaining friendly toward your colleagues, whether you are in political agreement with them or not; and speaking well of the Senate as an institution.[18]

Ralph K. Huitt describes the Senate type as:

. . . *a prudent man, who serves a long apprenticeship before trying to assert himself, and talks infrequently even then. He is courteous to a fault in his relations with his colleagues, not allowing political disagreements to affect his personal feelings. He is always ready to help another Senator when he can, and he expects to be repaid in kind. More than anything else he is a Senate man, proud of the institution and ready to defend its traditions and perquisites against all outsiders. He is a legislative workhorse who specializes in one or two policy areas. . . . He is a man of accommodation who knows that "You have to go along to get along"; he is a conservative, institutional man, slow to change what he has mastered at the expense of so much time and patience.*[19]

This image of the insider brings to mind the opposite role: the outsider, a senator whose eyes and mind are upon other political opportunities. Such men (often willingly) find themselves assigned to glamorous but relatively powerless committees. Hence the absence of the "household word" senators—McGovern, Muskie, Goldwater, Kennedy—from the inside club. Edward Kennedy is a particularly apt example, since he once successfully challenged the insular traditions of the Senate. Of Kennedy it was written:

On his own the amiable Teddy might someday have become at best a fringe member of the club, but he is associated with Robert F., who like John F., is the archetype of the national kind of politician that the club regards with suspicion. It's believed correctly that the Kennedy family has always looked on the Senate as a means to an end, but not an end in itself.[20]

Yet, shortly after this was written, Kennedy defeated Russell Long (D-La.), for the position of Majority Whip. However, Kennedy did not make good in his new role. He was soon replaced by a true Senate man, Robert Byrd (D-W.Va.).

Senators and prominent reporters have described the Senate "establishment" as the "inner club" where power in the Senate and in Washington is concentrated. The establishment is composed primarily of conservative senators from both parties who have acquired great seniority and control key committee chairmanships. The establishment consists of those senators who have learned the folkways of the Senate over a long period of time and who now appear to be running the Senate. In 1963, United States Senator Joseph S. Clark of Pennsylvania attacked the Senate "establishment" as "the antithesis of democracy."[21] He charged that it was composed of political conservatives from the Democratic South and the Republican Midwest who had acquired seniority and who controlled appointment to committees and other important posts. William S. White also talks of the "inner club" in the Senate, composed of those who "express consciously or unconsciously the deepest instincts and prejudices of 'the Senate type.'" For White, a Senate type is one who displays "tolerance toward fellows, intolerance toward any who would in any real way change the Senate," and commitment toward the Senate as "a career in itself, a life in itself, and an end in itself."[22]

Although the youthful Democratic Caucus won some victories over the "establishment" between 1974 and 1976, it soon became clear that moderate Democrats would halt further attempts at reform. In the House election for majority leader, a moderate, Jim Wright of Texas, defeated Phillip Burton of California, the symbol of liberal reform and chairman of the Caucus during its zenith of 1974. Thomas O'Neill of Massachusetts, veteran of twenty-four years' continuous service, became Speaker. The two new leaders crushed reformers' attempts to reduce their power. In the Senate, Robert Byrd (see above) replaced the retiring Mike Mansfield by defeating the more liberal Hubert Humphrey. The insiders were easily in command. The brief sway of the Caucus appeared over, and the jurisdiction of committees remains unchanged—each baron has his fiefdom.

In summary, it seems clear that there are elites within elites. There are elites within the House, the Senate, and the executive branch who exercise disproportionate control over government and who are not representative even of the majority of government elites. Power within the House and Senate appears to flow downward from senior party leaders and influential committee chairmen, whose dominance in congressional affairs is seldom challenged by the rank-and-file congressmen. Senator Clark writes: "The trouble with Congress today is that it exercises negative and unjust powers to which the governed, the people of the United States, have never consented. . . . The heart of the trouble is that power is exercised by minority, not majority, rule."[23]

Conflict and Consensus—Party Voting in Congress

p. 181- pol. dict.

Studies of roll-call voting in Congress show that the role played by political parties in legislative conflict depends on the issue.[24] _Party votes_, those roll-call votes in which a majority of voting Democrats oppose a majority of voting Republicans, occur on less than _half_ of all the roll-call votes taken in Congress. Roll-call voting follows party lines more often than it follows sectional, urban-rural, or any other divisions that have been studied. How much cohesion exists within the parties? Table 11–6 shows the number of party votes that have been taken in Congress in recent years and the average support Democratic and Republican congressmen have given to their parties. Democrats and Republicans appear equally cohesive, with members of both parties voting with their party majority more than two-thirds of the time. Party voting appears more frequent in the House than in the Senate.

Bipartisan votes, those roll calls in which divisions are not along party lines, occur most frequently in the areas of foreign policy and defense. Bipartisan agreement also appears on appropriation bills and roll calls where there is little dispute. Recently, bipartisan voting has settled issues of federal aid to education, highway beautification, water pollution, voting rights, presidential continuity, and increases in federal employees' pay and veterans' benefits.

Conflict between parties occurs most frequently over issues involving social welfare programs, housing and urban development, economic opportunity, medical care, antipoverty programs, health and welfare, and the regulation of business and labor. Party conflict is particularly apparent in the budget, the most important policy document of the national government. The budget is identified as the product of the president and carries the label of his party. On some issues, such as civil rights and appropriations, voting will follow party lines during roll calls

Table 11–6
Party Voting in Congress

	Party Votes as % of Total Votes	Party Support* Democrats	Party Support* Republicans
1970			
Senate	35	58	56
House	27	55	60
1971			
Senate	42	64	63
House	38	61	67
1972			
Senate	36	57	64
House	27	58	61
1973			
Senate	40	69	64
House	42	68	68
1974			
Senate	44	63	59
House	29	62	63
1975			
Senate	48	68	64
House	48	69	72
1976			
Senate	37	62	61
House	36	66	67

*Party support: Average percentage of times a member voted with majority of party of affiliation in disagreement with the other party's majority.

Source: Compiled from *Congressional Quarterly Almanac,* (Washington, D.C.: Congressional Quarterly Service, 1970–76).

on preliminary motions, amendments, and other preliminary matters, but swing to a bipartisan vote on passage of the final legislation. This means that the parties have disagreed on certain aspects of the bill, but compromised on its final passage.

Many of the issues that cause conflict between the Democratic and Republican parties are related to the conflict of government and private initiative. In general, Democrats have favored: lower tariffs; federal subsidies for agriculture; federal action to assist labor and low-income groups through social security, relief, housing, and wage-hour regulation; and generally a larger role for the federal government in launching new projects to remedy domestic problems. Republicans, on the other hand, have favored higher tariffs, free competition in agriculture, less government involvement in labor and welfare matters, and reliance on private action.

Further, each party supports the president to a different degree. The president generally receives greater support from his own party than from the opposition party in Congress, although party lines are hazy on issues involving veterans, civil service, public works, and states' rights; and partisan differences on foreign policy are practically nonexistent. Before World War II, Democrats tended to support U.S. international involvement, while the Republicans were heavily committed to neutrality and "isolationism." Now only the question of foreign aid divides the parties significantly in foreign affairs, Democrats generally supporting it more than Republicans.

To some extent, party influences check the decentralization inherent in the committee system; yet party votes do *not* occur on *most* of the issues voted on in a given session. The probability that a legislator will vote in accordance with the party leadership is only slightly better than chance. It seems that the feeling of party identification is more significant than actual party voting.

The Conservative Coalition

Although party voting appears more important than regional alignments, one regional voting block can be identified on a significant number of issues in Congress. As David Truman explains,

the evidence is clear that there [is] a solid and sharply identifiable die-hard element among the Southern Democrats, whose opposition extend[s] well beyond the issues of intense regional loyalty to almost a whole range of questions growing out of the strains and stresses to which the American society has been subjected in the mid-twentieth century.[25]

On the civil rights votes, this block of southern Democrats votes in opposition to a majority of both northern Democrats and Republicans.

More significant, however, is the "conservative coalition" of southern Democrats and Republicans who oppose the northern Democrats. In recent years this coalition has occurred on about 20 percent of all congressional roll calls (see Table 11–7). The coalition votes together on such issues as aid to depressed areas, minimum wage laws, federal aid to education, public housing, urban renewal, medical care for the aged, taxation, and other domestic welfare questions. Not all southern Democrats or Republicans vote with the coalition; a roll-call coalition is defined as any roll call in which a majority of voting southern Democrats and a majority of voting Republicans oppose a majority of northern Democrats. The coalition generally has resisted the expansion of federal power and the increase of federal spending programs.

The fortunes of the conservative coalition depend to some degree on the mood of the electorate. In 1974, for example, the ranks of the Democratic party were swelled; with fewer Republicans available to join forces with the southerners, and with most of the added Democratic congressional members being liberal northerners, the coalition made its

Table 11–7
The Conservative
Coalition in Congress,
1970–1975

	Percentage of Coalition Roll Calls to Total	Percentage of Coalition Victories on Coalition Roll Calls
1970		
Senate	26	64
House	20	70
1971		
Senate	28	86
House	31	79
1972		
Senate	25	63
House	29	79
1973		
Senate	23	54
House	21	67
1974		
Senate	21	54
House	26	67
1975		
Senate	28	48
House	28	52
1976		
Senate	26	58
House	22	59

Source: Compiled from the *Congressional Quarterly Almanac* (Washington, D.C.: Congressional Quarterly Service, 1970–76).

worst showing since 1965. Still, winning half the time in a mood of liberal reform is impressive. In 1976 the coalition displayed its resilience by regaining its earlier percentage of victories in both houses of Congress—conspicuous among them was defeat of attempts to delete funding for several new weapons (such as the B–1 bomber). Part of the reason for the continued success of the coalition is the moderation of the once-feared Democratic representatives elected in 1974; when they took office they helped oust these conservative committee chairmen and co-operated in strengthening the party caucus, but by 1976 they had become more cautious and notedly more supportive of the conservative coalition. The "Class of '74" voted 32 percent of the time with the coalition (up from 27 percent in 1974). Indeed, by 1976, they were no more liberal than their more experienced colleagues.

✳ Summary

This analysis of Congress produces several propositions that enable us to refine elite theory, and apply it to a specific institution:

1. Congress tends to represent locally organized elites, who inject a strong parochial influence in national decision making. Congressional members are

responsible to national interests that have a strong base of support in their home constituencies.

2. A member's relevant political constituency is not the general population of the home district but its elite. Less than half the general population of a district knows its legislator's name; fewer still have any idea of how he voted on any major issue. Only a tiny fraction ever express their views on a public issue to their legislators.

3. With the possible exception of civil rights questions, most congressional members are free from the influence of popular preferences in their legislative voting. However, a member's voting record generally reflects the socioeconomic makeup of the home district. Congressional members are products of the social system in their constituency; they share its dominant goals and values.

4. Congress seldom initiates changes in public policy. Instead it responds to policy proposals initiated by the president, executive and military elites, and interested nongovernment elites. The congressional role in national decision making is usually deliberative: Congress responds to policies initiated by others.

5. Congressional committees are important to communication between government and nongovernment elites. "Policy clusters," consisting of alliances of leaders from executive agencies, congressional committees, and private business and industry, tend to develop in Washington. Committee chairmen are key members of these policy clusters, because of their control over legislation in Congress.

6. The elaborate rules and procedures of Congress delay and obstruct proposed changes in the *status quo*, thus strengthening its conservative role in policy making. For a bill to become a law is a difficult process; congressional procedures offer many opportunities for defeat and many obstacles to passage.

7. An elite system within Congress places effective control over legislation in the hands of a relatively few members. Most of these congressional "establishment" members are conservative congressmen from both parties who have acquired great seniority and therefore control key committee chairmanships.

8. Most bills that are not killed before the floor vote are passed unanimously. The greatest portion of the national budget is passed without debate. What conflict exists in Congress tends to follow party lines more often than any other factional division. Conflict centers on the details of domestic and foreign policy, but seldom on its major directions.

References

[1]See Donald Matthews *Social Background of Political Decision Makers* (New York: Doubleday & Co., 1954).

[2]Heinz Eulau and John D. Sprague, *Lawyers in Politics* (Indianapolis, Ind.: Bobbs-Merrill Co., 1964).

[3]See Joseph A. Schlesinger, *Ambition and Politics* (Chicago: Rand McNally, 1966).

[4]Lewis A. Froman, *Congressmen and Their Constituencies* (Chicago: Rand McNally, 1963).

[5]Sam Kernell, "Is the Senate More Liberal Than the House?" *Journal of Politics*, 35 (May 1973), pp. 332–336.

[6]Committee on Government Operations, Subcommittee on Intergovernmental Relations, *Confidence and Concern: Citizens View American Government* (Washington, D.C.: Government Printing Office, 1973), pp. 72–77.

[7]Robert S. Erikson and Norman Luttbeg, *American Public Opinion* (New York: John Wiley, 1973), p. 281

[8]Warren Miller and Donald Stokes, "Constituency Influence in Congress," *American Political Science Review*, 57 (March 1963), p. 55.

[9]Raymond A. Bauer, Ithiel De Sola Pool, and Lewis A. Dexter, *American Business and Public Policy* (New York: Atherton Press, 1963), Chapter 35.

[10]Philip E. Converse, A. R. Clausen, and Warren E. Miller, "Electoral Myth and Reality: the 1964 Election," *American Political Science Review*, 54 (June 1965), pp. 321–336.

[11]V. O. Key, Jr., *Public Opinion and American Democracy* (New York: Alfred A. Knopf, 1961), p. 418.

[12]Charles O. Jones, "The Role of the Campaign in Congressional Politics," in M. Kent Jennings and Harmon Zeigler, eds., *The Electoral Process* (Englewood Cliffs, N.J.: Prentice-Hall, 1966), p. 21.

[13]Fred Westheimer, quoted in *Congressional Quarterly* (December 1, 1973), p. 3130.

[14]John W. Kingdon, *Congressmen's Voting Decisions* (New York: Harper and Row, 1973), p. 62.

[15]*Ibid.*, p. 88.

[16]Roger H. Davidson, David M. Kovenock, and Michael K. O'Leary, *Congress in Crisis: Politics and Congressional Reform* (Belmont, Calif.: Wadsworth Publishing Co., 1966), pp. 67–91.

[17]David B. Truman, *The Governmental Process* (New York: Alfred A. Knopf, 1955), p. 344.

[18]Donald R. Matthews, "The Folkways of the United States Senate: Conformity to Group Norms and Legislative Effectiveness," *American Political Science Review*, 53 (December 1959), pp. 1064–1089.

[19]William S. White, *The Citadel: The Story of the U.S. Senate* (New York: Harper and Row, 1956), Chapter VII.

[20]Cited in Nelson Polsby, "Goodbye to the InnerClub," in Lowi and Ripley, *Legislative Politics, U.S.A.*, p. 132.

[21]Joseph S. Clark, *The Senate Establishment* (New York: Hill & Wang, 1963).

[22]White, *The Citadel*, p. 84.

[23]Joseph S. Clark, *Congress: The Sapless Branch* (New York: Harper & Row, 1964), pp. 22–23.

[24]See Malcolm E. Jewell and Samuel C. Patterson, *The Legislative Process in the United States* (New York: Random House, 1966); William J. Keefe and Morris Ogul, *The American Legislative Process* (Englewood Cliffs, N.J.: Prentice-Hall, 1964).

[25]Truman, *Governmental Process*, p. 344.

Courts: Elites in Black Robes 12

The Supreme Court of the United States and the federal court system compose the most elitist institution in American government. Nine men—none of whom are elected and all of whom serve for life—possess ultimate authority over all of the other institutions of American government. These men have the power to void the acts of popularly elected presidents, Congresses, governors, state legislators, school boards, and city councils. There is no appeal from their decisions about what is the "supreme law of the land," except perhaps to undertake the difficult task of amending the Constitution itself.

Many of the nation's most important domestic policy decisions have been made by the Supreme Court rather than the president or Congress. It was the Supreme Court which took the lead in eliminating segregation from public life, insuring separation of church and state, defining rights of criminal defendants and the powers of law enforcement officials, insuring voters equality in representation, defining the limits of free speech and free press, and declaring abortion to be a fundamental right of women. Courts, then, are deeply involved in policy making—on such diverse issues as school segregation, busing, public school prayers, federal aid to church-supported schools, capital punishment, police brutality, crime and law enforcement, malapportionment of representation, pornography, censorship, and abortion. Indeed, sooner or later in American politics, most important policy questions are decided by judges—who are not elected to office and cannot be removed for anything other than "treason, bribery, or high crimes and misdemeanors." As de Tocqueville observed as early as 1835: "Scarcely any political question arises in the United States that is not resolved, sooner or later, into a judicial question."[1]

Judicial Review as an Elitist Principle

The undemocratic character of judicial power in America has long been recognized. The Founding Fathers viewed the federal courts as the final bulwark against mass threats to principle and property. In *The Federalist* No. 78, Hamilton wrote:

By a limited Constitution I understand one which contains certain specified exceptions to the legislative authority; such, for instance, as that it shall pass no bills of attainder, no ex post facto laws, and the like. Limitations of this kind can be preserved in practice no other way than through the medium of courts of justice, whose duty it is to declare all acts contrary to the manifest tenor of the Constitution void. Without this, all the reservations of particular rights or privileges would amount to nothing.[2]

In *Marbury* v. *Madison*, the historic decision establishing the power of judicial review, John Marshall argued persuasively that: (1) The Constitution is "the supreme law of the land," and the laws of the United States and of the states must be made in pursuit thereof; (2) Article III of the Constitution gives to the Supreme Court the judicial power, which includes the power to interpret the meaning of laws, and, in case of conflict between laws, decide which law shall prevail; (3) the courts are sworn to uphold the Constitution, therefore, they must declare void a law that conflicts with the Constitution.

Since 1803, the federal courts have struck down more than eighty laws of Congress and uncounted state laws that they believed conflicted with the Constitution. Judicial review and the power to interpret the meaning and decide the application of law are the major sources of power for judges.

The Founding Fathers' decision to grant federal courts the power of judicial review of *state* decision is easy to understand. After all, it is stated in Article VI that the Constitution and the laws and treaties of the national government are the supreme law of the land, "anything in the Constitution or laws of any state to the contrary notwithstanding." Federal court power over state decisions is probably essential in maintaining national unity, for fifty different state interpretations of the meaning of the U.S. Constitution or of the laws and treaties of Congress would create unimaginable confusion. Thus, the power of federal judicial review over state constitutions, laws, and court decisions is seldom questioned.

However, at the national level, why should an appointed court's interpretation of the Constitution prevail over the views of an elected Congress and an elected president? Congressmen and presidents are sworn to uphold the Constitution, and it can reasonably be assumed that they do not pass laws that they believe to be unconstitutional. Since laws must be approved by majorities of those voting in both houses and must have the president's formal approval, why should the Founding Fathers have allowed the decisions of these bodies to be set aside by the federal courts?

The answer appears to be that the Founding Fathers distrusted popular majorities and the elected officials who might be influenced by them. They believed that government should be limited so that it could not attack principle and property, whether to do so was the will of the majority or not. So the courts were deliberately insulated against popular majorities; to insure their independence, judges were not to be elected, but appointed for life terms. Originally, it was expected that they would be appointed by a president who was not even directly elected himself and confirmed by a Senate that was not directly elected. Only in this way, the writers of the Constitution believed, would judges be sufficiently protected from the masses to permit them to judge courageously and responsibly.

Find + Xerox

The Making of a Judge

The social backgrounds of judges reflect close ties with the upper social strata. John R. Schmidhauser reports that over 90 percent of the Supreme Court justices serving on the Court between 1789 and 1962 were from socially prominent, politically influential, upper-class families.[3] Over two-thirds of the Supreme Court justices ever serving on the Court attended prestigious or Ivy League law schools (Harvard, Yale, Columbia, Pennsylvania, N.Y.U., Michigan, Virginia, etc.). No blacks served on the Supreme Court until the appointment of Associate Justice Thurgood Marshall in 1967. Henry Abraham depicts the typical Supreme Court justice:

White, generally Protestant . . . ; fifty to fifty-five years of age at the ✳ *time of his appointment; Anglo-Saxon ethnic stock . . . ; high social status; reared in an urban environment; member of a civic-minded, politically active, economically comfortable family; legal training; some type of public office; generally well educated.*[4]

The Role of the Courts in the American System: Views of the Founders

Marshall in Support of Judicial Review:

It is emphatically the province and duty of the judicial department to say what the law is. Those who apply the law to particular cases, must of necessity expound and interpret that rule. If two laws conflict with each other, the courts must decide on the operation of each.

So if a law be in opposition to the constitution; if both the law and the constitution apply to a particular case, so that the court must decide that case conformably to the law, disregarding the constitution; or conformably to the constitution, disregarding the law; the court must determine which of these conflicting rules governs each case. This is of the very essence of judicial duty.

If, then, the courts are to regard the constitution, and the constitution is superior to any ordinary act of the legislature, the constitution, and not such ordinary act, must govern the case to which they both apply . . .

Chief Justice John Marshall in *Marbury* v. *Madison* (1803).

Gibson in Opposition to Judicial Review:

The Constitution and the right of the legislature to pass the Act, may be in collision. But is that a legitimate subject for judicial determination? If it be, the judiciary must be a peculiar organ, to revise the proceedings of the legislature, and to correct its mistakes. And in what part of the Constitution are we to look for this proud pre-eminence? Viewing the matter in the opposite direction, what would be thought of an Act of Assembly in which it should be declared that the Supreme Court had, in a particular case, put a wrong construction of the Constitution of the United States, and that the judgment should therefore be reversed? It would doubtless be thought a usurpation of judicial power. But it is by no means clear, that to declare a law void which has been enacted according to the forms prescribed in the Constitution, is not a usurpation of legislative power. . . . It is the business of the judiciary to interpret the laws, not scan the authority of the lawgiver; and without the latter, it cannot take cognizance of a collision between a law and the Constitution . . .

Chief Justice Gibson of the Pennsylvania Supreme Court, in *Eakin* v. *Raub* (1825).

Hamilton in Defense of Life Terms for Judges:

The standard of good behavior for the continuance in office of the judicial magistracy is certainly one of the most valuable of the modern improvements in the practice of government. In a monarchy it is an excellent barrier to the despotism of the prince; in a republic it is a no less excellent barrier to the encroachments and oppressions of the representative body. And it is the best expedient which can be devised in any government to secure a steady, upright, and impartial administration of the laws. . . . If then, the courts of justice are to be considered as the bulwarks of a limited Constitution against legislative encroachments, this consideration will afford a strong argument for the permanent tenure of judicial offices, since nothing will contribute so much as this to that independent spirit in the judges which must be essential to the faithful performance of so arduous a duty.

Alexander Hamilton, *The Federalist*, Number 78.

Hamilton on Behalf of an Elitist Judiciary:

Hence it is that there can be but few men in the society who will have sufficient skill in the laws to qualify them for the station of judges. And making the proper deductions for the ordinary depravity of human nature, the number must be still smaller of those who unite the requisite integrity with the requisite knowledge. These considerations apprise us that the government can have no great option between fit characters; and that a temporary duration in office which would naturally discourage such characters from quitting a lucrative line of practice to accept a seat on the bench would have a tendency to throw the administration of justice into hands less able and less qualified to conduct it with utility and dignity.

Alexander Hamilton, *The Federalist*, Number 78.

Drawing by David Yanzdon. © 1976
Punch (Rothco).

Of course, social background does not necessarily determine judicial philosophy. But as Schmidhauser observes:

If . . . the Supreme Court is the keeper of the American conscience, it is essentially the conscience of the American upper-middle class, sharpened by the imperative of individual social responsibility and political activism, and conditioned by the conservative impact of legal training and professional legal attitudes and associations. [5]

All federal judges are appointed by the president and confirmed by the Senate. The recruitment process that brings the names of potential appointees to the president's desk is highly political. Herbert Jacob reports that 80 percent of federal judges have held political office some time in their career prior to appointment.[6] (See Table 12–1.) Less than one-third of the nation's Supreme Court justices have had prior experience as judges. Few Supreme Court justices are promoted through the federal court system; political support and friendship with the president is a more promising avenue toward high judicial appointment. Generally, agreement with the political philosophy of the president is a necessary criterion for consideration. Of course, once appointed, a Supreme

Court justice can pursue a course of policy at variance with the president, and many have done so. The Attorney General's office assists the president in screening candidates for all federal judgeships; after the choice is narrowed, the president usually requests the American Bar Association to comment on the qualifications of the proposed nominees.

The president's formal nomination of a federal judge must be confirmed by a majority vote of the U.S. Senate. Until recently the Senate Judiciary Committee, which holds hearings and recommends confirmation to the full Senate, has accepted nominations by the president with a minimum of dissent. (The Senate has failed to approve only 28 of the 130 Supreme Court nominations ever sent to it.) The prevailing ethos was that a popularly elected president deserved the opportunity to appoint his own judges; that the opposition party in Congress would have its own opportunity to appoint judges when it captured the presidency; and that partisan bickering over judicial appointments should be avoided. But in recent years presidential-congressional cooperation on Supreme Court nominations has broken down on several occasions. In 1968 President Lyndon Johnson nominated his own lawyer, prominent Washington attorney Abe Fortas, to the Chief Justiceship of the Supreme Court. Fortas was already serving as an Associate Justice through an earlier Johnson appointment. A coalition of liberal (anti-Johnson) Democrats and Republicans in Congress complained of "cronyism," and information concerning Fortas's financial affairs was used to discredit his nomination and force his resignation from the Court.

Later, when President Nixon nominated two southern federal judges to the Supreme Court—Clement F. Haynsworth and G. Harold Carswell—similar tactics were employed in Congress to halt these presidential nominations. President Nixon charged that the Senate, by withholding confirmation of his southern conservative nominees, was infringing upon his "constitutional responsibility"; Nixon had actually campaigned for office pledging to alter the liberal stance of the Warren Court, and he believed he had a constitutional mandate to do so. Eventually, the Senate confirmed the president's nomination of other

Table 12–1
The Supreme Court

Justices	Position Held at Time of Appointment
Chief Justice:	
Warren Burger	Judge, U.S. Court of Appeals
Associate Justices:	
William O. Douglas	Member, Securities and Exchange Commission
Thurgood Marshall	U.S. Solicitor General
William J. Brennan, Jr.	Justice, Supreme Court of New Jersey
Potter Stewart	U.S. Deputy Attorney General
Byron R. White	U.S. Deputy Attorney General
Harry A. Blackmun	Judge, U.S. Court of Appeals
Lewis F. Powell, Jr.	Private practice
William H. Rehnquist	Assistant Attorney General

conservatives—Burger, Blackmun, Powell, and Rehnquist.

Presidents usually nominate judges who share their own political philosophy. Actually, this might be considered a democratizing influence on the Court, assuming that the people elect a president because of their agreement with *his* political philosophy. But Supreme Court justices frequently become independent once they reach the Court. Former Chief Justice Earl Warren, as Republican governor of California, had swung critical delegate votes to Eisenhower in the 1952 Republican Convention. When he was rewarded with the Chief Justiceship by a grateful president, there was little in Warren's background to suggest that he would lead the most liberal era in the Court's history. Later Eisenhower would complain that the Warren appointment was "the biggest damn mistake I ever made."[7]

The Special Style of Judicial Policy Making

The power of the courts to shape American life is cloaked in an *appearance of objectivity*. Because judges are appointed for life and legally accountable to no one, they maintain the fiction that they are *not* engaged in policy making but merely "applying" the law to specific cases. To admit otherwise would spotlight the conflict between judicial power and the democratic myth of policy making by elected representatives.

Former Supreme Court Justice Owen J. Roberts once defended the myth of judicial objectivity:

It is sometimes said that the court assumes a power to overrule or control the action of the people's representatives. This is a misconception. The Constitution is the supreme law of the land ordained and established by the people. All legislation must conform to the principles it lays down. When an act of Congress is appropriately challenged in the courts as not conforming to the constitutional mandate, the judicial branch has only one duty—to lay the article of the Constitution which is involved beside the statute which is challenged and to decide whether the latter squares with the former. All the court does, or can do, is to announce its considered judgement upon the question. The only power it has, if such it may be called, is the power of judgement. [8]

Carl Brent Swisher admits of some judicial policy making but still clings to the notion of judicial objectivity: "The court determines the facts involved in particular controversies brought before it, relates the facts to the relevant law, settles the controversies in terms of the law, and more or less incidentally makes new law through the process of decision."[9]

This mechanistic theory of judicial objectivity is acknowledged as a myth by many of the nation's better judicial thinkers. For example, former Justice Felix Frankfurter once observed:

The meaning of "due process" and the content of terms like "liberty" are not revealed by the Constitution. It is the Justices who make the meaning. They read into the neutral language of the Constitution their own economic and social views. . . . Let us face the fact that five Justices of the Supreme Court are the molders of policy rather than the impersonal vehicles of revealed truth. [10]

The courts also maintain the *fiction of nonpartisanship*. Judges must not appear to permit political considerations to affect their decisions. *After* they are appointed to the federal bench, they are expected to have fewer direct ties to political organizations than congressmen. They must not appear to base their decisions on partisan considerations, or party platforms, or to bargain in the fashion of legislators. Perhaps as a result of their nonpartisan appearance, courts enjoy a measure of prestige that other government institutions lack. Court decisions become more acceptable to the public if the public believes that the courts dispense unbiased justice.

Courts function under *special rules of access*. For example, courts seldom themselves initiate policies or programs in the fashion of Congress or the executive branch. Instead, courts wait until a case involving a policy question is brought before them. The Constitution gives jurisdiction to federal courts only in "cases and controversies." Courts do not issue policy pronouncements, rules, or order on their own initiative. For example, courts do not declare a law of Congress or an action of the president unconstitutional immediately upon its passage or occurrence. Nor do the federal courts render advisory opinions prior to congressional or executive action. Instead, the courts assume a passive role and wait until a case comes before them which directly challenges a law of Congress or action of the president.

To gain access to the federal courts, we must present a *case* in which the federal courts have *jurisdiction*. A case must involve two disputing parties, one of which must have incurred some real damages as a result of the action or inaction of the other. The *federal* courts will accept jurisdiction based on: (1) *the nature of the parties*—a case in which the United States government is a party; or a controversy between two or more states, or between a state and a citizen or another state, or between citizens of different states; or a case involving a foreign nation or citizen; or (2) *the nature of the controversy*—a case which arises under the Constitution (a "constitutional question") or under the laws and treaties of the United States. Congress has further limited the jurisdiction of federal courts in cases between citizens of different states by requiring that the dispute must involve over $10,000. All other cases must be heard in state courts.

Judicial policy making occurs in a *legalistic style*. Facts and arguments are presented to the courts in formal testimony, cross-examination, legal briefs, and oral arguments; all of these presentments are highly ritualized. Legal skills are generally required to make these presentments in a fashion that meet the technical specifications of the courts. Decorum in court proceedings is highly valued because it conveys a sense of dignity; legislative or executive offices rarely function with as much decorum.

These distinctive features of judicial policy making—the appearance of objectivity, the fiction of nonpartisanship, special rules of access, limited jurisdiction, and legalistic style—all contribute to the power of the courts. These features help to legitimize court decisions, to win essential support for them, and thus contribute to influence of judges in the political system.

The Structure of the Federal Court System

The federal court system consists of three levels of courts with general jurisdiction, together with various special courts (a Court of Claims, a Customs Court, a Patent Court, and the Court of Military Appeals). Only the Supreme Court is established by the Constitution itself, although the number of Supreme Court justices—traditionally nine—is determined by Congress. Article III authorized Congress to establish "such inferior courts" as it deems appropriate. Congress has designed a hierarchical court system consisting of nearly one hundred *U.S. federal district courts* and eleven *U.S. circuit courts of appeals,* in addition to the *Supreme Court of the United States.* (See Figure 12–1.)

Figure 12–1
The United States
Court System

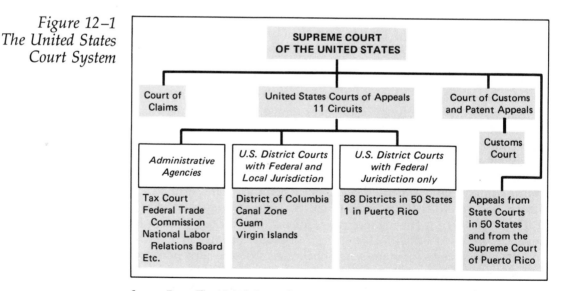

Source: From *The United States Courts: Their Jurisdiction, and Work,* Committee on the Judiciary, House of Representatives, Washington, D.C.: U.S. Government Printing Office, 1969, p. 3.

Federal district courts are the trial courts of the federal system. Each state has at least one district court, but larger states have more. (New York, for example, has four.) There are over three hundred federal district judges, appointed for life by the president and confirmed by the Senate. The president also appoints a U.S. marshal for each district court to carry out orders of the court and maintain order in the courtroom. Federal district courts hear criminal cases prosecuted by the U.S. Department of Justice, as well as civil cases. As trial courts, the district courts make use of both grand juries (juries composed to hear evidence and, if warranted, to indict a defendant by bringing formal criminal charges against him) and petit, or regular, juries (juries which determine guilt or innocence). District courts may hear as many as 300,000 cases in a year.

Circuit courts of appeals are appellate courts. They do not hold trials or accept new evidence but consider only the record of the trial courts and oral or written arguments (briefs) submitted by attorneys. Federal law provides that every individual has a right to appeal his or her case, so courts of appeals have little discretion in hearing appeals. There are nearly one hundred circuit court judges, appointed for life by the president and confirmed by the Senate. Normally, three judges serve together on a panel to hear appeals. Over 90 percent of the cases decided by circuit courts of appeals are ended at this level. Further appeal to the Supreme Court is not automatic, but must be decided by the Supreme Court itself. Hence, for most cases, the decision of the circuit court of appeals is final.

The Supreme Court of the United States is the final interpreter of all matters involving the U.S. Constitution and federal laws and treaties, whether the case began in a federal district court or in a state court. In some cases the Supreme Court has original jurisdiction (authority to serve as a trial court), but this jurisdiction is seldom used. Appellate jurisdiction is the Supreme Court's major function. Appeals may come from a state court of last resort (usually state supreme courts) or from lower federal courts. The Supreme Court determines for itself whether to accept an appeal and consider a case. It may do so if there is "a substantial federal question" presented in the case, or if there are "special and important reasons." Appeal can be granted by any four justices. However, most cases submitted to the Supreme Court, on "writs of appeal" and "writs of certiorari," are denied; and the Court need not give any reason for denying appeal or certiorari.

In the early days of the republic, the size of the U.S. Supreme Court fluctuated, but since 1869 its membership has remained at nine—a chief justice and eight associate justices. The Supreme Court is in session each year from October through June, hearing oral arguments, accepting written briefs, conferring among themselves, and rendering opinions.

Majority opinions of the Supreme Court are usually written by a single justice who summarizes majority sentiment. Concurring opinions are written by justices who vote with the majority but who feel the majority opinion does not fully explain their own reasons. A dissenting opinion is written by a justice who is in the minority; such opinions have no impact on the outcome of the case. Written opinions are printed, distributed to the press, and published in *U.S. Reports* and other legal reporting services.

Activism Versus Self-Restraint in Judicial Policy Making

Great legal scholars have argued the merits of activism versus self-restraint in judicial decision making for more than a century.[11] One view argues for self-restraint in judicial policy making: since justices are *not* popularly elected, the Supreme Court should move cautiously and avoid direct confrontation with legislative and executive authority. Justice Felix Frankfurter wrote:

The only check upon our own exercise of power is our own sense of self-restraint. For the removal of unwise laws from the statute books appeal lies, not to the courts, but to the ballot and to the processes of democratic government. [12]

But Frankfurter was arguing a minority position on the Court. The dominant philosophy of the Warren Court (1953–1969) was one of judicial activism. As Harvard law professor Archibald Cox asked:

Should the Court plan an active creative role in shaping our destiny, equally with the executive and legislative branches? Or should it be characterized by self-restraint, deferring to the legislative branch whenever there is room for policy judgement and leaving new departures to the initiative of others? [13]

Clearly the Warren Court believed it should shape constitutional meaning to fit its own estimate of the needs of contemporary society. In defense of a broad and flexible construction of the Constitution, it can be argued that if the fundamental law of the land does not change over time to fit a changing society, dozens of new constitutional amendments would be required each generation. The strength of the American Constitution lies in its flexibility—its relevance to contemporary society.

Nonetheless, the notion of self-restraint is reflected in a number of self-imposed maxims of interpretive philosophy—maxims which are generally, but not always, followed by the Supreme Court:

1. The Court will not pass upon the constitutionality of legislation in a nonadversary proceeding but only in a real case.
2. The Court will not anticipate a question on constitutional law in advance of the necessity of deciding it. The Court does not decide hypothetical cases.

3. The Court will not formulate a rule of constitutional law broader than is required by the precise facts to which it is to be applied.

4. The Court will not pass upon a constitutional question, if there is also present some other ground upon which the case may be disposed of.

5. The Court will not pass upon the validity of a law if the complainant fails to show that he has been injured by the law, or if the complainant has availed himself of the benefits of the law.

6. When there is doubt about the constitutionality of a law, the Court will try to interpret the meaning of a law so as to give it a constitutional meaning and avoid the necessity of declaring it unconstitutional.

7. All remedies available in lower federal courts or state courts must have been exhausted before the Supreme Court accepts review.

8. The constitutional issue must be crucial to the case, and it must be substantial rather than trivial, before the Court will invalidate a law.

9. Occasionally, the Court defers to Congress and the president and classifies an issue as a "political question," and refuses to decide it. The Court has stayed out of foreign and military policy areas.

10. If a law is held unconstitutional, the Court will confine the holding only to the particular section of the law that is unconstitutional, thus not affecting the rest of the statute.[14]

Courts are also limited by the principle of *stare decisis*, which means that the issue has already been decided in earlier cases. Reliance upon precedent is a fundamental notion in law. Indeed, the underlying *common law* of England and the United States is composed simply of past decisions. Students of the law learn what the law is through the case-study method—the study of previous decisions. Reliance on precedent gives stability to the law: if every decision is new law, then no one would know what the law would be from day to day. But the Supreme Court frequently discards precedent. Former Justice William O. Douglas, who seldom felt restrained by legal precedent, justified disregard of precedent as follows:

the decisions of yesterday or of the last century are only the starting points . . . a judge looking at a constitutional decision may have compulsions to revere the past history and accept what was once written. But he remembers above all else that it is the Constitution which he swore to support and defend, not the gloss which his predecessors may have put on it. So he comes to formulate his own laws, rejecting some earlier ones as false and embracing others. He cannot do otherwise unless he lets men long dead and unaware of the problems of the age in which he lives do his thinking for him.[15]

Distinguished jurists have long urged the Supreme Court to exercise self-restraint. A law may be unwise, unjust, unfair, or even stupid, and yet still be constitutional. One cannot equate the wisdom of a law with its constitutionality; and the Court should decide only the constitutionality and not the wisdom of a law. Justice Oliver Wendell Holmes once lectured his colleague, 61-year-old Justice Stone:

Young man, about 75 years ago I learned that I was not God. And so, when the people . . . want to do something I can't find anything in the Constitution expressly forbidding them to do, I say, whether I like it or not, "Goddamn it, let 'em do it."[16]

But the actual role of the Supreme Court in America's power struggles suggests that the Court is indeed prepared to equate wisdom with constitutionality. Broad phrases in the Fifth and Fourteenth Amendments establishing constitutional standards of "due process of law" and "equal protection of the laws" are frequently cited in attacks on laws believed to be unfair or unjust. Most Americans have come to believe that unwise laws must be unconstitutional, and that the courts have become the final arbiter of fairness and justice.

The Supreme Court in Elitist Perspective

The Supreme Court is best understood as an elitist institution, rather than as a conservative or liberal institution in American government. During the 1930s, the Supreme Court was a bastion of conservatism; it attacked the economic programs of the New Deal and clung to the earlier elite philosophy of rugged individualism. Yet the Warren Court was criticized as too liberal in its orientations toward equality of the law, church-state relations, and individual rights before the law. The apparent paradox can be understood if we view the Court as an exponent of the dominant elite philosophy, rather than as a constant liberal or conservative element in national politics. When the dominant elite philosophy was rugged individualism, the Court reflected this fact, just as it reflects a liberal philosophy today. Of course, owing to the insulation of the Court even from other elites, through life terms and independence from the executive and legislative branches, there is a time lag between changes in elite philosophy and the Court decisions reflecting these changes.

Before the Civil War, the Supreme Court spoke first for the Federalists under John Marshall and later for Southern planters and slaveholders under Roger Taney. Marshall, who served as Chief Justice for thirty-four years, helped to elevate the Supreme Court to a position of importance in American government equal to that of Congress and the president. Rulings by his Court helped establish the authority of the national government over the states and protect the rights of property. Taney, Marshall's successor, retreated from Marshall's nationalism and defended property rights in land and slaves. In *Dred Scott* v. *Sanford*, Taney declared that slavery was constitutionally protected and invalidated the Missouri Compromise by declaring that Congress did not have the power to exclude slavery from any of the territories.

Following the emergence of industrial capitalism in the second half of the nineteenth century, the Supreme Court became the spokesman for the prevailing elite philosophy of social Darwinism. The Court struck down the federal income tax; it prevented prosecutions of corporations under the Sherman Antitrust Act, while applying this act against labor unions; and it struck down child labor laws and laws limiting the work week. The Court interpreted the interstate commerce clause so restrictively that it prevented federal regulation of the economy. It interpreted the "due process" clause of the Fifth and Fourteenth Amendments and the contract clause of Article II, Section 10, in such a way as to protect business enterprise from almost any form of government regulation. Justice Oliver Wendell Holmes lamented, "the Fourteenth Amendment does not enact Mr. Herbert Spencer's *Social Statics.* . . . A constitution is not intended to embody a particular economic theory whether of paternalism . . . or of laissez faire."[17] But Holmes was writing a minority opinion. The majority impulse of the Court was to read social Darwinism into the Constitution itself and to give it constitutional protection.

The Supreme Court's greatest crisis occurred when it failed to respond swiftly to changes in elite philosophy. When Franklin D. Roosevelt became president in 1933, the Supreme Court was committed to the philosophy of rugged individualism. In a four-year period (1933–1937) the Court made the most active use of the power of judicial review over congressional legislation in its history, in a vain attempt to curtail the economic recovery programs of the New Deal. It invalidated the National Industrial Recovery Administration, nullified the Railroad Retirement Act, invalidated the National Farm Mortgage Act, and threw out the Agricultural Adjustment Act. Having denied the federal government the power to regulate manufacturing, petroleum, mining, agriculture, and labor conditions, the Court reaffirmed the notion that the states could not regulate hours and wages. By 1936, it appeared certain that the Court would declare the Social Security Act and the National Labor Relations Act unconstitutional.

The failure of the Court to adapt itself quickly to the new liberalism of the national elite led to its greatest crisis. Roosevelt proposed to "pack" the Court by expanding its size and adding new liberal members. But the nation's leadership itself was divided over such a drastic remedy; so well had the Court served the interests of the established order over its history that Congress was reluctant to accept Roosevelt's plan. Moreover, at a critical point in the debate, the Court changed its attitude, with Chief Justice Hughes and Justice Roberts making timely changes in their position. In *National Labor Relations Board* v. *Jones & Laughlin Steel Corporation*, the Court expanded the definition of interstate commerce to remove constitutional barriers to government regulation of the economy.[18] The power of the federal government to establish a social security system was upheld in a series of decisions that struck down the "due process" objections to social and economic legislation. And the contract clause was reinterpreted to permit Congress and the states to regulate wages, hours, and conditions of work.

A liberal concern for the underprivileged in America was reflected in the development of civil rights law by the Supreme Court under the leadership of Chief Justice Earl Warren. The Court firmly insisted that no person in America should be denied equal protection of the law. It defended the right of blacks to vote, to attend integrated schools, and to receive equal justice in the courts; it upheld the power of Congress to protect blacks from discrimination in public accommodations, employment, voting, and housing. It ruled that discrimination against any group of voters by state legislatures in the apportioning of election districts was unconstitutional. It protected religious minorities (and the nonreligious) from laws establishing official prayers and religious ceremonies in public schools. The Court also protected defendants in criminal cases from self-incrimination through ignorance of their rights, through the subtlety of law enforcement officials in extracting confessions, or through lack of legal counsel.

It is interesting, however, that the Court was noticeably less concerned with civil liberty when the liberal establishment's cold-war ideology was involved. In *Dennis* v. *United States* the Court permitted the prosecution of communists for merely "advocating" the overthrow of the government[19] and in *Communist Party, U.S.A.* v. *Subversive Activities Control Board*, it upheld the right of government to require the registration of "subversive" organizations.[20] It permitted congressional committees to interrogate citizens about their political views and upheld loyalty oaths and loyalty-security programs. But by the late 1960s, after a decline of cold-war ideology among the nation's elite, the Court began to protect "communists" and "subversives" from some of the harsher provisions of federal law.

Popular predictions that the Burger Court, with four Nixon appointees including Chief Justice Warren Burger, would reverse the liberal decisions of the Warren Court were based on a misunderstanding of the elitist character of the Court. Supreme Court efforts to end racial segregation under law, insure equality in representation, and maintain separation of church and state are fundamental commitments of the national elite. Hence, there was little actual likelihood of a rollback of the landmark decisions of the Warren Court in these areas. The Burger Court extended the doctrine of *Brown* v. *Topeka* to uphold Court-ordered busing of children to end racial imbalance in public schools with a history of segregation under law (Southern school districts).[21] However, the Court refused to extend the busing requirement to force independent suburban school districts to bus students into central cities to achieve racial balance in predominantly black city schools. The Burger Court also struck down state payments to church schools for nonreligious instruction.[22] Only in the area of rights of criminal defendants has the Burger Court altered the direction of Warren Court holdings; even here, the Burger Court has not reversed any earlier holdings but merely failed to extend them further.

Liberals were hopeful that the Burger Court would continue to expand the meaning of the Equal Protection Clause of the Fourteenth Amendment by ordering state funding of local schools because of financial inequalities in the property tax bases of local school districts. But the Court declined to do so, refusing to substitute its own judgment for that of state and local authorities about how schools should be financed.[23] Many civil rights groups also hoped the Burger Court would use the Eighth Amendment prohibition against "cruel and unusual punishment" as a device to strike down the death penalty. But the Court, while insisting on fairness and uniformity in application,[24] upheld the death penalty itself. Again, the Court declined to substitute its own notions about "cruel and unusual punishment" for the judgment of the many state legislatures that had voted to retain the death penalty.[25]

However, the Burger Court issued one of the most sweeping declarations of individual liberty in the Supreme Court's history: the assertion of the constitutional right of women to have abortions in the first six months of pregnancy.[26] The ultimate social impact of this decision—on population growth, the environment, and the role of women in society—may be as far-reaching as any decision ever rendered by the Court. Certainly this decision clearly indicates that the Supreme Court continues to be a powerful institution capable of affecting the lives of virtually all Americans.

Recognizing the elitist character of the U.S. Supreme Court, Professor John P. Roche once described the Court as:

. . . a Platonic graft on the democratic process—a group of wise men insulated from the people have the task of injecting truth serum into the body politic, of acting as an institutional chaperone to insure that the sovereign populace and its elected representatives do not act unwisely.[27]

Summary

Many of the nation's most important policies are determined by the Supreme Court of the United States. Indeed, most political questions sooner or later end up in the courts. Any fair examination of the court system in America will reveal the elitist character of judicial decision making.

1. The Supreme Court is established as the most elitist branch of the national government. Nine men—none of whom are elected and all of whom serve for life—can void the acts of popularly elected presidents, Congresses, governors, legislatures, school boards, and city councils.

2. The principle of judicial review of congressional acts grew out of the Founding Fathers' distrust of popularly elected officials who could be influenced by popular majorities. Judicial review enables the courts to protect constitutional principles against attacks by elected bodies.

3. The social backgrounds of judges reflect close ties to upper-class segments of society. Presidents may attempt to influence court decisions in their selection of judges, but life terms make judges independent of presidential or congressional influence once they are appointed.

4. Judicial decision making takes on an appearance of objectivity, maintains the fiction of nonpartisanship, employs special rules of access, and reflects a legalistic style. These features help to legitimize the decisions of men who have no electoral mandate.

5. Since judges are *not* popularly elected, some scholars and jurists have urged self-restraint in judicial policy making. This means the Court should decide only the constitutionality of a law, not its wisdom; the Court should not substitute its own judgment for the judgment of elected representatives. But over the years judicial activism has augmented the power of judges. Broad phrases in the Constitution such as "due process of law" and "equal protection of the law" have been used to strike down laws which the Court believed to be unfair or unjust.

6. Over its history the Supreme Court has not been consistently liberal or conservative, but rather reflective of dominant elite philosophy. The greatest crisis in the Court's history occurred in the 1930s when dominant elites accepted New Deal "liberalism," but the Court continued to reflect the "rugged individualism" of an earlier era. Contrary to popular beliefs, the Burger Court has not reversed any of the landmark decisions of the Warren Court. Instead, it has continued to reflect prevailing liberal establishment concerns for civil rights, equality in representation, and separation of church and state. The Burger Court's assertion of the constitutional right to have abortions may be one of the most important decisions in the Court's history.

References

[1] Alexis de Tocqueville, *Democracy in America* (New York: Mentor Books, 1956), p. 73.

[2] James Madison, Alexander Hamilton, John Jay, *The Federalist* No. 78 (New York: The Modern Library, 1937), p. 505.

[3] John R. Schmidhauser, *The Supreme Court* (New York: Holt, Rinehart and Winston, 1960), p. 59.

[4] Henry Abraham, *The Judicial Process* (New York: Oxford University Press, 1962), p. 58.

[5] Schmidhauser, *The Supreme Court*, p. 59.

[6] Herbert Jacob, *Justice in America* (Boston: Little, Brown, 1965), p. 95.

[7] Joseph W. Bishop, "The Warren Court is Not Likely To Be Overruled," *New York Times Magazine*, September 7, 1969, p. 31.

[8] *U.S.* v. *Butler*, 297.

[9] Carl Brent Swisher, "The Supreme Court and the Moment of Truth," *American Political Science Review*, 54 (December 1960), p. 879.

[10]Felix Frankfurter, "The Supreme Court and the Public," *Forum*, 83 (June 1930), pp. 332-334.

[11]Frank Jerone, *Law and the Modern Mind* (New York: Coward-McCann, 1930); Benjamin N. Cardozo, *The Nature of the Judicial Process* (New Haven: Yale University Press, 1921); Roscoe Pond, *Justice According to Law* (New Haven: Yale University Press, 1951).

[12]*West Virginia State Board of Education* v. *Barnette*, 319 U.S. 624 (1943).

[13]Archibald Cox, *The Warren Court* (Cambridge: Harvard University Press, 1968), p. 2.

[14]See Henry Abraham, *The Judicial Process* (New York: Oxford University Press, 1962), pp. 310-326.

[15]Justice William O. Douglas "Stare Decisis," *The Record*, New York City Bar Association, April 1947.

[16]As quoted by Charles P. Curtis, *Lions Under the Throne* (Boston: Houghton-Mifflin, 1947), p. 281; also cited by Abraham, p. 325.

[17]*Lochner* v. *New York*, 198 U.S. 45 (1905).

[18]*National Labor Relations Board* v. *Jones and Laughlin Steel Corp.*, 301 U.S. 1 (1937).

[19]*Dennis* v. *U.S.*, 341 U.S. 494 (1951).

[20]*Communist Party, U.S.A.* v. *Subversive Activities Control Board*, 367 U.S. 1 (1961).

[21]*Swann* v. *Charlotte-Mecklenburg Board of Education*, 39 L.W. 4437 (1971).

[22]*Lemon* v. *Kurtzman*, 403 U.S. 602 (1971).

[23]*Rodriguez* v. *San Antonio Independent School Board*, 411 U.S. 1 (1973).

[24]*Furman* v. *Georgia*, 408 U.S. 238 (1972).

[25]*Gregg* v. *Georgia, Profitt* v. *Florida, Jurek* v. *Texas* (1976).

[26]*Row* v. *Wade*, 410 U.S. 113 (1973); *Doe* v. *Bolton*, 410 U.S. 179 (1973).

[27]John P. Roche, *Courts and Rights*, 2nd ed. (New York: Random House, 1966), pp. 121-122.

American Federalism: Elites in States and Communities

13

In the United States there are nearly eighty thousand separate governments, over sixty thousand of which have the power to levy their own taxes; there are states, counties, cities, towns, boroughs, villages, special districts, school districts, and public authorities. Legally, states are important units of government in America; they are endowed with all government powers not vested specifically in the national government or reserved to the people by the U.S. Constitution. All other government jurisdictions are subdivisions of states; states may create, alter, or abolish these other units of government by amending state laws or constitutions. Over time, the number of local governments in America has been decreasing, mostly because of the consolidation of small school districts. Even so, the multiplicity of governments in America is still impressive.[1]

Decentralization—decision making by subelites—reduces strain on the national political system and on national elites by keeping many issues out of the national arena. Conflict among subelites is avoided by allowing each to pursue its own policies within the separate states and communities and not battling for a single national policy to be applied uniformly throughout the land. For example, subelites who wish to raise taxes and spend more money for public schools can do so in their own states and communities, and subelites who wish to reduce taxes and eliminate educational "frills" can also do so within *their* own states and communities.

The masses play an even smaller role in state and local politics than they do in national politics. The news media emphasize national politics rather than state or community politics. Very few citizens know who their *state* senator or *state* representative is, or who their councilmen or county commissioners are. We can expect 50 to 55 percent of the nation's eligible voters to cast ballots in presidential elections, but turnout in state gubernatorial elections in nonpresidential years is generally less than 50 percent. Municipal elections often attract fewer than 20 or 30 percent of the eligible voters.

Federalism: The Division of Power Between Nation and States

The Constitution divides power between two separate authorities, the nation and the states, each of which can directly enforce their own laws on individuals through their own courts. American federalism differs from a "unitary" political system in that the central government has no legal authority to determine, alter, or abolish the power of the states. At the same time, American federalism differs from a confederation of states, in which the national government is dependent upon its states for power. The American system shares authority and power constitutionally and practically. National and state power are sometimes considered as the opposite ends of a seesaw—if national powers are increased, then state power must decline. But, although national power has expanded over the years, so has the power of states and communities, which now perform more services, employ more people, spend more money, and have a greater impact on the lives of their citizens than they have ever had in the past.

The Constitution, in the Tenth Amendment, "reserves" to the states the power to protect and advance the public health, safety, welfare, or morals. The national government may therefore enact no laws dealing directly with housing, streets, zoning, schools, health, police protection, crime, and so on. However, the national government may *tax* or *borrow* or *spend money* to contribute to the general welfare. Thus, Congress cannot outlaw billboards on highways, because billboard regulation is not among the enumerated powers of Congress in the Constitution. But the national government, through its power to tax and spend, can provide financial grants-in-aid to the states to build highways, and then pass a law threatening to withdraw financial aid if the states do not outlaw billboards themselves. Thus, the federal government can indirectly enforce its decisions in such areas as highways and billboard regulation, even though these fields are "reserved" to the states.

The federal government is expanding its power in states and communities by use of grants-in-aid. During the Great Depression of the 1930s the national government used its taxing and spending powers in a wide variety of areas formerly reserved to states and communities. Grant-in-aid programs to states and communities were initiated for public assistance, unemployment compensation, employment services, child welfare, public housing, urban renewal, highway construction, and vocational education and rehabilitation. The inadequacy of state and local revenue systems contributed significantly to the increase of national power in states and communities. Federal grants-in-aid to state and local governments have expanded rapidly in recent years (Table 13–1) not only in dollar amounts, but also in percentage of the total revenue of states and communities that comes from the federal government.

Table 13–1
Federal Grants to States and Communities, 1932–1975

Year	Total Federal Grants (in millions of dollars)	Federal Grants as Percent of State-Local Revenue
1932	232	2.9%
1938	800	7.2
1942	858	6.5
1950	2,486	9.7
1955	3,131	8.3
1960	7,040	13.5
1965	10,904	14.6
1970	23,954	18.3
1975	51,732	22.4

Source: Special Analysis Budget of the United States Government 1975.

Whenever the national government contributes financially to state or local programs, the state or local officials are left with less discretion than they would have otherwise. Federal grants-in-aid are invariably accompanied by congressional standards or "guidelines" that must be adhered to if states and communities are to receive their federal money. Often Congress delegates to federal agencies the power to establish the conditions attached to grants. Federal standards are designed to insure compliance with national minimum standards, but they are bound to annoy state and local leaders, protests from whom are sometimes loud enough to induce Congress to yield to the views of subelites.

States or communities can reject federal grants-in-aid if they do not wish to meet federal standards, and some have done so; but most find it difficult to do. They are "bribed" by the temptation of much-needed federal money; and they are "blackmailed" by the thought that other states and communities will get the federal money if they do not, although the money was contributed in part by federal taxation of their own citizens.

In short, through the power to tax and spend for the general welfare and through the conditions attached to federal grants-in-aid, the national government can exercise important powers in areas originally "reserved" to the states. Of course, federal grants-in-aid have enabled many states and communities to provide necessary and desirable services that they could not have afforded without federal aid, and federal guidelines have often improved standards of administration, personnel policies, and fiscal practices in states and communities. Further, federal guidelines have helped to insure that states and communities will not engage in racial discrimination in federally aided programs. However, many commentators are genuinely apprehensive that states and communities have surrendered many of their powers to the national government in return for federal money. They argue that the role of states and communities in the American federal system has been weakened considerably by federal grant-in-aid programs and the conditions attached to them, because the centralization of power in Washington and the increased role of the national government in state and community affairs limits the individuality of state and local elites.

Elite Structures in the States

Elite structures vary among the fifty states, but it is generally agreed that economic elites are the most influential. The authors of *The Legislative System* interviewed state legislators in four states, asking them which interests were perceived as most powerful.[2] In all four states, business interests were most often named the "most powerful groups"; educational and labor interests, although important, had less perceived influence. Agricultural interests, government interests (associations of city, county, and township governments, and government employee associations), ethnic interests, and religious, charitable, and civic interests were given only minor mention by state legislators.

It is difficult to measure the relative strength of economic interests in all fifty states. The strength of any interest group is a function of many factors, including resources, organization, leadership, prestige, "cohesion" (unity), and "access" (contacts) to decision makers. Some years ago, the American Political Science Association questioned social scientists in the several states, asking them to judge whether interest groups in their state were strong, moderately strong, or weak.[3] Their judgments are open to challenge, but they are probably the best testimony of interest-group strength in the states.

Table 13–2 shows the relationship among the perceived strength of interest groups in the states, the levels of interparty competition and of party cohesion, and the socioeconomic environments in the states. States with stronger interest groups are more likely to be (1) one-party states, rather than competitive two-party states; (2) states in which par-

Social Conditions	Types of Pressure System*		
	Strong (24 states)†	Moderate (14 states)‡	Weak (7 states)§
Party competition			
One-party	33.3%	0.0%	0.0%
Modified one-party	37.5%	42.8%	0.0%
Two-party	29.1%	57.1%	100.0%
Cohesion of parties in legislature			
Weak cohesion	75.0%	14.2%	0.0%
Moderate cohesion	12.5%	35.7%	14.2%
Strong cohesion	12.5%	50.0%	85.7%
Socioeconomic variables			
Urban	58.6%	65.1%	73.3%
Per capita income	$1,900.	$2,335.	$2,450.
Industrialization index	88.8	92.8	94.0

*Alaska, Hawaii, Idaho, New Hampshire, and North Dakota are not classified or included.

†Alabama, Arizona, Arkansas, California, Florida, Georgia, Iowa, Kentucky, Louisiana, Maine, Michigan, Minnesota, Mississippi, Montana, Nebraska, New Mexico, North Carolina, Oklahoma, Oregon, South Carolina, Tennessee, Texas, Washington, Wisconsin.

‡Delaware, Illinois, Kansas, Maryland, Massachusetts, Nevada, New York, Ohio, Pennsylvania, South Dakota, Utah, Vermont, Virginia, West Virginia.

§Colorado, Connecticut, Indiana, Missouri, New Jersey, Rhode Island, Wyoming.

Source: Harmon Zeigler, "Interest Groups in the States," in Herbert Jacob and Kenneth Vines (eds.), *Politics in the American States* (Boston: Little, Brown and Co., 1965), p. 116.

ties in the legislatures show little cohesion and unity; (3) states which are poor, rural, and agricultural. Wealthy, urban, industrial states may have *more* interest groups, but no single one can easily dominate the political scene; whereas in the poorer, rural, agricultural states with relatively backward economies, interest groups may be fewer in number but stronger and able to exercise considerable power over public policy.[4] These findings lend some empirical support to James Madison's belief that "the smaller the society, the fewer the number of interests, and the greater the likelihood that a single interest will dominate."[5] Madison believed that the larger the political society, the less likely a single elite was to dominate its politics.

To better identify elite patterns in state politics, let us divide state elite systems into types. First, in the *single unified elite* system, usually found in a state with a nondiversified economy and weak, noncompetitive parties, a cohesive group of economic interests dominates state politics. A good example of this type of elite system is Maine, of which Duane Lockard writes: "In few American states are the reins of government more openly, more completely in the hands of a few leaders of economic interest groups than in Maine."[6] Specifically, power, timber, and manufacturing—"the big three"—have combined into a cohesive economic elite, due to their key position in the economy of the state. Over three-fourths of the state is woodland, most of which is owned by a handful of timber and paper companies. The timber interests, combined with power companies and textile and shoe manufacturers, control Maine politics to protect their own economic well-being. Challenges to the predominance of the big three are rarely well-organized or sustained efforts.

The Deep South states also display the cultural homogeneity and unified elites characteristic of nondiversified or agricultural economies. Occasionally, "populist" candidates have arisen from the masses to temporarily challenge the dominance of the planting, landowning, and financial elites in southern states. But once in power, the demagogues have seldom implemented populist programs; more frequently they have become instruments of the established elites whom they castigated in campaign oratory.

A second type of elite structure, *a dominant elite among lesser elites,* is also found in states with a nondiversified economy, although the states may display a reasonably competitive party system, with moderate party cohesion in the legislature. The distinctive feature of the dominant elite among lesser elites structure is the prevailing influence of a single industry.

There are many political histories of the power of Anaconda in Montana, Du Pont in Delaware, the oil companies in Texas and Louisiana, the coal companies in West Virginia, and so on. Doubtless, their reputations for absolute control of a state far exceeds their actual control over public policy; there are many issues in Delaware, for instance, in which the Du Pont Corporation and the Du Pont family do not become actively involved. Yet it is unlikely that the state of Delaware would ever enact legislation adversely affecting the Du Pont Corporation. Likewise, the reputation for oil control of Texas politics is exaggerated. The chairman of the Texas Democratic Executive Committee once said: "It may not be a wholesome thing to say, but the oil industry today is in complete control of state politics and state government."[7] This is an overstatement that one frequently hears in political circles; many issues in state politics are of little concern to the oil interests. However, it is unlikely that Texas politicians will ever oppose the oil depletion allowance in the federal tax structure, for this is a matter of direct and vital concern to the oil producers. The same may be said about the dominant interests in other states: While they may not control all aspects of state politics, they control those matters which directly affect them.

A *bipolar elite* structure is most likely to be found in an industrial, urban, competitive state with strong, cohesive political parties. Michigan is the prototype of this form of elite structure. While Michigan's economy is industrial rather than agricultural, it is nondiversified and heavily dependent on the automotive industry, the largest single employer. But automobile manufacturers do not dominate Michigan politics, because organized labor has emerged as an effective counterbalance to the automobile manufacturers. Joseph La Palombara concludes that "no major issues of policy (taxation, social legislation, labor legislation, etc.) are likely to be decided in Michigan without the intervention, within their respective parties and before agencies of government, of automotive labor and automotive management."[8] Labor and management elites in Michigan each have "their own" political party, and polarization in the elite system is accompanied by strong competition between well-organized, cohesive, and disciplined Democratic (labor) and Republican (management) party organizations.

A *plural elite* structure is typical of a state with a highly diversified economy. California may have the most diversified economy of any state in the nation, with thriving agricultural interests, timber and mining resources, and manufacturing enterprises that run the gamut from cement to motion pictures. The railroads, the brewers, the race tracks, the motion pictures, the citrus growers, the airplane manufacturers, the insurance companies, the utilities, the defense contractors, and a host of other economic interests coexist in this state. No one economic interest or combination of interests dominates California politics. Instead, a variety of elites govern within specific issue areas; each elite concentrates its attention on matters directly affecting its own economic interest. Occasionally, the economic interests of elites may clash, but on the whole elites coexist rather than compete. Political parties are somewhat less cohesive and disciplined in the plural elite system. Economic elites, hesitating to become too closely identified with a single party, even make financial contributions to opposing candidates to insure that their interests will be protected no matter which party or candidate wins.

One of the earliest studies of community elites was the classic study of Middletown, conducted by Robert and Helen Lynd in the mid-1920s, and again in the mid-1930s.[9] In Muncie, Indiana ("Middletown"), the Lynds found a monolithic power structure dominated by the "X" family, owners of the town's largest industry. Community power was firmly in the hands of the business class, which controlled the economic life of the city, particularly through its ability to control the extension of credit. The city was run by a "small top group" of "wealthy local manufacturers, bankers, the local head managers of . . . national corporations with units in Middletown, and . . . one or two outstanding lawyers." Democratic procedures and government institutions were window dressing

Single Elites in American Communities

for business control. The Lynds described the typical city official as a "man of meager caliber" and as a "man whom the inner business control group ignores economically and socially and uses politically." Perhaps the most famous passage from the Lynds' study was a comment by a Middletown man made in 1935:

If I'm out of work, I go to the X plant; if I need money I go to the X bank, and if they don't like me I don't get it; my children go to the X college; when I get sick I go to the X hospital; I buy a building lot or house in the X subdivision; my wife goes downtown to buy X milk; I drink X beer, vote for X political parties, and get help from X charities; my boy goes to the X YMCA and my girl to their YWCA; I listen to the word of God in a X subsidized church; if I'm a Mason, I go to the X Masonic temple; I read the news from the X morning paper; and, if I'm rich enough, I travel via the X airport. [10]

W. Lloyd Warner, who studied Morris, Illinois, in the 1940s, describes a power structure somewhat similar to Muncie's. About one-third of all of the city's workers had jobs in "The Mill," which Warner says dominated the town:

The economic and social force of the mill affects every part of the life of the community. Everyone recognizes its power. Politicians, hat in hand, wait upon Mr. Waddell, manager of The Mill, to find out what he thinks on such important questions as "Shall the tax rate be increased to improve the education our young people are getting?"—"Should the city support various civic and world enterprises?"—"Should new industries enter the town and possibly compete with The Mill for the town's available labor supply?" They want to know what Mr. Waddell things. Mr. Waddell usually lets them know. [11]

Hollingshead studied the same town (sociologists seem to prefer to disguise the names of towns they are studying: Warner called the town Jonesville; Hollingshead called it Elmtown), and his findings substantially confirmed Warner's. [12] And in sociologist Floyd Hunter's influential study of Atlanta, Georgia, [13] community policy is described as originating in a group composed primarily of business, financial, religious, and education leaders rather than from the people of the community.

According to Hunter, only those holding the right positions in the business and financial community are admitted to the circle of influential persons in Atlanta. Hunter explains that the top power structure concerns itself only with major policy decisions and that the leadership of certain substructures—economic, government, religious, educational, professional, civic, and cultural—then take their cues and communicate and implement the policies decided at the top level.

[The substructures] are subordinate . . . to the interests of the policy makers who operate in the economic sphere of community life in the regional city. The institutions of the family, church, state, education, and the like draw sustenance from economic institutional sources and are thereby subordinate to this particular institution more than any other. . . . Within the policy-forming groups the economic interests are dominant [p.94].

The top powerholders seldom operate openly. "Most of the top personnel in the power group are rarely seen in the meetings attended by the associational understructure personnel in Regional City [Atlanta] [p. 90]." Hunter describes the process of community action as follows:

If a project of major proportions were before the community for consideration—let us say a project aimed at building a new municipal auditorium—a policy committee would be formed. . . . Such a policy committee would more than likely grow out of a series of informal meetings, and it might be related to a project that has been on the discussion agenda of many associations for months or even years. But the time has arrived for action. Money must be raised through private subscription or taxation, a site selected, and contracts let. The time for a policy committee is propitious. The selection of the policy committee will fall largely to the men of power in the community. They will likely be businessmen in one or more of the large business establishments. Mutual choices will be agreed upon for committee membership. In the early stages of policy formulation there will be a few men who make basic decisions. . . . Top ranking organizational and institutional personnel will then be selected by the original members to augment their numbers; i.e., the committee will be expanded. Civic associations and the formalized institutions will next be drawn into certain phases of planning and initiation of the projects on a community-wide basis. The newspapers will finally carry stories, the ministers will preach sermons, the associations will hear speeches regarding plans. This rather simply is the process, familiar to many, that goes on in getting any community project underway [pp.92–93].

Note that in Hunter's description of community decision making, decisions tend to flow down from top policy makers (composed primarily of business and financial leaders) to the civic, professional, and cultural association leaders, the religious and educational leaders, and the government officials who implement the program. The masses of people have little direct or indirect participation in the whole process. Policy does not go *up* from associational groupings or from the people themselves.

The top group of the power hierarchy has been isolated and defined as comprised of policy makers. These men are drawn largely from the businessmen's class in Regional City. They form cliques or crowds, as the term is more often used in the community, which formulate policy. Committees for the formulation of policy are commonplace; and on community-wide issues, policy is channeled by a "fluid committee structure" down to institutional, associational groupings through a lower-level bureaucracy which executes policy [p.113].

According to Hunter, elected public officials are clearly part of the lower-level institutional substructure that *executes* policy, rather than formulating it. Finally, Hunter found that this whole power structure is held together by "common interests, mutual obligations, money, habit, delegated responsibilities, and in some cases by coercion and force [p. 113]."

Hunter's findings in Atlanta reinforce the elite model, and are a source of discomfort to those who wish to see America governed in a truly democratic fashion. Hunter's research challenges the notion of popular participation in decision making, or grassroots democracy; it raises doubts as to whether cherished democratic values are being realized in American community life.[14]

Plural Elites in American Communities

Pluralist models of community power stress the fragmentation of authority, the influence of elected public officials, the importance of organized group activity, and the roles of public opinion and elections in determining public policy. Who, then, rules in the pluralist community? "Different small groups of interested and active citizens [rule] in different issue areas with some overlap, if any, by public officials, and occasional intervention by a larger number of people at the polls."[15] Citizens' influence is felt not only through organized group activity, but also through elites anticipating the reactions of citizens and endeavoring to satisfy their demands. Leadership in community affairs is exercised not only by elected public officials, but also by interested individuals and groups who confine their participation to one or two issue areas. The pluralist model regards interest and activity, rather than economic resources, as the key to elite membership. Competition, fluidity, access, and equality characterize community politics.

In his significant study of power in New Haven, political scientist Robert A. Dahl admits that community decisions are made by "tiny minorities," who are not representative of the community as a whole in terms of social class.[16] However, Dahl challenges the notion that the elite system in American community life is pyramidal and cohesive and unresponsive to popular demands. Dahl studied major decisions in urban redevelopment and public education in New Haven, as well as the nominations for mayor in both political parties. In contrast to Hunter's highly monolithic and centralized power structure in Atlanta, Dahl found a polycentric and dispersed system of elites in New Haven. Influence was exercised from time to time by many elites, each exercising some power over some issues but not over others. When the issue was urban renewal, one set of leaders was influential; in public education, a different group was involved.

Business and financial elites, who in Hunter's study dominate Atlanta, are only two of many influential elites in New Haven. According to Dahl:

The economic notables, far from being a ruling group, are simply one of many groups out of which individuals sporadically emerge to influence the politics and acts of city officials. Almost anything one might say about the influence of the economic notables could be said with equal justice about a half dozen other groups in the New Haven community [p. 72].

Yet, Dahl also finds that all of the people involved in all community decisions in New Haven add up to only a tiny minority of the community. For example, Dahl writes:

It is not too much to say that urban redevelopment has been the direct product of a small handful of leaders [p. 115].

The bulk of the voters had virtually no direct influence on the process of nomination [p. 106].

The number of citizens who participated directly in important decisions bearing on the public schools is small [p. 151].

Moreover, Dahl notes that persons exercising leadership for each issue are of higher social status than the rest of the community, and that these middle- and upper-class elite members possess more of the skills and qualities required of leaders in a democratic system.

Obviously, Dahl's New Haven parallels the pluralist model. However, it is very important to observe that New Haven is not a democracy in the sense that we defined democracy earlier. Not all of the citizens of New Haven participated in the decisions that affected their lives, and not all of the citizens had an equal opportunity to influence public policy.

Aaron Wildavsky's study of Oberlin, Ohio, revealed, if anything, an even more pluralistic structure of decision making than Dahl found in New Haven. Oberlin was a reaffirmation of small-town democracy, where "the roads to influence . . . are more than one; elites and non-elites can travel them, and the toll can be paid with energy and initiative as well as wealth."[17]

Wildavsky studied eleven community decisions in Oberlin, including such diverse issues and events as the determination of municipal water rates, the passage of the fair housing ordinance, the division of United Appeal Funds, and a municipal election. He found "that the number of citizens and outside participants who exercise leadership in most cases is an infinitesimal part of the community,"[18] but that no person or group exerted leadership on *all* issue areas. The overlap that did exist among leaders in issue areas involved public officials—the city manager, the mayor, and city council members—who owed their positions directly or indirectly to "expressions of the democratic process through a free ballot with universal suffrage." Leaders often competed among themselves and did not appear united by any common interest. Persons exercising leadership were of somewhat higher social status than the rest of the community, but it was not status or wealth that distinguished leaders from nonleaders; it was their degree of interest and activity in public affairs.

Edward Banfield's excellent description of decision making in Chicago also failed to reveal a single "ruling elite," although the structure of influence was centralized. Banfield found that Mayor Daley's political organization, rather than a business or financial elite, was the center of Chicago's influence structure. According to Banfield:

Civic controversies in Chicago are not generated by the efforts of politicians to win votes, by differences about ideology or group interest, or by the behind-the-scenes efforts of a power elite. They arise, instead, out of the maintenance and enhancement needs of large formal organizations. The heads of an organization see some advantage to be gained by changing the situation. They propose changes. Other large organizations are threatened. They oppose, and a civic controversy takes place.[19]

It was not usually business organizations that proposed changes in Chicago; "in most of the cases described here the effective organizations are public ones, and their chief executives are career civil servants."

Though business and financial leaders played an important role in Chicago politics, they did not constitute a single elite.

After studying seven major decisions in Chicago, Banfield concluded that political heads such as Mayor Daley, public agencies, and civic associations employed top business leaders to lend prestige and legitimacy to policy proposals. The "top leaders" of Chicago—the Fields, McCormacks, Ryersons, Swifts, and Armours—and the large corporations—Inland Steel, Sears Roebuck, Field's Department Store, and the Chicago Title and Trust Company—were criticized less for interfering in public affairs than for "failing to assume their civic responsibilities." Few top leaders participated directly in the decisions studied by Banfield. Banfield admits that this fact is not proof that the top business leadership did not influence decisions behind the scenes; and he acknowledges the widespread belief in the existence of a ruling elite in Chicago. He quotes the head of a black civic association as saying: "There are a dozen men in this town who could go into City Hall and order an end to racial violence just like you or I could go into a grocery store and order a loaf of bread. All they would have to do is say what they wanted and they would get it."[20] Banfield states that top business leaders in Chicago have great "potential for power"—"Indeed, if influence is defined as the *ability* to modify behavior in accordance with one's intentions, there can be little doubt that there exist 'top leaders' with aggregate influence sufficient to run the city"[21]—but he maintains that these top leaders do not, in fact, run the city. Business leaders, divided by fundamental conflicts of interest and opinion, do not have sufficient unity of purpose in community politics to decide controversial questions. They have no effective communication system that would enable them to act in concert; and they lack the organization to carry out their plans, even if they could agree on what should be done.

The key to understanding community power, then, is relating the types of power structure to local social, economic, and political conditions. For example, we may find that large communities with a great deal of social and economic diversity, a competitive party system, and a variety of well-organized, competing interest groups have pluralist elite systems. On the other hand, small communities with a homogeneous population, a single dominant industry, nonpartisan elections, and few competing organizations may be governed by a single cohesive elite.

Thus, although descriptions of the power structures in American communities may differ only because social scientists differ in theory and methods of research, it is more likely that community power structures in the United States in fact range from monolithic elites to very dispersed pluralistic elites. Unfortunately, we do not yet know enough to estimate the frequency of different community power structures across the nation.

Summary The existence of political subelites within the larger American political system permits some decentralization of decision making. Decentralization, or decision making by subelites, reduces potential strain on the consensus of national elites. Each subelite is allowed to set its own policies in its own state and community, without battling over a single national policy to be applied uniformly throughout the land. Let us summarize the propositions that emerge from our consideration of American federalism and our comparative analysis of elites in states and communities.

1. Debate over state versus national power reflects the power of various interests at the state and national level. Currently, the liberal public-regarding elites dominant at the national level generally assert the supremacy of the national government. In contrast parochial, conservative, rural interests dominant in some states and communities, but with less power at the national level, provide the backbone of support for "states rights."

2. Although national elites now exercise considerable power in states and communities, particularly through federal "grant-in-aid" programs, this growth of national power has not necessarily reduced the power of state and local governments. State and local government activities are not declining, but growing and expanding.

3. Economic elites in states and communities are generally ranked as the "most powerful groups" by legislators.

4. States with the most cohesive elite system are likely to be one-party states, not competitive two-party states; states in which political parties show little cohesion and unity; and states that are poor, rural, and agricultural. Wealthy, urban, industrial states have more elite groups, but it is difficult for a single elite to dominate the political scene.

5. Scholars have described American communities in terms reflecting both single elite and plural elite models. Yet even the plural elite studies conclude that "the key political, economic, and social decisions" are made by "tiny minorities." They also find that these "tiny minorities" are recruited from the upper- and middle-class community. Few citizens participate in community decisions that affect their lives.

6. There is conflicting evidence about the extent of competition among community elites, the extent of elite concentration, the fluidity of elites, the ease of access to elite membership, the persistence of elite structures over time, the relative power of economic elites, and the degree of mass influence. Some scholars have reported a polycentric structure of power, with different elite groups active in different issue areas and a great deal of competition, bargaining, and sharing of power among elites.

7. Elite structures in communities are related to the community's size, economic function, and social composition. Small communities with a homogeneous population, a single dominant industry, a weak party structure, and few competing organizations are more likely to be governed by a single cohesive elite. Larger communities with social and economic diversity, a competitive party system, and well-organized competing interest groups are more likely to have plural elite systems.

8. Monolithic power structures are associated with a lack of political confidence among residents and with a widespread belief that political activity is useless. A plural elite system is associated with a sense of political effectiveness among citizens and with adherence to the rules of the game by leaders.

References

[1]For a comprehensive survey of government and politics in American states and communities, see Thomas R. Dye, *Politics in States and Communities* (Englewood Cliffs, N.J.: Prentice-Hall, 1969).

[2]John Wahlke, *et al.*, *The Legislative System* (New York: John Wiley, 1964).

[3]See Belle Zeller, *American State Legislatures* (New York: Thomas Y. Crowell Co., 1954), pp. 190–191.

[4]Harmon Zeigler, "Interest Groups in the States," in Herbert Jacob and Kenneth A. Vines (eds.), *Politics in the American States* (Boston: Little, Brown and Co., 1965), p.114.

[5]James Madison, Alexander Hamilton, John Jay, *The Federalist* No. 10 (New York: Modern Library, 1937).

[6]Duane Lockard, *New England State Politics* (Princeton, N.J.: Princeton University Press, 1959), p. 79.

[7]Robert Engler, *The Politics of Oil* (New York: Macmillan Co., 1961), p. 354.

[8]Joseph La Palombara, *Guide to Michigan Politics* (East Lansing: Michigan University, Bureau of Social and Political Research, 1960), p.104.

[9]Robert S. and Helen M. Lynd, *Middletown* (New York: Harcourt, Brace & World, 1929); and *Middletown in Transition* (New York: Harcourt, Brace & World, 1937).

[10]Lynd and Lynd, *Middletown in Transition*, p. 74.

[11]W. Lloyd Warner, *Democracy in Jonesville* (New York: Harper & Row, 1949), p. 10.

[12]August B. Hollingshead, *Elmtown's Youth* (New York: John Wiley, 1949).

[13]Floyd Hunter, *Community Power Structure* (Chapel Hill: University of North Carolina Press, 1953).

[14]For a more pluralist view of Atlanta's power structure, see Kent Jennings, *Community Influentials* (New York: Free Press, 1964).

[15]Aaron Wildavsky, *Leadership in a Small Town* (Totowa, N.J.: Bedminister Press, 1964), p. 8.

[16]Robert Dahl, *Who Governs?* (New Haven, Conn.: Yale University Press, 1961).

[17]Wildavsky, p. 214.

[18]*Ibid.*, p. 265.

[19]Edward Banfield, *Political Influence* (New York: Free Press, 1961), p. 263.

[20]*Ibid.*, p. 289.

[21]*Ibid.*, p. 290.

Protest Movements: Challenge to Dominant Elites

14

The place of blacks in American society has been a central issue of domestic American politics since the first black slaves were brought to these shores in 1619. The American nation as a whole, with its democratic tradition, has felt strong conflicting sentiments about slavery, segregation, and discrimination. But white America has also harbored an ambivalence toward blacks—a recognition of the evils of inequality but a reluctance to take steps to eliminate it. Writing in 1944, Gunnar Myrdal captured the essence of the American racial dilemma:

The "American dilemma" . . . is the ever-raging conflict between, on the one hand, the valuations preserved on the general plane which we shall call the "American creed," where the American thinks, talks, and acts under the influence of high national and Christian precepts, and, on the other hand, the valuation on specific planes of individual and group living, where personal and local interests; economic, and social, and sexual jealousies; considerations of community prestige and conformity; group prejudices against particular persons or types of people; all sorts of miscellaneous wants, impulses, and habits dominate his outlook. [1]

Myrdal's formulation of the American dilemma captures as well the more general attitudes of the American masses toward democracy: commitment to abstract ideals, but substantially less commitment to their practice. The struggle of blacks for full citizenship can be viewed as a dialogue—sometimes violent, sometimes peaceful—between the demands of black counterelites and the response of dominant white elites.

That there should be such a struggle at all in the United States demonstrates the precedence that racial feelings take over moral and constitutional requirements. The language of the Fourteenth Amendment leaves little doubt that its original purpose was to achieve full citizenship and equality for American blacks:

All persons born or naturalized in the United States, and subject to the jurisdiction thereof, are citizens of the United States and of the state wherein they reside. No state shall make or enforce any law which shall abridge the privileges or immunities of citizens of the United States; nor shall any state deprive any person of life, liberty, or property without due process of law; nor deny to any person within its jurisdiction the equal protection of the law.

However, one hundred years after the ratification of this amendment, the National Advisory Commission on Civil Disorders wrote: "Our nation is moving toward two societies, one black, one white—separate and unequal."[2] The commission strongly implicated whites in the failure of blacks to share equally in the affluence of American society.

What white Americans have never fully understood—but what the Negro can never forget—is that white society is deeply implicated in the ghetto. White institutions created it, white institutions maintain it, and white society condones it.[3]

The commission thus assumed that whites must solve the problem that they created. This assumption is a radical reversal of the American consensus that it is up to the *individual* to achieve personal goals in this open society. Government elites and masses frowned on the report of the Commission on Civil Disorders, thus indicating how radical is the idea that environmental rather than individual circumstances caused and sustain ghetto life and its violence.

In recent years, the civil rights movement has undergone a substantial shift in goals and techniques. Beginning with efforts to remove legal discrimination, principally in the South, the civil rights movement turned its attention toward economic inequalities in the North. As Bayard Rustin observes: "The very decade which has witnessed the decline of legal Jim Crow has also seen the rise of *de facto* segregation in our most fundamental socioeconomic institutions."[4] Americans can understand legal discrimination; and the majority—even a strong minority in the South—agree that such discrimination is inconsistent with the norms of a democratic society. However, the idea that society as a whole has a responsibility to reduce economic inequalities is alien to the myths and symbols of American individualism.

The Historical Background of Black Subjugation

The period of slavery is of more than historical interest; we are still feeling the impact of the brutality of this period. The scars of the rigidly enforced obedience system and the matriarchal family structure characteristic of slavery are still present today. Elkins has compared Southern slavery to Nazi concentration camps in its effects upon personality.[5] Both institutions were closed and highly authoritarian; both produced, for the most part, total obedience to the authority figure. In concentration camps, for example, guards were frequently viewed as father figures. Correspondingly, among slaves, the master often represented a father figure. Slavery, by rewarding obedience and compliance, negatively sanctioned individual effort and achievement.

Another factor with consequences that blacks are still struggling to overcome is the "deculturation" of the slaves. That is, blacks from many different African cultures were thrown together, and there was no common cultural buffer that enabled them to resist the psychological effects of the economic and social conditions of slavery. The condition of slavery became their dominant institution—an institution that molded black personalities. For example, to survive within the system, slaves developed childrearing practices that emphasized obedience over achievement.

McClelland, who developed devices to measure need for achievement, found that lower-class blacks, the group least removed from the effects of slavery, have the lowest need for achievement of any minority group. McClelland found, on the other hand, that middle-class blacks are uniformly higher in the need for achievement than are middle-class whites. This illustrates, first, that it is not being black that reduces the need for achievement and, second, that achieving members of the minority groups need to be more motivated than achieving members of majority groups. Since most blacks are lower class, however, they are unable to break out of the pathology of the ghetto. Ghetto norms reinforce the traditions of the past.[6]

Slavery also hindered the development of a strong family life. Since many slaveowners separated families on the auction block, the slave household developed a mother-centered pattern. After slavery was abolished, poverty in the ghetto strengthened the mother-centered tradition. Even now, about 35 percent of nonwhite families have female heads, compared to only 10 percent of the white families.[7]

In 1865, the Thirteenth Amendment abolished slavery everywhere in the United States. The Fourteenth Amendment, which was passed in 1867 by a Republican Congress that intended to reconstruct Southern society after the Civil War, made "equal protection of the laws" a command for every state to obey. The Fifteenth Amendment, passed in 1869, provided that the right to vote could not be abridged by either federal or state governments "on account of race, color, or previous condition of servitude." In addition, Congress passed a series of civil rights statutes in the 1860s and 1870s guaranteeing the new black freedman protection in the exercise of his constitutional rights. The Civil Rights Act of 1875 specifically outlawed segregation by owners of public accommodation facilities. Between 1865 and the early 1880s, the success of the civil rights movement was reflected in widespread black voting throughout the South, the presence of many blacks in federal and state offices, and the almost equal treatment afforded blacks in theaters, restaurants, hotels, and public transportation.

But by 1877, support for reconstruction policies began to crumble. In what has been described as the Compromise of 1877, the national government agreed to end military occupation of the South, give up its efforts to rearrange Southern society, and lend tacit approval to white supremacy in that region. In return, the Southern states pledged their support for the Union, accepted national supremacy, and agreed to permit the Republican candidate, Hayes, to assume the presidency, although the Democratic candidate, Tilden, had received a majority of the popular vote in the disputed election of 1876. The Supreme Court adhered to the terms of this compromise. In the famous Civil Rights Cases of 1883, the Supreme Court declared unconstitutional those federal civil rights laws preventing discrimination by private individuals. By denying Congress the power to protect blacks from discrimination, the Court paved the way for the imposition of segregation as the prevailing social system of the South. In the 1880s and 1890s, segregation was imposed in public accommodations, housing, education, employment, and almost every other sector of private and public life. By 1895 most Southern states had passed laws *requiring* segregation of the races in education and in public accommodations.

In 1896, in the famous case of *Plessy* v. *Ferguson*,[8] the Supreme Court upheld state laws requiring segregation of the races. Even though segregation laws involved state action, the Court held that segregating the races did not violate the equal protection clause of the Fourteenth Amendment so long as the persons in each of the separated races were treated equally. Schools and other public facilities that were "separate but equal" won constitutional approval.

The violence that occurred during this period was almost entirely one-sided: Whites attacked blacks. Grimshaw called this type of racial violence "Southern style."[9] The pattern of race relations at the turn of the century was clearly one of violent repression, the exclusion of blacks from jobs and labor unions, and rigid segregation. Blacks had lost most of what they had gained during Reconstruction.

The First Civil Rights Organizations

From the repressive pattern of the late nineteenth century the first black organizations emerged; the National Association for the Advancement of Colored People (NAACP) and the National Urban League were formed in 1909 and 1910, respectively. Both of these organizations reacted against Booker T. Washington's acceptance of the inferior status of blacks, and both worked closely with white liberals. These organizations, depending as they did on the goodwill of whites, chose a strategy of seeking black equality through court action and other legal means. They were (and still are) dominated by middle-class blacks and upper-class whites. They accepted the premise that meaningful change can be obtained within the framework of the American legal system. They were (and are) conservative in the sense that their techniques require commitment to the institutional *status quo*. They specifically disavowed any attempt to change or overthrow the basic political and economic structure of the society, for the changes they sought were limited to the inclusion of blacks in the existing society. In other words, they took literally the ideology and premises of the American democratic system.

When the concentration of blacks in northern cities increased the potential for mass action, a new style of violence began to emerge. A series of grievances, such as discrimination in housing and transportation, is expressed by the black community. As grievances build and expression becomes more aggressive, a precipitating incident occurs; and blacks respond by attacking whites or their property. The northern style riot differs substantially from the southern style violence; blacks no longer remain passive victims but become active participants. The "northern style" riot made its first appearance in Springfield, Illinois, in 1908.

Perhaps the first important black counterelite was Marcus Garvey. Since the NAACP was an elitist organization both in membership and appeal, the Universal Negro Improvement Association was organized by Garvey, a West Indian, to articulate the feelings of a latent black nationalism. Garvey's programs for a separate black nation in Africa held considerable appeal for impoverished blacks, especially as white bigotry, in the form of the Ku Klux Klan, spread north in the wake of black economic advance. Garvey's appeal essentially resembled that of the Black Muslims of the 1950s and 1960s and the more radical black nationalists of the late 1960s. Like the Muslims, Garvey urged his followers to practice personal frugality and establish a high level of morality. Like the nationalists, he sought to teach blacks that their color could be a source of pride rather than shame. At one time, Garvey had a following estimated at three million, but his movement collapsed in the middle 1920s. However, his appeal to the black masses was very important, for Garvey asserted that blacks would never achieve what the NAACP insisted that they could achieve—an equal share in the American economic system. As Myrdal observes, the Garvey movement "tells of the dissatisfaction so deep that it mounts to hopelessness of ever enjoying a full life in America."[10]

The period following the Korean War, marked by enormous legal and symbolic victories, was crucial in the development of the relationship between blacks and whites. The long labors of the NAACP paid off in the historic *Brown* v. *Board of Education of Topeka*[11] decision in which the Court reversed the *Plessy* v. *Ferguson* doctrine of "separate but equal." This decision symbolized the beginning of a new era of high expectations among blacks. While elected elites had remained silent on civil rights and, in fact, exhibited substantial hostility, an appointed elite, the Supreme Court, declared that blacks and whites were equal in the eyes of the law.

Brown v. *Board of Education of Topeka* marked the beginning, not the end, of the political battle over segregation. Segregation would not be abolished merely because the Supreme Court had declared it unconstitutional. Unless the political power of the white majority in the South were successfully challenged by another political elite with equal resources, the pattern of segregation would remain unchanged. Segregation was widespread and deeply ingrained. Seventeen states required segregation by law, and the Congress of the United States required segregation in Washington, D.C. Four other states (Arizona, Kansas, New Mexico, and Wyoming) authorized segregation at local option.

The Supreme Court, in not ordering immediate desegregation, snatched the tangible portion of the victory away from blacks. The Court placed primary responsibility for enforcing this decision upon local officials and school boards, thus in effect returning power to the white subelites in the South. As a result, during the 1950s the white South developed a wide variety of schemes to resist integration. Ten years after *Brown* v. *Board of Education of Topeka*, only about 2 percent of the blacks in the South had actually been integrated; the other 98 percent remained in segregated schools. In short, the decision meant nothing to the overwhelming majority of blacks, whose frustrations were intensified by the discrepancy between the declarations of the Supreme Court and the behavior of the local officials. Legally they were victorious, but politically they were impotent, since the South stubbornly refused to abide by the decision of the Court.

The continuation of this symbolic victory and tangible defeat reoriented the civil rights movement away from the removal of legal restrictions and toward the removal of *de facto* segregation and unequal socioeconomic institutions.

That this phase of the civil rights movement is strongly elitist should be carefully noted. The bargaining and exchanges took place largely between the NAACP and the Supreme Court, both of which were insulated from both white and black masses. The elite orientation of the NAACP, as previously noted, meant that its leadership accepted the prevailing values of white elites. Its attraction was to the "talented tenth"—the minority of upper-class, educated blacks. Its strategy was the "rules of the game"—litigation, not protest. White elites, especially those most removed from mass sanction, found NAACP values quite compatible with their own. The educated blacks of the NAACP sought only the removal of legal barriers to equality of opportunity. Being educated, they regarded education as the key to success. NAACP leadership, being economically successful on the whole, was better accepted by white elites and thus was culturally at the periphery of the black community. The NAACP's success depended largely on maintaining "good connections" with white elites, and the organizational leadership did not intend to risk its favored position by identifying with those sections of the black community unacceptable to the white elites.

Creative Disorder and Hostile Outbursts

The civil rights movement first became reoriented toward civil disorder in 1955, immediately after the *Brown* v. *Board of Education of Topeka* decision. Certainly the symbolic importance of this decision cannot be overestimated; and despite the paucity of tangible benefits, the decision undoubtedly stimulated the escalation of black expectations and demands. Black sociologist Kenneth Clark assesses the importance of official sanction as follows:

. . . This [civil rights] movement would probably not have existed at all were it not for the 1954 Supreme Court school desegregation decision which provided a tremendous boost to the morale of Negroes by its clear affirmation that color is irrelevant to the rights of American citizens. Until this time the Southern Negro generally had accommodated to the separation of the black from the white society. [12]

Dramatic support for Clark's hypothesis can be found in the 1955 refusal of a black to ride in the back of a bus in Montgomery, Alabama. Her act resulted in the Montgomery boycott and the first significant evidence of a shift away from the legalism of the NAACP. The Montgomery bus boycott illustrated the general relationship between elites and masses. The work of the NAACP was conducted exclusively by black elites. Their work stimulated mass behavior, which in turn required mass-oriented leadership. The need for mass-oriented leadership was filled initially by Martin Luther King, Jr., who was catapulted into prominence by the bus boycott. The Southern Christian Leadership Conference (SCLC) emerged in 1957 as the first southern-originated civil rights group. Although substantially more militant than the older black organizations, it was nevertheless explicitly nonviolent. Mass demonstrations were to be used to challenge the legality of both legal and *de facto* segregation and to prick the consciences of white elites.

The tactics of the SCLC were extended by the Student Nonviolent Coordinating Committee (SNCC), which was created from the next phase of direct action, the sit-in demonstrations and freedom rides of the 1960s. In February 1960, at Greensboro, North Carolina, the first sit-ins were conducted by North Carolina Agricultural and Technical College students. These sit-ins were followed by others, and SNCC was organized to coordinate this new student protest. SNCC, unlike the SCLC, encouraged blacks to feel proud of being black. The Congress on Racial Equality (CORE), which had been created in the 1940s, emerged from limbo to lead the freedom rides, which challenged the Jim Crow laws of transportation facilities. Many thousands of students participated in these extremely dangerous rides.

The vigor with which the freedom rides and sit-ins were pursued indicated that the civil rights movement was committed to direct action. However, even this new phase of the civil rights movement was not a mass movement; the participants were still relatively privileged in comparison to the black masses. The most frequent participants in the confrontations of the early 1960s were urban students, who were substantially less prejudiced and bitter against whites than were later leaders. These students had a very tolerant and optimistic attitude toward the white community. The freedom riders were not despair-driven anarchists but optimistic young people. The relatively privileged youths were disappointed in the unwillingness of the white society to recognize their merit.[13]

This phase of the black civil rights movement can thus best be explained by the relative-deprivation hypothesis advanced by Crane Brinton. He argues that revolutions are most likely to be led *not* by those at the bottom of the status pyramid, but by those who are more privileged than the masses they lead.[14] The psychology involved is simple; those who have nothing hope for nothing; those who have something see themselves as better off than the truly deprived but identify enough with the more advantaged to want more than they themselves now have.

In 1963, in Birmingham, Alabama, prolonged demonstrations were conducted on the broadest front yet conceived by civil rights leaders. Demands to end discrimination in public accommodations, employment, and housing were presented to the white elite of Birmingham. Under the leadership of Martin Luther King, Jr., these demonstrations were committed to nonviolence. Probably because of the broad nature of the demands, participation in these demonstrations reached the grass roots of the black community for the first time. All strata of the black community were involved.

Thus Birmingham was the beginning of a new militancy of all classes of blacks. But it was also the signal for an escalation of violence by whites. In Mississippi, Medgar Evers was shot; in Alabama, a white postman, participating in the civil rights march, was ambushed and killed. No one was punished for the murder of Medgar Evers, and Alabama Governor George Wallace stood at the door of the University of Alabama to prevent a black from entering. In Birmingham, a bomb killed four black girls who were attending Sunday school; and this was the twenty-first bombing and the twenty-first time that the bombers were not apprehended.

The Civil Rights Act of 1964

The Birmingham demonstrations were another landmark in the civil rights movement. As a partial consequence of the repressive behavior of southern elites toward these peaceful demonstrations, the Kennedy administration was moved to propose significant civil rights legislation. The Birmingham demonstration of 1963 stimulated what was to become the Civil Rights Act of 1964, the first significant entry of Congress into the civil rights field. The Act passed both houses of Congress by more than a two-thirds favorable vote; it won the overwhelming support of both Republican and Democratic congressmen. It ranks with the Emancipation Proclamation, the Fourteenth Amendment, and *Brown* v. *Board of Education of Topeka* as one of the most important steps toward full equality for blacks in America. The act provides:

I. That it is unlawful to apply unequal standards in voter registration procedures or to deny registration for irrelevant errors or omissions on records or applications.

II. That it is unlawful to discriminate or segregate persons on the grounds of race, color, religion, or national origin in any place of public accommodation, including hotels, motels, restaurants, movies, theatres, sports areas, entertainment houses, and other places which offer to serve the public. This prohibition extends to all establishments whose operations affect interstate commerce or whose discriminatory practices are supported by state action.

III. That the Attorney General shall undertake civil action on behalf of any person denied equal access to a public accommodation to obtain a federal district court order to secure compliance with the act. If the owner or manager of a public accommodation continues to discriminate, he shall be in contempt of court and subject to preemptory fines and imprisonment without trial by jury. [This mode of enforcement gave establishments a chance to mend their ways without punishment, and it also avoided the possibility that Southern juries would refuse to convict persons for violations of the act.]

IV. That the Attorney General shall undertake civil actions on behalf of persons attempting orderly desegregation of public schools.

V. That the Commission on Civil Rights, first established in the Civil Rights Act of 1957, shall be empowered to investigate deprivations of the right to vote, to study and collect information regarding discrimination in America, and to make reports to the president and Congress.

VI. That each federal department and agency shall take action to end discrimination in all programs or activities receiving federal financial assistance in any form. This action shall include termination of financial assistance.

VII. That it shall be unlawful for any employer or labor union with 25 or more persons after 1965 to discriminate against any individual in any fashion in employment, because of his race, color, religion, sex, or national origin, and that an Equal Employment Opportunity Commission shall be established to enforce this provision by investigation, conference, conciliation, persuasion, and, if need be, civil action in federal court.

While largely symbolic, the Civil Rights Act of 1964 did result in some tangible gains for southern blacks. The withdrawal of federal grant-in-aid money as a sanction was a remarkable innovation in federal enforcement of civil rights. When the United States Office of Education began to apply pressure in the South, progress was impressive in comparison with the previous ten years. The lessons of this astonishing increase are quite clear: To convert symbolic into tangible victories, a tangible sanction must be used. However, the Civil Rights Act of 1964 contained an amendment that forbade government agencies to issue any orders achieving racial balance in areas that did not have legally segregated schools in the past. Thus, the United States Office of Education could not issue desegregation guidelines outside the South, and the act, therefore, had no effect on the plight of blacks in the northern ghettos.

Nevertheless, the 1964 Civil Rights Act was a symbolic victory nearly equal to that of the 1954 *Brown* v. *Board of Education of Topeka* decision. One hundred years after the end of the Civil War, the three branches of the federal government had declared themselves to be in sympathy with black Americans.

In this phase of the civil rights movement, the dominance of the NAACP was broken, and more militant action was undertaken. Black elites, even those who successfully challenged NAACP hegemony, were still largely of middle-class origin. By appealing to the conscience of white elites they were able to extend symbolic victories to the legislative process. Though resulting in minimal tangible reallocations, such victories contributed to a loss of control by black elites of the black masses. The masses, activated by symbolic victories, began to rebel against black elites. This rebellion took place in the ghetto.

Life in the Ghetto

The ghettos were created when blacks migrated into, and whites out of, slum areas. This migration has gradually been declining, but the ghettos are well established. Only about one-half of the American black population lives in the South; the other half lives in the central cities of the North. Fully 98 percent of the black population increase in recent years has taken place in the central cities, while 77 percent of the white population increase has occurred in the suburbs.[15] Thus, the central cities are becoming black and the suburbs white.

All major American cities are characterized by a high degree of residential segregation. Sociologists Taeuber and Taeuber conclude:

In the urban United States there is a very high degree of segregation of the residences of whites and Negroes. This is true for cities in all regions of the country and for all types of cities—large and small; industrial and commercial, metropolitan and suburban. It is true whether there are hundreds of thousands of Negro residents or only a few thousand. Residential segregation prevails regardless of the relative economic status of the white and Negro residents. It occurs regardless of the character of local law and policies and regardless of the extent of other forms of segregation or discrimination.[16]

The physically crowded conditions in ghettos are pathological and conducive to violent collective behavior. Some of the more overt manifestations of the pathology of ghetto life can be observed in the remarkably high crime rate. (See Table 14–1.) Crimes against persons are ex-

Economic Makeup of Districts	Crimes against Persons	Crimes against Property	Patrolmen Assignments
High income white	80	1,038	93
Low-middle income white	440	1,750	133
Mixed high-low income white	338	2,080	115
Low income black	1,618	2,508	243

Source: *Report of the National Advisory Commission on Civil Disorders* (Washington, D.C., 1968), p. 267.

Table 14–1 Incidence of Crime and Patrolmen Assignments per 100,000 Residents in Four Chicago Police Districts, 1965

tremely high, and the presence of police seems to make little difference. Police departments apparently tolerate substantially more violence among blacks, even though they assign more patrolmen to ghetto areas.

Until the riots of the 1960s, there were no "law and order" protests against crime and violence in the ghetto. So long as the victims of black violence were blacks, the white society remained complacent. Similarly, although the victim of a violent crime is likelier by 78 percent to be nonwhite, it is the whites who now express concern about the maintenance of "law and order."

Continuing Inequalities Between Blacks and Whites

The poverty of the ghetto undoubtedly contributes to the high incidence of crime. While there has been substantial improvement in the economic position of blacks in recent years (Table 14–2), this improvement is not bringing the ghetto population appreciably closer to the white standard of living. It is customary to compare the ratio of white to black income to ascertain the extent of progress. Between 1947 and 1970 there was a gradual narrowing of the gap. Whereas in 1947 the median income of black families was only 51 percent of white family income, by 1970, it had risen to 64 percent. But this narrowing of the gap between black and white family incomes has not continued in the 1970s. Indeed, during the recession of 1974–75, black family income slipped back to 58 percent of white family income. Moreover, black unemployment remains about double that of whites, a ratio virtually identical to that of ten years ago; there is much additional evidence of a halt in progress toward equality. Thus, the percent of black persons below the poverty level, although reduced substantially (from 56 percent in 1959 to 32 percent in 1970), has now stabilized.

Another problem confronting the economic progress of blacks is the increase in black female-headed families—from 28 percent of black families in 1970 to 35 percent in 1974. As Table 14–3 shows, families, whether black or white, headed by females have lower incomes than families headed by males. The lowest position on the economic ladder is occupied by families with a black female head; 53 percent of such families were below the poverty line in 1974.

The problem of black poverty is largely—although not exclusively—concentrated among female-headed families, and seems most impervious to improvement. Hence, this change in family status seems to be why blacks have stopped improving their economic position. Unless this trend is reversed, or the economic position of black female family heads improves, the overall position of blacks may continue to deteriorate. Why, then, has there been a change? Most of the increase is due less to divorce than to the tendency of young black women to avoid marriage (21 percent, compared to 9 percent among white women).[17]

Table 14–2
Ratio of Black to White Median Family Income

1947	.51
1964	.54
1965	.54
1966	.58
1967	.59
1968	.60
1969	.61
1970	.64
1971	.60
1972	.59
1973	.58
1974	.58
1975	.58

Source: "The Social and Economic Status of the Black Population in the United States," *Current Population Reports,* U.S. Department of Commerce, 1975.

Table 14–3
Annual Income of Black
and White Families, 1974

	Black	White	Ratio
Male Head	$10,365	$14,055	.74
Married, wife present	10,530	14,099	.75
Working wife	13,982	16,825	.77
Nonworking wife	7,773	12,363	.63
Female Head	4,465	7,363	.61

Source: "The Social and Economic Status of the Black Population in the United States," Current Population Reports, U.S. Department of Commerce, 1975.

Police in the Ghetto

To many ghetto dwellers, the police are the symbol of white oppression. "Police brutality" has become a theme with enormous emotional impact among blacks. James Baldwin's description of the attitude of ghetto dwellers toward police cannot be improved upon:

. . . their very presence is an insult, and it would be, even if they spent their entire day feeding gumdrops to children. They represent the force of the white world, and that world's real intentions are, simply, for that world's profit and ease, to keep the black man corralled here in his place. The badge, the gun and the holster, and the swinging club make vivid what will happen should this revolution become overt. . . . He moves through Harlem, therefore, like an occupying soldier in a bitterly hostile country; which is precisely what, and where, he is, and is the reason they walk in twos and threes. [18]

Since the police role in the ghetto symbolizes white authority and repression, even the most exemplary police behavior would risk offense to the ghetto dwellers. And, of course, the behavior of many of the police is far from exemplary. The white masses strongly reject the idea that police behavior in the ghettos has been brutal or even discriminatory; only a small proportion of whites accept without reservation the possibility that blacks might be subject to rough treatment and disrespect by police. Seventy-two percent of the whites believe that blacks are treated the same as whites.[19] Of course, dissatisfaction with the police among the black masses runs very deep. (See Table 14–4.)

	Black	White
The police do not come quickly when called.	51%	27%
The police do not show respect and use insulting language.	38	16
The police frisk and search without good reason.	36	11
The police are too rough when arresting.	35	10

Source: Supplementary Studies for the National Advisory Commission on Civil Disorders (Washington, D.C., July 1968), p. 44.

Given this state of high tension between police and ghetto residents, it is almost invariable that a police action is the precipitating event immediately preceding a riot. A routine arrest made in an atmosphere of increasing tensions and black exasperation by previous perceptions of police hostility is usually the trigger for large-scale rioting. Blacks feel by a two-to-one margin that police brutality is a major cause of disorder, an idea that is rejected by whites by an eight-to-one margin.

Studies of police attitudes have uncovered substantial antiblack bias. For instance, Albert Reiss reported the following information to the Kerner Commission:

In predominantly Negro precincts, over three fourths of the policemen expressed prejudice or highly prejudiced attitudes towards Negroes. . . . What do I mean by extreme prejudice? I mean that they describe Negroes in terms that are not people terms. They describe them in terms of the animal kingdom. . . .[20]

Peter Rossi also studied the police in the cities that suffered violence. He finds that policemen feel that blacks are pushing too hard. Seventy-nine percent of the police do not believe that blacks are treated worse than the whites, and, like most whites, cannot see the need for any further push toward equality. They exhibit fairly strong antiblack attitudes; for example, 49 percent do not approve of whites and blacks socializing, and 56 percent are disturbed at blacks moving into white neighborhoods.[21] In an accurate estimate of black opinion, the police believe that only a small minority of blacks regard them as their friends, whereas a substantial majority of whites do so. However, policemen cannot understand why blacks resent them. Still, it is interesting that the police view themselves in much the same terms as blacks view them as to their status in the ghetto. The policemen feel alone in a strange and hostile land.

The goal of the police is generally not to reduce the long-term problems of the ghetto but to effect short-term control of riots. They wish to vigorously suppress riot activity, and they are angered by the leniency they perceive in judges and courts.* Police in the ghetto also have strong negative attitudes toward black civil rights groups and federal poverty agencies. They perceive the civil rights groups as contributors to vio-

---

*Because their occupation is a hazardous one that tends to develop strong in-group ties, the police also view lack of public support as a major problem. However, they need not worry about lack of support among the white community; 54 percent of the whites favored Major Daley's order to shoot looters on sight, and an even higher proportion favored a national holiday to honor the police (*Gallup Opinion Index*, Report No. 37, July 1968, p. 17). Clearly, the police are emerging as heretofore unappreciated heroes in the eyes of whites.

lence and the poverty agencies as misguided social reform institutions that do not understand the legitimacy of force.

The attitudes of the police are understandable in view of their recruitment and socialization processes. Police are recruited from the social classes most likely to have antiblack biases—the lower-middle and working classes. Moreover, very few police have had college training. Since we know that education is positively correlated with tolerance, we would expect that the police, being disproportionately representative of the uneducated classes, would be as typically intolerant as the average lower-class white.

In addition to the initial antiblack bias, occupational socialization probably strengthens the attitudes of policemen. The element of danger in policemen's jobs makes them naturally suspicious. Also, since policemen are engaged in enforcing rules, they become overly concerned with authority, and are politically and emotionally conservative. Jerome Skolnick observes: "It was clear that a Goldwater type of conservatism was the dominant political and emotional persuasion of police. I encountered only three policemen [out of 50] who claimed to be politically 'liberal,' at the same time asserting that they were decidedly exceptional."[22]

Add to these police attitudes the fact that the crime rate in ghettos is unusually high, and we have the makings of another vicious circle. One officer describes the operation of this circle:

The police have to associate with lower-class people, slobs, drunks, criminals, riff-raff of the worst sort. Most of these . . . are Negroes. The police officers see these people through middle-class or lower-middle-class eyeballs. But even if he saw them through highly sophisticated eyeballs he can't go into the street and take this night after night. When some Negro criminal says to you a few times, "Take off that badge you white mother fucker and I'll shove it up your ass," well it's bound to affect you after a while. Pretty soon you decide they're all just niggers and they'll never be anything but niggers. It would take not just an average man to resist this feeling, it would take an extraordinary man to resist it, and there are very few ways by which the police department can attract extraordinary men to join it.[23]

"Busing" and Racial Isolation in Schools

In northern ghettos, *de facto* school segregation—that is, segregated housing patterns coupled with neighborhood schools—has continued largely unchanged, even as integration has been achieved in the South. Approximately three-quarters of all black pupils in northern cities attend *de facto* segregated schools—that is, schools in which 90 percent or more of their classmates are black. Whereas in the South there has been progress toward integration, in the North segregation is actually increasing.[24] This increase in *de facto* segregation in the North has occurred because the black population in the central cities has grown as whites have vacated them, and because school officials have taken little action to achieve racial balance.

"I say to hell with racial imbalance—I'm through being bused in every day!"

Sidney Harris. Reproduced by special permission of *Playboy* Magazine; copyright © 1968 by Playboy.

Although the majority of both races state that they favor integration, white parents oppose many of the measures that would make integrated education possible. White parents have successfully fought busing of students in many northern cities. When whites say that it is permissible for blacks and whites to attend the same schools, what they have in mind is a balance in which most of the children are white. For example, although a majority of whites approve the idea of integration, two-thirds of them would not want to send their child to a school where more than half are black. One-third of the whites object to sending their children to schools in which approximately half the pupils are black.[25]

In 1971, in *Swann* v. *Charlotte-Mecklenburg*, the Court finally faced the full implications of the earlier Brown decision, with regard to *de facto* segregated schools. The school board of Charlotte, North Carolina, argued that their segregated school system was the innocent byproduct of a racially neutral neighborhood school policy: Since neighborhoods reflect economic status and income differences between blacks and whites, it was only "natural" that some schools would be overwhelmingly white and others overwhelmingly black.

The Court, however, rejected this defense and ruled that school authorities must do whatever necessary, including busing children to different schools outside their neighborhood, to achieve integration. If there had once been an official school policy of segregation, the Court reasoned that authorities had a positive obligation to integrate the schools immediately. It soon became apparent that this decision would have greater impact in the South than in the North, because segregation had never been an official policy in the North—although there was actually more segregation in northern than in southern states.

Political opposition to busing children to achieve racial balance in the school comes mainly from parents who fear their children will be transported into the violent crime-ridden culture of the ghetto. They fear that their children will be exposed to what black children have long had to cope with—rape, robbery, extortion, mugging, dope addiction— which have made ghetto schools blackboard jungles where surviving is more important than learning. Many white parents moved to the suburbs at great cost to themselves to obtain a better education for their children, and they do not appreciate the prospect of federal judges ordering their children back to ghetto schools. Generally, white parents are less fearful of black pupils being transported to white schools (as long as blacks remain a minority) than they are of white pupils being transported to predominantly black schools. Thus, limited one-way busing over relatively short distances is politically feasible. But the specter of large-scale two-way busing, transporting white children ten to thirty miles away from the suburbs to the ghetto, is another matter.

The widespread fear of busing between suburbs and central cities seemed to be at the heart of the Supreme Court's 5 to 4 ruling, in *Millikin v. Bradley* (1973), striking down Detroit's plan to integrate the school system by merging it with white suburban districts. The Court held that neither Detroit nor its surrounding suburbs had intentionally segregated the schools, even though most blacks attended city schools and most whites attended suburban schools. The Court, by effectively halting busing across school district lines, guaranteed continued segregation of northern cities. Since the suburbs are white and the central cities are black, the decision was a major victory for the white middle and upper classes. However, those whites, mostly the lower classes, still living within the central city (meaning those unable to afford the exodus to the suburbs), still faced the probability of busing. Hence, several major disturbances have occurred in Boston since intracity busing began in 1974. The Supreme Court decision—coupled with continuing protest by those whites remaining in the central city—solidified the division of metropolitan areas into black central cities and white suburbs.

Violence, Hope, and Trust

Urban violence was also a part of the social changes of the 1960s. Why did it occur in the 1960s, and why did it subside in the 1970s? (See Table 14–5.) Much of the decline in civil disturbances undoubtedly reflects the ending of the Vietnam War, but we might also infer that the nature of political protest is undergoing a dramatic change in this country. Since the essentially peaceful days of "nonviolent civil disobedience" characteristic of the late '50s and early '60s, political protest had grown steadily more violent in America in the late 1960s. In the 1970s, it moved underground as the established elites learned to cope more effectively with openly organized militant groups and mass protest demonstrations. Therein lies a possible explanation of the meaning behind the decline in mass protest. Another theory for the increased racial violence of the 1960s is related to the relative deprivation hypothesis mentioned earlier in the chapter. Totally subservient people seldom revolt; when things are looking up, but not far enough up, violence is likely to erupt. It is not those who have accepted poverty as a way of life but those who are

Table 14–5
Trends in Crime Statistics

Crime Rates			Total	Murders	Rape	Robbery	Assault
Crime Rate Per 100,000	1960		160	5	10	60	85
	1965		198	5	12	71	110
	1967		251	6	14	102	129
	1968		295	7	16	131	142
	1969		325	7	18	147	152
	1970		361	8	19	171	163
	1971		393	9	20	187	177
	1972		398	9	22	180	187
	1973		415	9	24	183	199
	1974		459	10	26	209	214
	1975		482	9.6	26.3	218	227
1960–1975 % Increase			201%	92%	165%	263%	167%

Civil Disturbances & Related Deaths				
Period	Total	Major[1]	Other[2]	Deaths
1967, June–Oct.	52	12	40	87
1968, all year	80	26	54	83
1969, all year	57	8	49	19
1970, all year	76	18	58	33
1971, all year	39	10	29	10
1972, all year	21	2	19	9
1973, Jan.–March	4	1	3	2

[1]*Major* = characterized by: 1) vandalism 2) arson 3) looting or gunfire 4) outside police used 5) more than 300 involved (excluding police) 6) 12 hours or longer duration.

[2]*Other* = Any of 1 to 4 above; duration at least three hours and more than 150 involved (excluding police).

Source: U.S. Fact Book, Bureau of the Census (New York: Grosset and Dunlop, 1977).

rising in the social order who become the most intense advocates of change. Thus, in the 1960s when hopes were highest for blacks there was a great deal of public protest; in the 1970s, black hopes for rapid progress declined, and so did protests.

Black aspirations were fired by the rhetoric of the Kennedy and Johnson administrations in the 1960s, but were not achieved; thus despite the policy positions of national elites, life did not improve, and by 1970 blacks were considerably more alienated than whites as is dramatically illustrated by Figure 14–1. Black trust in government was greater than white trust during most of the 1960s but declined sharply after 1968 because the expected more vigorous enforcement of integration never happened.

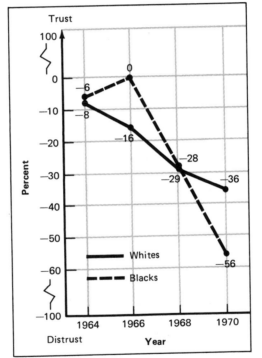

Figure 14–1
Index of Trust in Government, by Race, 1964–1970

Source: Arthur H. Miller, "Political Issues and Trust in Government," *American Political Science Review*, 68 (September 1974), p. 955.

Arthur Miller found that rising black distrust was directed first at political leaders and parties, and only later extended to elections.[26] However, by 1972, the majority of blacks (who changed from most trusting to least trusting in a few years) had lost faith in all democratic institutions, whereas whites still maintained a relatively high degree of trust in elections (although not in political leaders).

Protest Movements: Challenge to Dominant Elites   357

The economic discrimination against blacks, when coupled with the turmoil and hostile white response of the 1960s, enhanced black consciousness, which in turn propelled blacks toward more activism at the time. Upper-status blacks were also politically active. Thus, if the economic gap were to be closed, black activism might ultimately exceed that of whites; but such an occurrence erodes the basis for group consciousness. For whatever reason, the black movement had become quiescent by the middle 1970s. National Urban League affiliates, for instance, reported a substantial decline in militancy even as they reported a deterioration in black-white relations. Whites were reacting negatively both to random violence and to busing, Affirmative Action programs, and other government efforts. White images of black and government activity hamper the ability of black organizations—composed largely of more affluent blacks—to bargain with white elites: The coalition with liberal whites is made tenuous both by white backlash and black pride.

The Women's Movement

After more than two decades of highly visible protest, both peaceful and violent, the plight of blacks and other nonwhite minorities is well known. However, only within recent years have an increasing number of women come to view themselves as a distinct group facing economic and social discrimination similar to that suffered by blacks. It is not so much that the economic condition of women has worsened, but that some active women have moved away from the traditional stereotypes and role patterns defined for them by the dominant culture and are seeking new sources of identity.

Protest movements have a spill-over effect. As the traditional civil rights movement declined organizationally, its message of discrimination was received—and acted upon—by women. There are two components to the spill-over effect: First, politically active women—especially in the heated atmosphere of the 1960s—were quick to grasp the analogy between racial and sexual discrimination. Second, women were involved in the civil rights and antiwar protests. Thus, there was an established communications network that could be used to shift the focus of protest from any of the causes advocated by the "radical community" to women's rights. Discrimination against women was no more serious in 1965 than in 1955. What had changed was the ability of articulate, active women to respond. Ideologically sensitized and organizationally trained by the "radical community," the leaders of the women's movement succeeded in moving from one set of issues to another. However, as we shall see, women's movements have experienced problems that differ from those of other protest groups, due primarily to a problem of identification. Are women a "group"? That is, are their attitudes, behaviors, and problems unique to women *as* women? With blacks such a question is absurd; with women it is less so. Women, whether oppressed or not, are *not* a minority. Thus other shared group identities (Republican, Episcopalian, etc.) have minimized attitudinal differences between men and women. Examine any array of poll data comparing differences between blacks and whites; then compare differences in attitude between men and women. In virtually every case (with the notable exception of attitudes toward exclusively sexual issues, such as nudity in plays and movies), men and women have similar attitudes. Consider, for example, attitudes toward "the quality of life." Table 14–6 measures degree of satisfaction with a variety of conditions. In every case, women appear about as satisfied as men—hardly the conditions for radical protest. Further, there is some evidence that the general level of satisfaction among women is *increasing.* Take, for example, job satisfaction: Seventy-eight percent of the women polled were satisfied with their work; in 1949, only 66 percent of women were. In contrast, the percentage of blacks expressing satisfaction has not changed in that time.

	Male	Female	Black	White
Standard of living	71%	71%	48%	74%
The work you do	80	78	55	82
Your family income	62	60	38	64
The future facing you & your family	54	51	37	55
Your children's education	62	60	49	63
Your housing situation	73	74	52	77

Source: *Gallup Opinion Index* (December 1973).

Table 14–6
Percent Expressing
Satisfaction with Living
Conditions

Women, then, are a contented group—indeed, they are more content than men. Happy people are quiescent people. Further, the women's movement is frustrated by lack of a clear political ideology. Although the percentages vary somewhat from year to year, about the same proportion of women as men regard themselves as "conservative" (40 percent in 1977). About the same proportion of both sexes regard themselves as Democrats (42 percent of the males and 47 percent of the females in 1976). Similarity between men and women does not stop with political ideology and partisan identification. On a variety of issues, ranging from busing to defense spending, women and men are virtually identical. (See Table 14–7.) Indeed, on two questions of special significance to women—the Equal Rights Amendment and legalized abortion—men are more supportive than women of the official "women's position." Since these issues are defined by activists as crucial in the women's liberation movement, there is a gap between the articulated demands of women and the attitudinal basis for such demands.

Protest Movements: Challenge to Dominant Elites 359

Men are not the "enemy" (as are whites to black activists). Indeed, if men and women differ in their voting preferences (and they seldom do), women tend to vote slightly to the "right" of men as Table 14–7 shows with respect to various social issues. In 1976, women were more inclined to support Ford than Carter (51 to 48 percent) despite their belief that they would not be "better off" with him as president (they made no distinction between the candidates). Carter's vote was stronger among men (53 percent). (Ironically, men believed that women would be better off with Carter as president.) Carter's stand against abortion, contrary to the impression given by the media, was of low priority.

Through the years, women, unlike more cohesive blocs, have shown no clear voting preference. They showed slight preference for Republican candidates until 1960, displayed a very marginal preference for more liberal candidates until 1972, and chose the more conservative Ford in 1976.

The percentage of women who vote is only slightly lower than the percentage of men who vote. However, there have never been more than 19 women among the nation's 535 members of Congress. Many of them gained their seats through widowhood, having been appointed or elected to fill the term of a deceased husband. There have been four women governors in the states, but only one of these, Ella Grasso of Connecticut, did not serve in the shadow of her husband. Approximately 350 of the nation's 7,800 state legislators are women.[27]

	In Favor of	
Issue	Male (Percent)	Female (Percent)
Busing	33	36
Death Penalty	69	59
Wage/Price Controls	62	65
Diplomatic Relations with Cuba	65	61
Amnesty for Draft Evaders or Deserters	38	44
5% Surtax on Income for Social Programs	46	44
Reduction of Defense Spending	54	56
Reduction of Spending for Social Programs	37	32
Gun Registration	61	82
Marijuana Legalization	31	23
Aid to Parochial Schools	52	54
Legalized Abortion	54	48
Public Campaign Financing	71	72
Equal Rights Amendment	83	73

Table 14–7
Attitudes Toward Social Issues, by Sex

Source: *The Gallup Opinion Index*, Report No. 113, November 1974.

"Consciousness Raising" and Feminist Issues

Not surprisingly, women's organizations direct much of their activity toward "consciousness raising," that is, creating a group consciousness of the broadspread, deeply ingrained patterns of discrimination that purportedly operate against women not only in social arrangements and men's attitudes but in women's attitudes about themselves.

The raw material for such a group consciousness is there; for one, evidence of economic discrimination against women is easy to see. As Table 14–8 shows, female median income is about half the male. To some extent, such economic disparity reflects the difficulty women have in entering high-income occupations; they are forced to settle for more drudgery and less money. Some occupations (for example, nursing, secretarial work) are almost exclusively female; others (especially the more highly paid professions) are male dominated. However, even *within* occupational and educational categories, there is evidence of economic discrimination: The average professional woman's income is 60 percent of the average professional man's; the average female college graduate's income is 63 percent of her male counterpart. The trend, however, is clearly toward equal participation in higher education: In 1974, 44 percent of the college enrolled population was female (an increase of 6 percent in the last decade), and 42 percent of all bachelor degrees were earned by women, as were 40 percent of the masters degrees and 15 percent of the doctorates (in 1964, women earned 32 percent of the masters and 10 percent of the doctorates).

Year	Female Head of Family vs. Male Head with Working Wife	Female Head vs. Male Head, Nonworking Wife	Female vs. Male Individuals
1965	.41	.53	.55
1970	.41	.54	.54
1972	.38	.51	.57
1973	.39	.50	.58
1974	.39	.53	.58

Source: "A Statistical Portrait of Women in the United States," *Current Population Reports*, U.S. Department of Commerce (April 1976).

Table 14–8
Female Income as Percent of Male Income

Government and Women's Roles and Rights

Until recently, most state laws governing employment considered women frail creatures in need of special protections against long hours, heavy work, night work, and so on. Moreover, states did *not* guarantee equal pay and promotion opportunities for women or bar sexual discrimination in employment. But the federal Civil Rights Act of 1964, Title VII, prevents sexual (as well as racial) discrimination in hiring, pay, and promotions. The Equal Employment Opportunity Commission (EEOC), the federal agency charged with eliminating discrimination in employment, has established guidelines barring stereotyped classifications of "men's jobs" and "women's jobs." State laws and employer practices which differentiate between men and women in hours, pay, retirement age, etc., have been struck down. Under active lobbying from feminist organizations, federal agencies, including the U.S. Office of Education and the Office of Federal Contract Compliance, have established "affirmative action" guidelines for government agencies, universities, and private businesses doing work for the government; these guidelines set goals and timetables for employers to alter their work force to achieve higher female percentages at all levels.

At the center of feminist group activity in recent years is the Equal Rights Amendment to the Constitution (ERA) which would strike down *all* existing legal inequalities, in state and federal laws, between men and women. The amendment states simply: "Equality of rights under the law shall not be denied or abridged by the United States or by any state on account of sex." ERA passed the Congress easily and was sent to the states for the necessary ratification of three-fourths (thirty-eight) of them. The amendment won quick ratification by half the states, but a developing "Stop-ERA" movement slowed progress and threatened to prevent final ratification. Debate over ratification of ERA in the states has suggested that it may eliminate many legal protections for women—financial support by husbands, an interest in the husband's property, exemption from military service, and so forth. In addition to these specific objections, opposition to "women's liberation" in general has charged that the movement weakens the family institution, demoralizes women who wish to devote their lives to their family and children, and even encourages men to assert their masculinity in antisocial ways. Despite sometimes heated debate, it is impossible to predict exactly what impact ERA would have on state and federal laws,[28] much less the general condition of women in society.

Potentially the most important and far-reaching decision in the recent history of the Supreme Court is its action in the legalization of abortion.[29] Historically, abortions for any purpose other than saving the life of the mother were criminal offenses under state law. About a dozen states acted in the late 1960s to permit abortions in cases of rape or incest, or to protect the physical health of the mother, and in some cases her mental health as well. Relatively few abortions were performed under these laws, however, because of the red tape involved—review of each case by several concurring physicians, approval of a hospital board, and so forth. Then, in 1970, New York, Alaska, Hawaii, and Washington enacted laws that in effect permitted abortion at the request of the woman involved and with the concurrence of a physician.

The movement for liberal abortion laws in America, which began with a struggle for the liberalization of state laws, won a *national* victory when the Supreme Court ruled that the constitutional guarantee of personal liberty in the First and Fourteenth Amendments included a woman's decision to bear or not to bear a child. In the *Row* v. *Wade* and *Doe* v. *Bolton* decisions, the Supreme Court ruled that the word *person* in the Constitution did *not* include the unborn child. Therefore the Fifth and Fourteenth Amendments to the Constitution, guaranteeing "life, liberty and property," did not protect the "life" of the fetus. The Court also ruled that a state's power to protect the health and safety of the mother could not justify *any* restriction on abortion in the first three months of pregnancy. Between the third and sixth months of pregnancy, the state could set standards for how and when abortions can be performed, in order to protect the health of the mother; but the state cannot prohibit abortions in this period. Only in the final three months of pregnancy, the Supreme Court said, can the state ban all abortions to safeguard the life and health of the mother. Thus, the Supreme Court set national standards for state laws governing abortions.

Nonetheless, there are still many unresolved issues in state abortion laws.[30] "Right-to-life" groups have sprung up in many states to continue the fight against legalized abortion, as well as to push for a constitutional amendment to define the fetus as a "person." Some states have passed legislation protecting doctors and nurses from loss of jobs or other penalties for refusing to carry out abortions because of their moral and religious convictions. State laws are ambiguous about efforts to save aborted fetuses which emerge alive; it is still possible to convict a doctor of manslaughter if he fails to save a live aborted fetus. The Supreme Court has struck down state laws requiring husband or parental approval for abortions. However, state laws are still very restrictive in their definition of an "approved facility" for an abortion. Another unresolved problem is whether hospitals can refuse to allow abortions on their premises. In summary, abortion legislation is still an important item on the agenda of state legislatures and state courts.

Elite Dominance of the Women's Movement

Professional, educated, upper-middle class women comprise the heart of the women's movement. Lower- and lower-middle-class women are not attracted by its rhetoric and in fact still accept the idea of male dominance. Lower-class men receive deference as men. Middle-class men, by contrast, achieve status by their work. Lower-class women can hardly see themselves as men; but middle-class women can see themselves as professionals. Hence, "There is little distance between the rights a lower class woman has and the rights she feels entitled to. There is a great deal of difference between what a professional woman married to or simply associated with professional men has or can feel she is legitimately entitled to."[31]

The middle-class bias of the women's movement is well documented. After a survey in 1973, *MS* magazine found that its typical subscriber was: college educated (90 percent, compared to 20 percent of the female population) and employed (75 percent compared to 40 percent); two-thirds of the subscribers were in professional, technical, or managerial occupations with an annual personal income of $10,000 (or family income of $17,000). In 1974, a survey of NOW members revealed a similar class bias: Sixty-three percent were employed full time, and 66 percent were college graduates. They were also young and white.

Acceptance of discrimination is a partial consequence of the stability of the family as a preferred center of female activity. In spite of the increase of working women, most women feel that the ideal life is achieved through marriage and children. *Three out of four women believe that the family is more important than a job.* A career outside the home is less attractive than running a household. Hence, a plurality of women (44 percent) prefer not to work. Thirty-two percent prefer working in conjunction with a family. Pursuing a full-time career is not appealing to most women. Further, 60 percent of women (compared to 63 percent of men) prefer to work for a man. While "male chauvinist pigs" are the "villains" to active, professional, educated, upper-middle-class women, the *real* enemies of women's liberation are women. "Clearly, in the matter of overcoming sexual prejudices toward working women and in dealing with females already in the labor force, women are their own worst enemy and have a leading role to play if American society is to overcome these biases."[32]

The goal of women's movements is to "radicalize" the majority of women—that is, convince them of the necessity of concerted action in accordance with the values of the female elite. The vehicle for such accomplishment is the small group. Groups form, meet for a while, and disband, leaving the long-range development of goals and strategy in the hands of the active, professional minority. The ideas and goals of the active minority are, as we have seen, poorly understood by the passive majority. The average active life of a woman participant in small groups is about two years. Solidly in place, however, are local "oligarchies" whose goals are less ideological than those of transient activists.

While marriage and the family are still major factors for many women and older, married women are less attracted to women's movements, changes in marital states could provide some modest increases in the women's movement.[33] Divorces are increasing while first marriages and remarriages are not. Thus, more single women are available to participate in "consciousness raising."

On balance, however, the women's movement has not duplicated the intensity of group identity so characteristic of the black protests. It remains confined to an active, nonrepresentative, elitist minority. This dominance by an active minority is not, of course, unique to the women's movement. It is true of all political movements.

Summary

How do American elites cope with mass activism? Generally, established elites can depend upon mass apathy. But occasionally mass activism replaces apathy, and this activism is extremist, unstable, and unpredictable. America has experienced a long history of mass movements led by a wide variety of counterelites from Shays' Rebellion of the eighteenth century to recent black militancy. But the place of blacks in American society has been the central domestic issue of American politics. We chose to examine the movement for black equality within the context of elite theory to observe political activism among subservient people and the reaction of dominant elites to this activism. In many ways, the recent political activism among blacks is typical of mass movements—it is unstable and unpredictable; it expresses resentment toward the established order; it is made up of people who seldom participate in democratic politics and do not always understand the "rules of the game"; it is highly flammable and can produce violence; it has produced a variety of counterelites; and it has threatened the established order. However, we must be cautious in developing generalizations about mass movements based upon black experience in America. For blacks must contend not only with white *elites*, but also with white *masses*. Contrary to the general assumption of elite theory, the white masses *do* have opinions about civil rights and race relations, and elite behavior is more circumscribed by mass opinion than is normally the case. Hence, the relationship between white elites and black masses is complicated by the role of the white masses. Yet elitism offers many insights into the nature of the black struggle in America and the way in which this nation has responded to black demands.

1. Prevailing myths and symbols of the American nation are drawn from democratic theory; these include a recognition of the rights of minorities, a commitment to the value of individual dignity, and a commitment to the value of equal opportunity for all people. Although committed to these abstract ideals, white elites have consistently failed over the course of American history to implement these ideals in public policy.
2. Centuries of slavery and segregation have left black masses poorly educated, unskilled, poorly housed, poverty-stricken, frequently unemployed, segregated, and subject to a variety of social pathologies. White elites generally expect individual blacks to solve these problems individually. Black counterelites charge that white elites created these problems and are obliged to resolve these problems with black masses as a group.
3. White elites are willing to accept individual blacks on a near-equal basis only if these blacks accept the prevailing consensus and exhibit white middle-

class values. White elites are less willing to accept black masses who have not assimilated prevailing middle-class values.

4. Public-regarding liberal elites are prepared to eliminate legal barriers to provide equality of opportunity under the law for individual blacks, but they are not prepared to take massive action to eliminate absolute inequalities ("levelling"), which would bring black masses up to average white standards of living.

5. The first governmental institution to act and achieve equality of opportunity for blacks in America in the twentieth century was the Supreme Court. This institution was structurally the farthest removed from the influence of white masses, and was the first to apply liberal public-regarding policies to the blacks. Elected elites who are more accessible to white masses were slower to act on black rights than appointed elites.

6. Elected white elites did not respond to black requests until faced with a prolonged campaign of nonviolent civil disobedience, public demonstrations, and creative disorder and crises. Generally elites have responded by making the most minimal changes in the system consistent with maintaining stability. Often these changes are only symbolic. No revolutionary changes have been contemplated by elites even when they are faced with massive civil disorder.

7. The elimination of legal discrimination and the guarantee of equality of opportunity has been achieved largely through the efforts of black middle-class groups who share a dominant elite consensus and who appeal to the conscience of white elites to extend that consensus to include blacks.

8. The successes of black elites in achieving symbolic goals has helped to activate black masses. Once activated, these masses have turned to goals that went beyond accepted elite consensus—for example, demands for *absolute* equality have replaced demands for equality of opportunity. New mass-oriented black counterelites have emerged to contend with established middle-class black elites. Middle-class black elites have relatively little influence with masses in the ghettos. Mass counterelites have less respect for the "rules of the game" than either white elites or established middle-class black leaders.

9. Protest movements have a spill-over effect; they run from group to group in a ripple-like fashion. Groups only recently engaged in protest activity, such as women, have not developed the group consciousness of more severely repressed groups.

10. The women's movement is led by professional, educated, upper-middle-class women, whose views are not universally shared by the masses of women in America. Despite symbolic gains in the law, economic discrimination against women persists. Yet it is difficult to mobilize masses of women on behalf of feminist goals.

References

[1] Gunnar Myrdal, *An American Dilemma*, Vol. I (New York: McGraw-Hill Book Co., 1964), p. lxxi.

[2] *Report of the National Advisory Commission on Civil Disorders* (Washington, D.C., 1968), p. 1.

[3] *Ibid.*, p. 2.

[4]Bayard Rustin, "From Protest to Coalition Politics," in Marvin E. Gettleman and David Mermelstein (eds.), *The Great Society Reader* (New York: Vintage Books, 1967), p. 265. A short discussion of *de facto* segregation appears later in this chapter.

[5]Stanley M. Elkins, *Slavery: A Problem in American Institutional and Intellectual Life* (New York: Universal Library, 1963).

[6]David C. McClelland, *The Achieving Society* (Princeton, N.J.: D. Van Nostrand Co., 1961), pp. 376–377.

[7]U.S. Department of Commerce, Buearu of the Census, *Current Population Reports*, P-20, No. 125, 116, 106, 100, 88, 83, 75, 67, 53, 44, 33, and 26.

[8]*Plessy* v. *Ferguson*, 163 U.S. 537 (1896).

[9]Allen D. Grimshaw, "Lawlessness and Violence in America and Their Special Manifestations in Changing Negro-White Relationships," *Journal of Negro History*, 44, 1 (January 1959), 67.

[10]Myrdal, *An American Dilemma*, Vol. II, p. 749.

[11]*Brown* v. *Board of Education of Topeka*, 347 U.S. 483 (1954).

[12]Kenneth B. Clark, "The Civil Rights Movement: Momentum and Organization," in Talcott Parsons and Kenneth B. Clark (eds.), *The Negro American* (Boston: Beacon Press, 1966), p. 610.

[13]Donald R. Matthews and James W. Prothro, *Negroes and the New Southern Politics* (New York: Harcourt Brace Jovanovich, Inc., 1966), p. 424.

[14]Crane Brinton, *The Anatomy of Revolution* (New York: Vintage Books, 1965), pp. 100–105.

[15]Report of the National Advisory Commission on Civil Disorders, p. 390.

[16]Karl E. Taeuber and Alma F. Taeuber, *Negroes in Cities* (Chicago: Aldine Publishing Co., 1965), pp. 35–36.

[17]"The Social and Economic Status of the Black Population in the United States," *Current Population Reports*, U.S. Department of Commerce, 1974.

[18]James Baldwin, *Nobody Knows My Name* (New York: Dell, 1961), p. 62.

[19]"White Beliefs about Negroes," in *Supplementary Studies for the National Advisory Commission on Civil Disorders*, p. 30.

[20]*Report of the National Advisory Commission on Civil Disorders*, p. 306.

[21]*Gallup Opinion Index*, Report No. 25 (July 1967), p. 19.

[22]J. H. Skolnick, *Justice without Trial* (New York: John Wiley, 1967), p. 61.

[23]James Q. Wilson, *Varieties of Police Behavior* (Cambridge, Mass.: Harvard University Press, 1968), p. 43

[24]"Racial Isolation in the Public Schools," *A Report of the United States Commission on Civil Rights*, 1967, pp. 3–7.

[25]See Paul B. Sheatsley, "White Attitudes toward the Negro," in Parsons and Clark, *The Negro American*, pp. 303–324.

[26]Arthur H. Miller, "Political Issues and Trust in Government," *American Political Science Review*, 68 (September 1976), p. 955.

[27]Congressional Quarterly, *The Women's Movement*, pp. 56–59.

[28]See Shana Alexander, *Shana Alexander's State-by-State Guide to Women's Legal Rights* (New York: Wollstone Craft, 1975).

[29]*Row* v. *Wade*, 410 U.S. 113 (1973); *Doe* v. *Bolton*, 410 U.S. 179 (1973).

[30]Orma Linford and Naomi B. Lynn, "The Impact of the Abortion Decision: The States Respond," paper delivered at the Southern Political Science Association meeting, 1974.

[31]Stephanie Green, "Attitudes toward Working Women Have Long Way to Go," *Gallup Political Index*, March 1976, p. 33.

[32]*Ibid.*

[33] See *Gallup Political Index*, March 1976, pp. 14-20.

Epilogue: Dilemmas of Politics

If this book has left you with some uncomfortable feelings that:

neither elites nor masses can be fully trusted to preserve democratic values;

governments, corporations, banks, television networks, and other giant institutions cannot always be relied upon to protect liberty and insure justice;

ordinary individuals have a difficult task in holding these institutions responsible for their actions;

parties, elections, interest-group competition, and formal checks and balances are no guarantee of individual rights;

then the book has succeeded in its purpose: to make you feel uncomfortable about the future of democracy and the preservation of individual liberty.

Democracy is very fragile. Of the nearly 200 nations which claim independent sovereignty in the world today, no more than two dozen can be described as democracies. Nearly four-fifths of the world's population live under authoritarian regimes—where freedom of speech and press are curtailed, opposition parties are suppressed or eliminated, individuals play *no* role in the choice of their governments, and a single party and ideology controls all government offices and dictates public policy. Moreover, the number of these democracies has *declined* over time, and so has the number of people living under democratic governments. There is no unchanging law that says that democracy will always exist in the United States—or anywhere.

In Chapter 1 we defined democracy as:

popular participation in the decisions that shape the lives of individuals in society;

government by majority rule, with recognition of the rights of minorities to try to become majorities, including the freedoms of speech, press, assembly, and petition; and the freedoms to dissent, to form opposition parties, and to run for public office;

a commitment to individual dignity and the preservation of the liberal values of life, liberty, and property;

a commitment to equal opportunity for all people to develop their individual capacities.

Democracy is a noble ideal, even if it is not fully realized in the United States or anywhere else in the world. It should motivate our personal political activities—whether we are resisting the impulses of the masses to stamp out some despised ideas or trample the rights of minorities, or we are resisting the propaganda of elites or actions of governments intended to suppress our feelings about what is right and wrong in society.

There is no true "substitute" for democracy in the theories offered by pluralism that:

individual participation is antiquated in a large industrial society;

interest group leaders can bargain for us; we should dutifully vote in every election—even voting for the lesser of two evils when both candidates are distasteful to us;

we should join established interest groups and "work within the system" if we want change;

"private" decisions by large corporations, banks, television networks, and other nongovernment institutions are outside the boundaries of "politics" and political science;

we should not expect public policy to reflect majority preferences, but only the "equilibrium of group interests."

To accept these notions is to lose sight of the ideals of democracy.

The Inevitability of Elites

Yet we must also acquire the political maturity to know that democracy remains an ideal, and that nations are governed by elites, not masses. The elitism we have described in American society is not a unique corruption of democratic ideas attributable to capitalism, war, "Watergate," "the military-industrial complex," or any other events or group of people in this nation. Elitism is a necessary characteristic of all societies. There is no "solution" to elitism, for it is not the problem in a democracy. There have been many mass movements, both "left" and "right" in their political ideology, which have promised to bring power to the people. Indeed, many "successful" mass movements have overthrown social and political systems, often at great cost to human life, promising to empower the masses. To name just a few: Hitler promised to empower "der Volk" (the people); Lenin promised "a dictatorship of the proletariat" (the workers); and Mao Tse-tung promised a revolutionary, classless "peoples' democracy." But invariably they have created new elite systems which are at least as "evil," and certainly no more democratic, than the systems they replaced. Revolutions come and go—but the masses remain powerless. The question, then, is not how to combat elitism or empower the masses, or achieve revolution, but rather how to build an orderly, humane, and just society.

Let us summarize some of the obstacles to true democracy (that is, true popular participation and majority rule but with all individual rights and liberties protected and realized): One of the great obstacles to democracy in America is the sheer size of the nation and of its government and corporate institutions. In a large society, even assuming political equality, the individual's influence on societal decisions is so tiny as to render participation in mass democracy fruitless. As the society grows larger, the individual shrinks—in influence, power, liberty, and the capacity for shaping the decisions which affect the life of the individual. As the eighteenth-century philosopher Jean-Jacques Rousseau observed: "Thus, the subject remaining always one, the relation of the sovereign increases in proportion to the number of citizens. From which it follows that the more the state grows, the more liberty diminishes." The chance that any individual in a society of 215 million people can affect the outcome of an election or any other societal decision is infinitesimal. An individual who has less than one two-hundred-millionth of a say in the outcome of issues cannot be personally effective. This would be true even under conditions of perfect equality. Nearly half the eligible population did not vote in the 1976 presidential election. Many who abstained surely felt that their one vote in millions could not affect the outcome. This is a rational calculation. Size is one obstacle to effective individual participation in politics.

But another obstacle to effective individual participation in politics is *in*equality—not only in wealth but also in education, knowledge, intelligence, and leadership. Many social democrats in America and Europe complain about inequalities *among individuals*, especially inequalities of wealth. They propose to eliminate such inequalities by taking from the rich and giving to the poor, to achieve a "leveling," which they believe is essential to democracy. But the really dangerous inequalities in society are between *institutions and individuals*. If the government confiscated the wealth of every centi-millionaire in America, the total would amount to less than half of one year's sales of General Motors or Exxon, and less than 2 percent of the federal government's expenditures for a single year. In short, even very wealthy individuals are insignificant in relation to the wealth and power of the giant institutions of an advanced technological society. American democracy today faces the problem of controlling these giant institutions—corporations, banks, utilities, media networks, foundations, universities, and especially government itself.

Finally, the mature student of politics must confront "the iron law of oligarchy": Every political organization "becomes a minority of directors and a majority of directed." As each protest movement becomes organized and then institutionalized, its leadership gradually becomes a self-perpetuating oligarchy. The mass membership must delegate governing responsibilities to representatives, and by so doing they create a governing minority that will be distinguished from the masses in behavior, role, and status. This is true no matter what system of accountability is established: Delegation of authority creates a governing elite. Yet, delegation is essential, if only because people are unwilling to spend all of their time in decision-making activity—attending meetings, acquiring information, debating, and so on. Organization inevitably means oligarchy. Mosca demonstrated that even European socialist parties espousing democracy were in fact oligarchies:

When his work is finished, the proletarian can think only of rest, and of getting to bed in good time. His place is taken at meetings by the bourgeois, by those who come to sell newspapers and picture postcards, by clerks, by young intellectuals who have not yet got a position in their own circle, people who are glad to hear themselves spoken of as authentic proletarians and to be glorified as the class of the future. [1]

The authoritarianism of "revolutionary" parties today confirms Mosca's earlier observations. Participatory democracy is a romantic fiction.

The Frustrations of Politics

Many students who read this book lose their innocence. "How can I, an 18-year-old freshman from central Oregon, ever attempt to wage battle against the all-powerful elite?" "*The Irony of Democracy* certainly does not make me eager to take advantage of the opportunity to register to vote. I almost feel it is futile." Obviously, there is frustration, a sense of helplessness, and even anger over our claim that "the future of American democracy depends on the wisdom, responsibility, and resourcefulness of the nation's elite."

Even "revolutionary" movements are led by elites, and even the much-heralded "counterculture" of the 1960s and early '70s was dominated by a few intellectuals. When leftists shouted "power to the people," do not assume that the word "people" meant "masses," for it did not. Further, do not assume that the content of decisions would be altered appreciably by a shift in power from "capitalist" to "socialist" leaders.

One short-term method of change is protest. But protests are prima facie evidence of little political power. The protests of the 1960s and early '70s, beginning with the civil rights demonstrations and culminating in student uprisings, were all undertaken when it was realized that "normal" channels of political influence were not accessible.

Protest, even peaceful protest, has not been viewed with favor by either elites or masses. In spite of overwhelming evidence on this point, student protesters persist in the belief that their actions will "awaken the public." Indeed, they will, and the public's elite representatives will respond, but in grim and repressive ways. The backlash to protest, especially student protest, is inevitable. Take, for example, protests against the Vietnam War. According to the Survey Research Center, adult "doves" were quite antagonistic toward the protestors: A clear majority were negative, and almost one-fourth declared themselves extremely hostile. Thus, the natural target for a coalition—that part of the adult population opposed to the war—was alienated.[2]

Whether or not student protesters consciously sought coalition with those who shared their values, their tactics achieved the opposite effect. That any other protest tactics could succeed in building coalitions is doubtful. But clearly the fierce hostility of the mass suggests that it is in no mood to tolerate dissent, even when peaceful. It may be helpful to potential protesters to know that, in spite of media coverage sympathetic to the youthful protesters, adults (even doves) approved of what was labeled a "police riot" at the 1968 Democratic Convention in Chicago. The adult population also thought that the four Kent State students slain during a campus antiwar demonstration in 1970 *got what they deserved.* Less than 3 percent of the electorate was *not* alienated by students (and agreed with their goals).[3]

If there were to be "power to the people," then the student protesters would find themselves in a far worse situation than those who were attacked at the Chicago convention. A *genuine* "people's revolution" in America would begin (as we have argued in earlier chapters) with a reign of terror in which first radical students and then blacks would be threatened with brutal extermination. Of course, this is precisely the point of *The Irony of Democracy,* and why radical political movements accomplish only repressive political responses.

The Dilemma of American Politics

The dilemma of American politics today really differs little from that faced by the Founding Fathers in 1787—how to protect individuals in a majority-rule democratic system from the excesses and injustices of both mass *majorities* and elite *minorities*. James Madison warned that protection against *majority* oppression "is the real object to which our inquiries are directed." The question, however, is not only how to restrain the masses, but also how to control elites. The threat to democratic values arises not only from unrestrained majorities, but also from ruling minorities.

The masses, being antidemocratic, cannot be relied on to govern democratically. Despite a superficial commitment to the *symbols* of democracy, the people are not attached to the ideals of individual liberty, toleration of diversity, freedoms of expression and dissent, or equality of opportunity. On the contrary, these are more likely to be the values of elites. Masses are authoritarian, intolerant, anti-intellectual, nativistic, alienated, hateful, and violent. Mass politics is extremist, unstable, and unpredictable. The masses are not committed to democratic "rules of the game"; when they are politically activated, they frequently go outside these rules to engage in violence. Moreover, mass politics frequently reflects the alienation and hostility of the masses by concentrating on scapegoats, who can be any minority—Jews, blacks, Catholics, immigrants, students, intellectuals, etc.—somehow differentiated from the majority of the masses.

The masses are fatally vulnerable to tyranny. Extremist movements—reflecting authoritarianism, alienation, hostility, and prejudice—are more likely to be based in masses than elites. Hannah Arendt writes: "A whole literature on mass behavior and mass psychology demonstrated and popularized the wisdom, so familiar to the ancients, of the affinity between democracy and dictatorship, between mob rule and tyranny."[4] The masses, feeling in themselves the power of the majority, cannot be trusted to restrain themselves in dealing with dissenting minorities. Tolerance of diversity is a quality acquired only through years of socialization. The authoritarianism of the masses is unavoidable, given their authoritarian childhood experiences and family relationships, their limited education and restricted cultural opportunities, their monotonous job experiences, and their orientation toward immediate gratification. Efforts to reeducate or resocialize the masses are futile. Two hundred years ago Jefferson proposed universal free public education as a curative for mass ignorance, incompetence, and alienation. Today the masses in America average twelve years of free public education, but, if anything, they appear less capable of governing wisely and humanely than the masses of Jefferson's time.

Yet we have also learned that democracy is not always safe in the hands of elites—even democratically elected elites. Throughout this nation's history elites themselves have posed threats to democracy—from the Alien and Sedition Acts, to Woodrow Wilson's "Red Scare," to Roosevelt's incarceration of thousands of Japanese-Americans, to Truman's "loyalty" programs, to the recent Watergate "horrors." Restrictions on mass political activity—the forcible breakup of revolutionary parties, restrictions on the public appearances of demagogues, the suppression of literature expressing hatred or advocating revolution or violence, the equipping and training of additional security forces, the jailing of violence-prone radicals and their co-conspirators, and so on—are continuing threats to a democratic society.

Elite repression—its abandonment of democratic values—is a characteristic response to mass protest activity. While it may be comforting to argue that Watergate was unique and unprecedented, or that it was a product of a conservative ideology, neither statement is true. *All* elites are capable of repressive measures when they feel threatened by mass unrest.

Of course, repression in a free society is a contradiction. We cannot logically curtail liberty—even the liberty of a demagogue—to preserve a free society. James Madison considered and rejected repression as means of controlling mass movements, and pointed out the inconsistency of repression in a free society:

Liberty is to faction [mass movements] what air is to fire, an element without which it instantly expires. But it could not be less folly to abolish liberty, which is essential to political life, because it nourishes faction, than it would be to wish the annihilation of air, which is essential to animal life, because it imparts to fire its destructive agency.[5]

In short, repression is not really a serious instrument for an elite committed to the values of individual dignity, personal freedom, and tolerance of diversity.

If this dilemma—the protection of individual liberties against the assaults of majority and elite excess—is troublesome today, there is every indication that it may become even more serious in the next century. In recent times of affluence, government was said to regulate our lives "from the cradle to the grave"; but this charge lacked substance. There were regulations, yes, but there were freedoms, too: to live and work where you pleased; to build a house where you wished; to use land, air, and water on your property as you saw fit; to drive the kind of car you could afford; to heat your home to the temperature you desired; to have as many children as you wished; to select the career or profession which interested you.

Democracy and Technocracy in the Age of Scarcity

But the political freedoms of the twentieth century may prove to be luxuries beyond our means in the twenty-first century. In an age of affluence, democracies could be tolerated because there had been considerable slack in the system. The economic problems of industrial societies—how to achieve an appropriate distribution of existing and future wealth—could be debated and subjected to interelite negotiation. The problem was one of *distribution*. The stakes of the dispute were serious, but not fundamentally threatening to the social fabric. Thus, "wars on poverty" came and went, the distribution of wealth remained relatively stable, and protest was confined and isolated. However, in a future age of scarcity hardship will be much more widespread, as the problem shifts from distribution of abundant resources to conservation of scarce resources. And the scarce resources will no longer be only oil, natural gas, and some minerals but also food, fertilizer, clear air and water, and many other substances we now take for granted.

Continued inability of national governments to provide relief could lead to widespread civil unrest. Necessarily, governments' attention would shift from resource allocation to controlling civil unrest. In times of anxiety, the pressures toward authoritarianism are intense, as we learned from Watergate.

However, even assuming no widespread social unrest, there are other reasons why democracy may be unsuitable to an age of scarcity. Drastic restriction of individual liberty may be the only course available. As political economist Robert Heilbroner predicts: ". . . the passage through the gantlet ahead may be possible only under governments capable of rallying obedience far more effectively than would be possible in a democratic setting. If the issue for mankind is survival, such governments may be unavoidable, even necessary."[6]

If the present political game is survival, rather than the division of abundant resources, the power of *technological elites* over elected elites may relegate government "by the people" (even when "the people" are the elite) to antiquity. The greater the technological power we bring to bear in the struggle against scarcity, the more the political power of existing elites must be sacrificed to the technological elite. In a world where only the most careful planning can prevent rapid deterioration of the quality of life, social control, drastic restrictions on individual freedom, and rule by "experts" are inevitable.

Specifically, the twenty-first century may bring personal restrictions on freedom beyond those ever feared by nineteenth- or twentieth-century democratic philosophers: area population and growth-control laws may prevent us from choosing where we wish to live; restrictions on land use, water use, and air pollution may make property "rights" obsolete; the government may decide what kind of cars can be produced and driven; laws may regulate home heating, water, and utility use; tax penalties may be levied against large families; government "manpower" agencies may decide how many students can be admitted to what schools. More importantly, giant bureaucracies with great authority over our lives may be created to implement and enforce all of these new restrictions. Our lives may become a maze of permits, fees, licenses, regulations, guidelines, requirements, numbers, and forms.

What Is to Be Done?

If protest is largely futile, and "working within the system" a diversion of energy, what *can* concerned students do to maximize their political influence? First, they can lower their expectations regarding what can be achieved in the short run. Excessive idealism, coupled with a belief that society can be changed *NOW*, can only lead to bitterness and disillusionment. In the long run, these feelings may make you even less effective politically than need be. Excessive idealism can also expose you to the demagogic appeals of those politicians who would exploit your idealism for their own advantage. It is wise to understand your personal limits in shaping the world and resolving society's problems. It is time to reexamine adolescent optimism about "changing the world."

Drawing by Bernard Schoenbaum; © 1977 The New Yorker Magazine, Inc.

Second, it is important to learn about the world in which you live. This means reexamining for yourself the "truths" taught in the public schools—looking beyond the slogans of democracy (and of Marxism) to the realities of power in contemporary society. Just as this book has tried to reexamine our traditional teachings about American government, the concerned student should also critically reexamine the economic system, the social system, the communication system, and even the accepted "truths" of the physical and biological sciences. Developing your independent powers of social and political analysis can help you resist the floodtide of popular rhetoric, the symbolic posturing of politicians, the pseudo-science of the bureaucratic social engineers. You can learn to be wary of the politician or the bureaucrat who promises to solve society's problems with a stroke of the pen—to end racism, eliminate poverty, cure the sick, prevent crime, clean the air and water, provide new energy, and do so without imposing heavy new taxes or further restricting individual freedom. You will learn that there are no simple solutions to society's problems.

Third, it makes sense to try to master the technological revolution rather than let it master you. By this we mean you should endeavor to learn about one or more aspects of technology in the pursuit of your education. If your life is going to be directed by computers, why not learn some computer technology yourself? The same is true of social institutions. If laws are to regulate your life, why not master some aspects of the law yourself, even as an undergraduate? If you are going to be the object of the administrative, managerial, and budgetary practices of large bureaucracies, why not learn something about these subjects, for self-defense if nothing else? If you are not majoring in any of the physical and biological sciences, why not explore some of these courses—perhaps on a pass-fail basis if your school permits it? The more you know about today's technology, the less impressed you will be when someone tells you that their policies are "technological requirements."

Finally, it is essential that you become familiar with the meaning of individual freedom and dignity throughout the ages. This means reading and understanding the human quest for freedom in many times and cultures—from St. Thomas More to Aleksandr Solzhenitsyn, from Antigone to Galileo. It also means viewing American democracy from a world perspective—comparing the personal freedoms we enjoy with those existing in other nations. It is one thing to struggle against mindless corporate and government bureaucracies in this country, but quite another to conclude that America is "not worth saving"—especially when the personal liberties of Americans are compared with the personal restrictions in many other nations.

Perhaps increased suspicion and distrust of government is really a great blessing for democracy: Perhaps personal freedom is most endangered when we place too much trust in government, see great idealism in its actions, and have unquestioning faith in our public leaders. Perhaps democratic values—individual dignity, freedom of speech and press, rights of dissent, personal liberty—are better-protected when we are suspicious of government and its power, and are concerned with its size and complexity. Perhaps the most important danger to a free people is that they "politicize" all of the problems that confront them as individuals; that they blame government and "society" for the problems that beset them; and that they therefore excuse themselves from *personal* efforts to confront these problems. If we look to government to resolve all our problems, all forms of social dependency will increase, and individuals will assume *less* responsibility for their own lives—whereas the traditional democratic value is to encourage individuals to shape their own lives.

References

[1]Gaetano Mosca, *The Ruling Class* (New York: McGraw-Hill, 1939), p. 332.

[2]Philip E. Converse, et al., "Continuity and Change in American Politics: Parties and Issues in the 1968 Election," *American Political Science Review*, 69 (December 1969), 1087

[3]*Ibid.*, p. 1088.

[4]Hannah Arendt, *The Origins of Totalitarianism* (New York: Harcourt Brace Jovanovich, 1951), pp. 309–310.

[5]James Madison, Alexander Hamilton, and John Jay, *The Federalist*, No. 10.

[6]Robert L. Heilbroner, *An Inquiry into the Human Prospect* (New York: W. W. Norton & Co. Inc., 1974), p. 110.

Selected Additional Readings

Chapter One

The Origins of Elite Theory

Michels, Roberto. *Political Parties.* New York: Free Press, 1962. This book was first published in 1911 in German. Michels was a disciple of Mosca. Like Mosca, he sees elitism as an outcome of social organization. Michels argues that the very fact of organization in society leads inevitably to an elite. His often quoted thesis is "Who says organization, says oligarchy." Political scientists have called this "the iron law of oligarchy."

Mosca, Gaetano. *The Ruling Class,* ed. A. Livingston. New York: McGraw-Hill, 1939. This book was first published in 1896 in Italy. Mosca added to it later in a 1923 edition which reflects the impact of World War I on his ideas. Along with the work of Vilfredo Pareto, Mosca's *Ruling Class* forms the basis of what has been called "classical elitism."

Pareto, Vilfredo. *The Mind and Society: Treatise of General Sociology.* New York: Harcourt Brace Jovanovich, 1935. Originally published in 1915–1916 in four volumes. Pareto begins with a much broader definition of elite. He suggests that in any human activity, those who are the top practitioners are the elite in that activity. Elites can then be grouped into two classes—the governing elite and the nongoverning elite—depending on whether the activity of which they are a top practitioner is important to government or not. Pareto also introduces psychological notions into his work. He speaks of "residues" which are human instincts, sentiments, or states of mind. These remain constant over time and from state to state.

Parry, Geraint. *Political Elites*. New York: Praeger Publishers, 1969. An excellent discussion of classical elitism. Includes an extensive treatment of Mosca, Pareto, Michels, Max Weber, James Burnham, C. Wright Mills, and other elite writers.

Current Literature—Books: Elitism, Pluralism, and Democracy
Bachrach, Peter. *The Theory of Democratic Elitism: A Critique*. Boston: Little, Brown, 1967. In addition to giving a good review of classical elitist literature, Bachrach discusses the distinction between democracy, pluralism, and elitism. He observes that whereas pluralists claim that their model is the practical adaptation of democratic theory to the modern, technological state, pluralism in fact makes so many alterations in democratic theory as to render it unrecognizable. In fact, Bachrach coins a new term for the model produced by the combination of democratic theory with group theory—he calls it "democratic elitism." We call it "plural elitism."

Bell, Roderick, David V. Edwards, and R. Harrison Wagner. *Political Power: A Reader in Theory and Research*. New York: Free Press, 1969. This collection of important articles on power and elites includes works by Dahl, Polsby, Kornhauser, Simon, Banfield, and Bachrach and Baratz.

Dahl, Robert A. *Pluralist Democracy in the United States, Conflict and Consensus*. Chicago: Rand McNally, 1967. This is one of the few recent theoretical extensions of pluralism on the national level. Most of Dahl's important theoretical work has been at the community level. This book fills an important gap in pluralist literature.

Debman, Geoffrey. "Nondecisions and Power." *American Political Science Review* 69 (1975), 889–900. A defense of pluralism from attacks by "neo-elitists" who claim that nondecision-making is an important technique of elite dominance. A reply by "neo-elitists" Peter Bachrach and Morton S. Baratz follows the article.

Dye, Thomas R. and Harmon Zeigler, eds. *The Few and the Many*. North Scituate, Mass.: Duxbury Press, 1972. A series of important readings on elite theory and American politics describing the few who have power and the many who do not.

Kornhauser, William. *The Politics of Mass Society*. New York: Free Press, 1959. The argument in this book is that a "mass society" occurs when elites are obvious to masses and masses are accessible to elites. This situation produces a threat of tyranny. To prevent this situation from occurring, Kornhauser argues that intermediate groups are necessary to distract the attention of the masses from elite activities, to give the masses a sense of security and belonging at the local level, and to prevent demagogic manipulation of the masses by the elite.

Lipset, Seymour Martin and Earl Raab. *The Politics of Unreason: Right-Wing Extremism in America, 1790–1970*. New York: Harper and Row, 1970. This is a highly revealing historical account of extremist political movements in the United States.

Ricci, David M. *Community Power and Democratic Theory: The Logic of Political Analysis*. New York: Random House, 1971. This is an excellent review of both past and current philosophical, ideological, and methodological differences between elitists and pluralists of each theory, including the contributions of Joseph Schumpeter ("process" theory of democracy), David Truman ("group" theory of democracy), Floyd Hunter ("reputational" theory of elitism), C. Wright Mills ("positional" theory of elitism), and Robert Dahl ("pluralist" theory of democracy). Also included in the text are an excellent discussion of "the present scholarly impasse" existing between advocates of each point of view and an annotated bibliography of relevant literature.

Current Literature—Journal Articles: Elitism, Pluralism, and Democracy
Bachrach, Peter, and Morton Baratz, "Two Faces of Power." *American Political Science Review*, 56 (1962), 947–952. This article argues that power is tied to decision making, but power is also exercised when a decision can be prevented (called a "nondecision"). Thus, power has "two faces."

Dahl, Robert A. "A Critique of the Ruling Elite Model." *American Political Science Review*, 58 (1958), 369–463. This has become a classic critique of elitism from a pluralist point of view.

Walker, Jack L. "A Critique of the Elitist Theory of Democracy." *American Political Science Review*, 60 (1966), 285–295. This critique of both elitism and pluralism treats them as if they were two variations of the same theory. Walker argues that both make too many changes in classical democratic theory to allow it to serve as a meaningful model for government.

Chapter Two

Beard, Charles A. *An Economic Interpretation of the Constitution of the United States*. New York: Macmillan, 1913. A Free Press paperback edition was issued in 1965. Much of the second chapter of *Irony* is grounded in the data presented by Beard in this classic work. Beard traces the events leading up to the writing of the Constitution and the events surrounding ratification from an economic point of view. He discovers that economic considerations played a major, if not central, role in the shaping of the Constitution.

For several critiques of Beard see:

a. Benson, Lee. *Turner and Beard: American Historical Writing Reconsidered.* New York: Free Press, 1960.

b. Beale, Howard K., ed. *Charles A. Beard: An Appraisal.* Lexington: University of Kentucky Press, 1954.

c. McDonald, Forrest. *We The People: The Economic Origins of the Constitution.* Chicago 1958.

Corwin, Edward S., and J. W. Peltason. *Understanding the Constitution,* 6th ed. New York: Holt, Rinehart, and Winston, 1973. Of the many books dealing with explanations of parts of the Constitution, this paperback is one of the best. It contains explanations of The Declaration of Independence, the Articles of Confederation, and the Constitution in a section-by-section manner. The book is clearly written and is well suited for undergraduate as well as graduate and faculty use.

Lipset, Seymour Martin. *The First New Nation.* Garden City, N.Y.: Doubleday—Anchor Books edition, 1963. This book is a comparative treatment of the factors necessary for the development of a new nation. Lipset argues that any new nation must develop legitimacy of government, national identity, national unity, opposition rights, and citizen payoffs. The book is important because the United States is examined as the first "new nation" in light of these five factors and is then compared to other developing nations.

Madison, James, Alexander Hamilton, and John Jay. *The Federalist.* New York: Modern Library Edition, 1937. This is a collection of the articles published in support of ratification of the Constitution. They are perhaps the most important contemporary comments available on the Constitution.

Rossiter, Clinton L. *1787, The Grand Convention.* New York: Macmillan Co., 1966. This readable and entertaining account of the men and events of 1787 contains many insights into the difficulties the Founding Fathers had writing the Constitution.

Chapter Three Hofstadter, Richard. *The American Political Tradition.* New York: Random House—Vintage Books edition, 1948. This book is an important political history from an elite perspective. Hofstadter deals with the development of American political elites and their philosophies from Jefferson and the Founding Fathers through Jackson, Bryan, Wilson, and Franklin

Roosevelt. He emphasizes that at every stage of American history, elites have been in considerable agreement over major issues (with the possible exception of the Civil War). Finally, Hofstadter discusses the elite practice of incrementalism—i.e., that elite leaders have always moved to preserve the established order with as little change in the system as possible.

Lundberg, Ferdinand. *America's Sixty Families*. New York: Citadel Press, 1937. This is a classic work on elites which systematically traces the development of the entrepreneurial elite of the late nineteenth and early twentieth centuries.

Chapter Four

Elite Literature

Amory, Cleveland. *Who Killed Society?* New York: Pocket Books, Inc.— Giant Cardinal edition, 1960. This is a popularly written account of the "decline of high society" by an "insider." Amory is also the author of *The Proper Bostonians*, of which he is one. In *Who Killed Society?* he discusses the early sources of society in America, the most important families (the "400"), and the supposed decline of society in recent years. Note: Domhoff (below) disagrees with this latter aspect of Amory's work.

Andreano, Ralph L., ed. *Superconcentration/Supercorporation: A Collage of Opinion on the Concentration of Economic Power*. Andover, Mass.: Warner Modular Publications, 1973. The articles in this edited reader present a wide variety of opinions concerning the nature and implications of corporate concentration of economic power in America. Included are articles from such diverse sources as *Ramparts*, the *American Economic Review*, and *Hearings Before Antitrust Subcommittee on the Judiciary, House of Representatives*. As a result, the articles vary widely as to rhetoric, scholarship, factual content, and methodology, but they do present an interesting collage of opinions.

Baltzell, E. Digby. *Philadelphia Gentlemen: The Making of a National Upper Class*. Glencoe, Ill.: The Free Press, 1958. *The Protestant Establishment: Aristocracy and Caste in America*. New York: Random House—Vintage Books edition, 1964. The first of these books is a detailed analysis of how a national and associational upper class replaced the local and communal gentry in America between the close of the Civil War and 1940. The second book considers another question: Will the Anglo-Saxon-Protestant caste which evolved into a national upper class remain intact, or will the descendants of newer immigrants gain access to upper-class status? He concludes that this caste is still powerful but has lost its position as an authoritative aristocracy. This has left the upper class in an uneasy state with an uncertain future.

Berle, Adolf A. *Power Without Property*. New York: Harcourt Brace Jovanovich—Harvest Book edition, 1959. This work by a corporate lawyer and upper-class "insider" presents some interesting views of the American corporate economy. He argues that control of the corporate economy has passed out of the hands of owners and into the hands of managers. The effect of this change will be a return of the corporation to public accountability. This view has been widely debated. See, for example, the Kolko book cited below.

Domhoff, G. William. *Who Rules America?* Englewood Cliffs, N.J.: Prentice-Hall—Spectrum Books edition, 1967. *The Higher Circles*. New York: Random House—Vintage Books edition, 1970. In these books, Domhoff argues that there is a "governing class" in America. By this he means the part of the national upper class which holds positions of power in the federal government and industry and their upper-middle-class hired executives. He spends a great deal of time in both books developing the notion of social indicators. In *Who Rules America?* he examines elite control of the federal government, while in *The Higher Circles*, he develops in detail the role of private planning organizations in the formation of foreign and domestic policy.

Epstein, Edwin M. *The Corporation in American Politics*. Englewood Cliffs, N.J.: Prentice-Hall, Inc., 1969. A good introduction to the interdependence of government and corporations. It contains a historical overview of corporate political activities, a discussion of the types and general methods of corporate political involvement, and a discussion of pluralism vs. elitism.

Galbraith, John Kenneth. *The New Industrial State*. Boston: Houghton Mifflin—Sentry Books edition, 1969. Galbraith's book presents the notion of an intimate partnership between government officials and corporate specialists. General national goals (which Galbraith observes are "trite") are produced by this partnership. Decisions are made in this atmosphere of interrelationship between government and business. Needs and interests of the industrial system are "made to seem coordinate with the purposes of society" (p. 379).

Halberstam, David. *The Best and the Brightest*. Greenwich, Conn: Fawcett Publications, Inc., 1973. This book deals with the men who advised presidents Kennedy and Johnson with regard to the conduct of the war in Vietnam. Based on interviews of former *New York Times* Vietnam correspondent, David Halberstam, this book reveals an excellent view of the men and processes responsible for decision making at the highest levels of the federal executive.

Kolko, Gabriel. *Wealth and Power in America*. New York: Praeger Publishers, 1962. Kolko discusses the distribution of wealth and income in

America, the inequality of taxation, and the concentration of corporate power. He considers the questions: (1) Do a small group of very wealthy men have the power to guide industry, and thereby much of the total economy, toward ends that they decide upon as compatible with their own interests? and (2) Do they own and control the major corporations? He concludes both questions in the affirmative and then relates these facts to the problem of poverty in America.

Lundberg, Ferdinand. *The Rich and the Super Rich*. New York: Lyle Stuart, 1968. An extensive, well-documented, popularly written but unsystematic book which discusses both the corporate-governmental power partnership and elite life styles. Lundberg is the author of the more systematically written but dated book, *America's Sixty Families*.

Mills, C. Wright. *The Power Elite*. New York: Oxford University Press, 1956. This is one of the classics of elite literature. Mills takes an institutional approach to roles within an "institutional landscape." Three particular institutions—the big corporations, the political executive, and the military—are of greatest importance. The individuals who fill the positions within these institutions form a "power elite." These "higher circles" share social attributes (like similar life styles, prep schools, clubs, etc.) as well as positions of power. Thus, Mills' power elite is relatively unified. It is also practically free from mass accountability, which leads Mills to complain of the "higher immorality" of the power elite.

Pluralist Critique

Dye, Thomas R. *Who's Running America? Institutional Leadership in the United States*. New York: Prentice-Hall, 1976. A study of 5,000 top institutional leaders in industry, banking, utilities, government, the media, foundations, universities, civic and cultural organizations. The book "names names," studies concentration of power and interlocking at the top, examines recruitment and social backgrounds, discusses elite values, examines cohesion and competition among leaders, and shows how policies are decided upon.

Keller, Suzanne. *Beyond the Ruling Class*. New York: Random House—paperback, 1963. Keller presents an essentially pluralist group theory argument. She begins by adopting Pareto's notion of a series of elites—one for each type of human activity. The ones which are important to governmental and societal policy making are called "strategic elites." These strategic elites are becoming, according to Keller, more specialized and more isolated from one another. Thus, she disagrees sharply with C. W. Mills, who argues that interinstitutional elite movement is becoming easier and more common.

Rose, Arnold M. *The Power Structure*. New York: Oxford University Press—A Galaxy Book edition, 1967. This book is a more direct and systematic critique of elite literature as well as a restatement of pluralist theory. Rose presents the notion of "multi-influence" groups headed by elites. This notion is similar to Keller's strategic elite hypotheses. He asserts that the "power structure is highly complex and diversified," "that the political elite is ascendant over and not subordinate to the economic elite," and "that the political system is more or less democratic" (p. 492).

Chapter Five   Devine, Donald J. *The Political Culture of the United States*. Boston: Little Brown, 1972. Devine has provided an exhaustive analysis of the content of mass ideologies.

Edelman, Murray. *The Symbolic Uses of Politics*. Chicago: University of Illinois Press—Illini Books edition, 1967. Edelman deals with the general uses of symbols in society and then specifically the uses of political phenomena as symbols. He discusses the fact that myth and symbolic reassurance have become key elements in the governmental process. Edelman argues that the masses are generally uninterested in and inattentive to political phenomena as symbols. Only when the masses perceive symbolic or real threats or reassurances do they notice things political. Masses react to stimuli. Therefore, it is political actions which "shape men's political wants and 'knowledge,' not the other way around" (p. 172). Edelman also argues that mass demands, when they are articulated, are most often met with "symbolic" rather than "tangible" rewards.

Epstein, Edward Jay. *News from Nowhere*. New York: Random House, 1973. Epstein argues that television news is partially determined by the necessities of commercial television.

Erikson, Robert S. and Norman R. Luttbeg. *American Public Opinion: Its Origins, Content, and Impact*. New York: John Wiley, 1973. In this book, Erikson and Luttbeg have brought together and updated through 1970 several aspects of American public opinion research, including the formulation and content of opinion and the linkage between opinion and public officials. Especially important for the argument made in *Irony* are the chapters on political socialization, the potential of elections for "popular" control, and the impact of voter opinion on the policy choices of government officials.

Fromm, Eric. *Escape from Freedom*. New York: Avon Books, 1941. This book examines the notion of authoritarianism as an "escape" from the isolation produced by a large society. It is written primarily from a popular psychoanalytic point of view, interesting comparative reading with the political science and sociological works on authoritarianism.

Kornhauser, William. *The Politics of Mass Society*. New York: Free Press, 1959. (See Chapter 1, page 29.)

Lane, Robert E. *Political Ideology*. New York: Free Press, 1962, and *Political Life*. New York: Macmillan—Free Press edition, 1965. *Political Ideology* is a series of case studies, using in-depth interviews on 15 randomly selected "common men" in "Eastport." Lane attempts to probe the nature and extent of their political ideas. He finds that they do support the democratic ideal but that their political beliefs are held as a subpart of their job orientation and beliefs. *Political Life* was originally published in 1959. It is a diverse book with sections on the historical development of suffrage, conditions for the success of democracy, political behavior of the American people, etc. Perhaps the most interesting sections are those on the sociopsychological factors which affect political behavior. Lane discusses not only the *determinants* of man's political life but also the *effects* of social institutions (mass media, parties, economic organizations, etc.) on his political life.

Lipset, Seymour Martin. *Political Man*. Garden City, N.Y.: Doubleday & Co. (Anchor Books edition), 1963. This interpretation of American politics by an eminent political sociologist covers a myriad of factors that affect or are affected by the dynamics of political activity. Parts I and III—respectively entitled "The Conditions of the Democratic Order" and "Political Behavior in American Society"—are particularly germane to the discussion in this chapter.

Lipset, Seymour Martin and Earl Raab. *The Politics of Unreason*. New York: Harper and Row, 1970. A historical study of right wing extremism from colonial times to 1970.

Schattschneider, E.E. *The Semisovereign People: A Realistic View of Democracy in America*. New York: Holt, Rinehart and Winston, 1960. This book deals with the nature of conflict and change in America. Schattschneider argues against the pluralist-group theory bias which he perceives as the common view of the political system today. He also recognizes the elite-masses dichotomy which exists in the American social and political system. For example, he develops the notion that elites, by virtue of their organizational strengths, can manage conflict within the political system. They can alter it, exploit it, and/or suppress it (pp. 15, 17).

Stouffer, Samuel A. *Communism, Conformity, and Civil Liberties*. New York: John Wiley, 1966. This book, originally published in 1955, reports the results of a national survey of 6,000 persons which was designed to "examine in some depth the reactions of Americans to two dangers. One, from the communist conspiracy outside and inside the country. Two, from those who in thwarting the conspiracy would sacrifice some of the very liberties which the enemy would destroy." The study was one of the first systematic attempts to study the *intolerant* frame of mind and indicates that a large portion of America's masses would be willing to severely restrict even *legitimate* activities of unpopular minorities.

Chapter Six

Barnouw, Erik. *The Image Empire* (New York: Oxford University Press, 1970). A history of broadcasting since 1953, when television swept into America's living rooms. In this historical review, Barnouw shows how news is distorted and even manufactured to hold peak audiences.

Efron, Edith. *The News Twisters* (Los Angeles: Nash Publishing, 1971). A study of television coverage of the 1968 presidential elections and an expose of liberal bias in the network news that explores the myth of network "fairness."

Epstein, Edward J. *News from Nowhere* (New York: Random House, 1973). Discusses the "mirror" myth of television and discloses in detail how network television executives create "news."

Robinson, Michael J., "Public Affairs Television and the Growth of Political Malaise," *American Political Science Review* 70 (1976), 409–432. An examination of the impact of negative television journalism on mass attitudes, including increases in feelings of distrust, cynicism, and powerlessness.

———, "Television and American Politics 1956–1976," *The Public Interest* (Summer, 1977), 3–39. A thoughtful essay about "videopolitics"—the impact of both news and entertainment programming on mass attitudes.

Chapter Seven

Asher, Herbert. *Presidential Elections and American Politics*. Homewood, Illinois: Dorsey Press, 1976. An analysis of presidential elections since 1952.

Burnham, Walter Dean. *Critical Elections and the Mainsprings of American Politics*. New York: W. W. Norton and Co., Inc., 1970. Burnham argues that a realignment of party loyalties is probable.

Campbell, Angus, et al. *The American Voter: An Abridgement*. New York: John Wiley, 1964. This is an abridgement of the classic study of voting behavior in the United States conducted by the Survey Research Center at the University of Michigan.

Congressional Quarterly. *Dollar Politics*. Washington D.C.: Congressional Quarterly Inc., 1971. This short publication provides an excellent review of campaign fund raising, spending, and costs, as well as a chronological summary of federal legislation regulating campaign finances from 1945 through the 1971 Campaign Spending Act.

Flanigan, William H. *The Political Behavior of the American Electorate*, 2nd ed. Boston: Allyn and Bacon, 1972. In this short book, Flanigan draws on a wide range of previous voting studies in explaining American voting behavior. Of particular interest are the discussions in Chapters 3 and 4 of social, economic, and psychological correlates of voting.

Lipset, Seymour Martin. *Political Man*. Garden City, N.Y.: Doubleday (Anchor), 1963. (See Chapter 5, page 189.)

Milbrath, Lester. *Political Participation*. Chicago: Rand McNally, 1965. Milbrath presents a propositional survey of the literature on political participation through the early 1960s.

Miller, Warren E. and Teresa E. Levitin. *Leadership and Change: The New Politics and the American Electorate*. Cambridge, Mass.: Winthrop Publishers, Inc., 1976. An analysis of George McGovern's defeat in 1972.

Nie, Norman H., Sidney Verba and John R. Petrocik. *The Changing American Voter*. Cambridge: Harvard University Press, 1976. A description of the decline of political parties and the rise of ideology as influences in individual voter choice.

Niemi, Richard and Herbert Weisberg. *Controversies in American Voting Behavior*. San Francisco: W. H. Freeman, 1976. The best collection of the role of parties, issues, and candidate image.

Pomper, Gerald. *Elections in America: Control and Influence in Democratic Politics*. New York: Dodd, Mead, 1968. This is an outstanding study of the American electoral process. In addition to analyzing voting behavior per se, Pomper focuses on the impact of that behavior on public policy.

Pomper, Gerald. *Voters Choice*. New York: Harper and Row, 1975. Pomper argues that elections have become and will become, more ideological.

Pomper, Gerald, et al., *The Election of 1976*. New York: David McKay, 1977. Separately authored chapters on Congressional elections, the Carter victory, and state and local elections.

Chapter Eight

Crotty, William T. *Political Reform and the American Experiment*. New York: Thomas Y. Crowell Co., 1977. A provocative analysis of reform, including reform in political parties, as cyclical, frequently resulting in unanticipated consequences.

Downs, Anthony. *An Economic Theory of Democracy*. New York: Harper and Row, 1959. Downs develops an abstract model of party politics based upon traditional democratic political theory. The relationships among voters, parties, and governmental policy according to the democratic model are clearly presented, and empirical propositions are deduced therefrom.

Key, V. O., Jr. *Politics, Parties, and Pressure Groups*. New York: Thomas Y. Crowell Co., 1967. This work is a classic in the area of American party politics. Key traces the historical development of our present parties and discusses their role in the political system.

Ladd, Everett C., Jr. *American Political Parties*. New York: W. W. Norton and Co., Inc., 1970. The consensual nature of American parties is treated historically.

Michels, Robert. *Political Parties*. Glencoe, Ill.: Free Press, 1915. (See Chapter 1, page 28.)

Pomper, Gerald. *Elections in America: Control and Influence in Democratic Politics*. New York: Dodd, Mead Co., 1968. In focusing on the linkage between electoral behavior and public policy, Pomper discusses at some length the role of political parties, historically and within the contemporary context. Chapters 5, 7, and 8 are most useful in this regard.

Ranney, Austin. *Curing the Mischiefs of Faction*. Berkeley, Calif.: University of California Press, 1975. Essays concerning the role of political parties in the maintenance of political stability.

Sorauf, Frank J. *Party Politics in America*, 2nd ed. Boston: Little, Brown and Co., 1972. Sorauf employs the organizing concept of the political system in this theoretical work. He focuses on the parties within the American political system—their structure and the functions they perform.

Chapter Nine

Edelman, Murray. *The Symbolic Uses of Politics*. Chicago: University of Illinois Press (Illini Books edition), 1967. (See Chapter 5, page 188.)

Engler, Robert. *The Politics of Oil*. Chicago: The University of Chicago Press (Phoenix Books edition), 1961. Although somewhat dated, this book provides important historical background concerning the power of the American oil industry and its relationships to government—both at home and abroad. Particularly useful to the argument made in this chapter of the *Irony* are the sections on the oil lobby, the use of public relations, and the entry of oil corporation officials into appointive government positions.

Key, V. O., Jr. *Politics, Parties and Pressure Groups*. New York: Thomas Y. Crowell Co., 1967. (See Chapter 7, page 252.)

Olson, Mancur, Jr. *The Logic of Collective Action: Public Goods and the Theory of Groups*. New York: Schocken Books, 1968. This work is well written, dealing with the rational basis for interest-group activity. Individuals are the units of analysis, and Olson constructs a model of individual motivation for collective behavior based upon the assumption of rationality.

Schattschneider, E. E. *The Semisovereign People: A Realistic View of Democracy In America*. New York: Holt, Rinehart and Winston, 1960. (See Chapter 5, page 189.)

Scoble, Harry M. *Ideology and Electoral Action: A Comparative Case Study of the National Committee for an Effective Congress*. San Francisco: Chandler, 1967. A single interest group, the National Committee for an Effective Congress, is subjected to intensive study in this book. Scoble describes its history, its ideology, its organization, and its activities. Additionally, he relates his observations to interest group theory and compares the NCEC to other types of interest groups.

Verba, Sidney and Norman H. Nie. *Participation in America*. New York, N.Y.: Harper and Row, 1972. An examination of the causes and effects of political participation, including participation in organizations.

Zeigler, Harmon and Peak, Wayne. *Interest Groups in American Society*, 2nd ed. Englewood Cliffs, N.J.: Prentice-Hall, 1972. This comprehensive study of the composition and roles of interest groups in the political system of the United States discusses the development of interest group theory, the relationship of such theory to broader aspects of democratic political thought, and empirical data concerning group phenomena.

Chapter Ten

Barber, James David. *The Presidential Character: Predicting Performance in the White House*. Englewood Cliffs, N.J.: Prentice-Hall (paperback), 1973. This extremely readable book seeks to classify presidents along two continua—an "active-passive" baseline, according to the amount of energy and enthusiasm displayed in the exercise of presidential duties, and a "positive-negative" baseline, dealing with the degree of happiness or "fun" each president displayed in manipulating presidential power. Using these two baselines, Barber classifies the modern presidents into four types—active-positive (F.D.R., Truman, Kennedy), active-negative (Wilson, Hoover, Johnson), passive-positive (Taft, Harding), and passive-negative (Coolidge, Eisenhower). President Nixon was analyzed while in office to demonstrate the predictive capacity of these concepts.

Lindblom, Charles E. *The Intelligence of Democracy*. New York: Free Press, 1965. Lindblom analyzes the democratic decision-making process and prescribes the "best" way of making decisions. He discusses in depth the implications of incremental decision making.

Gold, Gerald, ed. *The White House Transcripts*. New York: Bantam Books, 1974. This is one of several publications which reproduce in its entirety the "Submission of Recorded Presidential Conversations to the Committee on the Judiciary of the House of Representatives by President Richard Nixon." Later versions of the recordings (including the House Judiciary Committee's version) contain some important variations from the material reported in this version.

Halberstam, David. *The Best and the Brightest*. New York: Random House, 1972. (See Chapter 4).

Neustadt, Richard. *Presidential Power*. New York: John Wiley, 1960. Neustadt focuses on the attributes of the individuals who occupy the office of the president rather than the attributes of the office itself. Instead of a discussion of the roles and formal powers attached to the presidential office, this book focuses on the ability of the president to use his personality, persuasive abilities, professional reputation, public prestige, etc., to increase his power and influence.

Rossiter, Clinton. *The American Presidency*, 2nd ed. New York: New American Library (Mentor), 1964. This classic traditional work on the roles and powers of the president was originally published in 1956. It discusses the several roles of the president (Chief of State, Chief Executive, Commander in Chief, Chief Diplomat, Chief Legislator, Chief of Party, Chief Manager of Prosperity, etc.). In addition, Rossiter discusses the several limitations of the president's powers, the historical and modern presidency and the "hiring, firing, retiring, and expiring of presidents."

Schlesinger, Arthur, Jr. *A Thousand Days*. New York: Houghton Mifflin, 1965, and *The Imperial Presidency*. Boston: Houghton Mifflin, 1973. *A Thousand Days* is an entertaining and instructive chronicle of the Kennedy Administration, devoted mostly to historical accounts of executive decision making, primarily in the area of foreign policy. In the *Imperial Presidency*, Schlesinger, Jr. describes the changes in the modern Presidency under Richard Nixon which he believes have resulted in an alarming concentration of power in just one man—Nixon. The argument runs directly counter to an earlier liberal point of view which held that the presidency—especially the presidency in the hands of Democrats—was not sufficiently powerful to push public-regarding public policy through a conservative, obstructionist Congress.

Wildavsky, Aaron. *The Politics of the Budgetary Process*. Boston: Little, Brown, 1964. An excellent book describing with considerable clarity the process of federal budgetmaking. He concludes "budgeting turns out to be an incremental process, proceeding from a historical base, guided by accepted notions of fair shares, in which decisions are fragmented, made in sequence by specialized bodies, and coordinated through multiple feedback mechanisms" (p. 62). The importance of this book is that it demonstrates the politics of policy formation and the extreme difficulties to be encountered in attempting radical change.

Clark, Joseph S., et al. *The Senate Establishment.* New York: Hill and Wang, 1963. Clark's book contains speeches made on the Senate floor that deal with power relationships in the Senate, especially the disproportionate power of the conservative coalition.

Davidson, Roger H. *The Role of the Congressman.* New York: Pegasus, 1969. Davidson's focus is upon the legislator's image of his job.

Huitt, Ralph K. and Robert L. Peabody. *Congress: Two Decades of Analysis.* New York: Harper and Row, 1969. Seven authoritative essays—Ralph K. Huitt's major contributions on the United States Senate and the executive-legislative process and Robert L. Peabody's critical review of scholarship and trends in legislative research during the last two decades—are collected in this volume.

Kingdon, John W. *Congressmen's Voting Decisions.* New York: Harper and Row, 1973. This book is the result of an intensive issue-by-issue examination of how decisions were reached by individual members of the U.S. House of Representatives in 1969. Focusing on one issue at a time, Kingdon employs interviews with selected congressmen to determine how they reached their decision concerning their vote on the issue. The result is a highly informative and readable text reflecting the complex relationships between the actors—the individual congressman, his constituents, fellow congressmen, party leaders in and out of Congress, interest group lobbyists, the executive branch, his staff, and the media—and the decision-making process—structural influences, information problems, and decision norms.

Nathan, James A. and James K. Oliver. *United States Foreign Policy and World Order.* Boston: Little, Brown, 1976. Chapter 13 is an analysis of congressional-executive relations and foreign policy.

Rieselbach, LeRoy N. *Congressional Reform in the Seventies.* Morristown, New Jersey: General Learning Press, 1977. Using responsiveness as an organizing concept, Rieselbach evaluates the reform efforts.

Ripley, Randall B. *Congress: Process and Policy.* New York: W. W. Norton, 1975. A comprehensive, historical analysis of the development of Congress institutionally.

Chapter Eleven

White, William S. *The Citadel: The Story of the U.S. Senate*. New York: Harper and Row, Co., 1956. Though White's attitude toward the Senate is reverential when compared to Clark's critical view, *The Citadel* contains much information in an easy, enjoyable, if somewhat dated book.

Chapter Twelve   Abraham, Henry J. *The Judicial Process*. New York: Oxford University Press, 1968. This book is one of the most comprehensive introductions to the basics of the judicial process. It provides both a sound theoretical introduction to the nature, sources, and types of law and a thorough "nuts and bolts" knowledge of the staffing, organization, and technical processes involved in the judicial process. There are four extensive bibliographies dealing with American Constitutional law, biographies and autobiographies of and by justices of the United States Supreme Court, comparative constitutional law, and civil liberties.

Jacob, Herbert. *Justice in America*. 2nd ed. Boston: Little, Brown, 1972. Jacob addresses this text to the question of how well American courts administer civil and criminal justice. He views the courts as political, policy-making institutions and examines their participants, procedures, and restraints. Special attention is given to "out-of-court settlements, plea-bargaining, and political justice and injustice."

Schmidhauser, John S. *The Supreme Court*. New York: Holt, Rinehart, and Winston, 1960. Although somewhat dated, *The Supreme Court* is still one of the best historical treatments of the development of the Court as an institution. It examines changes in the organization, procedures, and personnel of the Court over time.

Schubert, Glendon. *Judicial Policy-Making*. Glenview, Ill.: Scott, Foresman, 1965. This book by judicial behavioralist Glendon Schubert views the judicial process as an integral part of the political system. After first examining the relationship of the courts to other structural elements in the political system, Schubert focuses upon the judicial process itself as a policy-making system. He offers a "systemic model of judicial policy-making" and discusses it in terms of its "policy inputs, conversion, and outputs." Also included in the book is an evaluation of several approaches to the study of judicial policy making, including the "traditional, conventional, and behavioral."

Chapter Thirteen   Agger, Robert, Daniel Goldrich, and Bert Swanson. *The Rulers and the Ruled*. North Scituate, Mass.: Duxbury Press, 1972. This book presents an in-depth study of "power and impotence" in four American communities over a fifteen-year period.

Dahl, Robert A. *Who Governs?* New Haven: Yale University Press, 1961. This is perhaps the most important pluralist community power study. Using a "decisional approach," Dahl finds the existence of a number of elites making decisions in different issue areas.

Hunter, Floyd. *The Power Structure*. Chapel Hill: University of North Carolina Press, 1953. Although classical elitism has its origins in European sociological theory, much of the current American controversy over elitism has been the result of community power research. Hunter's *The Power Structure* was one of the first community power studies reporting elitist results. His use of the "reputational method" in this study of Atlanta set the scene for a heated debate with the pluralists Dahl and Polsby.

Ricci, David M. *Community Power and Democratic Theory: The Logic of Political Analysis*. New York: Random House, 1971. (See Chapter 1.)

Walton, John. "Substance and Artifact: The Current Status of Research on Community Power Structures." *American Journal of Sociology*, 72 (1966), 430–438. Walton makes an extensive survey of community power literature and finds that the use of the reputational method tends to yield elitist results, while use of the decisional method tends to yield pluralist results.

Chapter Fourteen

Banfield, Edward C. *The Unheavenly City Revisited: A Revision of the Unheavenly City*. Boston: Little, Brown, 1974. This book is an analysis, from a somewhat unusual viewpoint, of the problems of the people of urban America and of the cities in which they live. Banfield argues that the "poor" in America are not as unfortunate as they might first appear to be. It is only relative to the affluence of middle- and upper-class Americans that the poor seem deprived. In an absolute sense, however, they are not generally "poor," especially as compared to the poor of Europe or Asia. This book is frequently cited in our discussion of civil rights and the problems of the poor.

Clark, Kenneth B. *Dark Ghetto: Dilemmas of Social Power*. New York: Harper and Row (Harper Torchbook edition), 1967. *Dark Ghetto* is a particularly incisive analysis of the life of American blacks in urban ghetto areas and of the pathologies this life produces.

Congressional Quarterly. *The Women's Movement*. Washington, D.C.: Congressional Quarterly, Inc., 1973. An introduction to many political questions of special concern to women, including marriage laws, equal protection laws, child care, rape, women in politics, etc.

Freeman, Jo. *The Politics of Women's Liberation*. New York: David McKay, 1975. Freeman's analysis of the origins and consequences of the women's movement is the best available source.

Matthews, Donald R. and James W. Prothro. *Negroes and the New Southern Politics*. New York: Harcourt Brace Jovanovich, 1966. This is one of the pioneering works on the changing political role of the Southern black. It considerably updates some of Myrdal's earlier comments on Southern politics.

Myrdal, Gunnar. *An American Dilemma*, Vol I: *The Negro in a White Nation*. Vol. II: *The Negro Social Structure*. New York: McGraw-Hill, 1964. Originally published in 1944, this remains one of the most comprehensive studies dealing with the situation of blacks in America. It draws broadly from many disciplines.

Patterson, Ernest. *Black City Politics*. New York: Dodd, Mead, 1974. Discussion of urban organizations and political participation are especially useful.

Pomper, Gerald. *Elections in America: Control and Influence in Democratic Politics*. New York: Dodd, Mead, and Co., 1968. Chapter 9 contains a discussion of the development of the civil rights movement in America. The emphasis is on the changing status of blacks in American society and on the impact such change has had on American voting patterns.

Report of the National Advisory Commission on Civil Disorders. New York: Bantam Books, 1968. Popularly called "The Kerner Report," this volume is the most comprehensive study of major urban riots in the United States available today. It presents a detailed discussion of the factors underlying past riots and offers recommendations for avoiding such confrontations in the future.

Theodore, Athena, ed. *The Professional Woman*. Cambridge, Mass.: Schenkman, 1971. A collection of essays and articles dealing with the social, economic, political, cultural, and moral problems faced by women in their professional lives.

The Constitution of the United States of America

We the People of the United States, in Order to form a more perfect Union, establish Justice, insure domestic Tranquility, provide for the common defense, promote the general Welfare, and secure the Blessings of Liberty to ourselves and our Posterity, do ordain and establish this Constitution for the United States of America.

Article I

Section 1. All legislative Powers herein granted shall be vested in a Congress of the United States, which shall consist of a Senate and House of Representatives.

Section 2. The House of Representatives shall be composed of Members chosen every second Year by the People of the several States, and the Electors in each State shall have the Qualifications requisite for Electors of the most numerous Branch of the State Legislature.

No Person shall be a Representative who shall not have attained to the age of twenty five Years, and been seven Years a Citizen of the United States, and who shall not, when elected, be an Inhabitant of that State in which he shall be chosen.

Representatives and direct Taxes shall be apportioned among the several States which may be included within this Union, according to their respective

Numbers, *which shall be determined by adding to the whole Number of free Persons,* *including those bound to Service for a Term of Years,* and excluding Indians not taxed, *three fifths of all other persons.* [1] The actual Enumeration shall be made within three Years after the first Meeting of the Congress of the United States, and within every subsequent Term of ten Years, in such Manner as they shall by Law direct. The Number of Representatives shall not exceed one for every thirty Thousand, but each State shall have at Least one Representative; and until such enumeration shall be made, the State of New Hampshire shall be entitled to chuse three, Massachusetts eight, Rhode-Island and Providence Plantations one, Connecticut five, New-York six, New Jersey four, Pennsylvania eight, Delaware one, Maryland six, Virginia ten, North Carolina five, South Carolina five, and Georgia three.

When vacancies happen in the Representation from any State, the Executive Authority thereof shall issue Writs of Election to fill such Vacancies.

The House of Representatives shall chuse their Speaker and other Officers; and shall have the sole Power of Impeachment.

Section 3. The Senate of the United States shall be composed of two Senators from each State, chosen by the *Legislature thereof,* [2] for six Years; and each Senator shall have one Vote.

Immediately after they shall be assembled in Consequence of the first Election, they shall be divided as equally as may be into three Classes. The Seats of the Senators of the first Class shall be vacated at the Expiration of the second Year, of the second Class at the Expiration of the fourth Year, and of the third Class at the Expiration of the sixth Year, so that one third may be chosen every second Year; *and if Vacancies happen by Resignation, or otherwise, during the Recess of the Legislature of any State, the Executive thereof may make temporary Appointments until the next Meeting of the Legislature, which shall then fill such Vacancies.* [3]

No Person shall be a Senator who shall not have attained to the Age of thirty Years, and been nine Years a Citizen of the United States, and who shall not, when elected, be an Inhabitant of the State for which he shall be chosen.

The Vice President of the United States shall be President of the Senate, but shall have no Vote, unless they be equally divided.

The Senate shall chuse their other Officers, and also a President pro tempore, in the Absence of the Vice President, or when he shall exercise the Office of President of the United States.

The Senate shall have the sole Power to try all Impeachments. When sitting for that Purpose, they shall be on Oath or Affirmation. When the President of the United States is tried, the Chief Justice shall preside: And no Person shall be convicted without the Concurrence of two thirds of the Members present.

Judgment in Cases of Impeachment shall not extend further than to removal from Office, and disqualification to hold and enjoy any Office of Honor, Trust or Profit under the United States: but the Party convicted shall nevertheless be liable and subject to Indictment, Trial, Judgment and Punishment, according to Law.

Section 4. The Times, Places and Manner of holding Elections for Senators and Representatives, shall be prescribed in each State by the Legislature thereof; but

---

[1]Superseded by the 14th Amendment. Throughout, italics are used to indicate passages altered by subsequent amendments.

[2]See 17th Amendment.

[3]See 17th Amendment.

the Congress may at any time by Law make or alter such Regulations, except as to the Places of chusing Senators.

The Congress shall assemble at least once in every Year, and such Meeting shall be on the first Monday in December, unless they shall by Law appoint a different Day.[4]

Section 5. Each House shall be the Judge of the Elections, Returns and Qualifications of its own Members, and a Majority of each shall constitute a Quorum to do Business; but a smaller Number may adjourn from day to day, and may be authorized to compel the Attendance of absent Members, in such Manner, and under such Penalties as each House may provide.

Each House may determine the Rules of its Proceedings, punish its Members for disorderly Behaviour, and, with the Concurrence of two thirds, expel a Member.

Each House shall keep a Journal of its Proceedings, and from time to time publish the same, excepting such Parts as may in their Judgment require Secrecy; and the Yeas and Nays of the Members of either House on any question shall, at the Desire of one fifth of those Present, be entered on the Journal.

Neither House, during the Session of Congress, shall, without the Consent of the other, adjourn for more than three days, nor to any other Place than that in which the two Houses shall be sitting.

Section 6. The Senators and Representatives shall receive a Compensation for their Services, to be ascertained by Law, and paid out of the Treasury of the United States. They shall in all Cases, except Treason, Felony and Breach of the Peace, be privileged from Arrest during their Attendance at the Session of their respective Houses, and in going to and returning from the same; and for any Speech or Debate in either House, they shall not be questioned in any other Place.

No Senator or Representative shall, during the Time for which he was elected, be appointed to any civil Office under the Authority of the United States, which shall have been created, or the Emoluments whereof shall have been encreased during such time; and no Person holding any Office under the United States, shall be a Member of either House during his Continuance in Office.

Section 7. All Bills for raising Revenue shall originate in the House of Representatives; but the Senate may propose or concur with Amendments as on other Bills.

Every Bill which shall have passed the House of Representatives and the Senate, shall, before it become a Law, be presented to the President of the United States; If he approve he shall sign it, but if not he shall return it, with his Objections to that House in which it shall have originated, who shall enter the Objections at large on their Journal, and proceed to reconsider it. If after such Reconsideration two thirds of that House shall agree to pass the Bill, it shall be sent, together with the Objections, to the other House, by which it shall likewise be reconsidered, and if approved by two thirds of that House, it shall become a Law. But in all such Cases the Votes of both Houses shall be determined by Yeas and Nays, and the Names of the Persons voting for and against the Bill shall be entered on the Journal of each House respectively. If any Bill shall not be returned by the President within ten Days (Sundays excepted) after it shall have been presented to him, the Same shall be a Law, in like Manner as if he had signed it, unless the Congress by their Adjournment prevent its Return, in which Case it shall not be a Law.

---

[4]See 20th Amendment.

Every Order, Resolution, or Vote to which the Concurrence of the Senate and House of Representatives may be necessary (except on a question of Adjournment) shall be presented to the President of the United States; and before the Same shall take Effect, shall be approved by him, or being disapproved by him, shall be repassed by two thirds of the Senate and House of Representatives, according to the Rules and Limitations prescribed in the Case of a Bill.

Section 8. The Congress shall have Power To lay and collect Taxes, Duties, Imposts and Excises, to pay the Debts and provide for the common Defence and general Welfare of the United States; but all Duties, Imposts and Excises shall be uniform throughout the United States;

To borrow Money on the credit of the United States;

To regulate Commerce with foreign Nations, and among the several States, and with the Indian Tribes;

To establish an uniform Rule of Naturalization, and uniform Laws on the subject of Bankruptcies throughout the United States;

To coin Money, regulate the Value thereof, and of foreign Coin, and fix the Standard of Weights and Measures;

To provide for the Punishment of counterfeiting the Securities and current Coin of the United States;

To establish Post Offices and post Roads;

To promote the Progress of Science and useful Arts, by securing for limited Times to Authors and Inventors the exclusive Right to their respective Writings and Discoveries;

To constitute Tribunals inferior to the Supreme Court;

To define and punish Piracies and Felonies committed on the high Seas, and Offences against the Law of Nations;

To declare War, grant Letters of Marque and Reprisal, and make Rules concerning Captures on Land and Water;

To raise and support Armies, but no Appropriation of Money to that Use shall be for a longer Term than two Years;

To provide and maintain a Navy;

To make Rules for the Government and Regulation of the land and naval Forces;

To provide for calling forth the Militia to execute the Laws of the Union, suppress Insurrections and repel Invasions;

To provide for organizing, arming, and disciplining, the Militia, and for governing such Part of them as may be employed in the Service of the United States, reserving to the States respectively, the Appointment of the Officers, and the Authority of training the Militia according to the discipline prescribed by Congress;

To exercise exclusive Legislation in all Cases whatsoever, over such District (not exceeding ten Miles square) as may, by Cession of particular States, and the Acceptance of Congress, become the Seat of the Government of the United States, and to exercise like Authority over all Places purchased by the Consent of the Legislature of the State in which the Same shall be, for the Erection of Forts, Magazines, Arsenals, dock-Yards, and other needful Buildings;—And

To make all Laws which shall be necessary and proper for carrying into Execution the foregoing Powers, and all other Powers vested by this Constitution in the Government of the United States, or in any Department or Officer thereof.

Section 9. The Migration or Importation of such Persons as any of the States now existing shall think proper to admit, shall not be prohibited by the Congress prior to the Year one thousand eight hundred and eight, but a Tax or duty may be imposed on such Importation, not exceeding ten dollars for each Person.

The Privilege of the Writ of Habeas Corpus shall not be suspended, unless when in Cases of Rebellion or Invasion the public Safety may require it.

No Bill of Attainder or ex post facto Law shall be passed.

No Capitation, or other direct, Tax shall be laid, unless in Proportion to the Census or Enumeration herein before directed to be taken.

No Tax or Duty shall be laid on Articles exported from any State.

No Preference shall be given by any Regulation of Commerce or Revenue to the Ports of one State over those of another: nor shall Vessels bound to, or from, one State, be obliged to enter, clear, or pay Duties in another.

No Money shall be drawn from the Treasury, but in Consequence of Appropriations made by Law; and a regular Statement and Account of the Receipts and Expenditures of all public Money shall be published from time to time.

No Title of Nobility shall be granted by the United States: And no Person holding any Office of Profit or Trust under them, shall, without the Consent of the Congress, accept of any present, Emolument, Office, or Title, of any kind whatever, from any King, Prince, or foreign State.

Section 10. No State shall enter into any Treaty, Alliance, or Confederation; grant Letters of Marque and Reprisal; coin Money; emit Bills of Credit; make any Thing but gold and silver Coin a Tender in Payment of Debts; pass any Bill of Attainder, ex post facto Law, or Law impairing the Obligation of Contracts, or grant any Title of Nobility.

No State shall, without the Consent of the Congress, lay any Imposts or Duties on Imports or Exports, except what may be absolutely necessary for executing its inspection Laws: and the net Produce of all Duties and Imposts, laid by any State on Imports or Exports, shall be for the Use of the Treasury of the United States; and all such Laws shall be subject to the Revision and Controul of the Congress.

No State shall, without the Consent of Congress, lay any Duty of Tonnage, keep Troops, or Ships of War in time of Peace, enter into any Agreement or Compact with another State, or with a foreign Power, or engage in War, unless actually invaded, or in such imminent Danger as will not admit of delay.

Article II

Section 1. The executive Power shall be vested in a President of the United States of America. He shall hold his Office during the Term of four Years, and, together with the Vice President, chosen for the same Term, be elected, as follows:

Each State shall appoint, in such Manner as the Legislature thereof may direct, a Number of Electors, equal to the whole Number of Senators and Representatives to which the State may be entitled in the Congress: but no Senator or Representative, or Person holding an Office of Trust or Profit under the United States, shall be appointed an Elector.

The Electors shall meet in their respective States, and vote by Ballot for two Persons, of whom one at least shall not be an Inhabitant of the same State with themselves. And they shall make a List of all the Persons voted for, and of the Number of Votes for each; which List they shall sign and certify, and transmit sealed to the Seat of the Government of the United States, directed to the President of the Senate. The President of the Senate shall, in the Presence of the Senate and House of Representatives, open all the Certificates, and the Votes shall then be counted. The Person having the greatest Number of Votes shall be the President, if such Number be a Majority of the whole Number of Electors appointed; and if there be more than one who have such Majority, and have an equal Number of Votes, then the House of Representatives shall immediately chuse by Ballot one of them for President; and if no Person have a Majority, then from the five highest on the List the said House shall in like Manner chuse the President. But in chusing the President, the Votes shall be taken by States, the Representation from each State having one Vote: A quorum for this Purpose shall consist of a Member or Members from two thirds of the States, and a Majority of all the States shall be necessary to a Choice. In every Case, after the Choice of the President, the Person having the greatest Number of Votes of the Electors shall be the Vice President. But if there should remain two or more who have equal Votes, the Senate shall chuse from them by Ballot the Vice President. [5]

The Congress may determine the Time of chusing the Electors, and the Day on which they shall give their Votes; which Day shall be the same throughout the United States.

No Person except a natural born Citizen, or a Citizen of the United States, at the time of the Adoption of this Constitution, shall be eligible to the Office of President; neither shall any Person be eligible to that Office who shall not have attained to the Age of thirty five Years, and been fourteen Years a Resident within the United States.

In Case of the Removal of the President from Office, or of his Death, Resignation, or Inability to discharge the Powers and Duties of the said Office, the Same shall devolve on the Vice President, and the Congress may by Law provide for the Case of Removal, Death, Resignation or Inability, both of the President and Vice President, declaring what Officer shall then act as President, and such Officer shall act accordingly, until the Disability be removed, or a President shall be elected. [6]

The President shall, at stated Times, receive for his Services, a Compensation which shall neither be encreased nor diminished during the Period for which he shall have been elected, and he shall not receive within that Period any other Emolument from the United States, or any of them.

Before he enter on the Execution of his Office, he shall take the following Oath or Affirmation:—"I do solemnly swear (or affirm) that I will faithfully execute the Office of President of the United States, and will to the best of my Ability, preserve, protect and defend the Constitution of the United States."

Section 2. The President shall be Commander in Chief of the Army and Navy of the United States, and of the Militia of the several States, when called into the actual Service of the United States; he may require the Opinion, in writing, of the principal Officer in each of the executive Departments, upon any Subject relating to the Duties of their respective Offices, and he shall have Power to grant Reprieves and Pardons for Offences against the United States, except in Cases of Impeachment.

He shall have Power, by and with the Advice and Consent of the Senate, to make Treaties, provided two thirds of the Senators present concur; and he shall nominate, and by and with the Advice and Consent of the Senate, shall appoint Ambassadors, other public Ministers and Consuls, Judges of the supreme Court, and all other Officers of the United States, whose Appointments are not herein otherwise provided for, and which shall be established by Law: but the Congress may by Law vest the Appointment of such inferior officers, as they think proper, in the President alone, in the Courts of Law, or in the Heads of Departments.

The President shall have Power to fill up all Vacancies that may happen

---

[5] Superseded by the 12th Amendment.
[6] See 25th Amendment.

during the Recess of the Senate, by granting Commissions which shall expire at the End of their next Session.

Section 3. He shall from time to time give to the Congress Information of the State of the Union, and recommend to their Consideration such Measures as he shall judge necessary and expedient; he may, on extraordinary Occasions, convene both Houses, or either of them, and in Case of Disagreement between them, with Respect to the Time of Adjournment, he may adjourn them to such Time as he shall think proper; he shall receive Ambassadors and other public Ministers; he shall take Care that the Laws be faithfully executed, and shall Commission all the Officers of the United States.

Section 4. The President, Vice President, and all civil Officers of the United States, shall be removed from Office on Impeachment for, and Conviction of, Treason, Bribery, or other high Crimes and Misdemeanors.

Section 1. The judicial Power of the United States, shall be vested in one supreme Court and in such inferior Courts as the Congress may from time to time ordain and establish. The Judges, both of the supreme and inferior Courts, shall hold their Offices during good Behaviour, and shall, at stated Times, receive for their Services, a Compensation, which shall not be diminished during their Continuance in Office.

Article III

Section 2. The judicial Power shall extend to all Cases, in Law and Equity, arising under this Constitution, the Laws of the United States, and Treaties made, or which shall be made, under their Authority;—to all Cases affecting Ambassadors, other public Ministers and Consuls;—to all Cases of admiralty and maritime Jurisdiction;—to Controversies to which the United States shall be a Party—to Controversies between two or more States;—*between a State and Citizens of another State*[7];—between Citizens of different States;—between Citizens of the same State claiming Lands under Grants of different States, *and between a State or the Citizens thereof, and foreign States, Citizens, or Subjects.*[8]

In all Cases affecting Ambassadors, other public Ministers and Consuls, and those in which a State shall be Party, the supreme Court shall have original Jurisdiction. In all the other Cases before mentioned, the supreme Court shall have appellate Jurisdiction, both as to Law and Fact, with such Exceptions, and under such Regulations as the Congress shall make.

The Trial of all Crimes, except in Cases of Impeachment, shall be by Jury; and such Trial shall be held in the State where the said Crimes shall have been committed; but when not committed within any State, the Trial shall be at such Place or Places as the Congress may by Law have directed.

Section 3. Treason against the United States, shall consist only in levying War against them, or in adhering to their Enemies, giving them Aid and Comfort. No Person shall be convicted of Treason unless on the Testimony of two Witnesses to the same overt Act, or on Confession in open Court.

The Congress shall have Power to declare the Punishment of Treason, but no Attainder of Treason shall work Corruption of Blood, or Forfeiture except during the Life of the Person attainted.

---

[7]See 11th Amendment.
[8]See 11th Amendment.

Article IV   *Section 1.* Full Faith and Credit shall be given in each State to the public Acts, Records, and judicial Proceedings of every other State. And the Congress may by general Laws prescribe the Manner in which such Acts, Records, and Proceedings shall be proved, and the Effect thereof.

Section 2. The Citizens of each State shall be entitled to all Privileges and Immunities of Citizens in the several States.

A Person charged in any State with Treason, Felony, or other Crime, who shall flee from Justice, and be found in another State, shall on Demand of the executive Authority of the State from which he fled, be delivered up, to be removed to the State having Jurisdiction of the Crime.

No Person held to Service or Labour in one State, under the Laws thereof, escaping into another, shall, in Consequence of any Law or Regulation therein, be discharged from such Service or Labour, but shall be delivered up on Claim of the Party to whom such Service or Labour may be due. [9]

Section 3. New States may be admitted by the Congress into this Union; but no new State shall be formed or erected within the Jurisdiction of any other State; nor any State be formed by the Junction of two or more States, or Parts of States, without the Consent of the Legislatures of the States concerned as well as of the Congress.

The Congress shall have Power to dispose of and make all needful Rules and Regulations respecting the Territory or other Property belonging to the United States; and nothing in this Constitution shall be so construed as to Prejudice any claims of the United States, or of any particular State.

Section 4. The United States shall guarantee to every State in this Union a Republican Form of Government, and shall protect each of them against Invasion; and on Application of the Legislature, or of the Executive (when the Legislature cannot be convened) against domestic Violence.

Article V   The Congress, whenever two thirds of both Houses shall deem it necessary, shall propose Amendments to this Constitution, or, on the Application of the Legislatures of two thirds of the several States, shall call a Convention for proposing Amendments, which, in either Case, shall be valid to all Intents and Purposes, as Part of this Constitution, when ratified by the Legislatures of three fourths of the several States, or by Conventions in three fourths thereof, as the one or the other Mode of Ratification may be proposed by the Congress; Provided that no Amendment which may be made prior to the Year One thousand eight hundred and eight shall in any Manner affect the first and fourth Clauses in the Ninth Section of the first Article; and that no State, without its Consent, shall be deprived of its equal Suffrage in the Senate.

Article VI   All Debts contracted and Engagements entered into, before the Adoption of this Constitution, shall be as valid against the United States under this Constitution, as under the Confederation.

This Constitution, and the Laws of the United States which shall be made in Pursuance thereof; and all Treaties made, or which shall be made, under the

---

[9] See 13th Amendment.

Authority of the United States, shall be the supreme Law of the Land; and the Judges in every State shall be bound thereby, any Thing in the Constitution or Laws of any State to the Contrary notwithstanding.

The Senators and Representatives before mentioned, and the Members of the several State Legislatures, and all executive and judicial Officers, both of the United States and of the several States, shall be bound by Oath or Affirmation, to support this Constitution; but no religious Test shall ever be required as a Qualification to any Office or public Trust under the United States.

Article VII

The Ratification of the Conventions of nine States, shall be sufficient for the Establishment of this Constitution between the States so ratifying the Same.

Done in Convention by the Unanimous Consent of the States present the Seventeenth Day of September in the Year of our Lord one thousand seven hundred and eighty seven and of the Independence of the United States of America the Twelfth. In witness whereof We have hereunto subscribed our Names.

ARTICLES IN ADDITION TO, AND AMENDMENT OF, THE CONSTITUTION OF THE UNITED STATES OF AMERICA, PROPOSED BY CONGRESS, AND RATIFIED BY THE SEVERAL STATES, PURSUANT TO THE FIFTH ARTICLE OF THE ORIGINAL CONSTITUTION:

Amendment I

(Ratification of the first ten amendments was completed December 15, 1791.)
Congress shall make no law respecting an establishment of religion, or prohibiting the free exercise thereof; or abridging the freedom of speech, or of the press; or the right of the people peaceably to assemble, and to petition the Government for a redress of grievances.

Amendment II

A well regulated Militia, being necessary to the security of a free State, the right of the people to keep and bear Arms, shall not be infringed.

Amendment III

No Soldier shall, in time of peace be quartered in any house, without the consent of the Owner, nor in time of war, but in a manner to be prescribed by law.

Amendment IV

The right of the people to be secure in their persons, houses, papers, and effects, against unreasonable searches and seizures, shall not be violated, and no Warrants shall issue, but upon probable cause, supported by Oath or affirmation, and particularly describing the place to be searched, and the persons or things to be seized.

Amendment V

No person shall be held to answer for a capital, or otherwise infamous crime, unless on a presentment or indictment of a Grand Jury, except in cases arising in the land or naval forces, or in the Militia, when in actual service in time of War or public danger; nor shall any person be subject for the same offence to be twice put in jeopardy of life or limb; nor shall be compelled in any criminal case to be a witness against himself, nor be deprived of life, liberty, or property, without due process of law; nor shall private property be taken for public use, without just compensation.

Amendment VI   In all criminal prosecutions, the accused shall enjoy the right to a speedy and public trial, by an impartial jury of the State and district wherein the crime shall have been committed, which district shall have been previously ascertained by law, and to be informed of the nature and cause of the accusation; to be confronted with the witness against him; to have compulsory process for obtaining witnesses in his favor, and to have the Assistance of Counsel for his defence.

Amendment VII   In Suits at common law, where the value in controversy shall exceed twenty dollars, the right of trial by jury shall be preserved, and no fact tried by a jury, shall be otherwise reexamined in any Court of the United States, than according to the rules of the common law.

Amendment VIII   Excessive bail shall not be required, nor excessive fines imposed, nor cruel and unusual punishments inflicted.

Amendment IX   The enumeration in the Constitution, of certain rights, shall not be construed to deny or disparage others retained by the people.

Amendment X   The powers not delegated to the United States by the Constitution, nor prohibited by it to the States, are reserved to the States respectively, or to the people.

Amendment XI (1798)

The Judicial power of the United States shall not be construed to extend to any suit in law or equity, commenced or prosecuted against one of the United States by Citizens of another State, or by Citizens or Subjects of any Foreign States.

Amendment XII (1804)

The Electors shall meet in their respective states and vote by ballot for President and Vice-President, one of whom, at least, shall not be an inhabitant of the same state with themselves; they shall name in their ballots the person voted for as President, and in distinct ballots the person voted for as Vice-President, and they shall make distinct lists of all persons voted for as President, and of all persons voted for as Vice-President, and of the number of votes for each, which lists they shall sign and certify, and transmit sealed to the seat of the government of the United States, directed to the President of the Senate;—The President of the Senate shall, in the presence of Senate and House of Representatives, open all the certificates and the votes shall then be counted;—The person having the greatest number of votes for President, shall be the President, if such number be a majority of the whole number of Electors appointed; and if no person have such majority, then from the persons having the highest numbers not exceeding three on the list of those voted for as President, the House of Representatives shall choose immediately, by ballot, the President. But in choosing the President, the votes shall be taken by states, the representation from each state having one vote; a quorum for this purpose shall consist of a member or members from two-thirds of the states, and a majority of all the states shall be necessary to a choice. And if the House of Representatives shall not choose a President whenever the right of choice shall devolve upon them, *before the fourth day of March next following,* [10] then the Vice-President shall act as President, as in the case of the death or other constitutional disability of the President.—The person having the greatest number of votes as Vice-President shall be the Vice-President, if such number be a majority of the whole number of Electors appointed, and if no person have a majority, then from the two highest numbers on the list, the Senate shall choose the Vice-President; a quorum for the purpose shall consist of two-thirds of the whole number of Senators, and a majority of the whole number shall be necessary to a choice. But no person constitutionally ineligible to the office of President shall be eligible to that of Vice-President of the United States.

Amendment XIII (1865)

Section 1. Neither slavery nor involuntary servitude, except as a punishment for crime whereof the party shall have been duly convicted, shall exist within the United States, or any place subject to their jurisdiction.

Section 2. Congress shall have the power to enforce this article by appropriate legislation.

Amendment XIV (1868)

Section 1. All persons born or naturalized in the United States, and subject to the jurisdiction thereof, are citizens of the United States and of the State wherein they reside. No State shall make or enforce any law which shall abridge the privileges or immunities of citizens of the United States; nor shall any State deprive any person of life, liberty, or property, without due process of law; nor deny to any person within its jurisdiction the equal protection of the laws.

Section 2. Representatives shall be apportioned among the several States according to their respective numbers, counting the whole number of persons in each State, excluding Indians not taxed. But when the right to vote at any election for the choice of electors for President and Vice President of the United States, Representatives in Congress, the Executive and Judicial officers of a State, or the members of the Legislature thereof, is denied to any of the male inhabitants of such State, being twenty-one years of age, and citizens of the United States, or in any way abridged, except for participation in rebellion, or other crime, the basis of representation therein shall be reduced in the proportion which the number of such male citizens shall bear to the whole number of male citizens twenty-one years of age in such State.

---

[10]Altered by the 20th Amendment.

Section 3. No person shall be a Senator or Representative in Congress, or elector of President and Vice President, or hold any office, civil or military, under the United States, or under any State, who, having previously taken an oath, as a member of Congress, or as an officer of the United States, or as a member of any State legislature, or as an executive or judicial officer of any State, to support the Constitution of the United States, shall have engaged in insurrection or rebellion against the same, or given aid or comfort to the enemies thereof. But Congress may by a vote of two-thirds of each House, remove such disability.

Section 4. The validity of the public debt of the United States, authorized by law, including debts incurred for payment of pensions and bounties for services in suppressing insurrection or rebellion, shall not be questioned. But neither the United States nor any State shall assume or pay any debt or obligation incurred in aid of insurrection or rebellion against the United States, or any claim for the loss or emancipation of any slave; but all such debts, obligations, and claims shall be held illegal and void.

Section 5. The Congress shall have power to enforce, by appropriate legislation, the provisions of this article.

Amendment XV (1870)

Section 1. The right of citizens of the United States to vote shall not be denied or abridged by the United States or by any State on account of race, color, or previous condition of servitude.

Section 2. The Congress shall have power to enforce this article by appropriate legislation.

Amendment XVI (1913)

The Congress shall have power to lay and collect taxes on incomes, from whatever source derived, without apportionment among the several States, and without regard to any census or enumeration.

Amendment XVII (1913)

The Senate of the United States shall be composed of two Senators from each State, elected by the people thereof, for six years; and each Senator shall have one vote. The electors in each State shall have the qualifications requisite for electors of the most numerous branch of the State legislatures.

When vacancies happen in the representation of any State in the Senate, the executive authority of such State shall issue writs of election to fill such vacancies: *Provided,* That the legislature of any State may empower the executive thereof to make temporary appointments until the people fill the vacancies by election as the legislature may direct.

This amendment shall not be so construed as to affect the election or term of any Sentor chosen before it becomes valid as part of the Constitution.

Amendment XVIII (1919)

Section 1. After one year from the ratification of this article the manufacture, sale, or transportation of intoxicating liquors within, the importation thereof into, or the exportation thereof from the United States and all territory subject to the jurisdiction thereof for beverage purposes is hereby prohibited.

Section 2. The Congress and the several States shall have concurrent power to enforce this article by appropriate legislation.

Section 3. This article shall be inoperative unless it shall have been ratified as an amendment to the Constitution by the legislatures of the several States, as provided in the Constitution, within seven years from the date of the submission hereof to the States by the Congress.[11]

Amendment XIX (1920)

The right of citizens of the United States to vote shall not be denied or abridged by the United States or by any State on account of sex.

Congress shall have power to enforce this article by appropriate legislation.

Amendment XX (1933)

Section 1. The terms of the President and Vice President shall end at noon on the 20th day of January, and the terms of Senators and Representatives at noon on the 3rd day of January, of the years in which such terms would have ended if this article had not been ratified; and the terms of their successors shall then begin.

Section 2. The Congress shall assemble at least once in every year, and such meeting shall begin at noon on the 3rd day of January, unless they shall by law appoint a different day.

Section 3. If, at the time fixed for the beginning of the term of the President, the President elect shall have died, the Vice President elect shall become President. If a President shall not have been chosen before the time fixed for the beginning of his term, or if the President elect shall have failed to qualify, then the Vice President elect shall act as President until a President shall have qualified; and the Congress may by law provide for the case wherein neither a President elect nor a Vice President elect shall have qualified, declaring who shall then act as President, or the manner in which one who is to act shall be selected, and such person shall act accordingly until a President or Vice President shall have qualified.

Section 4. The Congress may by law provide for the case of the death of any of the persons from whom the House of Representatives may choose a President whenever the right of choice shall have devolved upon them, and for the case of the death of any of the persons from whom the Senate may choose a Vice President whenever the right of choice shall have devolved upon them.

Section 5. Sections 1 and 2 shall take effect on the 15th day of October following the ratification of this article.

Section 6. This article shall be inoperative unless it shall have been ratified as an amendment to the Constitution by the legislatures of three-fourths of the several States within seven years from the date of its submission.

Amendment XXI (1933)

Section 1. The eighteenth article of amendment to the Constitution of the United States is hereby repealed.

---

[11]Repealed by the 21st Amendment.

Section 2. The transportation or importation into any State, Territory, or possession of the United States for delivery or use therein of intoxicating liquors, in violation of the laws thereof, is hereby prohibited.

Section 3. This article shall be inoperative unless it shall have been ratified as an amendment to the Constitution by conventions in the several States, as provided in the Constitution, within seven years from the date of the submission hereof to the States by the Congress.

Amendment XXII (1951)

Section 1. No person shall be elected to the office of the President more than twice, and no person who has held the office of President, or acted as President for more than two years of a term to which some other person was elected President shall be elected to the office of President more than once. But this Article shall not apply to any person holding the office of President when this Article was proposed by the Congress, and shall not prevent any person who may be holding the office of President, or acting as President, during the term within which this Article becomes operative from holding the office of President or acting as President during the remainder of such term.

Section 2. This article shall be inoperative unless it shall have been ratified as an amendment to the Constitution by the legislatures of three-fourths of the several States within seven years from the date of its submission to the States by the Congress.

Amendment XXIII (1961)

Section 1. The District constituting the seat of Government of the United States shall appoint in such manner as the Congress may direct:

A number of electors of President and Vice President equal to the whole number of Senators and Representatives in Congress to which the District would be entitled if it were a State, but in no event more than the least populous State; they shall be in addition to those appointed by the States, but they shall be considered, for the purposes of the election of President and Vice President, to be electors appointed by a State; and they shall meet in the District and perform such duties as provided by the twelfth article of amendment.

Section 2. The Congress shall have power to enforce this article by appropriate legislation.

Amendment XXIV (1964)

Section 1. The right of citizens of the United States to vote in any primary or other election for President or Vice President, for electors for President or Vice President, or for Senator or Representative in Congress, shall not be denied or abridged by the United States or any state by reason of failure to pay any poll tax or other tax.

Section 2. The Congress shall have the power to enforce this article by appropriate legislation.

Amendment XXV (1967)

Section 1. In case of the removal of the President from office or of his death or resignation, the Vice President shall become President.

Section 2. Whenever there is a vacancy in the office of the Vice President, the President shall nominate a Vice President who shall take office upon confirmation by a majority vote of both Houses of Congress.

Section 3. Whenever the President transmits to the President pro tempore of the Senate and the Speaker of the House of Representatives his written declaration that he is unable to discharge the powers and duties of his office, and until he transmits to them a written declaration to the contrary, such powers and duties shall be discharged by the Vice President as Acting President.

Section 4. Whenever the Vice President and a majority of either the principal officers of the executive departments or of such other body as Congress may by law provide, transmit to the President pro tempore of the Senate and the Speaker of the House of Representatives their written declaration that the President is unable to discharge the powers and duties of his office, the Vice President shall immediately assume the powers and duties of the office as Acting President.

Thereafter, when the President transmits to the President pro tempore of the Senate and the Speaker of the House of Representatives his written declaration that no inability exists, he shall resume the powers and duties of his office unless the Vice President and a majority of either the principal officers of the executive departments or of such other body as Congress may by law provide, transmit within four days to the President pro tempore of the Senate and the Speaker of the House of Representatives their written declaration that the President is unable to discharge the powers and duties of his office. Thereupon Congress shall decide the issue, assembling within forty-eight hours for that purpose if not in session. If the Congress, within twenty-one days after receipt of the latter written declaration, or, if Congress is not in session, within twenty-one days after Congress is required to assemble, determines by two-thirds vote of both Houses that the President is unable to discharge the powers and duties of his office, the Vice President shall continue to discharge the same as Acting President; otherwise, the President shall resume the powers and duties of his office.

Amendment XXVI (1971)

Section 1. The right of citizens of the United States, who are 18 years of age or older, to vote shall not be denied or abridged by the United States or any state on account of age.

Section 2. The Congress shall have the power to enforce this article by appropriate legislation.

Index

Hoover, J. Edgar, 20
Housing Act (1937), 84
Housing discrimination, 151, 318, 349
Hughes, Charles E., 317
Huitt, Ralph K., 295
Humphrey, George M., 94
Humphrey, Hubert, 172, 178, 254, 256, 287, 296–297
"Hunger in America" (CBS), 147
Hunt, E. Howard, Jr., 20, 21
Hunter, Floyd, 330–332, 333
Hyman, Herbert H., 142 n.29

Idealism, 377
Ideology, political, 163–165, 171–172, 192; and election of 1972, 169–172
Ikard, Frank n., 220
Illinois, 287
Impeachment, 245–246, 252
"Implied powers," 60
Import taxes, 43
Impoundment controversy, 241–242, 280–282
Income levels, 78, 84, 128; inequalities, 100–101, 350, 351, 361; and voter turnout, 179, 181
Income taxes, 43, 101
Indentured servants, 25
Independent voters, 170, 171, 174, 199–200, 201, 202
Indians, 28, 44, 240
Individual liberty. *See* Rights
Industry. *See* Commercial interests
Inflation, 175
Institutional elites, 10, 11, 12, 89–120; corporate elites, 95–100; "Cowboys" and "Yankees," 115–119; govern-elites, 91–95; liberal establishment, 111–113; managerial elites, 102–105; military-industrial complex, 105–108; recruitment, 108–111; wealth of, 101–102
Insurance companies, 97, 98
Integration, opposition to: North, 353–354; South, 344–345
Intelligence gathering, 20, 21
Interest group theory. *See* Pluralist theory
Interest groups, 209–228
Interlocking directorates, 99
International Harvester Corporation, 75
Interstate commerce, 43, 317
Interstate Commerce Commission, 262, 265
Intolerance, 123–125, 139, 373, 374
"Iron law of oligarchy," 196, 213, 372
IRS, 18
Isolationism, 299
Israel, 180
"Issue voting," 171–172
Italy, 180, 212

Jackson, Andrew, 65–68, 254
Jackson, Henry, 254
"Jacksonian Democracy," 65–67
Jacob, Herbert, 308
Janowitz, Morris, 132
Japan, 180, 255
Japanese-Americans, internment of, 375
Jay, John, 41
Jay Treaty, 243
Jefferson, Thomas, 9, 23, 24, 34, 73, 240, 243; Jeffersonian vs. Hamiltonian policies, 60–63; presidential appointments, 67–68; Republican tax policies, 64–65
Jenkins, Walter, 261
Jenning, Kent, 193
Jews, 16, 271
Jim Crow laws, 342–346 *passim*
Johnson, Andrew, impeachment of, 245n
Johnson, Lyndon, 18, 94, 95, 117, 169, 178, 202, 203, 249, 261, 265, 275, 357; in Congress, 294; Fortas nomination, 309; and liberal establishment, 238; and TV, 145, 148; and Vietnam, 113, 145, 148, 152, 153, 154, 176, 240, 250
Johnson, William Samuel, 31, 38
Jones, Charles O., 276–277
Jordan, Hamilton, 256
Judges, federal: presidential appointment of, 308–310, 313; socioeconomic status of, 305–308
Judicial elite, 303–320
Judicial review, 49–50, 304–305, 306
Juries, 313
Juridiction, original/appellate, 313
Kansas, 70, 344
Kansas-Nebraska Act (1854), 70
Kariel, Henry, 11
Keech, William R., 178
Kennedy, David, 94
Kennedy, Edward M., 21, 139, 254, 256, 287, 295–296
Kennedy, John F., 18, 21, 94, 95, 112, 117n, 178, 245n, 264, 265, 296; and blacks, 347, 357; and Nixon, 247, 248
Kennedy, Robert F., 18, 296
Kent State student slayings, 373
Kentucky, 63
Kentucky Resolution, 63
Kerner Commission, 340, 352
Key, V. O., Jr., 2, 79, 80–81, 152, 169, 276
Keynes, John Maynard, 83; economic theory, 114–115
King, Martin Luther, Jr., 18, 110, 255, 259, 346, 347
Kirbo, Charles, 205n
Kissinger, Henry, 92, 95, 248, 249, 251
Klein, Herbert, 118
Kleindienst, Richard, 118, 245, 250